Whatever Happened to Raoul Wallenberg?

Morris H. Wolff, Esquire
Juris Doctor, M.A., J.D.

Whatever Happened to Raoul Wallenberg?

ISBN: 1-4701-9370-1
ISBN-13: 9781470193706

Dedications

To my two daughters Michelle and Lesley and to my brothers Carl, Richard and David and their wives, and my sister Ruth and her family for their continual love and support of my efforts on behalf of Raoul Wallenberg.

Acknowledgments

None of my rescue efforts could have been accomplished alone. I would like to thank the late Congressman Tom Lantos and his dynamic and supportive wife Annette whose strong encouragement has been a constant source of strength throughout this endeavor.

I would also like to thank my young colleague Jason Webster for his bravery and dedication to this cause with hopes that he continues to follow in my work in human rights.

And with appreciation to Patricia Pawlowski who has persevered with me in getting this book published so that all may know the truth about Raoul Wallenberg and his fate. Finally, my thanks to Terri Wilson and Judy Novak for their careful and patient assistance in editing this book.

Sincere thanks also to the Simon Wiesenthal Foundation and its leaders Rabbi Abraham Cooper and Marvin Hier who helped to raise Twenty Five Thousand Dollars to help cover part of the expenses. No legal fees were ever paid. I did all of my work *pro bono* for twenty-seven years. I want to thank President William J. Clinton for meeting with me at the White House and encouraging me to continue my work. President Clinton took a note to Premier Boris Yeltsin seeking Wallenberg's release in December of 1993. My thanks to the Mossad Intelligence Agency of Israel for mounting a raid on a Dacha near to Moscow in a valiant effort to rescue Wallenberg. They came within a hair's breadth of rescuing our hero. Finally, my thanks to my Germantown Friends School classmate and personal hero David Meredith Evans who, as the United States Ambassador to the Soviet Union, took a trip to Kazan Hospital on the Volga River five hundred miles from Moscow and met with Raoul Wallenberg in 1998. David Evans was the last person to see Raoul Wallenberg alive.

Whatever Happened to Raoul Wallenberg?

The Author, Morris H. Wolff

Raoul Wallenberg at his desk at the Swedish Embassy, November 26, 1944. The calendar served to conceal a wall safe where the "Brezhnev Diamonds" were kept, according to his photographer Thomas Veres.

Author's Note

I was retained in March of 1983 by the Wallenberg family to sue the Soviet Union in an effort to rescue Holocaust hero Raoul Wallenberg from Lubyanka Prison in Moscow. I was filled with dreams, hope and optimism. I was hopeful I would win the case and that the doors of the prison in Moscow, where Raoul had languished for 39 years under brutal conditions, would open and Wallenberg would be set free—an innocent man whose only "crime" was rescuing 100,000 Budapest Jews then headed towards the Nazi gas chambers at Auschwitz.

I nurtured dreams that one day Raoul and I, as "brothers in arms," would sit on the back of an open Lincoln Continental convertible and share a ticker tape parade down 5th Avenue in New York with grateful survivors and other Americans cheering him "Home." That was my dream. I held on to it through the long years of litigation and rescue efforts. I served *pro bono*. I never accepted money for this privilege of walking through the corridors of 20th century history as legal counsel for this great man. I became his voice in the courtroom and his quiet conscience in this world. My work led to the NBC TV series on Wallenberg starring Richard Chamberlain. From there a new awareness of Wallenberg developed.

Wallenberg was made an American citizen on August 5, 1981 at age sixty nine by President Ronald Reagan who said: "I hope the granting of citizenship to Raoul Wallenberg will hasten the day of his release, and that one day soon he will sit beneath the trees planted in his honor at Yad Vashem on the Avenue of the Righteous Gentiles in Jerusalem." The President went on to say to Wallenberg's brother, Guy Von Dardel, "Mister Von Dardel, we're going to do everything in our power so that your brother can sit beneath the shade of those trees and enjoy the respect and love that so many hold for him." **(See Reagan letter at the back of this book).**

I used Wallenberg's status as an American citizen, and other valid US laws, to win a precedent setting lawsuit in federal court in Washington, DC on October 18, 1985. Judge Barrington Parker, outraged by the Soviet misbehavior in kidnapping Wallenberg from Debrecen, Hungary on January 17, 1945, and holding him for 39 brutal years, ordered the Soviets to immediately release Wallenberg and to pay damages of 39 million dollars—the one million for each year of lonely captivity, which I had requested. It was a courtroom triumph. I was making plans to go to Moscow to bring Wallenberg home. **(See Judge Parker's opinion at the back of this book).**

You, as the reader of this book, will learn first-hand how governments often work at odds with their best intentions. Sometimes work done in secret is ill advised. Men working at the highest levels for President Reagan, including Fred Fielding, his White House Counsel, and John G. Roberts his White House

Whatever Happened to Raoul Wallenberg?

Assistant Counsel (now Chief Justice of The United States Supreme Court), have done our nation a great disservice. They covered up their own effort to sabotage my effort to rescue Wallenberg by failing to answer my letter to the President. I had asked the President, by hand delivered letter on November 11, 1983, to use his executive powers and his commitment to Wallenberg to demand his release. President Reagan carefully read my letter that was hand delivered by Faith R. Whittlesey, Assistant to the President for Public Liaison, and my personal friend from Philadelphia. The President wanted to follow my advice and demand the release of Wallenberg—but his aides countermanded the President's directive.

President Reagan had the moral power and the legal duty, under the *US Hostages Act* (22 US Code 1732) to issue an ultimatum and demand that the Soviet Union release Wallenberg. Supreme Court Chief Justice Roberts, then a White House lawyer, when specifically asked by the President for his candid legal advice, told Reagan:

"Mr. President you have not only the power but the duty under this law, as Morris Wolff has suggested, to demand the release of prisoner Wallenberg, now a US citizen."

Roberts, as White House lawyer acknowledged this awesome power and the correctness of my legal position. He should have used his courage to tell the president to do the right thing. In his memo to the President he states: "The federal law, Title 22 USC. 1732 by its terms, impose an explicit duty on the President. The duty to demand the release of a citizen and to take action is triggered, if he is being held by the foreign power (USSR) in violation of the rights of American citizenship."

Roberts was obligated to follow the courage of his convictions. But he failed miserably. Wallenberg could have been brought forward from solitary confinement of thirty-seven years and become a free man in November of 1983.

Raoul Wallenberg was only 73, in good health and alive, as you will learn in this book. But a small group of people in the White House and the State Department pressured Roberts and turned his courage to cowardice. These bad influences included State Department Legal Adviser, Dan McGovern who wanted to "refrigerate" Wallenberg. Thus, in a curious 180 degree turn, Roberts contradicted his memo to President Reagan and curiously stated:

"I nonetheless recommend a reply to Wallenberg family lawyer Morris Wolff essentially dodging the question of the applicability of 22 USC. 1732."

This critical White House memo was buried in the White House archives and later at the Reagan Library. It did not surface until John Roberts' confirmation hearing for appointment as Chief Justice of the Supreme Court. I never even received a courtesy letter answering my letter to the President. It was too hot to handle. Some very sensitive negotiations with the Russians were taking place in

November of 1985, at the time of my letter to Reagan. This was during the height of the Cold War. Reliable sources at the State Department kept me informed that my effort to rescue Wallenberg was being stymied by the US Department of State, which unfortunately had a record of insensitivity regarding matters involving the Holocaust. My 1983 letter to the President, and the internal secret White House staff reply, suggesting a "dodging of the issue," were not uncovered until the hearings of Justice Roberts in June of 2005. Mr. Roberts was being interviewed and questioned by the Senate on his qualifications as Chief Justice of the US Supreme Court. The Roberts/Fielding memo was discovered in the basement of the Reagan Library in California by an astute and professional journalist, E.J. Kessler, an investigative reporter with the *Jewish Forward*, a highly respect weekly newspaper.

Kessler called me long distance in Zurich, Switzerland in June of 2005. He came at me with a barrage of questions. He asked, "Do you know that your letter demanding action by President Reagan to gain Wallenberg's release was buried? It has now curiously surfaced, after being hidden for twenty years in papers at the Reagan Library. I was digging through them looking for evidence of courage and good character prior to the Roberts confirmation hearings. Can you confirm the contents of your letter and the Justice Roberts memo to Reagan on Wallenberg? Are you the Mr. Morris Wolff who wrote to the President? Do you plan to come back and testify at the Roberts' confirmation hearing? I hope you will!"

I was on assignment on an international law matter in Zurich. I often traveled in my international law practice. He asked me for my comment.

I was in a state of shock about this discovery. Yet, as I sat there having a coffee at an outdoor café in Zurich, I gathered my thoughts and replied.

"I never knew what happened to my letter to President Reagan. I simply went on with my pursuit of Wallenberg's freedom and wrote and filed my lawsuit suing the Soviets for his release. That lawsuit would not have been necessary had the President done the right thing in November of 1983 when he first read my letter. He should have taken action right away to demand the immediate release of Wallenberg under the existing law which I carefully quoted in my letter." I paused and drank some coffee and thought about his question on testifying.

I then replied," I will come back to testify. I will return. I plan to come back to my law office in Washington DC, and will now advance my schedule to return tomorrow. I want to know why Roberts did what he did."

I was amazed. Until that moment I had not been able to connect the dots. Roberts had endorsed and then jettisoned my November 11, 1983 letter to the President. He had countermanded Reagan's directive to answer me and to write a letter to the Soviets demanding the release of Wallenberg. Roberts through inaction and indifference had unwittingly signed Wallenberg's "death warrant".

This was Wallenberg's chance for liberation and freedom. Had Roberts and Fielding given the President encouragement and a strong and well-deserved green light—a 'do what you can do Mr. President to gain release' plea—Wallenberg would have been freed. The Russians at that moment were very sensitive to demands coming from the United States. They would have released Wallenberg, I am certain. Instead, the President's key advisors kept the President in the dark and thus guaranteed Wallenberg's continuing in custody. For inexplicable reasons they countermanded the President's first impulse and his directive to seek freedom for Raoul Wallenberg. They were insubordinate. They went against his instruction. Pressured by the State Department Legal Counsel, Dan McGovern, they developed a plan of do nothing inaction. They effectively destroyed my letter. But they did not destroy Roberts' self-damaging letter of advice. I never knew why I did not receive a reply. And now I knew why, . . twenty years later.

I called Senator Arlen Specter, who was then Chairman of the Senate Judiciary Committee. I asked to testify at the Roberts' confirmation hearing, and to find out why the Wallenberg scandal took place. Arlen Specter remains a close personal friend. He was a powerful United States Senator who grilled and destroyed Robert Bork as a Supreme Court candidate in the Senate confirmation hearings a few years earlier. I was hoping he would give Roberts a similar open and honest grilling. I had the fodder for his efforts but this was a new Specter. He and his clever associate David Brog knew I would be a hostile, but candid and honest witness. By now, thanks to Republican politics, Arlen owed his Senate Judiciary leadership position to Senator Orrin Hatch of Utah, a strong supporter of Roberts' candidacy. Hatch had stepped aside as Chairman of the Judiciary Committee and allowed Arlen to take his place. Arlen did not want me to testify. He knew I would expose Roberts and his peculiar White House behavior concerning Raoul Wallenberg. This would have a profound effect on the Jewish voters in Pennsylvania who were a mainstay of Arlen's coalition of support. He was not about to sully his image in the Jewish community. He knew in advance what I would ask Roberts and what Roberts would be obligated to say. It was already in the *Jewish Forward* article in which I had publicly labeled Roberts' actions as "cowardly."

Arlen knows my fighting nature and my ideals. We are good friends. We both graduated with honors from the Yale Law School. He swore me in as Chief Assistant District Attorney of Philadelphia before Judge Sloan when Arlen was District Attorney in 1965. Arlen has always been very supportive and respectful, including his full endorsement when I ran for the State Senate of Pennsylvania in 1970. He campaigned for me. He and his wife Joan attended my engagement party in March of 1965 and my wedding on May 15, 1965. I served him and the people of Philadelphia effectively, with honor and distinction. I told Arlen, "I want to ask Roberts if he might have any information on the whereabouts of

Raoul Wallenberg today. Roberts had access to State Department intelligence and to top secret CIA reports. I wanted to question Roberts on matters of courage, integrity and character. I want him to tell the public what he knew about the Wallenberg matter and why he did not encourage President Reagan to use the law I placed in front of him to rescue Wallenberg." I also wanted to ask Roberts whether as Chief Justice he would be willing to hear the Wallenberg case directly in the Supreme Court since the court has original jurisdiction in matters concerning Ambassadors. I was never given that opportunity. His assistant, David Brog, blocked my access to the panel, by delay after delay, claiming in phone call after phone call: "We are looking for the perfect spot on a panel for you to testify." That spot never materialized. David and Arlen called back a few days later:

"Morris, I'd like to invite you to testify on a panel. We have searched for the right panel, but we could not find one."

"That is just nonsense," I replied. "I believe you can find a five minute spot. Where there's a will, there's a way! Politics puts pressure on us all. It depends on how you respond."

I believed that my country would do everything possible to help achieve justice and to rescue Wallenberg. He was our *de facto* American diplomat—financed by the US Treasury, asked to act for our government in a time of tragic need. He was our diplomat in everything but his clothing. Our United States War Refugee Board went to Sweden and seduced Wallenberg to serve. They wined and dined him in a series of fancy dinners at the Bellsmanor restaurant in Stockholm, Sweden. We drafted him. We promised to cover for him and not leave him hanging out to dry. And yet for thirty-nine years—the number of years in Soviet custody when I answered the call—that is exactly what we did. Our State Department abandoned him in January of 1945 and allowed him to waste away in a Soviet jail. It was our duty to bring him home, and we failed. He is not merely a hero of Sweden and the United States but of the whole world — a man whose deeds speak volumes for his suffering, silent voice. He answered the call to end the suffering of others, and ironically was forced to suffer himself.

I hope this book will open the eyes of many people around the world, and be read especially by young people—our future leaders and decision makers. These will be men and women who never knew the Holocaust or World War II. It will be picked up and perused by good people who love to read of heroes. "It is better to light a candle than to curse the darkness," and that is what I have done as his torchbearer in the 27 years of effort I have put *pro bono* into the law case and my subsequent international efforts to rescue Wallenberg. I sued in US federal court and I won the lawsuit. I met with Presidents. I went to Israel and enlisted the Mossad Intelligence agency to implement a daring mission behind enemy lines in Russia to rescue Wallenberg. They almost succeeded. Israel is the only nation to ever make a true effort to rescue him.

Only Tom Lantos and a few good lawyers and courageous members of Congress, not the State Department, and not the White House, have worked with me for his release. And of course Judge Parker, who wrote a great and historic human rights opinion, which should have been taken by the President and presented to Premier Andropov and the Soviets in Reykavik at his summit meeting in the winter of 1985 when President Reagan first identified and excoriated the USSR as "the evil empire"

I write this book for the next generation of volunteers and political activists. I encourage you to step forward. Our young people need to rattle our government to do the right thing. Do something heroic with your life. Emulate the "can do", altruistic and courageous approach of Wallenberg. Give up your headsets, your video games, your material life, and your BlackBerries. Go into schools, go into neighborhoods, go the Peace Corps, and go to Africa and micro-finance women to start their own businesses. Serve and care about people the way Wallenberg cared. Give up cynicism and nihilism. Be pro-active. You can make a difference in the World.

And remember Dante's admonition in *The Inferno*: ... "that the hottest rim of Hell is reserved for those who in a moment of Moral Crisis suspended Judgment."

Reader's Praise

"I could not put this book down from start to finish. The readers will find compassion, intrigue, excitement, and truth all woven into a vital story. Morris Wolff uses his superb story telling ability to take you into his life experiences as he confronts the Soviet Union and wins. You will witness first hand his efforts to peel back the dark side of humanity in his numerous attempts to achieve Wallenberg's deserved freedom."

Sherry Wilson
Language Arts Teacher
Pioneer Central School District
Yorkshire, NY

"I loved this book. It's a riveting tale of human connections, legal creativity, diplomatic secrets, weird coincidences. Read if you hate lawyers, read if you like lawyers; it will influence your world-view, wherever you are. The book's lively tone and conversational narrative inspires, informs and entertains."

"Great for book clubs. Eminently readable, wide-ranging, mesmerizing. Dogged detective work and creative lawyering. Intrigue, real-life mystery, a secret international rescue raid. Shows how one man can make a difference: First the Swede Wallenberg—who engineers the rescue of some 100,000 Jews from Budapest at the end of World War II. Then, American attorney now author Morris Wolff— who engineers a "legal rescue" (and more) of the mysteriously-disappeared hero. Two "profiles in courage."

"Mr. Wolff tells of his conversations with well-known powerful public figures, some of whose decisions about Wallenberg will shock us. Mr. Wolff unflinchingly reveals how the mighty can fail us, but how good people appear amazingly and unexpectedly to answer calls to duty, rising to the occasion in surprising ways. As a reader, I am stimulated to want to learn more about human nature (good and bad), decision-making among the great nations, and how people of good will can use law to better protect individuals wrongfully spirited away."

Jody P. Williams, of Daytona Beach and Boston
Retired teacher and lawyer.

Whatever Happened to Raoul Wallenberg?

Story of a Hero for All Time written by a Hero for Our Time

"Raoul Wallenberg, 32 years old, left his home and wealthy family in Stockholm, Sweden in 1944 on a mission financed by the United States to save Jews from the Nazis in Budapest, Hungary. The Russians kidnapped him in January, 1945 and held Wallenberg for decades in Russian prisons. No one tried to gain his release, not his family, the Swedish Government, or the United States Government."

"Until in 1983, at the request of Wallenberg's brother, a young lawyer in Philadelphia, Morris Wolff, took on the case *pro bono*. After winning a lawsuit in US Federal Court against the Russian Government demanding damages and Wallenberg's release, his mission was frustrated and Wallenberg was never released. Many people are to be admired for their work on Wallenberg's behalf, and many to be reviled for their indifference or obstructions."

"Were this book just a brilliant thriller by Ben Macintyre or Alan Furst perhaps a happier ending could have been contrived. But this masterpiece is the work of Morris Wolff himself. Wolff's story of trying to free Wallenberg. So the outcome is dictated by history, not fiction. This is a true work of the soul written by a tenacious advocate: a testament to a truly wonderful person, as shown by excerpts from Raoul Wallenberg's own personal diary from June 1944."

Jim Magid
New York, NY
Amherst College
Classmate-Class of '58

"I have just finished reading your excellent book, the paperback version. You have achieved a marvellous level of research and writing. You have reason to be proud of your literary and legal effort. Congratulations and best wishes on its success."

Henry S. Bromley III
Germantown Friends School
Classmate-Class of '54

Table of Contents

Foreword
By Tom Lantos

 As a freshman member of the US Congress in 1981, I was proud to introduce legislation making Holocaust hero Raoul Wallenberg an honorary US citizen. My wife, Annette, and I were both ultimately saved by Wallenberg's valiant efforts in Hungary, and we have dedicated a good part of our lives both to preserving this hero's story and to finding out what became of him after World War II. This has been a long and trying road, but we have been fortunate to meet many fascinating and devoted Wallenberg historians along the way. Morris Wolff is one of the most distinguished among them.

In April of 1983, Morris came to Washington DC to meet with Annette and me regarding the fate of Raoul Wallenberg. His intent was to file a lawsuit against the Soviet Union seeking Wallenberg's immediate release. I invited him to testify before the House Foreign Affairs Committee, providing a platform to tell the Congress and the world of his plans. After his testimony, Morris received unanimous support from our committee and from Senator Claiborne Pell, then Chairman of the Senate Foreign Relations Committee.

Morris filed his complaint with the US District Court in February 1984. Then he and I appeared together on national television to explain the purpose of the lawsuit: Raoul Wallenberg was an innocent man who had been wrongfully imprisoned for nearly 40 years; he deserved to be freed and he deserved compensation for this egregious wrongdoing.

In this book, Morris has woven an intricate story that not only tells of Wallenberg's heroic efforts, but also includes personal accounts of those who knew Wallenberg, along with new information about the involvement of the US, Swedish, and Soviet governments.

This book will surely strike a chord with many audiences, ranging from students just learning about Holocaust history to historians interested in more deeply examining the roles of Holocaust heroes like Wallenberg. They will come away from this story with a greater understanding and more profound appreciation for a man who personified the idea that we truly are our brother's keepers. Raoul Wallenberg's story as a hero and humanitarian deserves to be told, and Morris Wolff has done so with dedication and skill.

Washington, DC
July 2007

1

Judge Barrington Parker Jr.'s Judicial Opinion

GUY VON DARDEL, on his own behalf and on behalf of his half brother, RAOUL WALLENBERG, and SVEN HAGSTROMER, Legal Guardian of RAOUL WALLENBERG, on Behalf of RAOUL WALLENBERG, Plaintiffs, v. UNION OF SOVIET SOCIALIST REPUBLICS, Defendant
Civil Action No. 84-0353
UNITED STATES DISTRICT COURT FOR THE DISTRICT OF COLUMBIA
623 F. Supp. 246; 1985 US Dist. LEXIS 14886
October 15, 1985

Ruling and Conclusion

In many ways, this action is without precedent in the history of actions against foreign sovereigns. It involves actions, which the Soviet Union has already admitted were unlawful. It involves a gross violation of the personal immunity of a diplomat, one of the oldest and most universally recognized principles of international law. Furthermore, this action involves a deliberate default by a defendant, which has repeatedly demonstrated its familiarity with the proper means for raising a defense of sovereign immunity under the *Foreign Sovereign Immunities Act.*

There can be little, if any, doubt that both subject matter and personal jurisdiction are conferred through that Act. Whatever sovereign immunity the defendant might have had, is, by the terms of the Act, subject to international [**53] agreements to which the United States was a party when the FSIA was enacted in 1976, which prohibit defendant's actions regarding Mr. Wallenberg.

Additionally, this Court determines that no applicable statute of limitations has begun to run against plaintiff's claims. Because Mr. Wallenberg is still being unlawfully held by the defendants, or alternatively, he is dead, the statute is tolled by the "discovery rule" and/or the law on tolling applicable when one party has fraudulently concealed facts.

For all of these reasons, default judgment is here by entered against the defendant.

Raoul Wallenberg's Personal Diary

Early June 1945. Stockholm Sweden (recovered Wallenberg Diary)
.*I am Raoul Wallenberg, 32 years of age and I am leaving in a few days to Budapest, Hungary to save the Jews. I have accepted this rescue assignment from the US government. This diary is for my personal use and confidential. If something happens to me I ask the finder to deliver it to Lars Berg at the Swedish Embassy in Budapest or return it to my brother Guy Von Dardel in Stockholm Sweden. I know I am headed into danger and may not return.*

The "offer" from the US War Refugee Board of their Treasury Department was formally presented to me last night at Bellsmanor Restaurant here in Sweden following several days of discussion. I will have unlimited funds to bribe the Horthy government officials to let the Jews remain in Budapest. My formal post: Secretary of the Legation of Sweden in Budapest, but working undercover directly for the US Government. I am to report directly to Cordell Hull Secretary of State, and to have the first $100,000 placed on my Stockholm Enskilda Bank account prior to departure. I can request, actually demand more money as needed for the success of my "save the Jews" mission. I hammered out the terms of my agreement last night. Ambassador Pehle, head of the USA War Refugee Board has promised to arrange my rescue when I fall into enemy hands. I do not believe them. But I now have no choice. I have accepted the assignment.

I will work with leaders of the Budapest underground in devising safe house and other schemes for saving the Jews and Gypsies of the city. Those Jews in the countryside have been destroyed, or shipped off to labor camps where they are gassed and die. This is Hitler's final country to dominate. Poland, Italy, Austria, Czechoslovakia and the rest of Europe has been conquered and made "Juden frei." (Clean of Jews)

I am 32. I hate standing by and having to watch the suffering and injustice visited on innocent people. No one here in Sweden, including my own family seems to care. They just want to make money. Feed the German war machine. They want to grow the Enskilda family bank with the sale of Swedish ball bearings and steel proceeds.

At age 26 I spent a summer in Haifa working in a Bank, sent there by my grandfather Gustav for "training." That was 1936 and Palestine was becoming a haven for refugees. With my lawyer friend, Moshe Landau, I went in the evening to watch the rusty, poor excuse for boats land and off load the poor Jews, with burlap bags, stuffed with their pathetic life possessions on their backs, disembark from ships in Haifa. They were escaping death, Hitler and Europe. They were in rags and hungry. I vowed that day to do something about it. Now is my rare and welcomed chance.

3

Whatever Happened to Raoul Wallenberg?

Now it is June 1944 and the situation for the very survival of the Jewish people and their civilization is much worse. Millions have died in the death camps, along the country roads and in large pits in the forests and no one raises a finger or shouts, "This is wrong. Stop it?" I have met three times with Ivar Olsen, the War Refugee Board representative here in Stockholm. We have had several dinners together. He is candid and honest with me. He says that Henry Morgenthau, the Jewish Secretary of Treasury, has pressured and pushed FDR to finally do something about the plight of the Jews in Europe. It is election year in America and FDR wants the Jewish vote in New York City.

This War Refugee Board, as they call the Genocide Prevention Program, should have been formed when the first Jews were taken away in 1933. Or at the latest, in 1938 when "Kristallnacht" first hit Germany with the destruction of the windows of all the Jewish shops. What were the Americans thinking? What were they waiting for?

Two nights ago on June 2, 1944 I was officially selected for this mission. I leave on June 6 stopping in Berlin on my way to Budapest. There I will visit with my uncle, the Swedish Ambassador to Germany. He says he is neutral and above the battle. He has written to my mother Maj to caution me to stay home and not to accept the assignment. His neutrality is a joke. He is the chief merchant, handling the sale of Swedish steel—Wallenberg family steel—to the Germans to make German tanks and parts for airplanes. My highly esteemed Wallenberg family is profiteering from the War!

June 4, 1944, My departure day

My beloved mother, Maj, and my brother, Guy, take me to the train station in Stockholm for my departure. I have my old tan raincoat, a knapsack, a change of clothes, and two loaded pistols, which I am taking for my own protection. My mother pleads one last time trying to talk me out of the mission. "Raoul, you are so handsome and so young. Why are you going? Can't you find something here at home? You have so much to live for here. Play polo, go out with your girlfriends Viveca and Ingrid. There will be summer parties. You have friends, parties and dances. And you have your favorite ladies. They adore you, two young and beautiful movie starlets Ingrid Bergman and Viveca Lindfors. They are clamoring for your attention. Aren't they and me and your brother and sister enough for you? Will you leave all this just to go to Budapest and save strangers, and probably get yourself killed?" My mother was prescient and clear. She knew the risk, but she also knew that once I made up my mind I would do it. She cries on my shoulder. I hold her close and comfort her. "Mama, I will be all right. I promise that I will write to you every day. I will not take chances. I promise you I will be home soon, and no later than Christmas. The war will be over. I promise".

4

June 4, 1944. On the train to Berlin.

I am on my way to Budapest. The train takes me first to Berlin. I have second thoughts about my mission now that I am away from my home and family in neutral Sweden. Soon I will journey into enemy territory in northern Germany. Soldiers will soon take over this train and occupy the cars, drinking and shouting to one another in the rough manner. Some of them will stare at my outfit, the slouch brown hat and the raincoat and ask if I am a war correspondent. But that is later. First stop Berlin, where I will be reunited with my sister Nina. I miss her gentle soul. She is like my mother, loyal, kind and caring.

June 5, 1944 Arrival in Berlin.

I am met at the train station by my sister Nina and her husband Nils Lagergren, who is assigned to work at the Swedish Embassy with my Uncle. Nils Lagergren is a lawyer, a stuff shirt who would never risk his life or choose what I am doing. He is stiff, rude and curt, and tries to tell me to have lunch with them and then get back on the train and go home. We have lunch on the Kurfurstendam and then I say goodbye and I walk to the Swedish Embassy, near to the ruins of the Reichstag. I am to be "briefed" by my uncle. I hate him. I hate what he is doing. He is helping the German war effort, up to his greedy armpits in war profits. That's why the Nazis tolerate him here.

I want to meet with him anyway. I can glean from him real news on how the war is going. I know the Germans are now suffering terrible losses in Russia and in France, and now are losing. I still want details on their operations in Budapest, and whether the Germans might be pulling out soon or entrenching. My uncle is on the inside, a favorite of the Germans. He has no scruples. Money, profit and parties are everything for him. He also hates the Jews.

June 5, 1944. Afternoon, with my uncle in Berlin

I enter the ivory white, high ceiling, ornate Swedish Embassy office at 3PM. He leaves me waiting, cooling my heels for a full half hour for no reason. He wants to show his colleagues who is boss, and that I am just a nephew; a person of little importance. He is fully aware that I want to take the night train to Budapest to start my work. I finally am ushered into his office at 3:45. He makes all kinds of excuses for the delay, asking, "How is your Mom? And your brother and sister?" Immediately he barrages me with questions; "Why are you going, what do you hope to accomplish? Are you to be the savior of the Jews?" He sneers at me, "Why don't you turn around and go home. This is not a game. It is being played on the bigger stage of life or death!"

I tell him that I am fully aware of the danger, and that "I plan to return home by Christmas with the War over. It matters. I have something I must do. These are innocent people who have done no harm. They deserve their life," We argue back and forth, trading invectives. After fifteen minutes of locking horns I *storm out. I do not have time to waste debating the issues. I am leaving tonight for Budapest. He is part of the enemy.*

June 7, 1944, Budapest Station

The train rattles on through the night. I see the lights of little towns, sleepy villages, huge fields of wheat, passing thru one sign says "City of Debrecen, 70 miles to Budapest." I open the paper map. I am sitting in the aisle outside the passenger cabin. I have taken an earlier train. No reservation. No seats left. I put my finger on Debrecen and trace my finger down the paper southeast to Budapest, the city on two sides of the Danube. I check my knapsack. Two pistols and a raincoat.

We arrive in the early morning before dawn, at the station at 6 AM. There are large yellow boxcars on the next track. I can distinctly hear the moaning and crying of people locked inside. Little children are screaming. Hands and fingers are thrust thru the slats of the boxcars, dropping paper notes down thru the slats to the ground. I get off and run over towards the departing train gather the scraps. "Remember me," one says. I am Lena Goldsmith. I live with my children and husband at Number 10 Alloi St. My children are with me. I do not know where is my husband. If you find him send him here. I need him."

These pathetic brief, hurriedly written scraps of paper, hand written victim notes make me sick in my stomach. Innocent families being pulled apart. One day living as a family, children coming home from school and playing in the back yard, living on a quiet street. Daddy going to work and coming home to read an evening paper. Mother cleaning the kitchen and preparing dinner. The next day the family pulled apart, some going to Oswiecism (Auschwitz) others to Dachau for "medical experiments". No explanation.

I have no time to waste. I must get to the Embassy and start my work. I hail a cab and am taken across the bridge over the Danube and from Buda up to Pest where I meet my new diplomatic team. Lars Berg is there along with several others. I have known Lars from before, at school. He will be my guide in these first few days.

Author's Note: The Wallenberg diary was found among his personal papers at the Swedish Embassy in Budapest at the end of the War.

Part I: Meeting Raoul Wallenberg

Whatever Happened to Raoul Wallenberg?

March 5, 1983
Philadelphia

The telephone rang in the darkness of a Saturday morning at my country home in Chestnut Hill, Philadelphia well before sunrise. After several rings, I woke up; clients would sometimes call at odd hours, when crises arose. It was 4 A.M. *"Who could be calling at this hour?"* I muttered to myself.

The first birds of morning—a mourning dove and a cardinal were singing in the darkness just outside my bedroom window. The soft pink flower of the mimosa tree moved gently in the breeze.

"May I speak with Professor Morris Wolff, please?"

"This is Professor Wolff speaking."

It was a rude interruption of a good night's sleep. My wife rolled over and muttered, "Who can that be calling?" She yawned and went back to sleep. I turned on the beam light, which focused only on my side of the bed and quickly grabbed a pen and a yellow pad of paper. I knew it must be a new client, or a client in trouble. At first the voice seemed gruff and arrogant, as if anyone had the right to call at four in the morning. But, as we spoke the man calmed down. It was a warm and soothing voice despite the early hour. There was music to it and a feeling of respect. It was a cultured and distinctive voice, reminding me of my dear friend in Germany, Ernst Voigt, who had been my "boss" during the summer of 1959, when I worked as an exchange student in Cologne at the Chamber of Commerce. It was also a bit imperial and condescending, especially calling at this early hour.

"Morris Wolff, this is Guy Von Dardel. I am the brother of Raoul Wallenberg."

"I know who you are. I was expecting your call at my office earlier this week. Professor D'Amato warned me that you would call."

I had been expecting this call, but was surprised that it hadn't come to my office during normal hours of the week, instead of interrupting a peaceful Saturday morning at home.

"Professor D'Amato, of the Northwestern Law School, called and briefed me on your complex legal matter. Your brother is the famous diplomat Raoul Wallenberg, and you have located him alive somewhere in the Soviet Gulag? I understand he has been salted away alive like the Count of Monte Cristo and has miraculously survived for thirty-nine years. Is that right?"

"Yes, thirty-nine miserable years, and now proof that he is alive has been brought to us."

"By whom?"

"By a prisoner recently set free by the Russians who shared a jail cell. He is known as the "Swede from Budapest." It is for sure my brother. I am certain

9

from the details and things these men have told me. He may not have long to live. Will you help us?"

Those were the magic words, the hook – "Will you help us?"

I put the phone back close to my mouth, "Of course, I will try to help you. I will do anything I can to get your brave brother released. But how can I assist? What can I do from here in the USA? This matter is between Sweden and the USSR. Your parents should have bribed the Russians years ago and brought him home. Why haven't Swedish lawyers helped you? Why me all the way over here in Philadelphia 39 years after the crime? And why did your wealthy family leave him to rot?" I was getting angry at the inaction of the family. I tend to be blunt where injustice is involved.

There was silence on the other end. "Some of my relatives never wanted him out. They did not want him released. They realized he would rat on them; tell of their complicity with the Nazis in selling Swedish steel for German tanks and pocketing the huge profits."

"The matter is quite complicated, Mr. Von Dardel, yes?"

"Yes, it is very complicated. But he is alive. And we want him home. Will you help us? A lawsuit demanding his release. We want you to sue the Russians. We are told you are smart, gutsy and Jewish – the man for this assignment."

"We will see," I responded. "My colleague Tony D'Amato has briefed me about your tragic situation. I will do what I can, and if I can help you, I will."

Professor D'Amato and I were colleagues and friends. I used his textbook on International law in my class. We both had been searching for a major human rights case to bring in our US federal court to test the limits of US jurisdiction, that is, to see how far a US Court would go to grant monetary relief and hold a foreign nation liable for violating the rights of its citizens or foreigners. I met Tony the year before at a piano playing of Cole Porter's "Night and Day," while playing hooky from a law lecture at the International Law Society meetings in DC.

He listened to my keynote address, and then Tony got up and left, walked down the hall to the grand ballroom and started playing the piano. I did not yet know him in person, only his famous and worthwhile book on international law. But I left the lecture a few minutes later, as fate would have it, heard the music, entered the starlit ballroom, sat down next to him and started singing. Our friendship started in song and ended up as partners in mounting the famous and historic Wallenberg lawsuit in federal court.

"So you were the famous keynote speaker, invited to address a crowd of smart lawyers and scholars from around the world." Tony chided as he riffed some notes. "I like your topic of going after rogue nations like Chile in a US Court. Maybe we can find a case and do it together, make some good legal noise, and walk together as famous jurists in the corridors of history, a team like Justices

Holmes and Brandeis. Wolff and D'Amato. I can see our names in lights!" Tony could poke fun at himself and others.

I had just returned from an American Bar Association assignment in Chile. I had been sent to investigate and report back on the torture and killings in the Santiago soccer stadium where hundreds of Chileans had been shot and mangled by Pinochet and his henchmen. It was a dangerous assignment. Chilean police followed me at every stage. My report went first to the ABA and with its unanimous endorsement forwarded to Congress. It led to Senate hearings and the passage of punitive new trade laws prohibiting the import of Chilean grapes to the United States. This was the first time the Congress asserted new laws and economic punishment for the violation of basic human rights.

My topic for the ABA and the American Society of International Lawyers—a crowd of about 200—was "What US laws can we creatively use to bring human rights violators in foreign countries in front of a US federal court in order to punish them severely?" I advocated bringing Pinochet, who like Eichmann was drugged and brought to Israel to stand trial and be executed for the genocide of the Jews—to stand trial in a US federal court and receive severe punishment for his barbaric acts of sending Chilean children to Buenos Aires – "los desparacidos," and then killing their parents in front of cheering crowds at the football stadium.

My audience of corporate and international lawyers was visibly shocked. This would be a major new reach of jurisdiction—a grab for judicial power to solve and eliminate human rights violations occurring anywhere in the world.

Some were intrigued by my novel and radical ideas for poking my unwelcomed nose into human rights violations occurring in other nations. Others were concerned that foreign governments might do the same if one of our presidents or vice presidents were traveling abroad—a complex issue in light of the US government's later behavior at Guantanamo, Abu Gharib and earlier in Vietnam.

Pinochet's brutal and murderous treatment of innocent Chilean mothers and children went unpunished. He, as dictator, decided there would be no freedom of the press or any other human rights in Chile. The courts were officially closed. I actually saw the huge black chain and large padlock on the front door of the Supreme Court building in Santiago.

I wanted to sue Pinochet, extradite him to the United States and put him away in a US jail. A radical idea at the time. But something like it had been done a few years earlier in the US federal court in *Pena Irala*. In that case a sadistic police chief, Pena Irala, killed the fifteen year old son of a popular newspaper publisher in Asuncion, Paraguay in an effort to stifle government criticism. The body of the boy, Jose Filartiga, was thrown on the front lawn of his home. Pena Irala fled to New York, thinking he would be safe from retaliation. The parents caught up with him and had him detained by INS immigration in New York. Pena

Whatever Happened to Raoul Wallenberg?

Irala, the killer of the fifteen year old boy, was tried in New York Federal District Court. Judge Kaufman found him liable for damages to the family, and subject to imprisonment under the *US Alien Tort Claims Act of 1790*, one of the first laws advocated by Thomas Jefferson. My thoughts were not radical or far-fetched. "We can do this," I told the audience. "It is just a matter of looking at history, and America's early commitment to prosecuting violation of human rights no matter where in the world they occurred. I am waiting for the right case and cause. It will come to me one day."

My talk was entitled "The Prospect of Suing Foreign Governments for Human Rights Misdeeds". It could have been called "Let's Stop the Public Killings and Hangings at the Stadium in Santiago by Suing Pinochet and his Henchmen in a US Federal Court." My long trip, commissioned by the American Bar Association, had left me shaken. I became devoted to the cause of locking up Pinochet, another Hitler on a slightly smaller scale. One night I had a private dinner in the home of two grieving parents whose three sons were gunned down in the streets of Santiago during a political demonstration against the Pinochet regime. The faces of the three young martyrs were painted on a large mural on the side of a three-story building, looming just outside the window of their home, as if to haunt them for the next ten years. After dinner, they showed me photos of eight other "disappeared children." The brutal tyrant in Chile must be stopped by his arrest, drugged and taken on a plane to New York, and then "found" by chance within the US jurisdiction. It was good enough for Eichmann; and it would be good enough for Pinochet.

Pinochet had abolished the Rule of Law. We had to stop him. I went for a dangerous two weeks with my colleague Juan Lareda Esq. of Philadelphia. We slept with the doors double locked and went everywhere with a bodyguard. He served as co-counsel and translator and helped me write the report to the US Congress which led the censure of the Pinochet government and a temporary suspension of grape imports to Philadelphia, a lucrative export trade for Chile.

Our report was carefully studied. Decisive action by Congress was taken. Laws were passed creating an economic boycott of Chilean imports until such time as corrections in government policy were made. In my speech I suggested a novel, new and different approach altogether—not government trade regulation but a grass roots citizen initiative: "Let's get a brave group of bright lawyers together—maybe eight or nine—and sue Mr. Tyrant Pinochet in a US court. We have no jurisdiction to bring legal action in a foreign country, not even if the people of that country are being tortured and killed by the thousands by the devil himself. Why not bring the devil/bastard here and hold him accountable for the torture he inflicted on his countrymen as a violation of international and US law?"

Preposterous, was what some of my colleagues thought of the idea. I am devoted to being provocative. I believe the law can be used courageously and creatively to achieve new precedents. We need not merely rely on the available cases and statutes. New frontiers of legal possibility can be created as I eventually accomplished for Wallenberg. Today it is used on a daily basis to protect the human rights of the underprivileged and less powerful.

It was 1983, and it would ultimately take years for this creative driving tactic to catch on. But I had planted the seed for a new legal idea. A huge field of positive jurisprudence has arrived in American federal courts over the past 35 years citing my case and following my lead. The Wallenberg victory spawned a whole field of new human rights cases, with injured litigants coming from places of abuse and torture, and then suing their homelands of Argentina, Turkey, Chile and elsewhere to nail "evil torturers" hiding out in American cities thinking they had escaped prosecution by leaving home.

It started with my Wallenberg case victory, with a verdict of 39 million dollars worth of damages and an order from federal court Judge Barrington Parker that Wallenberg be immediately released. Now victims of torture from other countries come to the United States seeking relief. In addition, other countries have now opened their courts for claims involving human rights crimes occurring in other countries. The example of Spanish jurist Baltasar Garzon is instructive. In 1998, his attempt to extradite Pinochet for crimes against Spaniards committed on foreign soil became an international cause célèbre.

Enough thinking ahead! Now back to my speech on Chile to the lawyers at the Shoreham Hotel in 1983. Undaunted, I walked out after my speech and down the red carpet toward an empty ballroom. Someone was playing the piano beneath a pool of white light. The tune was Cole Porter's *Night and Day*. I sat down beside him and started to sing along; not realizing it would be a fateful moment.

The man wore a black leather jacket covered with silver zippers. I learned later that the biker's jacket was a memento from his days as producer of the hit Broadway musical, *Grease*. That bonanza gave him enough money to retire and teach international law at Northwestern University. He also rode a Harley. His bushy black hair was salted with grey, as were his mustache and goatee. To my surprise, he had listened intently to my talk on Pinochet and felt as strongly as I did about the need to set international human rights law precedents in US federal courts. The piano man was Professor Tony D'Amato, whose textbook on public international law I happened to use in the classes I taught at the University of Pennsylvania Law School, and later at the Delaware Law School. We chatted and sang Cole Porter songs together. An instant friendship began to develop through music and laughter.

We went out for a beer that evening, and plotted how we might find the right test case to bring in a US court to challenge and to end human abuse and torture by a major foreign government, like the USSR or even our own government.

A few days before my pre-dawn phone call, Tony had called to alert me that I would be receiving a call from Guy Von Dardel, and why. "This is our chance," he said. In one of life's strange coincidences (many more of which form this story), it turned out that from their family home in Stockholm, Guy Von Dardel and his sister Nina Lagergren had read in the morning Dagbladet newspaper about D'Amato's work on what came to be known as the *Frolova* case.

The case of *Frolova v. Union of Soviet Socialist Republics, 761 F.2d 370 (7th Cir. 1985),* had arisen in the US federal courts of Illinois. A young American woman had gone to Moscow as a foreign exchange student and fallen in love with a Russian student named Yuri Frolova. The two married. The new Mrs. Frolova returned to her home campus of Northwestern University, where she awaited the arrival of her newlywed husband. When he failed to arrive as planned, she and her Jewish parents made inquiries. They discovered that he had been arrested as a political dissident, and was on a month-long hunger strike in a jail in Moscow.

The American woman found Tony D'Amato, then on the Northwestern Law School faculty. He helped her file a civil case against the Soviet government, justifying the suit on the basis of a treaty, the Helsinki Accords, which guaranteed the human right to reunification of families. D'Amato in a daring moment of chutzpah, asked the Judge: "Your honor, we are asking you to temporarily suspend all sales of wheat to the USSR now pending before the Chicago Board of Trade until Yuri Frolova is released from Soviet prison and allowed to rejoin his wife here in Chicago."

"The judge," according to D'Amato, "was quite taken aback by the request. He realized the international implications of suspending wheat sales during a winter of famine in Russia. He looked down at me over his horn rimmed glasses like I was vermin, and simply said he would take my request for sanctions 'under advisement'"

Hearing this radical request by counsel, the Russian legal defense quickly collapsed. Much as they wanted to continue to harass Mr. Frolova and others like him, they needed the wheat deals more; their own harvests of 1982 and 1983 had been disastrous. The very next day the Russians put Yuri Frolova on a one-way TWA flight to Chicago's O'Hare Airport where he rejoined his new wife and her family. Lesson learned: never aggravate a Jewish mother and her daughter. It may lead to new international law.

When Von Dardel and his sister read about the *Yuri Frolov* case they wondered if Tony D'Amato could start a legal action in an American court, threaten the disruption of wheat sales, and force the USSR to release their brother. They called Tony, whose response was quick and simple: "I am not the right man for this case. But I know who is. He is a lawyer with criminal trial experience as a Chief Assistant District Attorney in Philadelphia and years of success handling civil litigation. He is the lawyer I would choose if I were in your shoes. He shares my deep interest in human rights litigation. I will call and see if he will take your case. His name is Morris Wolff."

Another reminder that something needed to be done immediately had arrived at the Wallenberg home in Sweden in the form of a mysterious and anonymous phone call to Von Dardel only a few days prior to the article's appearance in the paper.

"Hello," a man's voice said in German, "I want to speak with Guy Von Dardel, the brother of Raoul Wallenberg."

Von Dardel had heard this sort of 'message from prison' call before. Something about the tone, the furtive and muffled nature of the voice, and the humorless urgency gave it away: another message from another ghost from the Gulag. It was the horror that never stopped; it only receded, or seemed to recede, when he turned his back on it.

"This is Von Dardel," he answered in German. "I am his brother. Who is this?"

"I can not tell you, Doctor Von Dardel. But, I have a message from your brother. He is alive. He wants you to rescue him."

Of course, just another message. They never dared to say who they were. Sometimes it was just a call. Sometimes demands for money were made. Von Dardel told me that he would typically go to the bus station at midnight to meet yet another stranger, and hand him some money, in exchange for a scrap of information about his brother. He would look in the stranger's eyes, trying to glimpse in them his brother Raoul. Then the stranger would say a few cryptic words of comfort, and board a bus and disappear back into the shadows.

This latest caller said what all the others had said: "Your brother is alive. I was with him three days ago in a cell at Lubyanka Prison. I promised him I would 'call you immediately upon my release. I am fulfilling my promise. Goodbye."

"No, wait," said Von Dardel. "Please, tell me about my brother."

The man was silent.

"Otherwise," said Von Dardel, "what am I to make of your phone call?"

"He is alive. He is in decent health. They still move him around inside the Gulag. Everywhere he goes, he is well known. The prisoners marvel that he has survived so long. They believe he has a secret power, and a strong will to live. He has shown great courage and an unusual sense of humor that keeps him alive. He is warmly received by the men in prison and has become an inspiration to live for them. He is known by residents of the Gulag as the Swede from Budapest."

"He says, 'As long as I communicate to the outside world, I am alive.'"

"He had one thing that he would repeat over and over again."

15

Von Dardel asked "What was that quote?"

"He would say 'turn your head towards God and God will turn his head towards you'"

Then the stranger hung up, after making no demands for money, or anything else.

It was a scintilla of hope, delivered alongside the *Yuri Frolov* case report.

Von Dardel immediately telephoned Professor D'Amato in Chicago. Tony immediately recommended me for the case, based on my background in international law with courtroom experience. "Morris Wolff is your man," he said. "I will provide back up for him as Second Chair. That means I will assist him with research but Morris will argue the case in court." Three days later Von Dardel interrupted my sleep with the case that no one else would touch.

The Wallenberg case struck me immediately as highly unusual. Over the phone that first morning I was not prepared to form an immediate legal opinion as to its viability. I needed to research the international and federal laws involved. I wanted to talk with colleagues in the international law field.

Von Dardel's phone call stirred up my emotions. Not just the cool tone of his voice, but waking me at home on a weekend. I knew hardly anything about him, just that he was one of the almighty Wallenberg dynasty, industrialists and statesmen, the Rockefellers of Sweden. My first impulse was to turn him down based on his presumptuousness and his arrogance—no matter how I felt about his brother.

Then I thought again about Raoul and his pitiable condition, sitting alone in a jail cell in Russia. I also thought about his historic deeds, as related to me by Tony D'Amato in his phone call a few days earlier, and now briefly recounted by his brother. To me, Wallenberg was the greatest hero of the 20th century. He saved thousands of Jews, all strangers. Now he needed to be rescued after thirty-nine years of unjustified imprisonment that violated every standard of human rights law.

From the beginning of my legal career, I have always welcomed the opportunity to help others less fortunate, and to assist victims of injustice. Here was my chance; a chance to become the voice for one of the great men of the 20th century. Despite my reservations, I seized the opportunity. This was a chance to make a difference –to walk in the corridors of history and to force the Soviets to release a great man. I would become Wallenberg's voice and his representative. Von Dardel was merely the messenger and my titular client, while his brother's plight became my true concern.

"I need to research the case," I told him. "We may have a chance." Immediately, I began considering a lawsuit plus other strategies. I thought to myself, what other ways could I pressure the Soviets to release the prisoner? Maybe I will go to Moscow and file a *habeas corpus* petition, best testing the legality of Soviet detention. I mused, that might be a losing effort but it will attract worldwide attention. I was already considering a multiplicity of strategies. I thought to myself he should have been freed years ago.

"Why are you acting so late?" I asked Von Dardel. "Why didn't your rich family offer a generous bribe to the Russians back in 1945? Why hasn't a Swedish lawyer stepped forward to help you with this national hero of Sweden in all these years? And finally, why me? Why have you come all the way over to the United States to find the right attorney?"

Von Dardel hesitated, and then explained with a hint of apology. "We should have acted sooner. I trust Professor D'Amato's advice. He has great respect for you. As to the family bribe, the rich part of my family refused to act. They don't care. As far as they are concerned Raoul can rot in prison."

"I am not a rich man. I work for very modest pay in Geneva as a nuclear physicist at the Center for Nuclear Research. I have no real money. But we want you to do this the right way. We want you to stick to principle, fight the Russians to release Raoul, and allow him to come home. We want you to sue the Soviets for their refusal to release my brother. From what we hear, you are the right man with the right skills to help us."

Although certain Wallenbergs are quite wealthy and powerful, those relations wanted nothing to do with Raoul. Some were actually mean spirited, and greedy only for money. They actively worked against Wallenberg's release. Raoul was considered a lost cause, an embarrassment. He was better dead than alive; a problem none of them were eager to deal with. This distance between members of the family was easily maintained, as it was Raoul's father who had been "The Wallenberg", but he had died before Raoul was born. Guy and Nina shared the same mother as Raoul, but had a different father. Guy had only his modest scientist's income while Nina was the wife of Gunnar Lagergren, a member of the European Court of Human Rights in Strasbourg. In addition to not being wealthy, Gunnar Lagergren too, it seemed, was embarrassed by the continued search for Raoul and wanted Guy and Nina to accept the manufactured idea that Raoul was dead. Gunnar could have maneuvered the case in front of the European Court many years earlier had he had any guts to do so. He could have used his prestige to signal the Swedish government to initiate the case against the USSR.

"In truth," Guy Von Dardel told me, "I am under pressure from all sides of the family and the government of Sweden to stop searching, but I refuse to give up. I have looked everywhere for help but no one in the family will assist me. I even solicited Kofi Annan, the Secretary General of The United Nations. He is married to my niece Nane Wallenberg, and neither one will lift a finger of assistance. As long as there is a one in a million chance I will go on. Will you please help us? Professor D' Amato says that you are the right man for this job. He has persuaded us that you have the backbone and carriage to go forward as our lawyer. He suggests that you even have a better brain than his. He told us of your work on Civil Rights with Bobby Kennedy in the Justice Department and that you reported to President Kennedy as well."

Von Dardel argued his own case for my coming on board pretty well. I was impressed by his sincerity. I was also impressed by his loyalty to his brother and his refusal to quit. Later he flew over from Stockholm and I met him in person in Washington, DC. We walked up the steps of the federal courthouse together on February 2, 1984 to file the lawsuit. We spent many hours together that snowy weekend in Washington walking to the Lincoln and Jefferson Memorials from the Hay Adams Hotel where we stayed. We walked at night, just the two of us. I learned all about his brother Raoul.

I began to imagine, during our first phone conference, the weight of his repeated disappointments—the blind alleys, the dishonest people, and the cowardice of Swedish Foreign Minister Unden. He met with Stalin and was intimidated in 1945—just weeks after Raoul's capture by the Soviets. Unden caved in, and refused to demand Wallenberg's release, thus sealing his fate to a barren jail cell, incommunicado for many years. I shared Guy's frustration with the run around and policy of craven abandonment by the Swedish and American governments, the excuses and lies and obfuscation of indifferent bureaucrats, and the money spent on promises. Now, the coincidence of the anonymous phone call from the released prisoner and the newspaper report of the *Frolova* case had offered Guy another glimmer of hope.

I spoke with Von Dardel for nearly two hours. I was spellbound by the human details of his story and his passion. By the end of our chat, faint rays of dawn had begun to filter through the window, lighting up the pink mimosa trees coming into bloom, and yellow forsythia bushes at my Devonshire country manor house in Chestnut Hill. My children were stirring looking for Saturday morning breakfast, always prepared by Daddy. It was 6 A.M. Von Dardel had talked for two hours. We bonded as friends and as attorney-client. I respected him as much as he respected me. After my initial burst of irritation with his voice, I began to find something familiar and trustworthy in it. At last it hit me. His voice was uncannily similar to that of an old friend of mine, Ernst Voigt. This pleasant association was one of the factors in my deciding to accept and prosecute the case.

Although Von Dardel's accent was Swedish, it was near enough to German that it had initially set off alarm bells in me. These alarm bells had been ringing for my family for at least two generations. Had my father as a bar mitzvah boy not left Germany in 1912, shepherded by his mother to start life over in America, he and our entire family might have ended as cinders in the Nazi crematoria. We might have been trapped, shipped off to a death camp, and obliged to hope against hope for a Wallenberg—someone brave enough to save our lives.

Fortunately, my grandmother could see into the future. She already felt the cold chill of anti-Semitism and the gibes and humiliation in her little hometown of Niedermarsberg. She had a severe limp from a birth defect leaving one leg shorter than the other, and the people teased her, called her "Gimpel Lena" to her face. At times they spit on her. Finally she had enough. She closed her successful millinery shop—the best one in town I was later told in 1959 when I visited my Dad's birthplace—and said "We're Going to America." Thank God!

My father held two passionate beliefs. They were the sun and the moon of my childhood. The first was his deep love and passion for America, his adopted country. He built a flagpole in the front yard and every Sunday morning and every holiday—my father would raise the American flag. The second passion was his deep loathing for Hitler and the Nazis, and the evil creators of the Holocaust. During World War II I traveled on a weekly basis from Philadelphia to Baltimore. He would stop at *Hausners* German restaurant in Baltimore. German sympathizers gathered there: they drank beer and spoke German. It was a well-known American gathering place of the *Bund*, German American sympathizers. My Dad, having been raised in Germany until age 13 spoke perfect German. He simply pretended to be what he was—a salesman stopping to sell dresses in Baltimore. He picked up loose talk about the German naval war effort and the night time movement and surfacing of German U-boats off the Atlantic coast near Baltimore. He overheard conversations in German about the U-Boats and their suspected movement. One night he listened in on a conversation focused on a Nazi plan to land sailors by rowboat from a surfaced German U Boat submarine. The plan, which was actually accomplished, was to land somewhere on a desolate stretch of beach near Montauk, Long Island in New York. He took this information the next day to the War Department in Washington. The landing of that rowboat was carefully monitored and the Nazi "invasion of Long Island" was thwarted. The four sailors of the U Boat were captured and later tried in an American court of law. My Dad became an unsung hero. He was given a Citation for Outstanding Citizen Service by President Harry Truman for his quiet, patriotic and unsung work. "It was my duty." These were his only words when asked.

Even after the war, *Hausners* restaurant remained a favorite place for Americans of German decent—loyal and otherwise. In the 1950s I traveled there with my dad during vacations on some of his business trips to Baltimore and Washington. As president of Form-Fit Dresses he was responsible for designing and manufacturing the popular women's dresses from the factory located at 148 W. 37th Street, New York City. I remember visiting his busy place of business and seeing the rows and rows of material, being cut by the women at their sewing machines, and the button sewers. Being a superb dress salesman on the road was his "cover" and also his actual business. It made it easy for him to be a spy since he also sold his dresses to the top department stores—Hechts, Woodward and Lothrop, Garfinckel's and other high-posh stores in Baltimore and Washington. He hated Hitler and the abuse of the Jews. He and my mom knew exactly what was going on, as did President Franklin Delano Roosevelt who failed to take prompt action to save the Jews.

In the spring of 1959 I observed a sign on the law school bulletin board at Yale: "Work Abroad-All Expenses Paid." That's all it said but it went right to my heart. I was looking for adventure and I didn't have the money to travel. This was my introduction to the AIESEC (Association Internationale des Etudiants en Sciences Economique et Commerciales) student exchange program. I signed the green forms and applied as my first choice to go to Israel. God has strange, and at times comedic plans for all of us. I signed up to go to Israel, Italy or Ireland. God decided on Cologne so that I could learn German. When I was offered a traineeship in Cologne, my father absolutely refused to allow me to go.

"No son of mine will ever set foot in Germany," he announced. I took this as a threat; an example of his desire to dominate and control his sons. I grew up against this strong personality and his strength made me strong.

As we argued about it, my mother interceded:

"This has nothing to do with you Leo, or your past. It is our son's choice not yours. I believe he has a mission. It is his time. The turn of the wheel now is towards peace. It is 1959, not 1943. Morris is destined to be a peacemaker between young people in America and Germany, and perhaps the whole world. He will go to a country still hostile toward Jews and he will make new friends. He will help to heal the wounds of the world and become a man of peace." My mother was right. She was broad-minded and spiritual. She placed her love and confidence in me. I thanked her for her courage and for standing up to my father. That is the only time I saw my dad speechless and at a loss for words. The only time he actually said, "Yes dear!"

In that memorable and life changing summer of 1959, just fourteen years after the end of World War II my idealism, and my ability to face a challenge, and make new friends in a hostile place was confirmed. Despite my father's strongly held and understandable beliefs, not only did I go to the land of my family's birthplace and enemies, but to the bustling cathedral city of Cologne on the beautiful Rhine River. It was just 40 miles from my father's country village of Niedermarsberg, where sadly no Jews lived anymore. I visited there on a forgiveness and healing trip. The mayor gave me a volume about the small village where my dad was born and spent his first fourteen years. I heard tales about my dad in his younger years from some of his friends who remembered him vividly as high energy, (the German word is "ausgelossen") full of life and a hell raiser who broke into the local sauerkraut factory one Saturday afternoon with his friend Percy Thorner. I learned my dad was also a rule breaker who set up his own code of conduct and his own rules, regardless of what society might have to say. As a result of my warm and positive welcome, my dad ultimately did return to his little village for a process of healing and reconciliation of his own. I treasure the postcard he sent to me: "This is from your mother and me. Here we are again standing and visiting old friends in Niedermarsberg."

During that summer of 1959 I immersed myself in the German language and became fluent in just two months. I also developed lifelong friendships, which continue up until now—some fifty good years later.

Ernst Voigt, head of the Cologne Chamber of Commerce, was my sponsor. His voice sounded just like Von Dardel's—one of the reasons I accepted the case. I remember approaching Herr Voigt's office door for the first time - with all my fears and prejudices aglow, my mind braced for images of Nazi brutality and fanatical regimentation. And there were the words, on the white closed door to Ernst Voigt's office. The scary and intimidating title, "Geschaftsfuehrer" confronted me. The sign simply meant managing director or chief executive, but my imagination ran wild!

I thought, "Well, here comes another fuehrer!" I was prepared to meet a control freak and a monster.

Instead I opened the heavy door and met a kind, joyful puckish man with a large radiant smile. Our friendship remained dear to me for fifty years. I traveled to Germany often to visit with him. My final visit was just before he passed away in 2009.

On the first day I arrived at his office he said, "Come in Herr Wolff. I have a great assignment for you." I sat on the edge of my chair as he went to his coat closet and emerged with a black English derby on his head, and a rust colored Burberry tweed sport jacket, with brown felt elbow patches—the perfect gentleman—and a long black closed umbrella draping from his arm. "I am the Duke of Bedford," he announced, in a moment of high parody. "And your assignment Herr Wolff during your traineeship with us this summer, will be to change my accent and to teach me the King's English." Needless to say, he already spoke a perfect English and French—and he announced my 'assignment' with a perfect Oxford English accent."

"But Herr Voigt," I replied. "I am just an American. I can not teach you the King's English." He laughed and replied, "Then you will just have to teach me American, I suppose." He broke the ice by making fun of himself. He put me at ease. He also broke the stereotype of what I expected a serious "fuehrer" to be.

Herr Voigt loved classical music and opera. I learned that summer about his deep regard for Jewish culture and Jewish people. "You are God's people, a very good and bright people. Hitler had it all wrong. I was held during the war in prison and was among a group of conscientious objectors numbered to be killed. Just before the end I was set free in the nick of time." During the war Herr Voigt, as general manager of the Cologne Chamber of Commerce, tried to save his

Jewish employees from deportation to the camps. Before the war he had collected priceless phonograph records of Jewish singers, some murdered in the Holocaust. He somehow kept his collection intact throughout the Nazi reign. Like Wallenberg he stood up to the Gestapo and was almost killed. He had tried to locate and rescue missing Jews who worked for the chamber of commerce by visiting Gestapo headquarters in person and asking for them by name. Later, he worked underground in the German resistance confronting the policies of the Nazis. Getting to know Ernst Voigt as my boss-friend melted my fears of being in a strange enemy land and dissolved my pre-conceived prejudices. One day on the way home from our regular Saturday afternoon visit to the sauna, the only afternoon we did not work, I confided to him:

"Ernst, I must tell you something so that you are not later embarrassed to find out."
"What is it?"
"I want you to know that I am Jewish."
"I did not know that until now."

He put his arms around me there in the street in front of his home on Sulzgurtel Ring. "It is good that you are here to see what we are trying to do in the new Germany. And it is good that young people and older people see that you are normal, not wearing horns." His lessons of tolerance and acceptance, and his ability to listen to other human beings and their stories, helped to make me a better person and a better lawyer.

Von Dardel and Voigt were cut from the same cloth—honorable European men of principle and devoted to justice. I agreed after my first conversation to take the case *pro bono*. I knew at the outset that it would be an important and historic case. I prayed that I might win.

I would make the victory and vindication a tribute to Raoul Wallenberg's great work; my way to shine a bright light, and the steady glare of good publicity on his dark and lonely prison cell. I did not harbor high hopes of victory, but I knew the international attention on Wallenberg might pressure the Russians to spit him out towards freedom. I gathered a team of bright and gutsy lawyers; they committed themselves to *pro bono* service and to follow my lead. They proved worthy of the task. The case was prosecuted with dignity, with knowledge of the law, and with no money involved.

In 1981, in the *Letelier* case, a US court held the government of Chile liable and responsible for the car bombing of former Chilean diplomat Letelier near DuPont Circle in Washington, DC. Pinochet's death squad went to Washington and planted the bomb. When the car started it exploded, sending debris spewing and falling among mothers and children playing near the fountain. Two Pinochet gangsters were identified as directly involved in killing the outspoken former Chilean Ambassador, who remained in Washington after Pinochet accomplished his military coup. The federal court award for the murder by car bomb was $11.4 million. This case became my model for Wallenberg in court.

The federal district court in Washington, DC enforced its judgment by confiscating two fully equipped and operative LACSA Chilean passenger planes at Dulles airport. Per court order, the US Marshal and the local sheriff simply went up to the fuselage and slapped a writ of attachment on each plane and ordered the planes sold, which they were, and the proceeds paid to the Letelier family. *Letelier* was admittedly an easier case, as the tort or injury had occurred in Washington, inside the borders of the US. Wallenberg was kidnapped from a point outside the USA and never brought here, thus making my case to free Raoul Wallenberg much tougher. Could I stretch this *Alien Tort* statute to include a tortuous wrong happening outside the borders and beyond territorial jurisdiction? We had nothing to lose by trying.

Five inspirational quotes drove me forward.
The first, from my father: "The only sin in life is low aim."
The second: "It Can Be Done," a motto framed above my grandfather's desk.
Third, "It is Better to Light a Candle than to Curse the Darkness,"
Fourth: "Know the Truth and it Shall Set you Free."
These last two mottos I learned from the Quakers at Germantown Friends School. I have adopted many of their values as my own.
Fifth: a quote attributed to British writer Edmund Burke, "The only thing necessary for the triumph of evil is for good men to do nothing."

I knew instinctively this would be a long shot case—but the legal challenges were only a small part of what we needed to overcome. The first line of attack was to get the public's attention and to shine a light on the brutal injustices in the Wallenberg case. This might force a political settlement and obviate the need for a confrontational legal action.

Von Dardel and I agreed to speak the following Saturday, once I had completed my research. We would re-engage in conversation and discuss our plans at a more reasonable hour. Von Dardel was embarrassed and apologized profusely when he finally realized midway through our two hour conversation that he had miscalculated the time difference and had awakened me in the wee hours of a weekend morning.

After I hung up I began thinking, could I win a lawsuit against the Soviet Union, against the nation itself, for a thirty-nine year old crime of kidnapping and assaulting a diplomat? Could the case survive an attack by Russian lawyers on the absence of power of the US federal courts to even hear the merits of my argument? As far as I knew, no United States court had ever taken jurisdiction over a case that happened beyond the territorial limit—that is, beyond the American shoreline. I would need some novel arguments and a miracle would also help. The right judge would make all the difference, one willing to hear our argument and not just dismiss the suit out-right as "a political question." Political questions cannot be addressed by a court, only legal ones. So I had to create or locate a relevant "legal question" or very relevant law. How do I do that, I wondered softly as I turned the light out and put the pad of yellow paper on the night table. And certainly I would need a judge with a fresh outlook. And even if I won the case... would that actually force the Soviet Union to free Wallenberg?

I sat there in the morning light looking through my pages of notes. *Sightings of Wallenberg: Lubyanka Prison, Lefortovo, Vladimir, Mordivinia, Gorky, Wrangel Island—thirty miles from Alaska. Von Dardel gave information to the Swedish ministry. Nothing done. Don't care. USA. - don't care.*

I realized our conversation had not begun to address the most maddening questions about this case. On the next page I wrote some of them: *Why are the Russians holding Wallenberg alive all these years? Why did they arrest him in the first place? Why won't they let him go? What do they get out of keeping Wallenberg? Is he still alive? Is this a wild goose chase, a quixotic notion of continued life? Even if I win, will this just be a pyrrhic victory?"* What did the Russians get out of burying a living man and then keeping him alive for four decades? If I took the case, my work would uncover some of the answers.

Even though it was Saturday, I decided to start my research right then and there that morning. I called my buddy Ted Heisler, a fellow member of the Germantown Cricket Club:

"Ted, I need to cancel our tennis date for this morning. I have a hot new law case involving a Swedish diplomat named Wallenberg. It needs my immediate attention,"

"Go to it. That's important. My wife Elisabet, a loyal Swede is interested in the plight of Wallenberg. She has been following his disappearance with interest. We will re-schedule for next week."

That Saturday morning I made breakfast for my two daughters. It was a weekly ritual and gave me a chance to assert my "fantastic gourmet cooking skills." I prepared my famous "a la Maurice shipwrecked egg special," as they called it adapting my first name to its French equivalent. This was a tradition I could not break even for Wallenberg. Then I would seek out Elizabeth Arnold, the "walking encyclopedia" at the Penn Law School Library, where I was a Professor of International Law and Ethics. Elizabeth Arnold had a passion for William Faulkner, the Swedish Nobel Prize winner for literature in 1950. I had published in 1983 an acclaimed scholarly article "William Faulkner and His Knowledge of the Law." We had bonded as Faulknerians, thus giving me very special library privileges, which were not granted to the general law faculty. She thought I was brilliant and told me so. She loved to tease me about being a "renaissance man." I would now tell Elizabeth, my fellow William Faulkner expert, that I needed a miracle—a law to protect international diplomats on assignment to a foreign country, even one who has been kidnapped. She was willing to go to the trouble of helping me on this special out-of-the-box mission. Would I be allowed to sue in an American court? Wallenberg was sitting alone in a prison somewhere five thousand miles away. What about territorial jurisdiction? Would that theory of international law pre-empt my chance to sue and be heard?

The Penn Law Library held a vast collection of international law materials. My case needed a miracle. My daughters Michelle and Lesley, fourteen and eleven at that time, teased me about working on a Saturday. "Come play with us. It is our day to play with you."

Feeling somewhat guilty about leaving my children on a Saturday, I went upstairs to get dressed and say goodbye to my wife, Debby. She is a practicing lawyer, specializing in tax, estates and family law. The daughter of a salesman, she has natural street sense. She was always the realist to my idealist. I shared the details of the phone call with her.

"Be careful," she said. "You're setting a lot of things in motion that have been dormant for many years."

"I have to do it," I said.

She said, "Make it quite clear. Get it in writing that Guy Von Dardel, as a representative of the powerful Wallenberg family, has come to you and has selected you as the one and only lawyer for this case. Let them know that once aboard you will be totally in charge, and that you will take complete charge as "Captain of the Ship", like a chief doctor in the operating room—what you say goes, with no interference. There will be a following of your orders and insubordination will not be tolerated."

Debby was tough and quite correct. I obtained the "Captain of the Ship" agreement in writing. All was in place before I proceeded with the assignment. I later obtained that agreement in writing and it proved to be important.

"This could become very dangerous," she said. "Taking on the Russians as Mister Nice Guy with no police protection may create harm for you. The Russians play hardball. They may try to muffle your voice and even kill you."

We cherished our privacy, safety and security as a close-knit family. I knew I would be threatened by taking on a politically explosive lawsuit. As a family, we did not want to lose these qualities of our privacy and our private life. The possibility of KGB surveillance was known to me as a serious risk. I was told that at the outset. But surveillance was only one of several possible invasions that this morning's phone call had invited into my home. We could have stopped to consider them all. But of course we did not.

Little did I know how much this cause and this case would personally cost me in terms of my family life and professional career!

Getting to Know Raoul Wallenberg

When I received that early morning phone call from Guy Von Dardel, I knew only what Professor Anthony D'Amato had told me of the Raoul Wallenberg story. As the case evolved, in addition to reading the published biographies, chronicling what was known of Wallenberg's life, I had the opportunity to hear stories directly from several key survivors rescued by Wallenberg. These private stories of men and women who worked with Wallenberg in Budapest have never been published before. I will relate some of them in these pages. These include the brave story of my new friend Bruce Teicholz who crossed the Carpathian Mountains and walked from Poland to Budapest in the dead of a cold winter to help Wallenberg. I met Teicholz on many occasions at his home in New York. He had survived through grit and determination as the head of Wallenberg's 440 person office staff. He was still in management in 1985 when I met him, but now on Park Avenue in property management rather than people management. We had dinner together. We shared his story and the dangers he faced as head of the underground in Budapest. I found him friendly, cooperative and humble.

In June of 1983, when I was invited by the House Foreign Affairs Committee to testify on my plan to sue the Soviets, I met several survivors including Agnes Adachi, a former secretary in Wallenberg's office. She and I remained friends for the next twenty-eight years. Both of us continued to search for Wallenberg. She died in 2011 after a full life in Forest Hills, New York. She always reminded me how lucky she had been to work with Wallenberg and to survive and to come and live in America. I met Wallenberg's chief assistant, the very beautiful Judith Yaron in Jerusalem in the summer of 1985. When she was nineteen, she was Wallenberg's personal secretary in Budapest. I also met Esther Weiss, Harry Spitz and other good souls saved by Wallenberg.

One of his most important survivors is his photographer Tom Veres, who supplied me with the photos for this book that he took as Wallenberg's photographer in Budapest. Tom survived the war and took up residence in New York City, working for the public relations firm of J. Walter Thompson. The forever loyal Tom Veres followed Wallenberg everywhere night and day, to the homes of Jews, to the train stations, to negotiations for the freedom of those trapped in the city and throughout the streets of Budapest, as Wallenberg pursued his effort to rescue Jews. Tom's priceless photographs of Wallenberg were personally given to me by him in his New York office in 1985. They are featured in this book.

Tom's last words to me were, "I want you to have these photographs for your book, Morris. You must write a book about what happened in Hungary and about what Raoul accomplished."

I am Wallenberg's lawyer and his would be rescuer. Others have written fine biographies, but they focus mainly on his work up to his capture in 1945 with a few speculations on his continuing in life. My book, for the first time, uncovers evidence of his remaining alive at least through the year 1998, when he was visited by our former United States Economic Affairs Officer at the Moscow Embassy, David Evans. This important and historic one on one visit took place in a second floor hospital room in Kazan, 500 miles east of Moscow on the Volga River.

Here in this chapter is a brief overview for those readers who may not be intimately familiar with or would like to be reminded of some of the key pieces of Raoul Wallenberg's story.

The tale begins in May of 1944, as Iver Olsen, Stockholm Chief of the US War Refugee Board, was looking for young, strong, and daring men of good will, from neutral countries, like Sweden, Turkey and Switzerland, to go into areas like Budapest and Greece, to save the Jews. The US War Refugee Board, headquartered in Washington, DC, and formed to save the last remnant of European Jewry, had branch offices in different neutral European countries, including Sweden, Turkey and Switzerland.

Two days after opening an office of the War Refugee Board on the Strandvagen in Stockholm, Olsen was agonizing over the difficulty of recruiting the ideal candidate for the mission, which was not without danger. In the elevator, on his way down stairs to buy some cigarettes, he ran into Kolman Lauer, a local businessman. On a whim, Olsen asked Lauer if he happened to know of a Hungarian-speaking Swede who might want to rescue the Jews of Budapest. Lauer did not scoff, as Olsen expected. Instead he asked questions about the War Refugee Board. It turned out that Lauer was Wallenberg's Jewish partner in an import export business with dual headquarters in Budapest and Stockholm. The family of Kolman Lauer's wife lived in Keckskemet in central Hungary. Lauer was frantically trying to get them out but could not go because he was Jewish. He had already discussed the problem with Raoul who volunteered to help rescue his partner's wife's family. Lauer, when the elevator reached the ground floor told Iver Olsen "I will put my mind to it." Lauer already had Wallenberg in mind. He knew the right person. He assured Olsen that he would not take long with an answer.

The next morning, Lauer phoned Olsen. "I have just the man for the mission," he informed Olsen. "He is my business partner, a young man named Raoul Wallenberg."

Bored and frustrated, Wallenberg had been looking for adventure. Because their export business had focused on Hungary, he was fluent in several languages, including Hungarian. Lauer promised Olsen that Wallenberg was cunning and intelligent. Lauer arranged for Olsen to meet Wallenberg the next morning. The young man showed up fashionably attired in a gray business suit, white shirt, blue tie and sunglasses. He told Olsen that he had Jewish friends with whom he did business in Budapest, and that he wanted to go and rescue the family of Lauer's wife. Wallenberg seemed to Olsen a down-to-earth businessman with good organization skills and a hard-nosed business sense. He believed he could complete his business rounds and still keep an eye out for the Jews. He also struck Olsen as having a strong desire to serve a higher purpose. As far as family ties…he had none, and could leave immediately. In fact, he had twice proposed marriage to the well-known actress Viveca Lindfors, and she had refused him both times. In addition to all the more noble reasons, this mission might prove an opportunity to win her back.

Olsen sent a cable to the US immediately:

"To Secretary of State Cordell Hull, and to Ambassador Pehle of the War Refugee Board:

We have found a new young eagle for assignment in Hungary. He is fearless. When he speaks of saving the Jews he gets a dark messianic look in his brown eyes and stares right through you. He is a man already obsessed with a sense of mission. His name is Wallenberg, a famous name here in Sweden. He has excellent family networks in Hungary, Sweden and Germany. He will be vetted tomorrow night at an inaugural dinner, and then flown to Berlin to visit his Uncle the Ambassador to Berlin from Sweden for a briefing, and then to Budapest to begin his work."

The next evening Olsen and Ambassador Herschel Johnson from the US Embassy in Stockholm met with Wallenberg and Lauer at the fashionable Bellsmanor Restaurant, Stockholm's fanciest restaurant, in the downtown area near the water. Wallenberg's motives became clearer to Olsen. He saw the mission as an opportunity to rescue thousands of human beings and walk into the history books as a hero. Wallenberg was driven by altruism, but something else as well. Olsen sensed that Wallenberg was also motivated by a determination to prove himself to his family.

Born just after his father died, Wallenberg grew up privileged, educated and talented. The Wallenberg's were a banking dynasty. Though he had the ability to succeed, his father's death left him without a connection to the family's inner sanctum, He'd been snubbed, ignored, and denied a place in the family business. By successfully completing a mission like the one proposed, he could rise above the fame of his family and make up for years of wounded feelings.

At the dinner, Wallenberg negotiated his own deal. He demanded a bank account in his name at the Wallenberg family's *Enskilda Bank* with an immediate payment of $100,000 in it, to be used for any purpose, including necessary bribes to Nazi leaders and Hungarian Arrow Cross generals. There was to be no interference, and no middlemen. Wallenberg would report by cable directly to Cordell Hull, FDR's Secretary of State, so as to avoid any breach in security. A guarantee of rescue was built into the package, an insurance policy of retrieval from either the Nazis or the Russians as needed. "The US will not leave you behind, if you are arrested. We will not leave you to twist in the wind." The US government was relying on Wallenberg and Wallenberg was led to believe that he could rely on the US. Ironically, it was the Nazis, not the Russians, whom Wallenberg feared most.

Wallenberg would be given full reign to run his own operation to save the Jews of Budapest. Iver Olsen, also a member of the Office of Strategic Services (OSS), a precursor to the CIA, may have added another assignment to Wallenberg's humanitarian mission—to supply information on German and Russian troop movements.

Ambassador Johnson wrote a cable to Secretary of State Cordell Hull regarding this meeting with Wallenberg that night:

There is no doubt in my mind as to the sincerity of Wallenberg's purpose because I've talked to him myself and was told by Wallenberg he wants to be able to help effectively save lives and that he was not interested in going to Budapest merely to write reports to be sent to the Foreign Office.

In July 1944, thirty-two year old Raoul Wallenberg arrived in Berlin from Stockholm. A young English-speaking Swede with an architecture degree from the University of Michigan, he had been working until then with Kolman Lauer in the import of goods from Hungary. He had traveled to Berlin to see his uncle, Jacob Wallenberg, the Swedish Ambassador to Nazi Germany. His stepsister Nina Lagergren, the mother of Nane Wallenberg, met him at Templehof Airfield. In her mid-twenties and six months pregnant with Nane, Nina was accompanied by her husband Gunnar Lagergren, a formidable lawyer, who represented the interests of countries whose diplomats had left Berlin.

Nina told me the following, "Raoul clutched a knapsack packed with his dinner suit and trench coat and a mix of other content: bundles of letters from Hungarians living in Sweden, a copy of a telegram sent by the king of Sweden to the Regent of Hungary, documents showing that the American Jewish Joint Distribution Committee had deposited $100,000 in his Swedish bank account, and a revolver older than he was."

At last the 32-year-old neutral Swede had found an important role to play in the world war. Dressed for the mountains in hiking boots and a slouch hat, carrying the stuffed knapsack and a sleeping bag, Raoul cut a conspicuously unconventional figure, in an airfield bristling with uniformed men dashing about and shouting orders.

As they drove away from the airfield, sirens began piercing the mid-day blue. Gunnar skidded the car to a halt on the shoulder of the highway. He pointed to a concrete bunker, shouting "run!" Explosions shook the ground around them. It was Raoul's first experience of bombings in war.

The American OSS Intelligence Agency had told Raoul that the war had turned, that the beaches of Normandy were now secured by the Allied British and American forces as a result of D-Day on June 6. He would be leaving for Budapest, via Berlin, just one month later on July 6, 1944 and was promised safe passage home following his dangerous assignment. He was surprised by the continued fighting. What's more, Gunnar told him, in Budapest, where Raoul was headed the next morning, he would have to wait for the Russians to arrive.

They dropped Raoul off at the Swedish embassy, on Embassy Row near the burned-out Reichstag. At the embassy, Raoul was told that his uncle, Ambassador Wallenberg, had vital business to conduct until three that afternoon. Could he return at that time? Later he told Nina he spent the afternoon walking along the mostly gutted buildings of Embassy Row. The former US and British embassies were closed. The Austrian embassy was open, as were the Japanese and Hungarian missions. Raoul considered introducing himself to the Hungarians, but decided against it. This would have been a major diplomatic gaffe. His duty was first to report to the Swedish embassy in Budapest and then present his credentials to the Hungarian Foreign Minister.

At 3 P.M., on July 6, 1945 Raoul sat in the office of his uncle, the Swedish ambassador to Nazi Germany. On the wall was a portrait of King Gustav V and out of the window behind the ambassador's desk was the Reichstag, charred and empty, since it went up in flames on February 27, 1933, shortly after the Nazis came to power. Maybe burned by the communists, as Hitler said, or maybe not, as Raoul and his Swedish friends thought.

Raoul's uncle asked about his family, his mother, his brother and sister, and the actress, Viveca, with whom Raoul was still smitten at the time. Then they spoke about Raoul's mission. Raoul saw it as opportunity to work for the Americans in Budapest against the Nazis; an opportunity to save the lives of Jews. Raoul compared his mission to that of the Scarlet Pimpernel in the recently released film of the same name, the story of a nobleman who saved lives during the French Revolution. Raoul had seen the movie with his brother Guy, and it had deeply affected him, Guy told me many years later.

Then, as a good nephew and as a young man who had never known his father, but still wanting to do him proud, Raoul asked his uncle for advice on his mission. His uncle was blunt and came right to the point.

"You are about to enter a dangerous game. Stay out of it."

His uncle vehemently opposed his mission. When Raoul tried to point out that one of the most famous of the Wallenberg ancestors, a great uncle Benedicts, had been a Jew, his uncle violently disagreed. To his uncle, the Wallenbergs were above all businessmen, not Scarlet Pimpernels. He advised Raoul to go back to Sweden.

What his uncle failed to disclose was his own ongoing violation of Swedish neutrality. Under his cover of "Ambassador," Jacob Wallenberg was responsible for selling the Germans the ball bearings that were the lifeblood of the German war machine. The story of the Wallenberg family's dark involvement in the war effort is proven a complex tale.

Instead of taking his uncle's stern advice, Raoul left the Swedish embassy and called Nina. "I'm leaving now." He said. "My uncle simply wants to brow beat me." He retrieved the luggage he had left with her and Gunnar and caught the first train to Budapest. With only standing room available, he stood for twelve hours through the night and finally reached his destination.

Raoul had often visited Budapest before the war, as president of the Central European Trading Company. He managed the exchange of home products—Swedish herrinsfilet and caviar—in order to provide fine-knit sweaters of Hungary, the superb salami, the apricot schnapps, and wines from the Tokay region. This time he arrived at a train station filled with families crammed into boxcars. He could hear their screams and cries. Many of them thrust papers scrawled with their names and addresses out through the slats of the cars. Notes read, "Please remember me. I am Greenbaum, or Gold or Veres, or someone else. I am so and so. I live at this street address. Contact my relatives." Raoul picked up some of these crumpled balls of paper as he stepped down from his own train. The rooms at the Majestic, the hotel where Raoul had stayed on past visits, belonged entirely to Adolf Eichmann and his minions, so Raoul found other accommodations.

Working at the Swedish Legation, up in the Buda hills, were, among others, Foreign Minister Ivan Danielsson, attaché Lars Berg, and Per Anger, who until then had been passively involved with helping the Jews. Per Anger showed Raoul examples of Swedish passports, visa certificates and Red Cross protection letters, all of which had been used to save a mere 700 Jewish lives thus far. Raoul would galvanize this team of diplomats into immediate action of saving even more lives.

Now, it was Raoul's turn to take over the effort of saving the Jews, financed by the War Refugee Board, a new branch of the United States Treasury Department. He was promised the protection and rescue if necessary by the United States according to words of promise given by Henry Morgenthau, Secretary of the Treasury, and by Cordell Hull, Secretary of State, and cabinet members under President Roosevelt. By October 1944, Raoul reported to the War Refugee Board that he had established Section C of the Swedish Legation, rented offices in three parts of the city, and recruited a staff of 400, financed entirely by the threatened community of Budapest. In other words, the Jews.

Admiral Horthy, acting regent of Hungary, and his government had accepted Section C personnel as protected citizens of Sweden. Raoul reported that his group had convinced the Horthy government to recognize 5000 new

A letter of protection (Schutzpass), issued by the Swedish legation in Budapest, to the Hungarian Jew Lili Katz. The document bears the initial W for Wallenberg in the bottom left corner.

protective passes, which Section C was making and issuing. These were the so-called "*Schutzpassen*." The Swedish government agreed to accept into its borders those Jewish Hungarians now protected by these passes. I wondered if the American government noticed the irony of the fact that Sweden, not at war with the Reich, was more willing to embrace the Jews than was the United States, a nation deeply at war with Germany. This willingness had not been tested much, as by then the journey from Budapest to Sweden was impossible because it required travel by train or car through German-occupied territory.

Section C solved that problem, buying Swedish safe houses, places where Jews were free to live under the protection of the Swedish flag. Wallenberg's staff went from home to home collecting canned goods, creating stockpiles of food and supplies to protect the populace until the inevitable arrival of Allied forces from Russia.

To the east, on August 23rd Romania defected to the Allied cause. Two days later, Adolph Eichmann, chief of the Gestapo's Jewish office, had vacated his quarters at the Majestic and left the country. He was certain to return. Since then Horthy's government had set its own policies. The deportations had stopped and the internment camps began releasing their prisoners. Raoul cut the Section C staff to 100, in preparation for finishing up their work. He even wrote his family that he expected to be home some days before the Soviets were to enter Budapest.

Then just as it seemed the war was about to end, the Nazis took control of the city, elevating the Arrow Cross, the armed Hungarian skinheads in

32

uniforms that bore a swastika-like insignia. Even their stiff-armed salute mimicked that of the SS troops who had suddenly made them powerful. In a day, members of the Arrow Cross were elevated from pariahs to bosses of the city. Their leader, Ferenc Szalasi, the closest thing Hungary had to Hitler, now ruled the country.

Section C reassembled. Quickly, the staff grew once more to four hundred. The operation worked twenty-four hours a day, as people lived in the offices. Wallenberg himself lived in the offices, or elsewhere in Pest, hiding.

He issued a memorandum to his staff: "This department must be in action day and night. There are no days off. If someone fails, he should not expect much help. If he performs well, he must not wait to be thanked." During my Tel Aviv interviews in Israel, in the summer of 1985 his assistant Judith Yaron explained:

"While Raoul Wallenberg was usually quite polite and professional,

Raoul Wallenberg in his Budapest office with his Jewish co-workers in November 1944. Pictured from left to right are: Dannonbergt, Hugo Wohl, Klein (behind), Forgacs (with V-neck sweater), and Paul Hegedus. Behind are Tibor Sandor and Dr. Otto Fleishmann.

under the stress of the moment he could be curt and brusque. He wanted everything to go well. He was determined to save every life possible. Sometimes I would go with him to the trains and watch him run along the top of the cars shoving new passports down through the openings to the Jewish families. Then he would jump off the train tops and rush to the doors of the closed cattle cars, open them and take the Jewish families out and 'home' to the new safe houses he had just purchased and over which he placed large Swedish flags of protection. He was a man possessed. He did not suffer fools gladly."

With this round the clock effort, in the six months between July 1944 and January 1945, Raoul Wallenberg and Section C saved the lives of thousands of Jews, possibly as many as one hundred thousand, according to reliable sources.

On January 17, 1945, Wallenberg was summoned to Debrecen on the border between Hungary and Romania, roughly 80 miles north of Budapest, for a meeting with the Russian military. His invitation to Debrecen came in the form of a note from Leonid Brezhnev, then General and Commander in Chief of the 18th Red Army Division, and later the Premier of the Soviet Union. The ostensible reason for the summons was a meeting of the Redevelopment Authority of the New Budapest, which would include a selection of people interested in the post-war rebuilding effort. Wallenberg was further instructed to come alone and not to bring any of his staff with him.

He may have gone voluntarily, and on his own, or he may have been coerced, under escort. We can't be sure. It is likely he knew the meeting did not bode well for him, but he did not let on to his staff the possibility that he was in danger. When he reached Debrecen, a group of Soviet soldiers forced Wallenberg into a military car, took him away through the woods, put him on a train headed to Romania under armed guard, and finally delivered him to Lubyanka Prison in Moscow. No decent or genuine explanation has ever been provided for his arrest, which was actually a kidnapping.

Was it because the Soviets knew that Wallenberg wanted to stay in Budapest after the war to help rebuild the city? Was it because Wallenberg was popular, and would expose the Soviet's true plan to take over Hungary and other eastern bloc countries? The Soviets recognized him as a potential thorn in their side and as an outspoken "troublemaker" when he told the invading Russian soldiers "Leave the women of Budapest alone. They are not here as your play toys. If you abuse any of them you will be subject to a war crimes trial just like the Nazis." After all, it was Wallenberg who, only the month before, in December 1944, at a Shabbat dinner of legend, had persuaded Eichmann, through the sheer force of his indomitable Swedish will, to call off the planned massacre of the Budapest Jewish Ghetto, thus saving 30,000 lives in one stroke. The Soviets didn't like popular figures and had already adopted an "iron curtain" policy, taking over each nation of Europe they "liberated," with plans to maintain their control after the war. They were amassing a host of satellite nations in Eastern Europe and they did not need a Swedish outsider like Wallenberg to interfere with and witness their efforts of conquest.

They may also have begun to believe that Wallenberg was working not just for Sweden, but for the American Office of Strategic Services espionage interests as well. According to former CIA Chief William Colby, with whom I met on several occasions, cables sent by Secretary of State Cordell Hull to Wallenberg congratulating him on his rescue work were intercepted and read by the Russians. This was most unfortunate since the interception compromised Wallenberg's true role as humanitarian and as savior of the Jews in Budapest. Briefly these exposed correspondences between the US government and Wallenberg may have been the trip-wire leading to suspicion and his capture.

It was not until two weeks later that the Wallenberg family officially learned of Raoul's abduction. In February 1945, the Wallenberg family received written word from the Soviet Union through the Soviet Ambassador to Sweden,

Madame Alexandra Kollontay that Wallenberg was in prison in Moscow, and would be released "as soon as papers could be processed." The family was asked to make no fuss and to allow the diplomatic process to correct a terrible "mistake."

"He will be back, but *schrei nicht,* don't make a fuss about it," Ambassador Kollontay told Raoul's mother, Maj Von Dardel. The Soviet authorities considered Mme. Kollontay's admission a major diplomatic error. No one was to admit to Wallenberg's presence in the USSR. The official lie was to be 'he is not known here.' No one was to confirm Wallenberg's capture, or presence as a prisoner. The Soviets recalled her from Stockholm. Her mission had been to lie and deceive and in that she had failed. She was stripped of her rank as diplomat and dismissed.

Prior to Kollontay's recall, she passed on this vital information about Wallenberg being a Soviet captive in Moscow. This was given to the wife of Christian Gunther, the Swedish Foreign Minister. On March 8, Hungarian Radio *Kossuth* reported falsely that Wallenberg had disappeared and probably been murdered by Gestapo agents on January 17th.

After this the family heard nothing more for two years. No news. Not until a letter from Soviet Foreign Minister Vishinsky, who issued the first official lie about Wallenberg in 1947. In his letter to the Swedish Prime Minister, he wrote, "Wallenberg is not known here." Ambiguous words to cover a terrible lie. In the letter, there was no admission that Wallenberg had ever been in Soviet custody—nor a claim that Mme. Kollontay's letter had been inaccurate.

There were quiet diplomatic efforts to free Wallenberg in the years following the abduction, but all failed. Only Raoul's mother pressured the Swedish Foreign Minister to act. Over the years that followed, opportunities to trade Wallenberg for Soviet spies captured in Sweden were badly bungled. In 1965 the Soviets wanted to retrieve Stig Bergling, a Swede who had been caught and jailed in Stockholm for spying for the USSR. They offered Wallenberg in a trade or 'spy-swap', as noted by Harvey Rosenfeld in his biography *Wallenberg: Angel of Rescue*. But the Swedish Foreign Ministry got greedy. They upped the ante and demanded a two-for-one deal. The Soviets refused and Wallenberg was left to rot in prison. When I noted this fact in a speech in 1993, the Swedes got huffy as if it were the first time the information had been revealed. My speech made front-page news in the *Swedish Dagbladet* and in other papers around the world on the AP wire, accusing the Swedes of dropping the ball.

The Swedish leaders turned their backs on Wallenberg. Raoul's mother begged them to find her son. Swedish Foreign Minister Unden refused to confront the government of Stalin. "It is not wise to question the Soviets," he announced.

When Unden met with Premier Joseph Stalin over the Wallenberg situation he fell apart, stating: "I think Wallenberg is dead." Stalin was amazed by the inept and cowardly behavior. To which Stalin responded cryptically with, "Wallenberg is not known in the Soviet Union." He later told aides, "I did not have to say anything. The man made no demand for Wallenberg's release. He just asked and answered his own question, and I sat there on my hands, needing to say nothing at all."

Even Dag Hammarskold, the lionized Secretary General of the United Nations, refused to trouble the Soviets on behalf of his vanished countryman. He told Raoul's mother: "It is a question of retaining an impartial role among the Big Powers."

For his part, the Swedish monarch Gustav VI Adolph told Raoul's mother, "What do you expect me to do? We can't just ransack the Russian prisons!" And Foreign Minister Unden griped about Mrs. Von Dardel, "What does she expect us to do, declare war just for the sake of her son?"

Despite their leaders' lack of effort, the Swedish people refused to forget Raoul Wallenberg. In the ten years following Raoul's arrest, public outrage in Sweden over the issue turned to political dynamite and threatened to undermine the control of the government held by the Socialist Democrat party. Stalin had died. Foreign Minister Unden and Prime Minister Erlander, with belated courage, pushed against the new Soviet leader, Nikita Khrushchev. Erlander told Khrushchev, "Raoul Wallenberg is casting a giant shadow over Swedish-Soviet relations!" Khrushchev considered that comment for ten months and then responded with a memorandum on February 6, 1957, carefully crafted by his deputy, Andrei Gromyko, then Foreign Minister of the USSR. The infamous pack of lies memo stated that, "Wallenberg died in Lubyanka prison in 1947 at the hands of one Smoltsov of the KGB, who subsequently had been put to death for his actions." The body, Russian officials claimed, had been cremated. All witnesses were said to be dead, purged, or discredited. This was a lie. Judge Barrington Parker later evaluated the report first hand and decided it was rubbish, not worthy of belief even for a moment.

The Gromyko memorandum was "truth—Soviet style," and a perfect alibi—except for one hitch. It was a pack of lies: "penaloka" a Russian word for fool the foreigners. No one in Sweden believed it. No one believed it, because the Swedish government had amassed evidence that Raoul had lived long after 1947.

In addition Judge Parker, during my oral argument before the court in 1985 stated: "the Gromyko letter is filled with falsehoods. It is unworthy of belief and carries no water in this court." He later confirmed this in writing in his brilliant written opinion published by the court on October 18, 1985.

Clues have arrived from different sources from 1945 up to the year 2011 indicating that Raoul Wallenberg might still be alive. As recently as April 26, 2011 a note stolen from a closed and still secret KGB file in Moscow reveals with certainty that Wallenberg was still alive in 1998 and was seen by David Evans at the mental hospital in Kagan on the Volga River. There is concrete evidence that he was still alive as recently as the year 2007. There have been reports from gulag escapees that they had worked alongside Wallenberg in Siberian work camps. There have also been admissions blurted out by officials who became talkative after drinking too much vodka; tidbits found by news reporters combing through KGB files at Lubyanka, and by the CIA. All the clues indicate that Wallenberg was alive long after 1947. By the early 1960's, many Swedes were furious, demanding to know the truth about the disappearance of Raoul Wallenberg.

Dr. Nanna Svartz, a leading Swedish physician, had a personal reason to care about the fate of her missing countryman. Her patient was Raoul's mother, Maj Von Dardel. In Mrs. Von Dardel she had observed the physical ravages caused by prolonged heartache. As a physician, she found the case illuminating. As a friend she found it very disturbing. As a human being, she hated the Soviets' cruelty and lying.

Dr. Svartz, had access to the highest levels of the Swedish government, and had studied the Wallenberg files herself. When in 1961 she received an invitation to speak at the Moscow Medical Congress—four years after the Gromyko memorandum—she decided immediately to use the occasion to try to personally rescue Raoul Wallenberg. She told his mother, "Maybe I can find his jail cell, pick the lock and set him free."

Arriving at the medical congress in Moscow, Dr. Svartz picked out the doctor she thought most likely to help her; Doctor Alexander Myasnikov. Myasnikov was her professional counterpart—just as respected and well connected in the Soviet Union as she was in Sweden. Based on their past discussions at professional meetings, she hoped he would be open with her. She approached him in the hotel lobby at the conference. To her surprise, when asked, he admitted that he not only knew Raoul Wallenberg, but also had examined Wallenberg as a prisoner in a mental hospital in Moscow in the past month. "Please send him home," she asked, "Or at least let me see him." Dr. Myasnikov said he would check with a senior Communist party colleague attending the same meeting.

Dr. Svartz waited anxiously; shocked that a Russian had actually admitted Raoul's existence, and had even confessed to examining him. She had asked the forbidden question and had received the beginning of a good answer. Or so she thought.

A few minutes later she was approached by a stranger who said Dr. Myasnikov had spoken to him of her request. He asked her to write down the name of the man she was after and where he was serving, then pocketed the message. She thanked the stranger, telling him she had also spoken, with Soviet Vice Premier Semionov in Stockholm about the case and that they had become friends. The stranger seemed to become uncomfortable at the mention of Semionov's name. He suggested she talk to Semionov about the case.

That evening at a banquet she spied Dr. Myasnikov once again. He too seemed tense and asked if she had spoken with Semionov. She said, "I have not, and when I tried calling Semionov I was told he was abroad." Dr. Myasnikov asked that she not use his name when she did reach Semionov.

The next day, upon her return to Sweden, she went to the office of Prime Minister Tage Erlander. She told Erlander everything. He insisted that she keep the matter secret. She agreed. Then, just days later, she received a letter from Dr. Myasnikov requesting that they meet again. She returned to Moscow only two weeks after the medical congress. This time they met in the privacy of a hotel room—she was not sure whether Myasnikov would be alone. Another nameless colleague sat in the room.

She asked to examine Wallenberg. Myasnikov said such a thing needed to be arranged at a higher level, "unless Wallenberg is dead." Then Myaniskov told Svartz that her conversation with Prime Minister Erlander had been reported to Chairman Kruschchev in a letter, who had then summoned Myasnikov to his office. Kruschchev pressured Myasnikov to change his story.

To Svartz's great shock, Myasnikov then accused her of fabricating a false story. He insisted that he had never heard of Raoul Wallenberg, until she mentioned his name. He denied everything they had spoken about just two weeks earlier and re-affirmed the party line, as propounded in the Gromyko memorandum. "Wallenberg has been dead since 1947," Myasnikov insisted. Myasnikov had been "turned", forced to change his story to protect his own life.

Several months later Prime Minister Erlander wrote to Khrushchev: "Foreign Minister Unden and I have discussed the most suitable way of transferring Wallenberg to Sweden. We have found that the best way would be if a Swedish physician were permitted to come to Moscow and discuss with his Soviet colleagues arrangements for transportation and interim medical care."

The Swedish ambassador in Moscow had hand-delivered the letter. Khrushchev told the waiting ambassador, "There is nothing to add to the Gromyko memo."

Now more years elapsed. Erlander thought it best not to create a public flap. But then, perhaps under political pressure from a questioning population, on September 16, 1965, Erlander appeared on Swedish television and told Nanna Svartz's story publicly for the first time. He ended the story with these words: "The Swedish government considers further approaches to the Soviets on the subject of Raoul Wallenberg's disappearance useless. We have done our best to reopen the search and rescue operation, as a duty of the Swedish government."

As far as Erlander's administration was concerned, the case was closed. Several months later Dr. Myasnikov died suddenly and under strange circumstances. He had been drugged, and a possible murder was involved.

After 1961 numerous sightings of Wallenberg were made in various prisons in the Soviet Union, by prisoners who were later released from Soviet custody. These sightings were reported as late as 1981. Despite the slivers of evidence that Raoul was alive somewhere, the Wallenberg family seemed to withdraw gradually from the emotional see-saw. Perhaps successive disappointments had left them resigned. Raoul's stepfather died first, then his mother. It was left to his sister Nina and his brother Guy to continue pressuring the governments of Sweden and the US to seek Wallenberg's release.

In 1970, the US State Department had a chance to retrieve Wallenberg in a swap for Soviet spies held in US prisons. This responsibility was entrusted to Henry Kissinger and his staff. Nothing was done. There was no new inquiry and no trade. The American government at the time thought any efforts to confront the Soviets on the Wallenberg matter would be considered "an act of provocation."

Only a few people knew the real story. Brezhnev by 1970 was now Premier, the same greedy Brezhnev who had broken into Wallenberg's office in January of 1945 and stolen the so called "Wallenberg diamonds," a pile of valuable jewels entrusted to Wallenberg by the Jews leaving for the death camps. Brezhnev, a captain with the 18th Red Army waited until after Wallenberg's trip to Debrecen. He had been tipped off about the large cache of jewels in Wallenberg's safe. The CIA knew that Brezhnev had lined the pockets of his army coat and taken a wheelbarrow at night to empty the safe. On his return to Moscow, Brezhnev moved up as a greedy politician, using the Wallenberg jewels to bribe his way to the top. Nixon was asked by the Wallenberg family to ask Brezhnev to release Raoul. He told others he simply could not discuss the matter of Wallenberg's release with Brezhnev, that it would be an embarrassment. Kissinger was out of the loop. The CIA had not briefed Henry Kissinger but the president had been fully informed that any mention of Wallenberg's name and fate would be a source of deep embarrassment to Brezhnev. Brezhnev was a common thief dressed as a Soviet leader. Brezhnev still held some of the Wallenberg diamonds in his bank vault, which should have been returned to their rightful Jewish owners as war reparations. Kissinger knew nothing of the Wallenberg diamonds, and yet Nixon had been correctly briefed carefully on this sensitive matter by the CIA. Since *Détente* was important and Brezhnev's anger was not to be engaged, Nixon's lips had to be sealed on this issue, and he could not allow Kissinger to mention the Wallenberg name in front of Brezhnev.

Nixon pointedly told Kissinger: "If you or I start with 'the Wallenberg Question' Brezhnev will walk out, creating a precarious situation in US-USSR relations. Brezhnev is here to sign the *Non-proliferation Treaty*." Kissinger was confused but he said nothing. He knew that Detroit industrialist Max Fisher, a strong Nixon supporter had urged the re-opening of the Wallenberg question as a way to stimulate the support of Jews to vote for Republicans. Max Fisher told Nixon: "Since FDR courted the Jewish vote, first in New York, and then in the nation, Jews have chosen to be Democrat and to vote mainly for democratic candidates. If you want to woo the Jewish vote, you can do so effectively by making Wallenberg your hero and making his rescue your top priority." Max Fisher told me of his Nixon conversation in March of 1988 during a dinner at his luxurious home in Palm Beach and how he fervently tried to persuade Nixon to urge the Russians to release Wallenberg. But cynically Wallenberg had been taken off the chessboard of international negotiations between US and Russia. He would no longer be used as a pawn for possible exchange.

In 1975, Jan Kaplan was jailed in Russia on currency charges. When he was released eighteen months later, he brought out with him another ray of hope that Wallenberg was indeed still alive. He called his daughter, Anna Bilder, in Israel, to tell her the good news of his release. Then he told her about the Swede he'd met in the prison infirmary, a man who had been held for 30 years. He promised to send his daughter a letter with more details. However, unwilling to trust the regular Soviet mail system, Kaplan gave the letter he had written for his daughter to a "Swiss couple" whom he met on the outside steps of the main synagogue in Moscow. They represented that they were leaving that night for Israel. Kaplan believed they were concerned about the plight of Raoul Wallenberg. He had chosen his new messengers very poorly. Not Swiss tourists at all, the KGB agents arrested Kaplan immediately. Jan Kaplan's family never saw him again.

Several months later Kaplan's wife Eugenia wrote to daughter Anna in Tel Aviv. She put the letter in the regular mail and it arrived unmolested. "I have lost all hope," she wrote. "All of this happened because of a letter concerning a Swiss or a Swede named Wallenberg whom your father knew in prison. Your father had written to you about this Wallenberg and tried to get it to you. Since then your father has been in Lefortovo and Lubyanka and now I have lost all hope of ever seeing him again."

Anna Bilder took this letter to the Swedish Embassy in Tel Aviv. She asked for help, but no one responded to her plea.

Then, in October of 1981, there was a new ray of hope. In a White House Rose Garden ceremony, President Ronald Reagan made Raoul Wallenberg a citizen of the United States with full rights. The ceremony happened two years before my becoming the lawyer for the family and being personally involved in the lawsuit and the Wallenberg story. Guy Von Dardel and Nina Lagergren later described the conversations at the Rose Garden ceremony to me in detail.

In the Oval Office, President Ronald Reagan took tea with Nina and Guy just before the citizenship ceremony. He poured the tea himself and carried it to them, then sat in a blue armchair with his own cup of tea. The President told them their brother was a personal hero of his. At his urging, they told the American President about Raoul. They spoke of Raoul's love of theater, the pranks he loved to play, his innate ability to make others laugh, his charisma with women, and others. They spoke of Raoul's compassion as a child, bringing home birds whose wings needed mending. There was his curiosity about people, so different from the typical arrogance or imperious nature of many others in the Wallenberg family. They spoke, too, of Raoul's ambitions; his desire to live up to his father's legacy, a military hero who died before Raoul was born, and of Raoul's desire to help others. He loved to be heroic. He pretended to be the new Scarlet Pimpernel. The Scarlet Pimpernel was the rescuer of aristocrats loyal to the King and facing the guillotine during the French revolution in 1791. The Pimpernel devised clever strategies for taking French aristocracy out of Paris by stagecoach and transporting them at great personal risk to England in order to avoid death by the guillotine.

Nina and Guy told President Reagan how much Raoul had loved America, starting with his years of studying architecture at the University of Michigan. They could not resist telling the President how one day a group of youths offered Raoul a ride, and he hopped into their car. They drove him to a deserted spot and robbed him of everything. They even made him strip off his clothing. They were about to drive away and leave him like that, but Raoul got in front of their car and began negotiating with them—completely naked. Whatever he said to the thugs, he ended up back on the main highway, somewhere between Chicago and Ann Arbor, Michigan, with his clothes, his suitcase, and a few dollars. Apparently Raoul considered this a great victory, one of his best experiences in America. He continued hitchhiking, and returned to the university in time for the next school term. This misadventure had begun with Raoul Wallenberg's 1934 visit to the Chicago World's Fair. The incident happened on the way back to Ann Arbor.

Reagan promised to help rescue Raoul. When they were summoned to the Rose Garden for the official citizenship ceremony, Reagan's final words to Nina and Guy were, "You have my word." Reagan considered the citizenship to be full "first class" citizenship with all rights included. "There is nothing symbolic or part-way about it," Reagan said, "This is full citizenship, with all the rights of any American citizen."

In the Rose Garden that afternoon, a military band broke into the first bright bars of "Hail to the Chief," and Guy felt tears coming spontaneously to his eyes. The White House had scheduled the ceremony for 5 P.M., in part to take full advantage of the dramatic end of day's sunlight, and also to capture the national television networks, all of which were present. News anchors Dan Rather and Tom Brokaw were there.

Reagan sat outdoors in the Rose Garden at a mahogany desk with twenty-seven pens to sign the law making Raoul Wallenberg an official US citizen. "This day is long overdue," he told the small crowd. The President used the first of the pens, and then handed it to Nina as a gift. The second pen went to Guy. Next to Guy stood Congressman Tom Lantos, who had introduced the legislation to make Wallenberg an honorary citizen; next to him stood his wife, Annette.

Reagan told the audience of the Lantos' personal interest. As endangered Jewish children in Budapest, Tom and Annette Lantos had witnessed firsthand the courageous actions of Raoul Wallenberg. In fact, Wallenberg saved them. They each received a pen.

Senator Claiborne Pell of Rhode Island, chairman of the Senate Foreign Relations Committee, also received a pen. Pell's father had been the last United States Ambassador to Budapest from 1938 to 1941, just before the outbreak of World War II. Pell had vivid boyhood memories of the city where Wallenberg, just a few years later, would devote six intense months to heroic acts. Pell had sponsored the bill in the Senate. Pell had also crossed over to the House to give testimony at one of Lantos' hearings. Present, too, were Senators Daniel Patrick Moynihan, Democrat from New York, and Rudy Boschwitz, Republican from Minnesota, who had pushed the bill from either side of the party divide.

Reagan recalled the only other person in history who had ever been made an honorary American citizen—Sir Winston Churchill. He quoted the words spoken about Sir Winston by President John F. Kennedy at the signing ceremony for Churchill: "'Indifferent himself to danger, he wept over the sorrows of others.' That compassion also exemplifies the man we are gathered here for today."

Then the President described the debt of honor owed by the United States to the absent Swede. In 1944 the War Refugee Board of the United States wished to protect the lives of Hungarian Jews who faced extermination at the hands of the Nazis. The US looked for help in the neutral country of Sweden. Wallenberg had volunteered for the task. In the months that followed, the United States supplied the funds and directives, and Raoul Wallenberg supplied the courage and the passion.

Reagan asked: "How can we comprehend the moral worth of a man who saved tens of thousands of lives?" And then the President spoke of Wallenberg in the present tense. "Wherever he is, his humanity burns like a torch."

Although this sentence was quotable and inspiring, it was also much more. For in his use of the present tense, the President directly contradicted the official Russian line that Wallenberg had died thirty-four years earlier. If anyone knew of Wallenberg's whereabouts, the Soviets must, for they had kidnapped him. The President's statement suggested a confident knowing on his part that Wallenberg was still alive.

The lie of Wallenberg's death had festered so long it had taken on a mythic reality. One could not say for sure he was dead, but nor could one act with certainty that he was alive. One could only imagine Wallenberg trapped, perhaps forever, in a shadowy paralysis and meager hope. The lie had smothered the truth. Under that shadow Wallenberg had existed for three dozen years—half his possible lifetime.

President Reagan deftly avoided the issue. Instead, he ornamented the myth of Raoul Wallenberg. "I heard someone say that a man has made at least a start on understanding the meaning of human life when he plants shade trees under which he knows he will never sit. Raoul Wallenberg is just such a man. He nurtured the lives of those he never knew at the risk of losing his own. And then just recently I was told that in a special area behind the Holocaust Museum in Israel, Hungarian Jews, now living in Sweden, planted ten thousand trees in Raoul's honor."

He ended with a vow: "Mrs. Lagergren, Mr. Von Dardel, we're going to do everything in our power so that your brother can sit beneath the shade of those trees and enjoy the respect and love that so many hold for him."

As the President clasped Von Dardel's hand, he vowed, "This ceremony is not the end. This is not the end of an old story. No—this is the beginning. We will rescue Raoul Wallenberg."

"We are counting on you, Mister President," Guy said. "It's in your hands."

Yet, nothing was done. And I was soon to find out why.

Whatever Happened to Raoul Wallenberg?

Part II: Raoul Wallenberg versus USSR

Whatever Happened to Raoul Wallenberg?

March 5, 1983
Philadelphia

Yellow forsythia blossoms had gathered on the windshield of my car, along with the pink blossoms of the cherry trees that lined the driveway of my Devonshire Country Manor House in Chestnut Hill. It was a tranquil Saturday morning in Philadelphia. The abundant blossoms looked like the aftermath of a ticker-tape parade; like confetti of bright flowers welcoming Wallenberg to America. I had a vision of myself and Wallenberg seated in the back of an open convertible, the triumphal return of a celebrated hero with confetti fluttering from the office windows along Manhattan's Fifth Avenue. But the parade was to be a date in the future, as I pulled my lime green Pontiac Grand Prix from the rounded driveway and headed to the city.

During my thirty-minute drive to the law library at Thirty-fourth and Chestnut Streets in downtown Philadelphia, Canadian geese seemed to follow me in a "V" formation overhead. They knew where they were going. I hoped that I did, too. I needed a point of focus for the Wallenberg case, a lead bird for the "V" formation. Were the geese an omen, or was I embarking on an absurd and wild goose chase?

The parking lot and the law library were quiet. Students had emptied out for the spring holiday.

"What was Wallenberg doing at this very moment I wondered?" "Was he sitting in some two-by-four cell, eating slop for dinner, dressed in gray prison garb, a bare light bulb always on above his bed?"

Could Wallenberg be helped after thirty-nine years of abandonment? The crime committed against him, the kidnapping of a diplomat, had occurred long ago and thousands of miles beyond US jurisdiction. Wasn't this after all, a matter between Sweden and Russia? The United States had no direct responsibility for Wallenberg's fate. At that moment, I still didn't know how wrong appearances could be.

I imagined the courtroom scene. The judge saying:

"Mister Wolff, you seem to be suing an entire country."

"That's right, your honor."

"And not a small country, or even a mid-sized one. No. You're going right for the largest country on Earth?"

"So you say that this gigantic country committed a crime in or around Budapest. Now let me ask you. Where in United States jurisdiction does Budapest lie? I've heard of Paris, Tennessee. And Athens, Texas. Is there, perhaps, a Budapest, Arizona?"

"No. As we know, your honor, Budapest is in Hungary. In Europe."

"And the injured party is native to none of these places?"

"Well, actually, your honor...."

"Do you have a precedent for this case, Mister Wolff?"

"No, sir, there is no precedent for this case."

"I beg to differ, Mister Wolff. There is a precedent—a perfectly good precedent known as 'territorial jurisdiction.' Are you aware of territorial jurisdiction?"

"Yes, your honor. It says that the border of a foreign state is closed to judicial scrutiny."

"That is correct. And under the *Act of State Doctrine,* no state can interfere with or sit in judgment upon the actions of another state, no matter how heinous or illegal these actions might be."

"But, sir, the Law of Nations...."

"What? That ancient law? It's over 200 years old! Who's your client?"

"A heroic Swede sitting for many years with no visitors in a series of Soviet jail cells."

"What - not even a US citizen?"

"He is by law a US citizen and I contend that he has full rights as a citizen to be rescued by the US Army if necessary. There is even a specific law. The Hostages Act of 1868 actually requires our President of the United States to take every measure possible to rescue United States citizens held illegally in prisons in foreign countries. Wallenberg is not a half-breed; he is a full citizen with full legal rights of protection and the right of retrieval as a citizen through a special law enacted by Congress. Wallenberg was made a citizen in 1981 after we knew he was illegally captured and thrown into Lubyanka prison in Moscow. It is the duty of our government to locate and rescue him."

"This is clearly a political situation. You're presenting your complaint to the wrong branch of the government, Mister Wolff. Why don't you walk this case over to the State Department, where they will continue their excellent work of giving you a run around and a fancy legal argument for why they are doing nothing to retrieve your noble client, your hero of the century?"

Wallenberg had indeed been declared a citizen of the United States by Act of Congress and by the President's signature in a formal Rose Garden White House ceremony on August 5, 1981, Wallenberg's seventy-first birthday. Congressman Thomas Lantos of California, the sponsor of the bill—a man saved by Wallenberg as a sixteen year old in 1944 in Budapest, who later migrated to the USA and got himself elected to Congress on a "Save Raoul Wallenberg" platform—made it very clear: "The reason we are passing this law today is to give an unequivocal legal basis for demanding and obtaining his freedom. This is now a matter of law. President Reagan will honor and enforce this commitment by signing this law passed by both houses of Congress. This is not a gesture of appreciation. This law is a leveraged tool to pry Wallenberg loose from the brutal conditions of a Soviet jail in Moscow or the barren cold solitude of Siberia."

I considered the legal heft and power of that Act of Congress as I walked toward the ivy-covered law library. Why hadn't it been used before now? Who had buried and forgotten this legal tool for Wallenberg's freedom? Was I to learn that people in the White House or State Department had conspired to bury this law, and to abandon Wallenberg to his fate?

I took the time to read the inscription carved into the marble slab across the top of the magnificent Penn Law Library. "From those to whom much has been given, much is expected." I took the admonition personally, and used it as my guide. I first read it as a high school senior when in the spring of 1954 I visited this library to research and predict the probable vote outcome of the Supreme Court's verdict in *Brown vs. Board of Education*. Already as a senior in high school I was interested in how human rights decisions were reached in a US court of law. I predicted an eight to one outcome. I was intrigued and curious about our Supreme Court and how it reached decisions. I was off by one vote. The actual vote was 9-0 as Chief Justice Earl Warren arm twisted Felix Frankfurter to change his obstinate vote against desegregation. The Brown decision was a great moment in legal and social history. I had predicted all the justices, other than Frankfurter, would vote to repeal school segregation.

Inside, the bright morning sun light streamed through stained-glass windows flickering on the bronze busts of illustrious law-givers—Holmes, Brandeis, Cardozo, Disraeli, Demosthenes, Socrates. Framed in glass on wooden display stands were the legal briefs from famous cases done *pro bono*—without fee, for the good of humanity and the cause of justice—providing inspiration to idealistic students. I was destined to find a case such as the one I held in my hand as I walked up the white marble stairs to the law library entrance. No, not just a law case but also a cause, a scream for justice and an important story to be told to the world. Was it merely a case or was it an enduring cause? What was the difference? Only the middle letter "U."

It was for this kind of case or cause that I became a lawyer. My passion for law and justice started over sixty years ago, way back during my student days from 1950 to 1954 when I was fifteen years old and starting my education at the Germantown Friends School, a Quaker school of high principles. We were taught that war is not the answer and that simple basic values of fairness, integrity, honesty and service must prevail. Teachers like Ed Gordon and David Mallery imbued me with a sense of justice and a knowledge of politics and an urgent invitation to pursue what is right. Even in my GFS graduation yearbook, under my photo as Student Council President, the student editor David Evans had inserted a quote from Lord Shallcross: "He sees the right and he pursues it too!" Why else had I chosen the profession of law? This same David Evans became our Economic Affairs Officer at the Moscow Embassy. He took a special train trip to

Kazan and was the last man to see Wallenberg alive in the year 1998. More on this later.

I did *pro bono* work, representing juvenile defendants on a regular basis. But most of my work had until recently been of the in-box-out-box variety, helping clients chase after money, cases that lacked any genuine appeal to justice. Before 1983, I spent a solid fifteen years as an international lawyer, negotiating contracts in Paris, Cologne, Germany, Mexico City, Saudi Arabia, and Beijing, China.

My legal negotiations were exciting. I would negotiate with ministers and presidents of companies in foreign countries. I was involved in the formation of international contracts to sell wholesome consumer products that people needed: chickens for the school lunch program in Saudi Arabia, Bahrain, Lebanon and Iran in 1975, before the fall of the Shah. Also I went back to Cologne to draft the legal documents for the sale of swimming pools. My major client was the $5 billion dollar SC Johnson and Son Company, and their 17 overseas subsidiaries. I strategize their plan to market in Europe the manufacture of "Johnson Wax" for floors, "Pledge" polish for furniture, smooth "Edge" shaving cream and "Simonize" for cars. My client's consumer products were innocent and useful, but still there was no idealistic purpose for my work, nothing that would survive me in the memory of others.

I chose not to deal with guns or tanks or other items that harm people. I speak French, German, and Spanish in many business matters. This facility with languages helped me to negotiate contracts, form joint ventures, and open doors for clients so they can sell their products effectively in foreign countries.

But then suddenly one day in the spring of 1979 I woke up in a cold sweat in a far away hotel room in Jeddah, Saudi Arabia. I asked myself, "What the hell are you doing here? You are a Jewish lawyer in a hostile Arab country. You can quite easily hear a knock on the door in the middle of the night and get yourself killed. If someone discovers your religion you are fair game for terrorists. This is not funny. Even if there is a big fee involved, get out of here now! This is a danger much too great for a family man with a young wife and two young children. If terrorists break into this hotel room, you are dead." On that same trip I witnessed a Holiday Inn in Beirut burn down, while simultaneously watching the same event on CNN. It was a worldwide and important event. I also watched helplessly as a terrorist passed beneath my window of the hotel lobbing grenades from his passing car into the department store windows. Loud bombs went off. I thought the hotel was about to collapse. I was traumatized. Right then and right there I decided to return home to Philadelphia. I had enough Middle East travel to last a lifetime—seeing the walls of hotel rooms and conference rooms—but missing the joy of growing up with my family. I decided to limit my international law practice to negotiations in Philadelphia, and trials before the federal courts in Philadelphia, New York and Washington DC. This would also give me time to branch out and accept an invite from Law Dean James Freedman to teach international law and ethics at the nearby University of Pennsylvania School of Law. So I decided to give up international travel temporarily.

On the flight home from Saudi Arabia that eye-opening day in 1979, I began to make my transition, leading to teaching International Negotiations and Public International Law at the University of Pennsylvania Law School in my home city. This gave me more time to be with my family, to play tennis, to see friends, and to live a real and genuine life.

The law for me is a noble calling and a profession: it is a creative and a positive field of work. You can help people with your knowledge. You can help and counsel them in a good direction. You can make a difference. And you can be held in high esteem by yourself and others if you do it the right way. To be permitted to work to rescue Wallenberg, and to use my legal acumen in the process was to work for the cause of justice. This is God's work here on earth for those who choose to do it. "Justice, justice shall thou pursue," according to the prophet Isaiah. For me the pursuit of justice is a creative act of the heart.

On that Saturday in March of 1983 in the quiet of the empty law library, I paused before the bust of Oliver Wendell Holmes, one of the great Chief Justices of the Supreme Court, and read his inscription: "The life of the law is not logic; it is experience." What about the lonely experience of a man held incommunicado for thirty-nine years? Perhaps Justice Holmes would send me an idea about how to correct that.

The great power of the law is its ultimate fairness and its reliable certainty. But this certainty can stifle the development of new laws to take care of the emerging needs of justice. The stifling effect of precedent can also be the law's curse. For Wallenberg and for the cause of justice, I needed something new. I was searching for a new argument that would allow me to argue this case in a federal court. Chief Justice Earl Warren, in my visit with him in chambers in the spring of 1962, said:

"The law is a living organism. It expands to meet the necessities of justice. We expanded the law in 1954 in *Brown vs. Board of Education*. We overturned fifty-six years of the insidious practice of school segregation. Separate but equal could never be equal. Separating little school children in segregated schools infuses a sense of inferiority in the minds of small children that can never be undone. Plain and simple. Social discrimination and slighting people cannot be remedied. The Supreme Court reversed school segregation in 1954 because it was unfair. It was not right. It was not just. And we created new findings and new judicial law to challenge segregation and to change it. Our decision was partly based on the sociological findings of Gunnar Myrdal, a Swedish sociologist, and an intelligent man. By reversing the 1898

51

verdict in *Plessy v Ferguson*, which allowed southern states to enforce segregation in schools and on railroad cars, we shattered precedent. We invented new law. We created new precedent."

Warren became my hero. Some people carried posters outside the Supreme Court building: "Impeach Earl Warren." Justice Warren continued, "I did not care. I knew we were on the side of history and we were simply doing the right thing. We removed the illegal state-enforced practice of segregation leading to Martin Luther King and the Civil Rights Movement."

That was 1954 and 1961 I thought to myself. This is 1983. "I wish Warren was still on the Supreme Court. The activists are all gone," I muttered. "This is a different court; a court of pygmies rather than giants. No more Hugo Black, no William O. Douglas and no Bill Brennan or Earl Warren. I would have brought the case right to the Supreme Court if these men were still alive. But now that court is quite conservative. Judicial activism has changed to judicial restraint. But we still need judges dedicated to Justice. I said to myself 'God please send me the right judge.'"

Little did I know that first day that God *would* send me the right judge for my case—a man consumed by an interest in justice and fairness and in freeing Wallenberg."

I spoke my prayer out loud to the deserted library, the quiet shelves, the desks, empty of their usual law students, "*a little madness in the spring…*"

The librarian, who sat in her glass-lined office to the right, heard my prayer—"God, send me the right Judge"—and glanced up at the sound of my voice. It was Elizabeth Arnold, a beautiful woman close to eighty years old, who had served as chief librarian here for more than thirty-six years. I always suspected that she held more legal information inside her head than the entire faculty of the law school put together.

"Did you say something, Professor Wolff?" She said.

I poked my head inside her office.

"*A little madness in the spring…*how does the rest of it go, Mrs. Arnold?"

"*Is wholesome even for the King…*You meant Emily Dickinson?"

"Why yes, I suppose it is. I thought for a moment it was Edna St. Vincent Millay."

"Oh no. Millay was never that cheerful. Are you bringing a bit of March madness with you, Professor Wolff?"

"Why yes, my dear Mrs. Arnold. I am going to introduce your library to the spirit of the irrational."

I gave her the background on Wallenberg. I said: "Marie, I am going to need a lot of help. But first I need to get myself oriented. Where does the law talk about diplomats? Where does it actually say in a law book that it is illegal to kidnap one? I'd better start at the beginning, with the heavy old digests of international law, like Grotius, from 1643. And then the question arises—which court will be willing to even hear my new case? Whose national or international law gives guidance on how to spring a Swedish diplomat languishing for thirty-nine years in a Russian jail? Certainly there must be some treaties of recent record. Or with your love of the human imagination in William Faulkner, Mrs. Arnold, perhaps you can find me some musty old statute in the rare book room from Thomas Jefferson or Ben Franklin that speaks to the outreaching idealism of our American legal system in the days after the American Revolution?" She laughed as I delivered my diatribe, frustrated by the enormous and quixotic nature of my new burden and responsibility. I now carried on my solitary shoulders the duty to free Wallenberg from jail.

This situation was clearly *sui generis*—this was a case of first impression. I had before me an empty slate—*tabula rasa*. There was almost nothing to build upon, no precedents. The kind of thing you don't hear about much. I said out loud: "Safeguarding diplomats must be important in the law. It has to be written somewhere."

"So Professor Wolff, may I call you Morris—it is a Saturday—you know. Morris, is it your view that Wallenberg was definitely one of our diplomats?" said Elizabeth.

"Yes, we seduced him into diplomatic service and promised him rescue if he was caught during his dangerous mission. The situation was unique. He was our *de facto* US diplomat dressed in Swedish clothing. We sent him to Hungary. His overcoat was Swedish. His clothing was American. His family feels we sent him there and it is our duty to bring him home. It stands to reason that he had diplomatic immunity as an official member of the Swedish legation at the Swedish Embassy in Budapest."

I wondered silently how this crime could have happened. Obviously, the promise of protection, and the guaranty of retrieval if captured, as made by the United States State Department and the White House, had been a lie. These were empty words used to manipulate Wallenberg to do something for our war effort, and to garner the Jewish vote for FDR in 1944. Had the United States Green Beret crack commando group ever been ordered to storm the Russian prison where Wallenberg was held? No. Nothing that heroic was even thought of or put in motion.

The government of Israel's crack commando Mossad unit flew into Entebbe Airbase, stormed the airport in there in Uganda and rescued hostage Israeli tourists. They went and rescued their own without fanfare. But had there been any behind the scenes effort to rescue Wallenberg? If not, *why* not? And why would the Russians arrest and detain Wallenberg, and keep him alive? Among the many puzzles of the Wallenberg story, this was the strangest. But I did not have time to address it now. The Russians had no right to hold him for even one day. I just had to prove it and I thought I had a good shot at doing so.

I looked in Borchard's tome on diplomatic law. Borchard says: "The kidnapping of diplomats clearly violates all tenets and principles of basic international law. If abductions go unpunished, the pool of applicants for the job of foreign diplomat would be considerably reduced."

I put back the book and pondered his thoughts. Who would want to represent a country when that country did not safeguard its representatives? And from the country's point of view, if you lost your messengers, pretty soon you stopped getting needed information. The city-states of Athens and Sparta had figured this out thousands of years before Wallenberg. You can't let another city-state imprison or kill your messenger.

The musty old books piled up before me—Hackworth, McDougal, Vattel, Lauterpacht—venerated voices of international law; McDougal from 1962, my professor at Yale, and the older great ones from the past three centuries. It was easy enough to show a tradition. Countries tend to respect each other's diplomats. But beyond tradition and common sense, I also needed a specific law to argue in court. Otherwise I would be thrown out before starting my argument. Judges would always start by asking, "What's the law in this case Professor? What is the governing law? What are you asking us to decide and based on what specific law?"

"What was the most fundamental law in this case?" I asked myself. "What the hell can I say in court with a straight face" —The Law of Nations. *I don't think so!* That is, the operating agreement of all civilized countries. I imagined a judge scoffing: "Law of Nations? Where is it enforced? The law of nations is brute force, dog eat dog." And yet here was Hugo Grotius, in 1643 advocating "the requirement of civilized behavior between civilized nations" with his *Mare Liberum*—the doctrine that the seas as a matter of law were open to all nations.

Elizabeth Arnold came over to my desk.

"Are you stuck?"

"Yes, I am stuck. I have no idea where to go."

"I suggest you look at Blackstone's chapter on diplomatic immunity."

She placed a large green covered volume in front of me.

"These are the writings of Sir William Blackstone, the great English jurist, and a contemporary of Mozart. His legal voice remains the unrivaled authority on international law even after two hundred years."

I opened his *Commentaries* and she, leaning over my shoulder, followed her long, bony finger to an index entry. I read it. It was the proclamation I needed:

Since the time of Alexander the Great, it has been the law of nations to provide protection for diplomats who travel on behalf of their nation. The protection of such persons shall be inviolate.

This was a good beginning; a bit old, but solid. For Blackstone, there were only two unbreakable laws of civilized nations. One was the law that any nation could assert international law against captured pirates. No need to return them to the scene of the crime.

The other was the protection of diplomats. The antique fundamentals: Don't touch my ships; don't touch my ambassadors. It gave me a sense of hope in the darkness, the helpful statement: "The kidnapping of diplomats can be prosecuted wherever the defendant is found."

Except that Wallenberg was in Russia, not in the United States. But could the defendant USSR "be found on the map, or at the Soviet Embassy in Washington, and brought into a US federal court in the District of Columbia and punished?"

I researched existing treaties between the United States of America and the Soviet Union. Treaties are nothing more than signed agreements between countries. With any luck I would find a treaty that reiterated Blackstone's rule on diplomatic immunity, and would also carry the binding signatures of the United States and the Soviet Union. With that treaty in hand as an exhibit to my written brief and complaint, I could enter a courtroom and remind the judge that Article Six of the United States Constitution, clearly and unequivocally states that all treaties are to be considered the "supreme law of the land." Very clever. Very original. Our case appeared to be doomed on first glance, but now with Blackstone's help, I had an interesting possibility of success. At least, no law professor could laugh at my assertions of diplomatic immunity on prisoner Wallenberg's behalf. Sympathy if not the law would be clearly on our side. And what if I lost? I still would have made a major statement about the scandalous behavior of the Soviets in kidnapping Raoul Wallenberg. I would have reminded the world that a great man sat in chains while the world ignored his plight. I would raise a hue and cry that would force the President to do something.

Even a doomed case might help Wallenberg by bringing attention to his plight - as long as we presented a dignified and respectable argument and left no room for cynics to mock our effort. My main goal was to stir things up, arouse interest and create enough positive publicity to force my government to take action. I never expected to win the case. It would be only during the presentation of my arguments before Judge Parker that I dared to believe I could win this one. Parker took my legal arguments with a seriousness I had never anticipated. He was the one judge on the twelve judge panel sent by God to hear the facts and rule on the evidence. Now, back in the law library I began to build my case like a sculptor taking grey clay and forming a work of art. I decided I would present the case as a treaty violation of diplomatic rights, and then surround the judge with supportive law, with precedent, with whatever else I could find.

Whatever Happened to Raoul Wallenberg?

I imagined that it would take more work to lose this case with dignity than it took to win most others.

I found three treaties to start. The first was a 1927 agreement for the protection of diplomats, signed by Sweden and the Soviet Union. The next two were my real score: the *Vienna Convention of 1961* and the *Vienna Convention for Protecting Diplomats,* signed in 1973. Both bore the signatures I needed. Officials from Sweden, the USSR and the United States State Department had signed each one.

The 1961 Vienna Treaty guarantees the safety of diplomats while executing their responsibilities. Wallenberg was such a diplomat working for the Swedish Embassy in Budapest at the time of his kidnapping. The 1973 *Vienna Treaty* expanded that to define the rights of all "internationally protected persons." Wallenberg fully qualified as one of those. This was binding US and Swedish Law. I did not want to go to Moscow to prosecute the case. I was looking for a hook to try the case in federal court in Washington, DC, where the USSR Embassy could be served with my complaint.

Under theories of universal jurisdiction, the crime of kidnapping is considered to be so serious that the felon can be punished universally, that is wherever he is caught. In a case like this, the USSR and the KGB were the active felons. They could be "caught" in the USA, or at least so I could argue. And our federal district court, under theories of universal jurisdiction, can take jurisdiction at will - at least, that's what I will suggest to the court. And to prove the point, I would cite the case of *Israel v. Eichmann.*

During World War II, Adolph Eichmann, the chief architect of the Holocaust under Hitler, was placed in charge of making Europe "juden rein"— "free and clean of all Jews." There was to be a systematic cleansing of the Jews, a genocide of all members of this historic human race. After his work in Budapest, where he confronted Wallenberg directly by phone and in person, Eichmann managed to escape arrest by fleeing with the help of Nazi sympathizers through the Vatican in Rome. He was then given a new passport and persona/identity in order to travel to a Nazi haven for criminals, in Buenos Aires, Argentina. The Mossad tracked him down, captured him near his home at 10 Lombardi Street at 5:21 one evening in 1960 as he got down from the bus and was walking to his home. The capture was timed perfectly. They drugged him, knocked him out, put him on a plane seated upright but "asleep" between two Israeli MOSSAD agents, and brought him to Israel to stand trial for his crimes. Gideon Hauser, the Israeli Minister of Justice, justified the action by invoking the *Law of Nations.* After Eichmann was convicted in 1961, Israel hanged him. The only hanging in Israel's history, and a good one.

If Israel could be so bold in pursuing justice in Eichmann's case, could not the US be just as bold in pursuing justice for Wallenberg, Eichmann's moral opposite-the classical difference of good confronting evil?

Would the United States ever take such a bold step? Who would they arrest? Could an entire country be punished for a crime? Would a law-flouting government such as the Soviet Union qualify under this law as a legal "person?" If the Soviet Union were found guilty, who exactly would be punished?

Criminal cases are normally tried close to the scene of the crime. Bringing the case in Moscow was out of the question. My law professor Telford Taylor had tried that and was thrown in jail for a month in Moscow and then thrown out. As he writes in his book *The Reign of Terror*, "Russia, and especially Moscow, is no place to try a human rights case. It can be dangerous for both the client and the attorney." I called Taylor. He said, "Don't do it. The Soviets will make a mockery of your case. They will deny everything. They even have a special word for it—Peneloka—fool the foreigner with an abundance of lies."

Taylor had gone to Moscow hoping that due process might prevail. He had tried to call witnesses, subpoena records, and engage in cross-examination. He told me, "The whole proceeding was in the hands of someone called a 'procurator' who called witnesses as he saw fit, cut them off when he chose, considered the evidence of his choice, and wrote a report that condemned three men to death after a two-day trial. It was a living nightmare. It was rigged from the beginning. The presence of legal counsel for the defendants meant nothing to the procurator. We were simply an annoyance to be brushed aside."

"Morris, I suggest you bring this important lawsuit in the federal district court in Washington, DC. That's your best chance. You might get a judge who will listen to your case. Sweden should have taken it to the World Court and sued the USSR—nation to nation, but they have no balls, no guts, no sense of doing the right thing. Do what you have to do. Consult with me as you move forward. I will be your loyal back-up man."

Taylor became a good back-up man, a good blocking back to guide my running with the ball. As a young man he had been a prosecutor at the Nuremberg trials of the top Nazis in 1945-46. He confronted Goering and Himmler directly and convicted them of war crimes.

He was my favorite law teacher along with Fred Rodell, who changed his name from Rodelheimer to be allowed into the Yale Law School faculty in the 1950s as their first Jew. In his unique and maverick style Rodell held his constitutional law seminar at the bar at historic Mory's, with pitchers of beer for his students. It was my favorite class and he was my most brilliant professor. It was Rodell who took five of us to Washington, all expenses paid, in order to meet individually for forty-five minutes with several Supreme Court Justices—Chief Justice Earl Warren and Justices Potter Stewart, John Harlan, Hugo Black, Byron "Whizzer" White and William O. Douglas.

I continued to cast about for a friendlier venue than a US district court, which was likely to act as surprised as if I were bringing a Sherman tank down to the local used car lot. I spoke the next day with Guy Von Dardel about using the

57

International Court of Justice at The Hague. We quickly agreed against it. As a private lawyer representing a family and a missing brother, I could not come to the International Court of Justice at The Hague as a group of individuals. In the World Court the complaint had to be brought by one nation against another. Von Dardel and I agreed that neither the United States nor Sweden could be relied upon to take the initiative, not after four inert decades.

I challenged Von Dardel, "Why didn't your brother-in-law Nils Lagergren, a member of the European Court of Human Rights in Strasbourg, use his influence? Why did he not go behind the scenes to the Swedish Ministry of Justice and prod the Swedes?"

"Are you kidding? My brother-in-law is a snake. He pretends to be interested in Raoul but he actually ignores the whole matter. He urges me not to call you. So does my sister. Everyone has fallen away from the effort since my mother died."

The International Court of Human Rights in Strasbourg offered me another unique court for human rights advocacy. It was open to the claims of individuals. This court heard cases presented by any individual whose human rights were violated. But they usually just filed reports. They did not have the power to order a nation to release someone from jail. It could order, for example, a surprise visit to all Soviet jails in a blitz search for Wallenberg. This court had shown some teeth in defending the rights against torture brought by Irish Resistance freedom fighters, men imprisoned in Northern Ireland. But I thought carefully about the difficulties of litigating in Strasbourg. What would it cost? How many months would it go on? How could I possibly afford that?

The more I thought about venues, the more I warmed to the United States as the right place to bring the case. Wallenberg had been officially made an American citizen by act of Congress; let America stand up for him. The plan had an element of drama and surprise. Wallenberg had been forgotten for 39 years, now suddenly I would bring a lawsuit to rescue him. My plan had daring. The only thing it didn't have was "legs," no solid precedents. No matter how sturdy the ride, it would require a trial judge who had courage and vision. One of my various gut feelings told me to take the case directly to the US Supreme Court. Roll the dice. Try to nail the Russians with a haymaker. The Constitution, Article Six, says that a case involving a foreign diplomat could be brought originally in the US Supreme Court.

But then I remembered Article Three, Section Two, which lays out the ground rules for jurisdiction. I went and checked it again. Title 28, Section 1331: All matters arising out of treaties should be tried initially in the district courts, then move upstairs to a Court of Appeals and then to the Supreme Court if need be.

I needed the bright glare of publicity and a heavy dose of public interest. I pictured those Supreme Court justices peering at me as I came into court with my appeal. No Earl Warren there now to ask the poignant question cutting through the legal garbage: "But Counselor, is it fair." The liberal activists had been replaced by a stodgier conservative court. Warren, Black, Brennan and Douglas were gone. Who would listen to my argument for jurisdiction?

"I need the impossible," I said to Elizabeth. "I need a law that says a US federal district trial court can take jurisdiction and hear arguments in a civil action against our major enemy of the Cold War. What can you do to help me stir up tension and brouhaha enough to create a release and have us bring our diplomat home. If you just happen to have the right case or statute lying around, please let me know."

"Is that all?" she asked me, with a wonderfully innocent expression, and a sly smile. She was dressed like a Main Line Matron, her gray hair carefully coifed, a grey sweater joined by a pin of red roses and a pink blouse and a gray long skirt to contain her modesty. She was every inch a lady and a great legal scholar as well. She should have been a law professor, and not merely a law librarian. But she loved her work: even came in on Saturdays to help students. She knew the law. I'll never forget the furrowed brow thinking, and the open look of wonderment on Elizabeth Marie Arnold's face. Hers was a look of profound self-amusement. I revisit it many times in my memory.

She reached into her desk drawer and produced a bailiff's-ring of strange, long keys.

"I believe I have just what you need. Come with me."

Elizabeth and I squeezed into the staff elevator, scarcely big enough for two, and headed silently and pneumatically up to the fifth floor of the Penn Law Library building—heading to the Rare Book Room which only she could access that day. She remained mum the whole time, humming "Fly Me to the Moon," a Sinatra tune. She maintained a wry twist of a smile barely detectable on her lips. The elevator opened. She led me to a hermetically sealed room. No outside air ever touched these precious books. She used two keys to release the locks and push open the heavy door. The air surging in my face smelled like a windless morning in the high desert. Sunlight leaked into the chamber from high windows, illuminating glass display cases and a few shelves of beautiful, leather-bound books.

I looked into the lighted cases. Displayed were an original Gutenberg Bible, hand-written drafts of pages from Whitman's *Leaves of Grass,* and a first edition of *Don Quixote.* Nearby were handwritten letters and notes of Benjamin Franklin, James Madison, and Thomas Jefferson—all authors of the US Constitution. On a shelf were the books that Edgar Allan Poe had written in Philadelphia.

She opened a glass case. "One of the two originals left in the world. Take a look at this."

59

It was a large leather bound volume from the ancient year 1789. It was the first US code of laws written by America's first Congress. The tome was so fat that she could barely get her long, thin fingers around the width of the volume. She held the book against her chest, closed the glass lid, and set the book on top of the display case. The paper was parchment, thick and supple. The *Alien Tort Claims Act*, the first law authorized and actually written by the newly elected President Thomas Jefferson of Virginia. It was a law Congress passed even before it voted for the Bill of Rights. To see it in the original was an enormous privilege.

"Read it aloud," Elizabeth said.

I read the exact wording. *"Federal District Courts shall have original jurisdiction of any civil action by an alien*—in other words, Wallenberg or his brother Von Dardel - for crimes *committed in violation of the law of nations or a treaty of the United States."*

"In other words," I said to myself "the United States must defend the law of nations, no matter where it's transgressed. And what did the Law of Nations say about someone like Wallenberg? After all, wasn't he a diplomat?"

"Blackstone said that kidnapping a diplomat was a specific violation of the Law of Nations. Diplomats needed protection or immunity from arrest. Violation of a diplomat was taboo number one. And, Elizabeth, I imagine that Jefferson would have been familiar with Blackstone, because Blackstone was the undisputed authority on international law at the time."

Even though it had scarcely been used, the *Alien Tort Claims Act* was good law in 1789 and remains good law today in 2011. It has never been repealed or modified. It is to this day still a good law. I always marvel at this law's idea of inviting foreigners to come to America for protection and for justice. The law epitomized Jefferson's faith in the American experiment. What foresight.

"Imagine if every victim of tyranny responded to this invitation," I said. How would the courts handle it? How would other countries handle it? Legal systems as we know them would be challenged to ascend to the next level. It might even lead to an International Court of Criminal Justice."

"I know," She said, her eyes twinkling. "Don't you just love being an American sometimes?"

When I left the University of Pennsylvania's Law Library late that afternoon, I was elated. I had found the basis for a sober and persuasive case. I had enough law to survive in my opening procedural argument of jurisdiction, and be permitted to present my substantive argument on Soviet liability for the acts of false arrest, kidnapping, torture and violation of *habeas corpus*—the right of any defendant to be given a hearing within 24 hours after his arrest. Now I had my "ticket" to argue my case. I had been given a mission, a purpose, a meaning and a goal!

April 1983
Washington, DC

I drafted my complaint against the Soviet Union seeking Wallenberg's release. I worked day in and day out for three full months on the research and writing of the argument. I reviewed my several drafts with Philadelphia lawyer Juan Laureda, who was my co-investigator of Pinochet's violation of human rights during our two-man trip to Chile. I decided to use claims for damages that would immediately engage the Soviets—including a request that the federal district court in Washington, D.C. immediately suspend American wheat sales to the USSR, pending the outcome of the suit. I also asked in the complaint for one million dollars in damages for each of the thirty-nine years of Wallenberg's illegal arrest and detention. These were tough and real demands, right from the get-go. We would also arouse and enlist the support of the various Wallenberg committees around the world. Numbering perhaps three dozen, these were volunteer committees formed to help me to secure Wallenberg's release. They included the large and vibrant New York committee headed up by master violinist Isaac Stern and his wife Vera, and supported financially by Henry Kissinger and the prestigious Counsel on Foreign Relations.

In New York, I met twice with Nobel Peace Prize winner Elie Wiesel, a survivor from Hungary and the author of *Night,* and other books on the Holocaust. Wiesel encouraged my lawsuit. He gave me good advice and told me his personal story of survival as tears moistened his cheeks. I was privileged to share time again with him in the month of March, 2011 when he and I were both awarded with the humanitarian service medal by Chapman University of Orange, California.

I met with Henry Kissinger, who volunteered to contact his Soviet counterparts and friends in Russia in an effort to find out which prison camp presently housed Wallenberg. I was given great support on research and law arguments from my mentor and international law professor from Yale, Myres McDougal. New York law firms were also enlisted including Paul, Weiss, Rifkind and Garrison and Morris, Ernst and Greenbaum. Simon Wiesenthal, the famous Nazi hunter, and his foundation gave me $25,000 to defray the heavy expenses. "We will work together to rescue this brave hero," Wiesenthal told me. A high-profile panel of well-respected, diverse human beings volunteered to support my effort.

I asked the White House, through Chief Presidential assistant David Gergen, to get the State Department and the White House to file an *amicus curiae*—friend of the court—brief supporting my civil complaint. Gergen was enthusiastic and very supportive. He tried his level best, but his efforts in November of 1983 were undercut and sabotaged by White House Counsels Fred

Fielding and John G. Roberts, for reasons then unknown but later learned and explained in detail in the later pages of this book.

John G. Roberts today sits on a self-constructed throne as the Supreme Court Chief Justice of the United States. This is an awesome and powerful position. I have repeatedly asked Justice Roberts to explain his behavior in telling President Reagan not to touch the rescue of Wallenberg issue. I believe Roberts sabotaged Wallenberg's chance for freedom. I have been met by his cold shoulder, silence and no reply. Roberts realizes today that he could have been instrumental in creating Wallenberg's rescue. He regrets not having helped to rescue Wallenberg. He has even stated: "I support the strong and robust use of presidential power," yet later on in his memo to the President on January 25, 1984, he caves in and 'recommends a reply to Wolff over your signature (Mr. President) essentially dodging the issue and the applicability of the just law.'

I felt it was the natural thing for the United States government to support my effort. Wallenberg was our American *de facto* diplomat. We financed and sent him to Budapest. It was the duty of my government to bring him home. FDR had established the US War Refugee Board in 1944 at the urging of Secretary of Treasury Henry Morgenthau, in an effort to rescue the remaining Jews of Europe. The Americans enlisted and funded Wallenberg for his dangerous mission to Hungary. After all, not only had the US government sponsored Wallenberg's mission financially; the US War Refugee Board was the initiator of the idea and plan. It recruited him and promised to rescue him if he fell into enemy hands. The Swedish government was used as a point of access into Budapest since the US was officially "at war" with Hungary. Sweden was a neutral country still maintaining diplomatic relations with Hungary.

I met with D'Amato soon after the first phone call from Von Dardel. We chose as our venue an Indian restaurant across from the Shoreham Hotel in Washington DC. Tony was brash, gutsy, unconventional, and eager to go against the grain. He loved inventing lawsuits to disturb foreign governments. He brought a copy of a book, *Raoul Wallenberg: The Righteous Gentile* by John Bierman to show me. He opened it and pointed to a picture of a balding man with an earnest look, and an unmistakable sense of mission. He was handsome, with a strength and openness about his face that I liked. It was Wallenberg, frozen in time at the age of 32. He looked like me at that time and I felt an immediate sense of connection and kinship. The same photo and others appear in this book, thanks to the Holocaust Museum in Washington, DC.

I asked Tony to leave the book open to the series of pictures. I wanted to get to know Wallenberg, feel his personality through his pictures. I saw the picture of Wallenberg that I have placed with mine at the front of this book. He looked healthy and "on the job," busy on the phone finding the time of train departures so he could rush to Hagysholom train station and get the Jews off the train before it left for Auschwitz. I had been told that he could be warm and charming, but also impatient and demanding. He looked charming and self-assured as he stood there on the phone listening. I tried to imagine him as he'd been first as a 32 year old fearless savior of human lives, and then, later as a 71-year-old man—probably grey hair, wrinkled, gaunt face and frame from years of rotten prison food. I pictured him with a stubbly beard and whiskers, impatient for release. I moved him forward from a young and aggressive 32 to a resilient 72 of today. I somehow knew he was still alive, and waiting by his prison door for his rightful release. I saw him still alive, but suffering and waiting, patiently waiting. I saw him alone in a prison camp, dressed in prison rags, and wasted after all of his desperate 39 years in the Gulag. Tony reached into the inner pocket of his leather jacket and placed a worn, brown leather billfold on the table. Inside were two passports. *Schutzpassen.* One bore a photo of a man, the other a woman. They were a couple who lived in Chicago, Tony told me. They had asked Tony to advise me that they did not want their names made public, but that they were prepared to assist with the case in any way.

Wallenberg had designed these Swedish protective passports to help protect the Jews in their dealings with the Germans and the Hungarian Arrow Cross fascists. Wallenberg had previously learned that the German and Hungarian bureaucracies had a weakness for external symbolism. So he had the passports attractively printed in blue and yellow (Sweden's national colors) with the Three Crowns coat of arms in the middle, and he furnished them with the appropriate stamps and signatures. Of course Wallenberg's protective passports had no value whatever under international law, but they commanded the respect of those whom they were designed to influence.

As I looked at the pictures in the *"Schutzpass"* I saw faces of two frightened parents and their son. The passport was marked August 6, 1944. The young boy in the photo in the passport was approximately eight years old. I thought back to when I was eight in the summer of '44, my eighth summer. What was I doing that summer? I was with my family at our summer home at Camp Sandyville, a colony of Jewish families from Philadelphia and New York who fled to the cooler altitude of the Pocono Mountains in the northeast corner of Pennsylvania.

I was looking closely at the faces of this Hungarian family saved by Raoul Wallenberg, and funded by money from the US War Refugee Board. I thought of a strange coincidence.

My mind went back to August of 1944. I was eight and a half years old. My family was staying for the summer in the Pocono Mountains of Pennsylvania, ninety miles from Philadelphia. The summer camp of log cabin bungalows was a safe haven and meeting place for survivors and other first generation Jews who had fled the pogroms in Poland, Lithuania, Russia and Germany.

Whatever Happened to Raoul Wallenberg?

On an August morning my mother woke me early. It was 6 A.M. and it was cold, but I had to get up. She leaned down to my bed and whispered "Morris, it is time for you to get up and to become a champion." I had accepted a mission. I had given my word and made a promise. I had no choice but to keep it—just like Wallenberg after he accepted his mission to go to Budapest. We both had appointments. These appointments were about to converge.

I had agreed in a moment of impulsive altruism and madness to swim the two and one half mile length of Lake Tamiment, from Nature's Rock to the Sandyville shore on a "would you dare" challenge and a $3,300 bet. In some ways it was not exactly a bet, but it was a commitment on my part to swim the length of the lake in order to stimulate a charitable response from the Jewish families. I wanted the families to give money to help rescue the Jews of Europe from the rapacious momentum of the Holocaust. Each of the thirty-three families had pledged one hundred dollars in support of my marathon swim. I selected The War Refugee Board as the destination for the funds since it was committed to rescuing families besieged by The Holocaust. The bet was whether I could swim the two and a half miles alone, with just my mom alongside in a rowboat. I had promised not to touch the boat during my long journey. I decided the money would go to help Jewish children in Europe being terrorized by the Nazis.

The Jewish families from our summer mountain community got up at 6 A.M. in the early morning light just to watch me swim the lake—even the lifeguards. I was happy to know that I was swimming to raise money for the US War Refugee Board, money that would go to Jewish refugee children. They were so vivid in my imagination. They had no homes, no parents. They were little prisoners sitting in refugee camps behind barbed wire.

Even at age eight and one half, I was already a precocious student of world events and world history. My Mother made sure of that. Forwarded from our home the "Weekly Reader" arrived each Monday and it actually covered the story of the Holocaust more completely than the New York Times. The prestigious New York Times is partly to blame for the apathy and failure of citizens in the United States to respond to the terrible plight of European Jews. The New York Times made it a practice to bury information on the Holocaust in the back pages of the paper. Ironically, the Sulzbergers, the Jewish owners of the New York Times did not want to ruffle feathers, and wanted to pass as "Good Americans" rather than as "Good Jews."

The pictures which I saw in the Jaqcues Bierman's book Raoul Wallenberg: The Righteous Gentile were of Jewish refugee children, clinging to barbed wire in concentration camps. There were other photos of adults saved by Wallenberg at the Budapest train station. These photos in 1983 reminded me of the pictures I had seen during the summer of 1944 in my Philadelphia Inquirer. Those 1944 photos had stimulated my decision to swim the lake and to raise money for children whom I did not know and would never meet. When I first took the case in 1983 I told my mother of the coincidence—of the photos in 1983 and the memories of '44, and of our famous swim-the-lake experience.

At age eight and one half I was already an advanced young swimmer, and running long distances. My mom, a water-safety instructor, pushed my athletic abilities to the limit. I remember climbing into our Chevy station wagon wearing my maroon bathing suit and terry cloth bathrobe. As we drove down the hill to the lake, the headlights of the car scared a small deer. At the lake, cars were already parked in long rows occupying what was normally the green grass of the baseball field.

They had gathered to cheer, drink coffee, kibitz and watch me swim or drown. There were mixed feelings in the crowd, but most wanted me to win!

I walked through the crowd; people parted to make space for me. I walked down to the water with my mother behind me holding towels and a thermos of hot tea. There were candles floating on the lake purchased by the families for an extra five dollars. Each candle floated on a small square piece of plywood, and on the underside were prayers for relatives of the camp families still living in Europe.

As I sat and shivered, my teeth chattering, my mother rowed the yellow wooden boat the two and a half miles out to our "Nature's Rock." The sun was rising, reflecting bright yellow off the yellow color of the wooden boat, and casting long rays of glimmer on the water. The white mist was just rising as we embarked. As we reached the large boulder that was "Nature's Rock," I got out and plunged into the icy water, going completely under for a moment. I surfaced, gasping for air. "Start swimming Morris." "It can be done," my mother said. "Swim hard, but come up for air. Just lie on your back when you get tired. Regain your strength and push on!" My mother gave me more instructions: "Swim systematically without touching the boat. Stay alongside me. I will row slowly. Be patient; one stroke at a time. We will make it together, all the way back to the Sandyville shore, where everyone is waiting for you to win."

I swam, changing strokes from time to time, my teeth chattering; first the front crawl, then breaststroke, and at times resting on my back to catch my breath. I swam, and I swam, and I swam. The water seemed to get warmer as I kept going. I could see the headlights of the cars on the distant shore. My mother whispered words of encouragement from the boat, "You can do it." I could still hear her words of encouragement years later as I looked at the faces in the *Schutzpass*.

After two hours in the water, I reached the Sandyville shore, and the sandy beach leading up to the line of cars. The families had stayed to watch my arrival. They cheered and reached out to help me, handing me fistfuls of cash, as I staggered up on the sandy beach, the sun pouring its light all around me.

The next day I took the money to the post office to mail it to the War Refugee Board in Washington, stuffed into two fat green Camp Tamiment emblazoned envelopes. One held checks. The other had all the cash. All together it was $3300.

As I walked to the post office, drivers honked and waved. "Go, Morris, go!" they cheered. The community was united with pride, after months of being haunted by newspaper photos of little children and their families carrying huge burlap bags, walking away from their homes, staring blankly, not knowing where they would sleep that night. We received daily news about the labor camps and death camps. We felt uneasy and guilty—living peaceful, safe and comfortable lives while others suffered. Now we had struck back at the horror.

At the post office Werner Sperling, the postmaster, a Jewish refugee from Austria, counted out the cash and wrote a money order for it, fitting everything into one large envelope. His wife, also a Jewish refugee from Austria, asked me which Jews in Europe specifically I wanted to help. She said I ought to specify it in a letter, not just send the money. In a copy of *The Jewish Forward,* her husband showed me a headline that read, "Hungary's Jews Hang onto Thread of Hope."

And so I wrote a cover letter to the War Refugee Board: "Dear Sir, please use this money to help the Jewish children of Hungary. They need to be saved." I sealed the green envelope myself and placed it in the mail slot of the little wood cabin post office that served as the sending station, and walked around the lake back to my home. My solitary swimming journey was now complete. Mission accomplished!

Now, sitting at a small table in the Indian restaurant, as the sun was setting on the trees surrounding Rock Creek Parkway, with the red and white checkered table cloth and the multi-colored candle dripping silently into a white dish, I found myself thinking about my new silent, voiceless and absent client Raoul Wallenberg, and about my first contact as a child with the War Refugee Board. I remembered that slender green envelope, with the Tamiment Tomahawk in the upper left corner. My imagination followed the path of the envelope on its journey to Washington, DC, and then direct to Budapest. I imagined Raoul Wallenberg sitting at his desk, opening his mail, and seeing the tomahawk logo of Camp Tamiment. And he would have taken out my letter and read it with care. For a moment his hands touched the same paper that my hands had touched. That would have been a kind of handshake—the start of a relationship, and the beginning of a life of converging destinies. I returned from thinking about my swimming experience in 1944 to the business at hand.

It was after midnight when Tony and I got up to leave the Indian restaurant. We both had similar perceptions of the Wallenberg scandal. The American government should have acted to rescue Wallenberg but it did not. Wallenberg was a World War II M.I.A. hero. His family had been patient. They had mistakenly placed their trust in governments, and the diplomatic process, believing they would ultimately obtain Wallenberg's return to Sweden. Now it was time to consider tougher and more confrontational action.

"There is evidence that he is still alive." were Tony's parting words, as he gripped my arm and looked one last time into my face.

"Yes," I answered. "I sense he is very much alive. Something dramatic and concrete needs to be done—now!"

I left the restaurant, and walked under the antique streetlights that graced Connecticut Avenue, and then crossed the street to enter the Shoreham Hotel. When I got to my room, I ruminated over the case, and made some notes. Lawyers normally rely on facts they can see, testimony they can hear, and people they can cross-examine. I sensed that Wallenberg was still alive; otherwise, what would be the reason for suing the Soviets for his release? Evidence had been gathered from several sources suggesting that he was alive, despite four painful intervening decades. But I knew that, as much as I wanted to speak with him firsthand, I might never see or speak with Raoul Wallenberg until I had rescued him through court action from his lonely vigil in the gulag. Still, I longed to know firsthand from him just what he wanted me to do.

Then, I set aside my legal pad, with all the notes on Wallenberg's heroism. I thought to myself, "Morris, you plan to go to all this effort, but for what? Who is this for? Is it for Wallenberg himself, or just a desperate effort to remind people that there was once a Holocaust, and that a few brave souls tried to save Jews? Is my client alive? Could he have survived 39 years of detention, confined alone in a small one-man cell, at times shipped around to various labor camps within the gulag, and suffering the cold winters of Siberia at hard labor? How could he have survived? What mental and physical program could he have put in place to accomplish this? I had read Viktor Frankl's. *"Man's Search for Meaning."* Frankl found a reason to live and a meaning to his unjust imprisonment. "I am here so that I may testify when the War is over about the horrors and brutality that I have seen with my own eyes. I shall be historian of the Holocaust." Perhaps Wallenberg, as he invented his own twenty-four letter alphabet, and tapped messages on the pipes for fellow prisoners to "hang in" and survive found a similar energy and purpose. I hope so. Could he possibly be alive?"

It was then that I experienced the most amazing encounter of my life. Nothing like it had ever happened to me before, nor has anything like it ever happened since. What I am about to describe is something I would have never thought possible, but it was very real at that moment. Some have called it a messianic moment, others consider it an altered state of consciousness, when we are in touch with powers and people in a manner beyond our normal senses of sight and sound. But I can assure you it was a very real moment. It was also an exciting peak experience in my life. And it strengthened my resolve to do everything in my power to pursue this case of rescue to the end.

Whatever Happened to Raoul Wallenberg?

A warm spring breeze filtered through the window of my hotel room on the second floor of the Shoreham, lifting the light curtains. I heard sounds, a creaking of the floorboards of the old hotel and a movement as if someone else was present in the room. I sensed I was not alone, but I also felt I was not in danger. These were benign and safe sounds. I looked under the bed and in the bathroom. Nothing. No one. I went into the bathroom and stood in front of the sink and mirror. I heard footsteps. Again, I felt as if someone else was in the room, but it was a peaceful presence. I did not move.

I opened my Dop Kit, took out my toothbrush, unbuttoned the top button of my blue pajama and I began to brush my teeth, looking at myself in the mirror over the sink.

Then I looked up and saw a man with sun-burned cheeks and a grizzled beard quietly coming up just three or four feet behind me. He was advancing quietly towards the door of the bathroom. I did not feel threatened. I stared into the mirror and I saw him; Wallenberg. I saw the face I had seen earlier in the John Bierman book. It was now a much older face with hollowed cheeks and grey whiskers and vacant blue eyes. He was aged now, the haunted blue eyes of a man standing directly behind me—his face reflected in the mirror above the sink. Our eyes met in the mirror and our heads began to move up and down gently in harmony—moving slowly with one another. I was communicating with him through eye contact and body language. I was aware of his presence. I acknowledged his silent message: "Take my case. Please take my case. Get me out of here." He stood still and again he motioned. I sensed if I turned, he would no longer be there. He raised his head slowly up and down again, as if to say "yes" in silence. "Yes, please take my case to court. I need your help. I need your voice. I am still alive."

I found my head again moving up and down in tandem with his; it was a crazy, surreal, hypnotic moment of connection. His eyes and mine maintained contact in the mirror for a few moments. I did not turn around. I somehow sensed that if I turned, I would have broken the spell. As I looked into his eyes and saw his haggard face, shaped by years of imprisonment, he seemed to be saying again without words, "Please take my case. I am very much alive. Please help set me free. Come rescue me soon."

His last words, "rescue me soon," had a sense of deep insistence and pressure. As if to say I do not have much time. I select you and trust you. In the wake of this inexplicable moment, I felt a sense of direct appointment. The man himself had drafted me into service.

From that day forward, I dedicated my life to finding Raoul Wallenberg. **I promised him directly, man to man, that I would come for him.**

April & May 1983
Philadelphia

I worked alone in my study at home reviewing international law cases and crafting the Wallenberg brief. In feverish moments of creativity, it was all coming together. *The Alien Tort Claims Act* of 1790, Jefferson's dream tool for the promotion of human rights in American Courts was a bonanza for me. Many quiet human rights cases from the 19th and 20th centuries, like *Santissima* in 1823, long dormant, now seemed to be awakening. Like friends, they were stepping forward and taking up strategic positions of responsibility within my brief. I felt as if they were whispering, "We are your pillars of strength. We are here for you. We are still good law. We have been ignored for years, but never overturned, never reversed."

I accepted an invitation from the US Congress to testify and share facts concerning Wallenberg's survival and location, where he'd been seen, and to lobby the members of the House Foreign Affairs Committee.

August 3, 1983 was scheduled by Congressmen Peter Kostmayer, of Bucks County, Pennsylvania, and Tom Lantos, of San Mateo, California, for my report on my draft complaint and plans to sue the Soviets for his release. The date would coincide with the "Raoul Wallenberg Oversight Hearings" scheduled by the House Foreign Affairs Committee. This was to be the second time that Congress, at the urging of Congressman Tom Lantos and Senator Claiborne Pell of Rhode Island, would try to investigate and find out what happened to Wallenberg and determine the degree of responsibility our government should now assume to achieve his release. After all, we had appointed Wallenberg an American emissary in 1944 and had long since failed to gain his freedom.

The oversight hearings were the brainchild of Congressman Tom Lantos and his wife. As children in Hungary, they were both rescued by Wallenberg. As Lantos tells it, he was a blond haired messenger boy in Budapest, an innocent child whom the Nazis never thought to stop. He was running messages between Wallenberg and the Budapest underground. He fooled the Nazis every time with his story of running to the store on an errand for his sick mother. One time he was playing stickball on an empty lot. "I thought because I had blond hair, and looked Aryan, that the Nazis would never figure me for a Jew. I was wrong. Wallenberg saw the Hungarian Arrow Cross grab and question me. He ran out of the safe house, grabbed me from their arms, scolded them and me, and hustled me into safety. Don't ever assume you are one of them, he told me. You may be blond, but you are Jewish and fair game. Without Wallenberg's quick action I would have been shot and killed, or at least taken away."

Whatever Happened to Raoul Wallenberg?

After the war Lantos and his dynamic and diminutive (4' 10" tall) wife Annette stayed in Budapest. They left when the student uprising of 1956 failed to throw off Communist rule. They moved to America and settled in San Mateo, California, where Lantos ran for Congress, and based his campaign on a "Free Wallenberg" ticket, attracting the financial and voting support of many wealthy Jews in the San Francisco area. He won and moved to Washington, DC.

True to his word, Lantos made his first official act as a member of Congress the filing of a bill naming Wallenberg as a citizen of the United States. Reagan signed the bill into law on August 5, 1981 and stated: "This law must be used as a tool to pry this hero out of the hands of the Soviets, and to secure freedom for Raoul Wallenberg. I sign it with the hope and prayer that he will one day sit beneath the tree planted for him at Yad Vashem on the Avenue of the Righteous Gentiles in Jerusalem." Reagan got mileage with the Jewish vote for this Rose Garden ceremony—a great actor at work, but little else.

Support for my lawsuit grew. There was a generous gift of $25,000 from the Wiesenthal Foundation in Los Angeles, to cover part of the expenses of the litigation - not legal fees, just court costs, translation of documents Xerox materials, travel to court, and expenses. The assistance of the foundation's Rabbi Hier and Rabbi Abraham Cooper remains to this day of great value.

An impressive array of distinguished lawyers and law professors joined me. They agreed to volunteer their services on a *pro bono* basis. This included Myres McDougal, Sterling professor of International Law at Yale, my law school mentor; and Louis B. Sohn, Bemis Professor of Law at Harvard. We began to build a team—a "noble band of brothers" and later, sisters. Murray Levin of the law firm Pepper, Hamilton and Sheetz in Philadelphia saw me one afternoon about to dive into the swimming pool at the Germantown Cricket Club. When I came up to poolside I saw that he was reading a biography of Wallenberg.

"My, oh, my, I just happen to be his lawyer and here I find you reading his biography. What a coincidence."

"That's a God-incidence," he answered. "Can I work with you on the case?"

"By all means. I need all the help I can get. Murray Levin was the first lawyer to sign on."

Professor Tony D'Amato of the Northwestern Law School in Chicago and Professor Jordan Paust of Houston Law School were next. They were followed by the Hon. Earl Silbert, the courageous Watergate prosecutor, who took a genuine interest in the Wallenberg case from the beginning. I went to Washington, DC to consult with him about the issue of jurisdiction. We had been colleagues and friends since we both worked in Washington in the 1960s as prosecutors for David Acheson (Dean Acheson's son) the US Attorney. He was also my tennis partner every Sunday in Georgetown, where we often watched former CIA head Allen Dulles, Secretary of State Dean Rusk or Defense

Secretary Bob McNamara out for their separate Sunday walks. We were young lawyers, at times awed by watching these great figures, "the covers of *Time* Magazine" walk by in real life, often saying hello or sometimes stopping to watch.

Earl was known to his friends as "Earl the Pearl," a term of endearment. He was also known as "goody two shoes." These references to Earl's reputation for honesty were borne out by his brilliant and tireless work on the Watergate investigation, leading to criminal convictions of John Ehrlichman and H.R. Haldeman, and their subsequent prison terms.

"This will really be a tough case to sell!" Earl said when I first consulted him about the Wallenberg case. "You are going to go to court to try to persuade a US federal judge to take jurisdiction over a human rights crime that occurred 39 years ago, in a foreign country. But what the hell, it's worth a shot, and who knows—you might win. I will help you go for it. We can't let him stay there."

Other friends from the teaching profession joined, including James Freedman, President of the University of Iowa and Professors Harold Lesnick, John Honnold, and Covey Oliver of the University of Pennsylvania Law School, where I taught international law and ethics.

From this talented and dedicated team I was able to draw on a wealth of research talent and legal insight. My esteemed law partners, former Governor Harold Stassen and Ted Kostos, worked with me to sharpen and refine drafts of the legal documents and oral arguments. It was an extraordinary collaborative effort. Together we did everything we could to free Raoul Wallenberg.

May 1983

Philadelphia: The Frank Ford Show

His name had been Frank Goldstein in the 1930's, but to "pass" and get jobs in radio and television he had "anglicized" his name. Now, Frank Ford had the most popular talk radio show in the Philadelphia-New Jersey area, with big names with interesting causes invited to appear. I had known Ford, a fellow Jew and the "dean of talk shows" in Philadelphia, for more than fifteen years. I had last been on the show in the spring of 1972 to report back on my work on the United Nations Law of the Seas Conference in Caracas, Venezuela.

He called me to appear on his show again after reading of my upcoming testimony before Congress about my plans to sue the USSR for Wallenberg's release. This fit perfectly with my secondary strategy. Because of my concern that the court would refuse to accept jurisdiction in the case, I was simultaneously gathering publicity support, hoping, if legal avenues proved fruitless, to use 'shame' as the tool for discovering Wallenberg's fate.

"This case is not just about winning," Ford said to me on the phone. "This case is about publicity. Motivate the American public. Get them riled up. They have to feel Wallenberg's pain and his frustration, sitting in that stinking hole of a Russian prison with nothing to do, no one to talk to, and no reason for being held captive. Create a deep sense of outrage. Demand his release. Tell me the background. How did you get involved? Is there any precedent for suing the USSR in a US federal court? Do you think he's still alive?"

Frank's on-the-air rapid-fire method was to ask a series of questions and let you pick up on the one you felt like answering. That way he got his guests talking and keyed up to answer a raft of questions. I could tell that Ford had caught the same "bug" I had about Wallenberg's fate and the need to rescue him and bring him "home" to America or Sweden.

I told Frank how I had been asked by the Wallenberg family to put pressure on the Russians to disclose the truth; how the family had reports of recent, credible sightings of Raoul. I admitted that almost nobody thought we could win a lawsuit against the Soviet Union, but that many, including me, believed we could prod President Reagan to take action and demand that Yuri Andropov, the Russian President and former KGB chief, open the gates of Lubyanka and send Wallenberg home to Stockholm.

"Publicity is your most effective tool," Ford said. "Get confrontational. Stir things up. Call them to account. I would like you to appear on my show as soon as possible."

I reminded him that I was scheduled to testify before Congress on June 18th, in just three weeks. If I could, I wanted to use my guest appearance on his show to reach out to his audience, tell them a little about a great man, and see if there might be some survivors in the Philadelphia area who knew Wallenberg, especially any recent Russian Jewish immigrants who might be survivors of the Gulag, or a real long-shot, perhaps some Russians who were prison guards, or who knew Wallenberg and his location through the release of Jewish political prisoners like Sakharov and Scharansky.

Later I met Anatole Scharansky, a political prisoner held in Russia incommunicado. I met him in Washington, DC and he inscribed his book: "To Morris Wolff. Freedom fighter for Raoul Wallenberg. Never give up. Bring him home. I want you to win"

There were large numbers of Russians coming into Philadelphia and settling in the greater Northeast. They were becoming, as Frank told me, butchers, cab drivers, doctors—hard-working people trying to get ahead. These people were out there in Ford's huge radio audience.

Ford invited me to be a guest on his WCAU show that Friday, the day they got their biggest listener audience.

I was running late, but I pulled into the radio station parking lot at ten before two and screeched into the radio room at three minutes before the hour, just enough time to re-connect with Frank and review what we wanted to talk about. He was a handsome man, with sharp blue eyes and a full head of hair - grayer now than when I had last seen him. It had been years, but his friendly intensity made me feel welcome.

"Just the mere mention of Wallenberg's name," he marveled, "and we have had ten phone calls from people who owe their lives to him, from right here in Philadelphia. Can you think how many there must be across the country? Once you get this thing going, it will spread like wildfire. These people want to know what you are doing as his lawyer, and how you plan to rescue him." He looked at me. "Are you prepared to answer that? Maybe you'll need the Mossad, or some other intelligence group to locate him and hijack him out of there. It will have to be stealth and trickery. These Russians aren't going to just open the door to Lubyanka and let him go."

The red light went on outside the booth.

"Okay, we are on the air!" Frank swiveled in his cushioned armchair and brought the mike closer. "Friends of Freedom from Radio Land," he began as he turned and winked at me, "we have a very special guest for you this afternoon. A lawyer from Philadelphia in the tradition of Andrew Hamilton. Just as Hamilton stepped forward in 1773 to defend John Peter Zenger and freedom of the press against the tyrant King George III of England, Morris Wolff, a distinguished member of the Philadelphia Bar, is stepping forward to sue the Soviet Union for the release of a World War II hero who has been literally sitting in chains in a Russian prison for the past 39 years. You may ask, what was his terrible crime that has warranted such a jail term? His only crime was to rescue more than 100,000 Jews in Budapest in 1945. And, you may ask, what was his reward?"

Whatever Happened to Raoul Wallenberg?

Frank stopped for a moment and lit an unfiltered Camel cigarette. "His reward has been thirty-nine years of incommunicado imprisonment, no visitors, no family, no friends, no communication—all for just doing this one good deed to save lives. America selected Wallenberg for this assignment. We paid his expenses. We set him up. We applauded his work and then we abandoned him at the end of the war. Now a man with backbone and 'batzim, a Yiddish word for balls, has come forward to take on the Russians and hold them accountable in a US federal court for this gross violation of Wallenberg's human rights. Morris Wolff, welcome to the show."

"It's good to be here with you, Frank," I said, and we were off.

I started by giving Frank's listeners an idea of who Wallenberg was, why he went to Hungary, and why he was taken prisoner by the Russians and held captive. I spoke, too, about the legal theories I planned to use, what I was asking for by way of damages, and I mentioned the Congressional hearings.

"What do you have for us today Morris? Do you have any new information about your client Mr. Wallenberg and his whereabouts? How can our listeners help you?"

I took a document from my brown leather brief case and put it in front of Ford. I cleared my throat and continued. "We have a sworn statement by a survivor who was just released last month after many years in Russian prisons. He was with Wallenberg in a cell at Mordivinia Prison—a special place within the Gulag for political prisoners. They were together for three months—January, February, and March of this year. We are working on that specific report." Then I continued, "You have a lot of listeners, Frank. And I would like to hear from your listeners if some of them, or any of their parents, were saved by Wallenberg. If any of your listeners knew Wallenberg firsthand and can give statements about his work in Hungary, it would be helpful to our case."

The phone lines began to light up like lights on an air traffic control panel. For the next hour I took calls from survivors and people who had been with Wallenberg in Hungary. Countless people called in with testimony of their association with Wallenberg - those who had themselves been with him during that period or those who had close relatives he was able to save. I gratefully jotted down names, feeling energized and optimistic.

Toward the end of the hour Frank's assistant slipped us a note: "A woman in Atlantic City, Mrs. Esther Weiss, says she was with Wallenberg in Budapest as a young girl." Frank wrote across the top of the note in red pen: "PUT HER ON!"

"Hello, Mrs. Weiss. This is Frank Ford here with Morris Wolff. Please tell us your Wallenberg story."

"This is wonderful," she said. "After all of these years, we have someone who wants to find Mr. Wallenberg! I agree with Mr. Wolff, the lawyer there on your show. I believe he is still alive. I was a young girl in Budapest when Mr.

Wallenberg first arrived. He was the first person to ever come to help us. We were doomed. The Nazi noose was tightening around Budapest. All the Jews in the countryside were already dead or in concentration camps. He was a ray of hope in a frightening world."

And so Esther Weiss told all Ford's listeners her story.

"I was fifteen at the time, a young girl in school, but I volunteered. I was very attracted to Wallenberg immediately. He was shy and reserved, but strong and decisive. He was magnetic, drawing people to help him from all over Budapest. At one point he had four hundred volunteer employees, and three offices. He took charge immediately."

"He set up his first office at 43 Tatra Ulloi, and had messengers running in and out of there every day with new passports to give to Jews to save their lives. My home was right next-door. There was a large garden behind his office with trees and swings and a small water fountain; very peaceful."

"One day I was playing and singing in the garden with my two sisters. We would read together and sometimes sing as well. I looked up at the window in the building above the garden and saw Wallenberg. It was a hot day, with the window open and no screens. We girls went to the kitchen to get some lemonade and cookies for him. He sat down on the wooden bench they normally reserved for our father Apuka, and Wallenberg asked us three girls to sing for him."

Esther paused and began to cry. We could hear her sigh and cry through the phone. We waited. She rejoined us. Frank lit another cigarette and waited. Esther picked up where she had left off.

"This is such a relief from my daily schedule," Wallenberg said to us. "Sing anything." So we sang some songs from our school. He unbuttoned his suit coat and his shirt collar and loosened the blue and gold tie that he loved to wear. He smiled at us to keep singing. "I rarely take time from my work. This is wonderful."

"He smiled and ran his fingers through my hair. No one else was there, just me, my sisters and Wallenberg. We spent an hour that way together. He seemed so happy. He was so relaxed. We saw him smile, and he tried to hum the songs with us. He had a good voice and a playful manner. After about an hour one of his aides, from next door, came into the garden to get him. "I am being marched off," he said, "but I would rather stay with you children here. I will visit again sometime."

"It was the last time we saw him in a relaxed situation. He was two different people. The official person, who barked orders at his staff and berated the police, and forced the Arrow Cross soldiers to release Jews at the train station, and then the sweet man we met in the garden that day."

"He often seemed so sad," Esther said, "as if something important was missing from his life."

75

Ford intervened. "But do you really think he is still alive, Mrs. Weiss, after all these years?"

"Yes, I do." she answered. "Mr. Wallenberg was a sacred soul, an avatar sent by God to assist the Jews in despair. He was for us a Messiah. Messiahs do not die. They are given special gifts of Life. I feel Mr. Wallenberg is alive, just as I first felt his eyes on me that day in the garden before he came down to spend time with us. I feel his energy. When he leaves this earth I will feel that energy as well. We know he is alive. Others feel the same way. There will be a shift in energy when he dies and that shift has not yet taken place."

"And I want to say to your Mr. Wolff do not give up. Whatever you do, do not give up. We are with you, and God will guide you to victory. Persevere with this. Mr. Wallenberg is waiting patiently to be rescued." She sighed and began to cry again, overwhelmed by feelings. "This is a sign." Esther Weiss continued, "I think we should send an investigation team to Russia to find him. We should rescue him while he is still in good health. Mr. Ford, you should go and take your talk show to Russia, in Moscow, with Mr. Wolff, and ask the Russian people to help you to find him."

"I agree," Ford responded. "That is exactly what we should do. We will have to get some clearance from the governments but I am ready to try this new approach. We will appeal at the grass roots directly to the people. What do you think, Morris?"

I paused and took a breath. "In theory, I love the idea," I replied. "But in practice, we couldn't just show up in Red Square and start talking to people; we'd get arrested by the KGB. The Cold War has never been icier than right now. But other than those minor details, I would be happy to go there with you as part of a citizens' delegation. I want to find him and bring him home."

WCAU Talk Radio in Philadelphia was a power station, with a national listening audience of over 12 million.

Frank Ford gave us the first mass-media publicity support for the Wallenberg case, helping us "get our act on the road" and in front of the listening public. His "Talk of the Town" show gave wide exposure to the hushed-up story and scandal of Wallenberg's plight. Then, the nationally aired morning TV shows, including ABC's Good Morning America, and NBC's Today Show, aired many of the interviews with Wallenberg survivors, and invited me on as a morning guest. I heard from friends I had not seen in years from all over the country. When I was on CNN I heard from friends in Europe from my AIESEC student days. Later on, CNN again carried the story of our lawsuit, and I received letters from Wallenberg survivors in 25 different countries. The publicity gave our effort support and sober minded credibility worldwide.

Soon after the radio show I visited Esther Weiss in Atlantic City, and we became friends. She arranged a special banquet at the nearby Margate Synagogue in 1985 where Wallenberg was honored in absentia, and I was given the National

Counsel of Christian and Jews Award of New Jersey for humanitarian work. I shared the podium that night with Rosa Parks, and found her to be a quiet, determined, humble woman—an icon in history and a courageous leader of the Civil Rights movement.

I stayed in touch with Esther for several years after our first Talk Radio "meeting." She kept a picture of me and one of Wallenberg next to her bed. She died in 1993 after a full life, leaving five children and 13 grandchildren. Three of her children became teachers, one of whom designed a curriculum on Wallenberg and Human Rights for her school. Esther helped start the Holocaust Center at Stockton State College, near Atlantic City.

My annual meetings with Esther helped me to persevere in my effort to find Wallenberg. She pushed me, and gave me hope and inspiration to carry forward. She never let me forget my obligation. She once said, shortly before she died, "As long as there is one ray of hope that he is alive we must carry forward and find him. And you, Morris, must be the beacon of light to the world and the permanent torchbearer."

She always told me to remember Winston Churchill's speech at the Harrow School in 1941, when he famously stood up and said, "Never give up; never give up, never give up," and then abruptly sat down. She found out I was born on Sir Winston's birthday, November 30th, and never let me forget that "coincidence," as she called it.

She was like an older sister and friend to me, and my link to the tender and caring aspect of Wallenberg's persona so often overlooked in the clinical recounting of his work. To this day, I treasure the mental picture of him sitting in relaxation, sipping lemonade, and having fun with Esther and her sisters, just sitting in the afternoon sunlight and singing in the garden next door.

Near the end of the Frank Ford Show, Reba Levine called in.

"I was actually born in Wallenberg's private apartment on August 5, 1944. I owe him my life. I was listening to your show while driving out to Wynnewood for my voice class. I had to pull off the road and call you and offer my support." She began to cry. "My mother often told me how and where I was born, and the sacrifice of this man for me and for others in Budapest."

She told us her story. "Above a Viennese bakery located on a small cobblestone street near his office in the center of Budapest, Wallenberg kept a small flat where he slept each night, often for just a few brief hours. The flat was sparsely furnished with a bed, kitchen table, and a few chairs. On his night table were pictures of his mother, brother and sister in small gold frames, and a small bedside library: books by Kant and Spinoza, the plays of Ibsen and Strindberg, and the poems of Rilke. Each morning a Jewish shopkeeper left Wallenberg loaves of bread and his favorite, "elephant ears" pastry. Food provisions included coffee for mornings and his favorite chamomile tea to help him to ease off to sleep after his "normal" 18-hour days. Twice a week Judith Yaron, his personal secretary would come to clean the flat, wash the windows, change the sheets, and put a few items of food on the shelves and in the refrigerator. On some nights Wallenberg slept on the sofa at his office, especially when he anticipated an early morning visit to the train station to haggle for the release of another train load of Jews."

One of the first volunteers, who arrived with Judith Yaron, was a tall, 22-year-old woman with blonde hair and blue eyes. She was a quiet person who kept the files for every Jewish family that came to the office for assistance. She was seven months pregnant, her husband having gone to fight with the resistance in the Carpathian Mountains on the Romanian-Hungarian border east of Budapest. Her baby was due August 5th. Wallenberg, on being told the mother had no place to have the baby, immediately offered her his flat for the clandestine delivery. That night, from midnight until dawn, he simply walked the streets of Budapest. At 7:00 A.M. he returned to his office to begin his daily round of meetings with the Jewish Counsel, which that day had purchased three new properties to serve under the blue and gold flag of the Swedish Legation—three more safe houses for Jewish families needing sanctuary. Both Reba and her mother survived the war, and were joined by her returning father. After being processed as "family" through the Joint Distribution Center in Vienna, they moved to Toronto. Reba, named after Raoul, developed a career as an opera singer and voice teacher in Toronto. She had now moved to Philadelphia, where she taught voice at the world-famous Curtis Institute for Music and sang solos with the Philadelphia Orchestra.

"I want to help. Wallenberg made life for me possible," Reba said.

The next week Reba started a Save Raoul Wallenberg Committee in Philadelphia, attracting over 100 members to her cause. To help pay the costs of litigation, she gave benefit dinners and concerts featuring musicians she had enlisted from the Curtis Institute and the Philadelphia Orchestra. The events helped focus the attention of the people of Philadelphia on the Wallenberg case.

In addition, Reba raised money to cover the travel expenses of Wallenberg survivors who wanted to accompany her to the House Foreign Affairs Committee hearings on June 18, 1983 where, with her help, I asked for congressional support for the Wallenberg litigation.

August 1983
Washington, DC

After the Frank Ford show, more radio interviews and television appearances in the weeks leading up to the hearings helped increase public awareness and build support. Meanwhile, I made my final preparations for the hearings, another key building block in the architecture of my 'shame' strategy. Win or lose the case, I was determined to focus a bright public spotlight on the Soviet behavior towards Wallenberg. The Wallenberg family lawyer Claes Cronstedt flew to Philadelphia from Stockholm to meet with me at my home for three hours to discuss the case, and to carefully review with me each point I was planning to raise in my federal complaint. I had already written nine separate drafts of the complaint. My wife Debby arranged and hosted a party for Cronstedt and for Szen Hagstromer, Wallenberg's closest boyhood friend. We invited a few of our closest friends over to meet these two distinguished representatives of the Wallenberg family. "You have done excellent work in crafting this historic complaint," Cronstedt told me. He gave me the Wallenberg family's vote of approval for the lawsuit and their prayers and blessing.

During a visit to Washington, DC, I rehearsed my speech and testimony with Tom Lantos, Wallenberg's chief advocate in the US Congress.

"Speak for Wallenberg," he told me. "You sound like him; you even look like him—refined, urbane, witty and persuasive. Become his voice. Use the fact of his citizenship in your speech. Wallenberg is now an American just like you and me. The only difference is that he is not here with us to celebrate his freedom... at least not yet."

Tom Lantos made me feel good about my work. He was always available, along with his wife, Annette. His words were always a strong encouragement.

I lobbied for a Congressional resolution endorsing and supporting the litigation in the US federal court. I had written the following letter to every member of Congress and to the President: "Help me to free Wallenberg now! He needs your support, members of Congress, as I press this litigation in the federal court in Washington, DC. I need your unanimous resolution supporting my litigation. I want the resolution signed by every member of Congress."

I met with key senators and congressmen. First was Senator Claiborne Pell of Rhode Island, chairman of the Senate Foreign Relations Committee. Pell's father Herbert was the last US Ambassador to Hungary before the war. He admired Wallenberg's heroic work in Hungary. He agreed to cosponsor a Senate resolution supporting the Wallenberg hearings and our litigation efforts to rescue him. Senator Arlen Specter of Pennsylvania, my former boss when he was District Attorney of Philadelphia, also agreed to support the resolution.

On the House side, Representative Jim Leach of Iowa, a ranking member of the House Foreign Relations Committee, lent his support, as did Representatives Peter Kostmayer of Pennsylvania and Barney Frank of Massachusetts. Leach's support became valuable as he stepped forward to suggest a suspension of wheat sales to Russia "pending Wallenberg's release." The State Department had expected—and hoped—that because Leach represented the Wheat Belt state of Iowa, he would oppose the resolution. His suggestion took them completely by surprise. I had two strategic meetings with Representative Leach, who agreed actively to support my plans to sue the Soviets for Wallenberg's release, and to introduce me to the Congress on June 18. I was flattered by his offer of support; a sharp contrast to a quite different meeting I had shortly before the hearings.

Congressman Lantos had earlier called the White House and spoken with Chief of Staff David Gergen. With President Reagan's full approval, Gergen had scheduled for me a 3 P.M. appointment with Assistant Secretary of State Richard Fairbanks, who was in charge of European Affairs. Fairbanks had been selected as the point man within the State Department to handle the resistance effort against my lawsuit and to take sides with the USSR. Lantos had also secured a promise from Gergen that my request for an *amicus curiae* 'friend of the court' brief would receive a full and fair hearing at the State Department. No such hearing ever happened. Little did I know that the State Department would oppose my case behind the scenes.

I had great trepidation as I approached Fairbanks' office. Informed sources had confirmed to me that the State Department considered the case a "hot potato." Then there was Jim Leach's phone call just the day before.

Leach had told me that the US State Department was apparently more interested in appeasing the USSR than in finding Wallenberg. The Legal Counsel's office at State had analyzed the problem carefully. They knew that suspension of wheat sales—our strongest leverage to free Wallenberg—was a real threat to U.S-Soviet relations.

Thus State Department Legal Counsel Ed Derwinski had just gone to Leach's office and angrily confronted him. "We can hurt you Mr. Leach," Derwinski said. "Matters are hot; the situation is quite tense with the USSR right now. The Soviets consider this lawsuit a serious blunder. And the Soviets think we are behind this. They don't understand that a private citizen lawyer has the right to stir things up and create a potential international crisis beyond our control."

Leach replied: "By the way, don't try to frighten me Counselor Derwinski. I am not worried about my political future. Morris Wolff's lawsuit comes at the right time. It is all part of the Congressional Oversight Committee meeting to find out if you guys at State are still dragging your heels. You have had three years to do something since the first Wallenberg oversight hearing. You promised us action; nothing concrete has been done. Now here we are in 1983 and you have done nothing. You have just shuffled papers. Wolff is stirring things up. Yes, indeed he is. But he is acting in the great tradition of an outspoken citizen fighting against injustice and I plan to support him all the way. I am circulating his complaint against the Soviets to all my colleagues. We have 133 Members of Congress already signed on. In the next days we will have 100 more. This lawsuit is not an affront to anyone. You help us get the Soviets to open the prison door! Good day Mr. D."

Leach called and related to me the above conversation, which I recorded with his permission. I like the part of his calling him Mr. D. After all Mr. D. or Derwinski had been a "D rated" machine politician of Mayor Daley, a ward heeler from Chicago who somehow made it to Congress for a brief time, before taking his cushy joke of a job at the State Department where his chief duty was to make sounds but do nothing.

Congressman Leach warned me that the State Department was taking a hostile position, trying to achieve a cover up of the Soviet's outrageous action. Instead of supporting the lawsuit and a stoppage of wheat sales, Derwinski and forces in the State department and the White House wanted, for some reason, to sabotage and crush my lawsuit. But it was too late. Momentum was on our side. My appearances on national TV had unleashed a tirade of angry letters to members of Congress: "Do Something. Do Something Now!" This was the new clarion call.

And thus the second round of Wallenberg hearings before the US Congress was called. The State Department wanted to crush my effort to bring litigation against the Soviet Union. At the same time, the Congress was ready to unanimously support my lawsuit. How ironic—The United States government was on a collision course with itself. Congress, and the Executive Branch were at odds with each other—all because a private citizen was planning to bring an important human rights lawsuit.

The State Department wanted full management of the Wallenberg issue. They had already sided secretly with the USSR. They actually went out and retained Eugene Theroux Esq., an experienced and greedy, expensive senior attorney with Baker and McKenzie, a Washington, DC law firm, to represent the Russians against me!

Leach said, "Be careful. They play hardball, not principle. I just wanted to give you a heads-up that the pinstripe boys at the State Department are not your friends."

These worries ran through my mind as the taxi approached the entrance of the State Department in Foggy Bottom. I got my "pass" and went to Fairbank's office.

I intended to make a reasoned, low-key but impassioned plea for Fairbanks' cooperation. At the very least, even if I could not enlist his support, I definitely wanted his tacit approval and an assurance he wouldn't blindside my lawsuit. I knew Fairbanks behind the scenes was already helping the Russians.

At precisely 3 P.M. his secretary ushered me into Fairbanks' office and offered me a cup of coffee. "He'll join you momentarily," she said. I rehearsed again what I was planning to say. "I need your help, Mr. Fairbanks, in giving us an *Amicus Brief* supporting our effort to rescue Ambassador Wallenberg." I sat there waiting. Fifteen minutes later the secretary returned to warm up my coffee. "I am sure he'll be here very soon," she said. I looked at my watch. I wouldn't have much time before the hearing.

Twenty minutes late, Fairbanks entered his office and mumbled an phony apology; something about the press of duties and other responsibilities. He was dressed in the standard State Department uniform of blue pinstriped suit, white shirt and red tie-the incredible conformity of State Department types. His first words shocked me.

"Why are you filing this lawsuit?" he said accusingly. "Why are you trying to stir up bad feelings between our country and the Soviet Union?" His tone was cold, hostile and belligerent. He threatened me.

"You have no idea what might happen to you! And we will not be able to protect you. The Russians play hard ball and they may decide to kill you."

"Are you saying my life is in danger if I bring this lawsuit?"

"I am just saying go back to Philadelphia, Professor, and practice law. Leave international matters in our hands. We are the Executive Branch. You are interfering with the conduct of foreign affairs. This is an internal matter for the Russians to resolve, and for us to work out through secret diplomacy."

"Are you saying Wallenberg's kidnapping from Budapest, and being drugged and dragged to Moscow is merely an internal matter? I don't think so. I think it is a criminal matter. I wish we could conduct a criminal prosecution of those involved in his abduction. As it is, I will file a civil action under the *Alien Tort Claims Act*. In addition I have a new law in my corner. It is *the Foreign Sovereign Immunities Act*, and it effectively takes away the cloak of immunity for foreign nations who commit crimes against foreign diplomats"

Fairbanks face reddened. He did not anticipate this blow back.

He took another tack. "Listen Herr Professor. You have a lot of friends here at State. The Chief Legal Adviser went to law school with you, but he will oppose your lawsuit at my request. Other people here know that you mean well. But you have no idea what a serious reaction your lawsuit will cause. The Soviets will think we put you up to this."

"Then disabuse them," I said. "Tell them that you can not control private lawsuits. That's what the separation of powers is about. We have an independent judiciary. Let them decide if I have a good cause of action."

I reminded Fairbanks of President Reagan's remarks in the Rose Garden on August 5, 1981—just two years earlier—when he signed the law making

Wallenberg a full United States citizen, with all rights of rescue under the *US Hostages Act of 1868*.

I told Fairbanks:

"I will write a letter to President Reagan asking him to put the Soviets on notice that Wallenberg is now both a US citizen and a US Hostage under 28 US Code 1732. As such President Reagan has an affirmative duty to demand his release. He actually has no discretionary choice. He has a legal and binding duty to demand the release of Wallenberg, just as President Jimmy Carter demanded the release of the embassy employees held hostages in Tehran, Iran a few years back."

Fairbanks eyes widened. Now I was on the offense. I was the one delivering the 'threats.'

"Only a bullet will stop me," I said. "And you guys are not about to order that."

"Do not under estimate what we might do."

"Why not follow the President's lead?" I asked. "He has signaled to you and the State Department that rescuing Wallenberg is a priority matter. Or was it all just show: something for public relations, and nothing else? Besides, isn't this a good time for the State Department to redeem itself for its inactivity and apathy shown over the years since Wallenberg's capture in Budapest?" I asked. "You have the power—and I believe you have the duty—to file an *Amicus Brief,* a friend of the court brief supporting our litigation initiative."

I reminded him that David Gergen, the Chief of Staff at The White House had sent me to see him for just this purpose. "We need your support, and not your resistance and opposition. Wallenberg was practically a US State Department diplomat and employee paid by the US State department from a private and secret account." I said. "It will strengthen our claim to have you and the State Department on board, supporting your *defacto* diplomat. It will show the Court that our government is backing the rescue effort and wants him sent home to his family. The President cannot lose on this one. Help me send a message to the Soviet Union that our government stands four square behind this initiative," I continued.

"No way," he replied. "This is a closed issue. It is our official position that Wallenberg is dead."

His curt, quick, and defensive reply stunned me. Why should he want Wallenberg to be officially dead? Soviet Premier Andrei Gromyko had claimed in 1957 that Wallenberg died of a heart attack ten years earlier, but this version of Wallenberg's death had been fully discredited. Why should a healthy man have a heart attack at age 34? More importantly at the moment, why was Fairbanks buying into this lie?

"How do you know?" I challenged him. "How can you be certain? What is your proof? Show it to me. Is that an official State Department position, or just your opinion?"

He did not answer my question. Instead he turned and looked out the window. He then shuffled some papers on the credenza behind his desk. I could see his hands shaking as he lifted the papers and turned towards me. "This is my private Wallenberg file," he said.

"May I see it?" I asked.

"No, you may not," he replied. "It is an official confidential file for my eyes and the Secretary of State only."

"What are you afraid of?" I asked. "What is there to hide?"

His face turned crimson. His right eye suddenly began to twitch nervously. He tugged at his collar and unbuttoned the top button. Then he loosened his tie and took off his suit coat. He took off his horn-rimmed glasses and waved them in my direction. He got up from his chair. He came at me, stopped, while glowering and towering over me.

"You will drop this lawsuit if you know what's good for you. You are fishing in troubled waters."

I stood up and faced him. "Are you going back to intimidation? Are you trying to scare me off the property?"

"I expect my American government to support my effort in court," I answered, staying calm and focused on the purpose of my visit. "Wallenberg is our man. He was almost an employee of your State department. He was our diplomat dressed up as a Swede. We went to him and seduced him with promises and assurances of protection. He was our 'soldier,' drafted during wartime for a dangerous mission. It is the duty of our government to rescue this soldier, still missing in action."

I reminded him of my professional experience as a lawyer with the Office of Legal Counsel within US Justice Department and as a member of Attorney General Robert Kennedy's legal team.

I had filed several *amicus briefs* in support of citizen lawsuits during the civil rights movement in the sixties. Now, I told him, it was time for the State Department to show some backbone and do the right thing.

I left the acrimonious meeting frustrated by Fairbanks' belligerence. His opposition baffled me, since my visit had been arranged by David Gergen and approved by the President. The reason for his behavior did not become clear to me until later.

I had been aware, of course, that in certain matters the State Department had a historically poor record, dating back to the 1930s, when it came to supporting and protecting Jews. Its feeble effort to save the Jews of Europe during and after World War II is well documented.

I had read David Wyman's revelatory book *The Abandonment of the Jews,* which documented the effect of the anti-Semitism that was rampant among key figures in the State Department before and during World War II. Wyman cited as one example the adamancy of Assistant Secretary of State Breckinridge Long, who in 1939 successfully urged President Roosevelt not to permit the landing of the "St Louis," a refugee ship that set sail from Hamburg, Germany filled with more than 900 German Jews fleeing the Nazis. The ship hovered for a week off the coast of Florida, before the ship and its human cargo was forced to return to Hamburg, Germany—and to the death of each person on that ship. The people standing on the deck could actually see the bright lights of Miami and its tall buildings and pleasure yachts. They were almost close enough to touch American soil. So near, and yet not near enough. A nod from the State Department could have saved all of those lives, and allowed these poor souls to land at the harbor of Miami. Why not? "Give me your tired, your poor, your huddled masses yearning to be free." Did these words have meaning?

This same strain of anti-Semitism still permeated the upper ranks of the State Department professionals in 1983 when we started to prepare our lawsuit. Since Fairbanks at that time had achieved the rank of Assistant Secretary of State for European Affairs, it was natural for the Wallenberg case to be placed in his hands by the Reagan Administration. (The Carter Administration, on the other hand, would probably have assigned it to Stuart Eizenstadt, Assistant Secretary of State for Human Rights, with a much different reception and outcome.) But we happened to be filing our lawsuit during one of the most frigid years of the Cold War. Our timing was not auspicious, but we had no choice.

I later learned Fairbanks had earned a reputation among members of the State Department for being hostile to Jewish interests and "all matters Israeli," especially if they ran counter to the interests of the Iraqi, Libyan or Soviet governments. "He hated Israel," one informed source, a lawyer at the State Department, told me. "He sides with the Syrians and Iraqis on all issues where the vital interest of Israel is involved," my source elaborated

Fairbanks aggressively fought to kill my case. He killed the initiative within the State Department to file a much-needed Wallenberg *amicus brief* actively supporting my case. My law professor friends in the Office of Legal Advisor within the State Department told me they were eager to file, but Fairbanks vetoed it. I was told that Fairbanks was an unprincipled opportunist with no ideals - that he sometimes had deep conflicts of interest between his duties and the interests of Americans.

My sources also believed that he used his position at the State Department to cater to the interests of the USSR, Syria, and Iraq, carefully preparing to make big money by serving as a lobbyist for one of these foreign nations once he retired. Opposing the *amicus brief* was one such occasion in which the interests of a foreign nation, the Soviet Union, were given priority over the true interests of the citizens of the United States.

Fairbanks, from the year 1982 forward, was apparently looking out for himself, and how he could profit from his contacts once he left government.

It is now clear to me that when I met Fairbanks he was already trying to determine which foreign nation would be the highest bidder for his post-government services. He had already narrowed his focus to Russia and Iraq. Accordingly, his actions at State were tailored as much as possible to the interests of these potential future employers.

Andrew Cockburn, in his book, *Dangerous Liaison: The Inside Story of the US-Israeli Covert Relationship,* describes Fairbanks pragmatic exit strategy in this way: "Richard Fairbanks was the State Department official who directed Operation Staunch. This was a project for the construction by Bechtel Corporation of a pipeline to transport Iraqi oil across Jordan to the Gulf of Aqaba, an outlet desperately needed by the Iraqis, since Hafez al-Asad had cut the line across Syria in 1982. Fairbanks retired shortly thereafter from government service and went to work at a salary in excess of $350,000 per year for the Iraqi government of Saddam Hussein as its lobbyist and diplomat in Washington D.C. He was obviously a turn-coat serving Iraqi, Libyan and Soviet special interests long before he left the State Department."

State Department sources later advised me as to how Fairbanks sold his soul. "He was like a college football player in 1983—a high draft pick looking for the team or nation most willing to pay his price. It came down to the Russians and the Iraqis. Richard took the Iraqis. He felt they would be a more stable source of money for him from oil revenues. He was right. The Russians were not reliable or loyal to their American lobbyists. The Iraqis were. He made a fortune as a lobbyist. Your plea for Wallenberg and the *amicus brief* never had a chance. He parked your case in his office and took away the keys. Between Fairbanks and McGovern at State and Fielding and Roberts at the White House your case was a dead duck."

I did not get shot. Fairbanks' threats of bodily harm did not occur. I could still move forward with my case, even if my government would not lift a finger to help me. And so I did.

August 3, 1983
The House Foreign Relations Committee

My testimony before the House Foreign Affairs Committee was on a bright and sunny day in Washington, DC. Bright and clear, a day for lucid comment and clarity in the Wallenberg case. At last, the scandal of the Wallenberg story and cover up would be told before the world, and carried on CNN, C-Span, ABC and CBS. The courtroom was packed. People continued to stream into the large room as the ten o'clock time for oral testimony of my plan to sue the Soviets would be revealed. Hundreds of people from various "Save Raoul Wallenberg Committees" had come to Washington, DC from around the world: Hungary, the Czech Republic, Slovakia, Ukraine, Poland, Russia, Venezuela, the United Kingdom, Canada, Belgium, France, Australia, Netherlands, Chile, Italy, Germany, Israel, and Argentina—all survivors, or children of survivors who kept the flame alive. There were state delegations from New York, California, Texas, Florida, Vermont, Georgia, and Pennsylvania—all supporting the litigation and putting pressure on their senators and members of Congress to support our effort. A broad base of national and international grassroots support was in place to hear my argument for a Congressional resolution to support my lawsuit, and to hear selected holocaust survivors—saved by Wallenberg—testify about Wallenberg's self sacrificing deeds. All of this in one bright spring morning—June 18, 1983— before the House Subcommittee on Human Rights of the Committee on Foreign Affairs.

Marvin Makinen, a professor of biophysics at the University of Chicago, who had been imprisoned in Lubyanka as an American spy, and who met Wallenberg there in 1958, agreed to testify. He had encouraged the Wallenbergs to select me as their lawyer. He also helped to obtain the $25,000 from the Simon Wiesenthal Foundation, which would help defray legal expenses of the lawsuit. Reba Levine and several of her closest friends from Budapest were in the audience. So was Agnes Adachi who worked with Wallenberg in his office in Budapest, and who in 1989 wrote *Child of the Wind: My Mission with Raoul Wallenberg*.

My papers of research and the draft of my complaint—Von Dardel vs. the USSR—stuck to the green felt on the mahogany table as I unpacked my briefcase and prepared to testify. One by one the members of the House Foreign Affairs Committee came over to shake my hand and congratulate me and express support before the testimony began. They had read my prepared statement and a copy of my draft complaint a week earlier, as distributed in advance by Annette and Tom Lantos. The legal complaint had gone through eight drafts, been reviewed by Ivy League professors and top trial lawyers, and was fresh and new and ready for filing.

Whatever Happened to Raoul Wallenberg?

C-Span, NBC, CNN and ABC flipped their cameras on. Journalists were in the audience, including one from Pravda (who was also a KGB agent, as I later learned). The white klieg lights flooded the chamber. I was the leadoff witness. A finger from a TV cameraman pointed in my direction. "You are on in ... five, four, three, ..."

"Members of Congress, and learned members of this House Foreign Affairs Committee, I first want to thank Committee Chairman Gus Yatron, from Scranton, Pennsylvania, and Congressmen Tom Lantos of California and Peter Kostmayer of Pennsylvania for their invitation to testify about my work before the House Foreign Affairs Committee and its sub-committee on human rights. I realize that today's hearing is totally devoted to 'What Happened to Raoul Wallenberg?' and how an American President, and our White House, the Congress and the State Department can do more to achieve his rescue."

I pulled the microphone close to me as the klieg light of the cameras went on. "For the record, my name is Morris H. Wolff. I am a lawyer from Philadelphia. I have been retained by the Wallenberg family on a *pro bono* basis to find an answer to that question. I have also been instructed by the Wallenberg family to file a law suit demanding their brother's immediate release from Soviet prison and his safe return home, a right he enjoys under the *Helsinki Accords*, a treaty signed by the USA, the USSR and Sweden, and therefore binding law, on all nations. This law requires nations to protect the human right of family re-unification, and to avoid unlawful detention of family members. There are other strong laws involved, including the protection of diplomats on assignment and the *Alien Tort Statute* written by Thomas Jefferson in 1789 and still on the books. There are many laws which require his release, including the *US Hostages Act of 1868* which requires our President Reagan to demand Wallenberg's immediate release as a US citizen—a status granted specifically to Raoul Wallenberg by this Congress and signed into law by our esteemed President Ronald Reagan on August 5, 1981—just two years ago." This call for immediate action created a loud murmur and a stir in the audience behind me.

"Why hasn't the President acted?" asked Congressman Gus Yatron. "Why are we here today discussing this matter if the President has had the power to demand his release for almost two years?"

"I have asked the same question of members of his White House staff, including White House Chief of Staff David Gergen," I replied. "As yet I have been given no answer. I will write a formal letter to President Reagan asking him to use his specific legal powers to demand the release of Wallenberg. But first I am asking this Congress for a Unanimous Resolution supporting my lawsuit."

"That is what we are here for today, Mr. Wolff. Please proceed with your testimony, and pardon my interruption."

"I have accepted this assignment on a *pro bono* basis. I consider it to be an honor to be entrusted with this sacred responsibility. But I need your help, and the help of all of these Wallenberg survivors who have traveled great distances at their own expense to be here today." I turned behind me and saw the rows and rows of people who came to support my testimony before the Congressional Committee.

"Copies of my prepared testimony and a copy of my prepared legal complaint have been distributed to all members of Congress, and delivered to each member of the House Foreign Affairs Committee. I welcome your suggestions members of Congress on how I might make it stronger. I am here to answer your questions concerning my plan and its strong legal basis, and to gain your support for the filing of my action. I want all of you to be my symbolic and actual co-counsel in this historic human rights litigation. I believe your support is vital. Wallenberg as of August 5, 1981 is a full United States citizen, just like you and me and many of his supporters in this room today. He is entitled to full privileges of his citizenship, including the right to enter and leave the United States as he chooses. He is not merely an American citizen, but he is an American patriot as well in the tradition of the Marquis de Lafayette and Sir Winston Churchill—the only other individuals granted this extreme honor."

I then took thirty minutes to outline the facts of the case and reviewed the law for the benefit of the members of the Committee. They listened quietly and took notes, and from time to time questioned me on the application of a specific law, and how it would be legally applied in an American federal court of law.

I began by reciting key parts of the law known as the *Act for the Prevention and Punishment of Crimes Against Internationally Protected Persons*: "Foreign governments have no right to interfere with the immunity of a diplomat."

"Even if Raoul Wallenberg is a Swedish citizen, he is also an American citizen. He has dual citizenship. It is the duty of both countries to do all within their power to achieve his rescue. Even if the offense began in Hungary, by his abduction, he is now in what might be labeled so-called 'protective custody' within the Russian prison system. What are the Russians protecting?"

"The citizenship granted by Congress and by President Reagan provides the same rights and privileges of citizenship as those granted to any natural or naturalized citizen."

I pointed out the irony that it was "Wallenberg's courage, in printing Swedish passports that gave Swedish citizenship to Hungarian Jews so that they could live" and how we, the United States, "must be ready and willing to assert the same beneficent and generous rights of citizenship tc Raoul Wallenberg!"

"We originally promised him and guaranteed him protection, through a letter from Secretary of State Cordell Hull in 1944 before Wallenberg left Sweden for Budapest. We failed him. The behavior of our US government has been atrocious. It involves cover-up, denial, deception and abandonment. His family and people around the world expect this committee to do more than give lip service and expressions of gratitude for his service. I will now turn to the federal courts for relief. The case has been entrusted to me as family appointed legal counsel. I believe that our courts will do better. I have clear evidence that Wallenberg is miraculously still alive. He has been held for thirty-nine years in Lubyanka prison in the heart of Moscow under a different name, Sven Andersen. We must take steps through the Congress, the President and the Courts of the United States to set him free."

I concluded: "As we put our best foot forward, I ask the members of this committee to pass a unanimous resolution condemning the behavior of the Russians in holding Wallenberg under brutal incommunicado conditions for the past thirty-nine years. I also urge the Congress in its resolution to ask President Reagan and his State Department to put full pressure on the Russians to release Wallenberg immediately and to account in writing the reasons for his shameful detention."

"Finally, I ask the Committee to ask the State Department and the White House to specifically support and endorse my lawsuit in the federal courts by coming on board as *Amicus Curiae*—friend of the Court—on our side of right and justice and all things decent as we present this historic landmark case in the federal courts."

There was a complete silence in the room for what seemed like two to three minutes. There was a murmur of outrage in the audience. "How can this be? How can there be laws for this, and no one to act for all these years. Something must be done." The members of the panel looked at each other, wondering who would be first to speak. Finally, Congressman Jim Leach rose to speak for the Committee.

"Mr. Wolff, we thank you for coming here in your capacity as legal counsel for Raoul Wallenberg and for briefing us on your plans. You have my endorsement of your lawsuit, and I am sure that you will have the complete support of this panel. Raoul Wallenberg is a Swedish hero, a world hero, a true humanitarian, and a man in chains who has risked his life to save thousands of strangers—people he never knew." He continued, "In my district in Iowa we have many Swedes and many farmers. Congressman Derwinski, who since his loss in the last election now serves as Counselor for the State Department, in a cynical moment of petty sarcasm, wonders if we are willing in Iowa to give up our wheat sales to Russia until this crucial human rights issue is properly resolved. The answer of my constituents is 'Yes, we are.' The farmers of Iowa and the other people of my state are prepared to ask the President to stop the sale of Iowa wheat—and all US wheat—to Russia, until Wallenberg is released, and to support your litigation to the hilt—100%. If you need us to stop selling wheat to Russia until this matter is resolved, we are prepared to advise the President and the USDA—the Department of Agriculture to do so. This may go against our own economic interest and the USDA and US State Department policy, but action—positive action—is now the best immediate policy. We will support your litigation and boycott of wheat sales and put pressure on the Russians to shape up and do the right thing. 'Free Wallenberg now,' as you have said. We agree with you."

One by one the twelve members of the committee got to their feet. All the other people in the hearing room got up as well. Jim Leach started to clap his hands. Soon all members of the committee were standing up and clapping, and then the whole room was standing and clapping. The applause lasted for several minutes and I felt vindicated in my work, and exhilarated, high and happy. This is what I had been working for all along—public recognition of Wallenberg's plight and support by the United States Congress, the peoples' house in our system of government.

Gus Yatron banged down his wooden gavel on a white piece of marble. "Thank you Mr. Wolff. You are a citizen patriot in the lineage and tradition of Raoul Wallenberg. This session of the House Foreign Affairs Committee is hereby officially closed *sine die.*"

Congressmen Lantos, Weiss of New York, Yatron of Pennsylvania and Jim Leach of Iowa all approached me at the witness table and shook my hand. Yatron put his arm around me and squeezed. I forgot to tell you he said, "I am a former linebacker of football at Penn State." From the strength he showed, I did not need a reminder.

"We will see this through," Leach said. "State Department has been dragging its feet on this issue for three years, trying to curry favor with the Russians by sitting on its hands, and ducking this issue. We won't let them sweep it under the carpet this time. We fully support your action. We will circulate our petition asking members of Congress to sign on as co-counsel. If you need me, I will come to the trial to testify in support of your argument in federal court."

"That will be great to have your actual support in court," I replied. "We are looking for all the support we can find and this will be a big boost."

I packed up my brown leather brief case; a good day's work done; much more to do, but for now, a deep feeling of a major milestone reached—a moment of quiet satisfaction.

Tom Lantos came over and took my arm, like an older brother. We walked together, arm in arm, out of the House Caucus Chamber Room 125, then slowly walked down the white marble steps of the Capitol. I looked back at the American flag above the Capitol flowing out in the breeze. The sun was shining. Tom had tears in his eyes. "I wish my mother and Wallenberg could have been here today to see and hear you testify," he said. "You had the courage of a lion in there. You put all of the cynics and non-believers back on their heels. They were speechless. I want you to know that there were members of the Russian embassy in the audience listening intently to your words. They are afraid of what you are doing, and its potential power in world opinion. They even know that you as a private citizen are doing this for the good of the cause, and not at the request of our government. Be careful in the coming days. I want no harm to come to you. If you sense you are being followed, or your work interfered with in any way I want you to let me know."

"Now it will be up to them, the federal court and then the Supreme Court," he said, pointing to the Supreme Court building. "You have won round one. Public opinion and outrage will be a positive factor. You have created it and we in the Congress will encourage it as you bring your case into the justice system. But be careful. I know the two KGB agents in the room today posing as 'reporters'. They were sitting in the back row. They are concerned about this case and where it might lead, in terms of the scandal of it all, and being shown to the world for the terrible tyrants they are. You may even open up the discovery of Soviet state secrets. You are now on their list. Watch what you do and with whom you talk. And whenever possible don't be alone."

We walked over to Union Station. I looked at the small monument where Abraham Lincoln first arrived by train from Springfield Illinois to begin his presidency in 1860. I looked into Tom's bright and sparkling blue eyes. I envied his handsome head of white hair. We hugged each other. I welcomed his warmth.

Years later I was invited by his feisty and charming wife Annette to attend Tom's birthday party in the capital. I reminded him of that first great day in 1983 when we joined forces to move the lawsuit from the Congress towards the courts. Annette gave him a brightly wrapped white ribbon and pink paper birthday card. On the front was written four words: "This is God speaking!" Tom gently opened it up to hushed silence and he read the cryptic funny note: "See you soon!" We laughed together and had a great birthday party. But dear Annette, the woman who worked with him day and night in his office, serving as his buffer zone and best friend, knew something that the rest of us did not know. Tom had cancer. A year later he passed away. Saved by Wallenberg he came to America and lived a miraculous and productive life. He became a lifelong friend and courageous supporter of my lawsuit for Raoul Wallenberg and for all causes of human rights.

That day way back in June of 1983, Tom Lantos and I shook hands and hugged one another in the busy corridors of Union Station. We parted for the second of many good times together. I walked alone up the train platform and happily took the Metroliner fast train back home to Philadelphia.

October 1983
FDR Library, Hyde Park

After the June hearing, I immersed myself again in writing and finalizing the brief in support of my complaint and learning more details about Wallenberg's life. I worked from sun up to sun down every day on preparing the complaint. Except for a game of tennis or a walk with my wife and children, my time was consumed by the case. I checked with Professor Jordan Paust of the University Houston School of Law on some of the finer points of treaty law that might govern the case. I became aware that the Soviets might try to defeat my claim with a preliminary objection that the "Act of State" doctrine prevented any consideration by the United States Federal Court of any activity within their borders. The policy also protected criminal behavior by the state and made the enforcement of international law a toothless tiger. In other words, the Soviets could engage in any form of criminal behavior in its own territory and no foreign state or person could contest it, nor could a United States federal judge analyze its quality of legality. Of course, part of the misbehavior in this case involved the Soviet's kidnapping of Wallenberg while on diplomatic assignment in Hungary— outside Soviet territory. Part of the crime happened in Hungary and part in Russia. Therefore, I was not worried about this weak defense. I was certain there would be other legal excuses presented.

I took concrete steps to gather as much support for my case as possible. I contacted my friend Professor Elie Wiesel of Boston University, a Nobel Prize winner for Literature, and Philip Roth, author of *Portnoy's Complaint* and *Goodbye Columbus*. Both offered their support. I called Wiesel, "Professor Wiesel, I am gathering a group of scholars, writers and authors to support my law case and my book. Would you be willing to help me?"

His soft melancholy voice: "Professor Wolff, I will not only help you. I will give you a list of survivors whom I personally know from Budapest. You may want to talk with them. They knew and worked closely with Wallenberg. They were lucky, like me, and escaped the horrors of the Holocaust. It is important that you keep notes and that you write a book as you go along and publish it when your lawsuit ends in triumph and victory. Your Congressional testimony has created a national victory already. Just by initiating your lawsuit, you are charting out new ground for human rights. It is important for the world to see how Wallenberg, as one man, made such a difference. It is of equal importance that the law remains as a very honorable profession as exemplified by what you are doing in the justice system to rescue him. When you finish writing your book, I will endorse it. Get it on paper, and write this book about your human rights experiences in Chile and Hungary." *That is how his endorsement twenty-five years later occurred.*

Whatever Happened to Raoul Wallenberg?

Professor Wiesel was good for his word. He sent me a list. One man was Janos Beer, at that time 86, and living in Winchester, Massachusetts, not far from Brandeis University in Waltham, Massachusetts. I called and spoke with Janos Beer.

Here is his report:

"In November 1944, I was a university economics student in Budapest. One day, I bumped into my friend Tom Veres, age 19, who invited me to the nearby Swedish legation where Tom worked as the official Wallenberg photographer. I then met Raoul Wallenberg, a very strong willed but courtly man with good manners. He was obviously fond of Tom and told me 'Tom Veres must record everything I do on film, every rescue mission, so that we develop archives of the terrible things happening here. Someday people may doubt that this horror ever happened. We will have it on film and will show it everywhere once this war is finally over.'"

Somehow the Russians sensed this open attitude towards publicity in Wallenberg after he was taken into custody. A secret KGB memo was obtained by my research assistant at the Woodrow Wilson International Center in the year 2007. That secret memo stated: "The prisoner Wallenberg will never be released to the west because his behavior would be uncontrollable. It is anticipated that he would make a major publicity tour and reveal the abuses and torture which he observed while in custody."

Janos Beer continued, "Wallenberg excused himself after our brief exchange claiming he had important work to do. I walked around the legation and met some of the other diplomats. I did not tell Wallenberg I was Jewish but I think he knew. After all, I had received a forged Swedish passport made by Wallenberg. Wallenberg was very resourceful when it came to volunteers. Before he left that day, he corralled me and talked me into working in the 'Schutzling Protokoll,' which was an elite secret group of strong young men which he had created for the sole purpose of rescuing Jewish families and to transfer them from the ghetto enclave in central Budapest to the internationally protected ghetto, which Wallenberg ingeniously created under the neutral flag of the Red Cross. Wallenberg co-opted everyone and every organization he could get his hands on. He created places like 'the Swedish Library' and the 'Swedish Sports Center' and placed dozens of families of Jews in those locations under the officially neutral blue and yellow Swedish flag."

Beer continued, warming up to the conversation: "This volunteer activity sounded very dangerous and very romantic. With Wallenberg always showing up everywhere in the background we felt very safe. If we were not back on time from a work assignment or dangerous mission Wallenberg would come and find us. He was like a demi-god. He treated everyone with patience and a kindly and respectful attitude. We were very important people to him, not the "Jewish scum" which the Nazis called us. Wallenberg was optimistic, calm, reassuring and full of humor. On November 28, 1944 I went with Wallenberg and Veres in his Studebaker car to the Josefvaros railway station where the Nazis had packed Jews into a cattle car for deportation. Wallenberg and I spent hours negotiating the release of those Jews who held the *"schutzpasse"* document. These were the passports Wallenberg had created to claim that the Jews were actually Swedish citizens under Swedish jurisdiction. Several hundred people were taken out of the railway car and sent home."

It was stories like Janos Beer's report that kept me in the game, keeping me working on the case despite the lonely vigil and the solitude involved.

One night in October, I was asleep when the telephone rang. It was midnight. *"Who could be calling at this hour?"* I wondered. *"Guy Von Dardel wasn't going to make that mistake again,"* I muttered. I picked up the phone and remained silent. I heard heavy breathing and fear, followed by a strong German accent. It was a man's voice. He simply said:

"Lawyer Wolff?" his deep voice had a sense of menace.

"Hello, who is this?" I asked, guardedly.

"A friend of Raoul Wallenberg. It doesn't matter who I am."

"What do you want?" I said.

"I want to help you find your hero. I was sitting in the room when you testified before the Foreign Affairs Committee. I can help your case. I want you to win."

He had my full attention. Was he a spy for the KGB or just what?

He told me that there were certain vital government papers called *"Wallenberg Papers."* These included US State Department cables from Roosevelt's time as President written in '44 and '45, now hidden away by the US State Department for over 40 years. He told me he would arrange for me to review a secret file to be found in the Hyde Park archives of FDR, papers so hot that they were moved out of Washington, DC to Roosevelt's remote but safe Hyde Park Presidential Library on the Hudson River north of New York City.

"The government doesn't destroy things, it just conveniently 'loses' them into out-of-the-way places," the man told me. "The file contains secret cables sent from the US Secretary of State Cordell Hull and later Under Secretary of State Edward Stettinius which were sent directly to Wallenberg in Budapest during the war, telling him to speak to Hungarian resistance leaders, and specifically what to do, where to go and with whom to speak. Wallenberg was to deliver specific vital messages to aid the US interest in the war, aside from saving Jews. I had never heard of this file; I began to make notes. The man sounded credible, as if he had

95

something I could use to show that Wallenberg was working directly as a US diplomat. I told him I wanted to see the file.

"You are to go to Hyde Park this coming Monday," he said. "You are to wear a white shirt and a red and blue tie. As a professor at the University of Pennsylvania you should be able to find a tie with your school colors." He laughed. He was obviously familiar with the details of my life, and with my work. I wondered what else he knew about me.

"You will ask for the Chief Librarian, and you will show him any biography you already have of Wallenberg. He will let you in. He will hand you a few folders, plus a box of materials," the voice continued. "You will have just three hours to sift through and read them. You will find there some very valuable documents supporting your argument that though he appeared to be with the Swedish Foreign Service, he was in fact a United States employee and diplomat paid by the United States."

I was intrigued. "Why are you doing this?" I asked him.

"Let's just say I don't like buried documents and seeing men buried alive. I know that our US State Department and President Reagan and his White House will try to bury your case, and possibly you with it. They will buy judges if they have to defeat you in the name of 'National Security.'"

I wondered if the caller was on the level. If so, these secret cables would provide proof of Wallenberg's actual role as a *de facto* US diplomat, working for and being paid by the government of the United States; this was something crucial that I wanted to argue in court. I barely slept the rest of the night.

In the morning, I immediately made plans to visit the library. Then I realized there might be a good way to verify the accuracy of the phone call through other channels—George Ball was on the Board of Trustees of the Hyde Park library. I could call him without disclosing the secret tip of the midnight phone call, now that the midnight caller had tipped me off about the documents' existence. There might be an easier way for me to gain access. I called George Ball in New York City.

I had known George Ball as an esteemed friend and colleague since 1959, when he was managing partner of the Paris office of the New York law firm Cleary, Gottlieb, Steen and Ball. George Ball served as Undersecretary of State under Presidents Kennedy and Johnson before returning to his New York law practice. He had courageously come out in opposition to the Vietnam War in the Johnson administration in 1967 and promptly lost his job. We had lunched together in Paris in 1959 and again in New York in 1967. Fortunately, he was also a trustee of the Hyde Park Library.

He answered his private phone at the office. I told him of my desire to visit the Hyde Park library as part of my research. I also told him about the midnight phone call. "Let me clear the path and make sure you get what you need. I will get back to you as soon as possible," he said. "I won't have you make a long trip unless it is worth it. I know the chief librarian very well. No need to follow some cloak and dagger routine. If the documents are there I will surface them for you. Good to know someone wants to help you. I will alert the librarian to what you need and he can pull up the materials in advance."

Two days later Ball called back. "Bingo," he said. "We have actually located the documents you need. They will be laid out for you on a table in a quiet private room of the library. You are to go there next Monday morning at 10 a.m. as you have already planned.

That next Monday, my law assistant Richard Katz and I set out in a fierce rainstorm at five in the morning. The rain was hard and steady; the streets and highways were wet. We drove over the George Washington Bridge and up the Hutchison River Parkway—rain and more rain. When we arrived, I parked the car in the circular gravel driveway outside the main entrance. The rain stopped. The sun came out creating a slight fog surrounding the imposing former residence of President Roosevelt, alongside the Hudson River. The large public parking lot was empty. I rang the small brass doorbell. A short, balding man dressed in a black three-piece suit with watch fob, opened the door, looking down his nose at both of us through his pince-nez glasses.

"I am here to see Mr. David Lloyd," I said. "I am sent by trustee George Ball."

The man arched his eyebrows. "And you are ...?"

"Morris H. Wolff and this is my assistant Richard Katz. I showed him my ID Driver's License and photo. "George Ball has sent me."

I produced George Ball's letter of introduction, typed on Hyde Park Library stationery. He read it carefully, and then opened the door further, looking around to make sure no one else was there.

"Mr. Wolff, I happen to be David Lloyd. We have been expecting you. Please follow me. You may take all the time you need to sift through the documents." He took us to a large ballroom with a crystal chandelier and a huge royal blue, light blue, and orange saffron Persian rug extending for the forty foot length of the huge room. This was the President's ballroom where he entertained Sir Winston Churchill, Josef Stalin and others. David Lloyd returned a few minutes later and walked with us down the hallway, and past a large room with a spectacular view of the Hudson River. I glanced out at the riverboats and sailboats slowly sailing past. "Mr. Wolff, you must be a very special friend of Ambassador Ball." He smiled and explained, "We don't get many visitors who know about the FDR and Cordell Hull secret Wallenberg cables even being here."

Next he led us through the rooms of the oak paneled library. The first was lined with books on history, diplomacy and politics. Lloyd cleared his throat as he walked and continued, "I have gone through the files and records, culling out for you all the cables between Ambassador Wallenberg and the Secretary of State's office dealing with Ambassador Wallenberg's work for the United States' government in Hungary. Most of them are marked 'Secret and Confidential.' but I have been advised by Ambassador Ball that you are working to find the man himself."

"Ambassador Wallenberg," I mused to myself. Yes, that would definitely be a proper title for the man. He had never gained that title during his service in Hungary. But "Ambassador of Peace" or "Special Ambassador of Goodwill." Something better than just Secretary of the Legation, which sounded so pedestrian, like a paper pusher—not at all in the grand style of Raoul Wallenberg.

We passed through another library room filled from floor to ceiling with bookcases of leather-bound books of the philosophers—Spinoza, Hume, Maimonides and Berkeley. In the final room were the poets—Wordsworth, Keats, Byron, and Coleridge.

We stopped at a long walnut table, where Lloyd showed us the original cables laid out chronologically in three careful rows: 31 cables from Wallenberg and 28 replies to him. There were several more boxes of documents, in addition to the thick tan cardboard box on the table, which had presumably held the cables now spread before us.

We started to read the cables, marked "Top Secret." None had been censored or marked. These were the originals. We were not allowed to make copies; I took notes from these important documents.

The first one was a cablegram dated September 18, 1944, from US. Secretary of State Cordell Hull, congratulating Wallenberg on setting up safe houses and inventing fake Swedish passports to save the Jews.

In a later cable, the State Department had again noted Wallenberg's performance. This one was sent from the new Acting Secretary of State Edward R. Stettinius, Jr. to Iver Olsen in Stockholm, asking that he convey to Wallenberg the US Government's *"sincere appreciation for the humanitarian activities of the Swedish Government and the courage and the ingenuity displayed by Mr. Wallenberg himself."* I picked up another cable. In it Wallenberg was asked to deliver a note to a Hungarian citizen living in Budapest, who was working underground with the US and its allies. The cable asked Wallenberg to get an answer and cable back to Stettinius.

Richard Katz showed me a cable dated October 5, 1944, commending Wallenberg for his courage in rescuing Jews from the trains headed for the death camps. It saddened me to see this fresh evidence, as if it were needed, that the Americans knew all along about the death camps, but never bombed the tracks leading there, letting the Jews die in the camps.

Another cable from Wallenberg included a request that he be allowed to return to Sweden for Christmas to be with his family, and to complete his mission before leaving. The reply from Washington was marked *"Rejected: Wallenberg agrees to stay and report on the Russians."*

Next we turned to a cardboard box with black felt tip marking on the outside, identifying the contents as Office of the Secret Service, OSS cables and correspondence from and to Wallenberg from July of 1944 up to January 12, 1945. The box was sealed. Richard took a pair of scissors from his briefcase and slit open the top. Inside was a red leather three-ring binder book. On the front in bold letters it read: "Intercepted Cables."

I read an internal Office of Strategic Services cable dated January 6, 1945, which reflected an urgent tone: *"Please ask Ambassador WALLENBERG to comment to us DIRECTLY on the number of Soviet troops coming into Budapest. Can he estimate the tanks and the artillery, and the number of Russian soldiers now with the 18th Red Army coming into Budapest? Can he discern their intention? Do they intend to stay?"*

The OSS, which gathered intelligence during World War II and at the end of the war, was renamed the Central Intelligence Agency (CIA).

At the time I first read this cable, I was deeply shaken. Now I knew why the Russians wanted to remove him from Budapest. After his humanitarian work he was now becoming a spy against Russia for the United States and his undercover position was being compromised and exposed by the open and unencrypted cables. I knew that Wallenberg may have been on a double mission for the United States. I was shaken because these were the unencrypted cables, negligently sent, that had aroused the Russian's suspicion that he was an American spy, not just a humanitarian. These cables caused the Russian to arrest Wallenberg.

Mr. Lloyd that moment re-entered the room. He noticed my troubled expression and walked over to glance at the date on the cable. "It was not encrypted. This one and several others," Lloyd said, pointing to three more cables in the book. "This got Wallenberg in trouble. We now know that they were intercepted by the Russians. They thought his 'saving the Jews' program was merely a cover. They did not believe that anyone would come that far just to save the Jews. They decided he must be a spy and locked him up expecting to force out valuable answers to help them in the Cold War."

Of course the Russians thought he was a spy. How could our government have been so inept in transmitting raw and exposed cables? None of the cables had been encrypted?

Another cable asked Wallenberg to stay in Budapest and help rebuild the city, and *"to keep an eye on the Russians. We need to know what they are doing with their invasion. Do you think they are planning to overtake and colonize Budapest and Hungary? Be our eyes. Tell us what you see!"*

The final cable in the book was from Washington, dated January 18, 1945, the day after Wallenberg's capture at Debrecen. It simply asked where he was. There was, of course, no answer.

We continued sifting through the other boxes and found a copy of a receipt for a check for $100,000 drawn on the US Treasury, War Refugee Board Account, made out to "Swedish Rescue of Jews in Budapest." It was cashed in Sweden on June 5, 1944, just before Wallenberg's trip. His name was on the check as the endorser.

Since Wallenberg was being paid by the Americans, not the Swedes, the Russians assumed that he was a spy, not a diplomat. That was why the Russians still wouldn't release him. Was he, even now in 1983, still considered trade bait? Had the US and Sweden simply never come up with the proper spy to trade?

We also found two of the "Swedish" passports Wallenberg had created. They represented the gift of life he had given to others while losing his own freedom. If only one of those passports could have been used to redeem Wallenberg's life, I thought. We also discovered two previously known documents recorded in Harvey Rosenfeld's book, *Raoul Wallenberg, Angel of Rescue.* These included a letter from Wallenberg's mother to Henry Kissinger begging him to find her son, and the 1957 Gromyko memorandum claiming that Wallenberg was dead.

In a small separate file marked "US War Refugee Board 1944-45" we found a photo of Wallenberg having dinner with a group of what appeared to be American diplomats and Kolman Lauer, his Jewish business partner, at a restaurant called Bellsmanor in Stockholm. It was signed *"To Raoul, with best wishes for your humanitarian work and your high adventure in Budapest, Iver Olsen, American War Refugee Board."*

I then opened a new separate green folder, with a copy of a type written letter sent to Wallenberg from the War Refugee Board in Washington, DC in late August of 1944. *"To Raoul Wallenberg, Please find enclosed a special check of $3,300 US dollars representing donations from a unique group of American Jewish contributors, including money specifically for the children of Budapest. These monies were raised as a prize that was won by a courageous eight year-old boy who gained the donations in August of this year of 1944 by swimming across the cold waters and the whole distance of Lake Tamiment in the Pocono Mountains of Pennsylvania."* "Oh my God!" I said to myself. "Can this be possible? How is this possible?" The brief note in the green folder sent chills up my spine. Here was history reaching out to touch me, to connect Wallenberg and me. I was that young boy. My mission had started years earlier. I was now reconnecting with Raoul Wallenberg forty-one years later.

My mind traveled back to that day of swimming the lake and how tired I had been. Tired? Nothing compared to what Wallenberg had gone through all these years, and maybe even now. Sending money was easy. If only it were as easy to win Wallenberg's freedom.

Just before 4:30 we repacked all the documents carefully in the box and thanked Mr. Lloyd. We had promised to take nothing with us but our notes. He shook my hand and offered me a black velvet case. It contained an engraved picture of FDR seated in a wheelchair, with braces visible on his legs, afflicted by polio but carrying on his duties. FDR normally did not show his legs in photos. On the back was FDR's famous quote from his Franklin Field speech of 1936 in Philadelphia: *"We have nothing to fear but fear itself."*

Richard and I drove back from Hyde Park to Philadelphia in the gathering darkness. We now had our argument for jurisdiction in an American court: Wallenberg was clearly our US government representative camouflaged as a Swedish diplomat. He was employed and paid by the US government. We had seen the receipt for the $100,000. There was the photo of his send-off party. Any federal judge would be able to see the close connection of Wallenberg's activity with the United States government. The United States sent him to Hungary, placing him in danger. It was the duty of our government to bring him home.

We arrived back in Philadelphia before midnight. I felt that the case was gaining a very positive momentum. We had nailed down a vital legal issue: Wallenberg was a US diplomat on foreign assignment during World War II, and thus a "soldier left behind." The international duty of rescue under the *Geneva Convention*, and the *US Hostages Act of 1868*, could become a cornerstone of my argument in federal court.

Could he still be alive? Could U-2 reconnaissance flights over the Gulag camps help to locate him? The Defense Intelligence Agency in 1972 had taken pictures of US soldiers left behind in Laos and Cambodia. They were able to identify individual faces of American prisoners. Could our lawsuit help mobilize a similar effort for locating Wallenberg?

I couldn't sleep that night. I got up, went downstairs, made myself a cup of tea, and walked out into the garden to watch the full moon rising over the pine and mimosa trees. I wondered about the midnight caller. Who was he, and what was his interest in our case? Why did he choose to help? He focused my attention on valuable information for the lawsuit. I have never learned who he was.

October 1983
Philadelphia

A few days after our successful Hyde Park expedition, I went to Philadelphia's 30th Street Station to meet Wallenberg's first biographer, the award-winning writer Elinor Lester, a journalist at *Newsday*. Her well-documented book, *Wallenberg: The Man in the Iron Mask*, had for millions of readers and survivors brought this hero back from the living dead.

Elinor was small but had a dynamic presence. One of the first things she said to me was, "It's my pursuit of the holy grail. I have spent my life pursuing Wallenberg and his freedom. It has consumed me and I shall soon die. My one desire is to get Wallenberg known," she began, "and now it is for you to rescue him."

She was, by her own account, a woman obsessed, convinced, as I had become, that Wallenberg was still alive. Her book had started as an article in the Sunday *New York Times Magazine*. The article broke the ice, exposed the scandal and raised the consciousness of people in New York and elsewhere to the fact that Wallenberg was not dead. And that something needed to be done.

"The whole attitude of the government has been smug indifference," Lester said to me that day over lunch. "They used this man like a disposable paper cup, then crumpled him up and threw him away. I encountered all kinds of resistance in writing my book. The State Department refused me official access to their cables. I am glad you found some of them in your trip to Hyde Park. The government has a secret central archive on Wallenberg. No one knows this. They should be hammering for his release day and night. He was a US diplomat, plain and simple, on a US mission, with US financial backing. The insensitivity of the United States government towards Wallenberg's fate is demonstrated over and over again from 1945 to the present," she said. "But nothing was worse than the indifference shown to the family by our government in May of 1973. Wallenberg's mother, Maj Von Dardel, then in her eighties, wrote a personal letter to Henry Kissinger. She asked him, in his capacity as United States Secretary of State, to find out the truth about her son. I mention the letter in my book. So, of course, you know about it."

Elinor opened her briefcase and showed me a copy of the letter written by Wallenberg's mother to Kissinger. I had seen it at the library in Hyde Park:

"I ask you, who have by virtue of your extraordinary efforts, liberated thousands of prisoners, against the background of my tragic ignorance of what really happened to my son after he was arrested, to inform me if you have the possibility to undertake something which can throw new light on my son's fate, and if he is still alive, to return him to liberty."

Elinor pulled another paper from her case and handed it to me. "Five State Department officials examined the case and recommended that Kissinger take appropriate action. Here's a copy of the letter they drafted for his signature." The letter read:

"Against the background of the humanitarian nature of the case and your son's efforts for the Hungarian Jews during the last war, the United States government is prepared to ask the Soviet government via the American Embassy in Moscow what happened to your son."

I knew from Elinor Lester's biography on Wallenberg that the letter was never sent. Kissinger read it. It was then marked 'rejected by Kissinger' and returned to the file without explanation. Inquiries to his office were met with a response of "no comment."

"What do you think was the reason?" I asked.

"I suppose Wallenberg was considered to be off the chessboard," she replied. "He was expendable, and no longer a player. In the world of power politics, he was simply not important. There was no room for sympathy or family concern. We are still in a Cold War—a competitive war with Russia. They can still stir up major trouble and potential war, as they almost did with their missiles in Cuba. That's why our government is trying to soothe their feelings in this new don't-rock-the-boat policy. Your lawsuit, though, will certainly rock the boat. Our government does not want you to make discoveries about this case. They want it to be considered a closed chapter. I think you must be careful as you proceed. Our government may not like the whole idea of discovery."

Lester suggested I meet with Kissinger. Who knew? Maybe with no more axes to grind he might be willing to help. I told her about my own strange midnight caller and my Hyde Park visit. Together we looked again at the Gromyko memorandum, which I had also seen in Hyde Park, and which Lester had located through other sources at the State Department and described in her book. The significance of the Gromyko note was the admission, for the first time, that Wallenberg had been imprisoned in the USSR. The Soviets had never before acknowledged even having Wallenberg in custody—let alone having "killed" him. The note was the most revealing "admission against interest" that the Russians had provided—a document vital to our case. Fortunately its accuracy had been validated by its discovery in the two different locations—at the State Department and at Hyde Park.

Lester promised to help me in any way she could, whether it was verifying research or providing information.

"I have brought a copy of my notes for you." Lester told me late in our lunch. "Keep them carefully. Do not show them to anyone. They could be tracked back to my sources at the State Department. I don't want that to occur. By the same token, be careful whom you bring in to help you with the case. Make sure you know them. The Russians may try to infiltrate your efforts. Keep your team of lawyers small."

"Isn't it ironic," I said, "that the Soviets expend so much effort hiding a prisoner they claim is dead?"

"Well, the State Department knows he's alive," she handed me some papers.

I glanced through them. They were State Department records of where Wallenberg was detained in the Soviet Union during the past thirty years. Harvey Rosenfeld's biography had brought them to light. Still, to see them in bold print was a new shock. Why were these secret notes buried for so long? What did our government have to fear?

Lester's notes helped me to write a strong first draft of the complaint one week later. The documents she had shown me, and the ones I had seen at Hyde Park, became valuable building blocks for our litigation. Lester helped us to broaden the grounds for the civil suit to include the negligence of the US government as well as the criminal behavior of the Soviets. We would use these documents in a court of law to assign the Soviet government legal responsibility for Wallenberg's abduction and detention.

Elinor Lester was a battler. Her support did prove invaluable in preparing the case. What she told me at the time was that she herself was battling cancer. A year and a half later, she died. I admired her insight and strength. She is one of my inspirations to keep fighting forward.

December 1983
New York City

"You are going to need to nail the Soviets in their tracks. Hoist them by their own petard. I will help you get some Wall Street lawyers who have daily dealings with the powers in Moscow. They will add real clout for this case," I was speaking with Norman Redlich, brilliant trial lawyer and Dean of the NYU School of Law. He had invited me to address the NYU Alumni and certain Wall Street experts on my case.

Redlich offered to help me with his valuable advice, and he actually contributed his writing skills to the development of the *Wallenberg v. USSR* historic complaint. We were having dinner at the NYU Law School, in the room where Henry James wrote his novel *Washington Square*. Redlich had just reviewed the latest draft of my complaint. He suggested that I select a prestigious Wall Street law firm to step up and help me with the final draft. In that way there would be some power names signed on to the bottom of the complaint, such as Paul Weiss, Cravath, or Shearman and Sterling.

"They'd be honored to join you; and they can provide substantial assistance with a suit of this magnitude. It will affect the court's perception of your serious purpose, and will influence the final count. It will also increase your standing in the general public's opinion," Redlich said.

I didn't have to look very far. I was surrounded by lawyers. Redlich had invited legislators from several major Wall Street firms to join us for dinner. The theme of the weekend seminar was Transnational Litigation. Most of the litigators present were greedy moneymen. I was the only *pro bono* human rights lawyer invited to the dinner. Some of the lawyers found this to be quite unique—and I did as well. It felt like the legal Hall of Fame was present: Cravath, Swain and Moore; Sullivan and Cromwell; Davis Polk & Wardwell; and Cleary Gottlieb. Each of these firms had sent high-powered lawyers at one time or another to serve our country in senior Foreign Affairs or State Department positions. John Foster Dulles, Eisenhower's Secretary of State, came from Cravath. My friend George Ball, who opened the archives at Hyde Park, had been JFK's most trusted advisor on foreign affairs and also Undersecretary of State. He was from the Cleary Gottlieb law firm. In deciding to enlist a prestigious Wall Street law firm, I was following the advice of Dean Redlich, while still remembering Elinor Lester's admonition to keep the circle of lawyers small. I simply felt that we needed the clout and muscle of a major law firm.

"Take your pick," Redlich said. "I will twist some arms if need be. They're all chasing dollars, clients and publicity. But you are the only one here embarking on a ground-breaking, precedent-setting human rights trial. They should volunteer their young brains for your case."

Redlich congratulated me on recruiting Nobel Prize winner Elie Wiesel and his foundation to support the cause. He suggested I go further, "Get some senators, law professors, even Hollywood movie stars. Add some 'sizzle and sex appeal' to whet the public's curiosity. Enlist other public figures, each signing on as an *amicus curiae*."

After dinner I headed to the law library. I was scheduled to speak the next day on "The Wallenberg Initiative: Suing the Soviet Union for Human Rights Violations." I had reserved a study carrel where I could put the final touches on my talk.

I climbed the stairs to the faculty study room on the third floor, where a carrel and writing materials had been set aside for me. I began to outline my talk. I heard sharp, staccato, almost metallic footsteps coming up the stairs. A door to the suite opened. The footsteps stopped behind me.

I turned to find a tall man in a dark blue pinstriped suit, white shirt, and red tie standing behind me. He had been at the dinner table earlier, but I hadn't had a chance to speak with him. I noticed a tan-colored hearing aid in his right ear and a gold watch fob on his vest. He was obviously rich. His hair was parted in the middle, perfectly up-to-date for the 1920s.

"My name is Oswald." he said. "David Oswald. Dean Redlich said I could find you here. I am managing partner of a 250-member law firm. Eight of our lawyers are fluent in Russian. We do business with Russia and represent several banks with dealings in Russia. We know the terrain. I speak Russian."

"That could be useful," I said. "Right this moment, though, I'm busy preparing a…"

"We can translate all your documents, including the complaint, into Russian," he interrupted, and sat down next to me. "You will need that. Under the *US Foreign Sovereign Immunity Act of 1976* you are obliged to serve the Soviet Foreign Ministry in Moscow with three copies of the complaint in Russian, supported by a note that indicates why a US court has taken jurisdiction. I can personally translate the documents for you. Our firm has an office in Moscow. They will serve the papers on the Soviets as required by law. We will cover all of your filing fees and other expenses. This is an important human rights case. We want to see you win." This man was coming on much too strong. What was his angle? What was his real interest? He seemed *"gung ho"* to get involved. "For us it is positive public relations. A strategy for attracting raw talent—beef by the carload." He laughed with a cynical curl of his upper lip as if he were sneering. "We use *pro bono* work like this to attract the brightest law students for the summer. We wine and dine them and hook them for the following year. Not pretty, but effective."

At least he was honest. He did not give me any 'good for mankind' BS.

This seemed too easy, and yet too good to be true.

"What else is in it for you?" I asked.

"Well, it's a good cause, right?" he replied.

I wasn't convinced.

"Beyond that, what does your firm get out of this?"

He let a tight smile show. "Good publicity. We can use this to boost the image of our firm to graduating law students from Yale, Harvard, Columbia and Virginia. That's where we go big game hunting for next year's recruits. Competition is keen. The Wall Street firms all want an edge, or a leg up. This Wallenberg case is a card we can play during interviews up at Yale, your alma mater. We want the students to know we do the best *pro bono* work, and that we also believe in justice and in the value of your case."

I wanted the power and prestige of a major Wall Street firm to support my litigation. I knew that a big firm could be of great value. They majored in brains and hard work at the big firms.

"I'll have to give it some thought," I said. "I don't know you. The Wallenberg family is very careful about who they want associated with this case."

"I can understand that" he answered. "Due diligence is a virtue."

He started to get up; then he grimaced with pain. He had a bad leg. The lights in the room made him appear to glitter as they reflected off his gold watch, tie pin and fob chain. A Richard Corry maniacal grin spread across his face. I sensed he was motivated by greed only and not altruism. Yet I reasoned to myself that his law firm had clout, power, prestige and prominence. Most of all, they would be taken seriously by any federal court. He exuded a certain negative energy that felt mesmerizing and dazzling, yet strangely cold. He smiled awkwardly, shook hands stiffly, and walked off.

I went to the bookcase and took down the Martindale-Hubbell Directory of Lawyers in New York. I turned the pages to his Wall Street law firm and ran my finger down the page until I reached his name.

"Hmmm. Mother's maiden name was Tolstoy."

I wondered for a moment whose side he would be on once the suit was filed. Was he here for sabotage and espionage or to help? I remembered Elinor Lester's admonition and warning that the Russians might try to interfere.

He had climbed very quickly from associate to partner in five years. It would normally take an associate eight years in a firm of that size. His specialties were Litigation and Corporate law. The law directory indicated his fluency in French and Russian.

The resources of his law firm could be valuable in a *pro bono* lawsuit. I decided to check with the Wallenberg family the following day, to see if they had any objections. I would then cross check him out with Dean Redlich and with other lawyer friends in New York.

I completed the notes on my talk. As I left the library, Oswald was still lurking there in the shadows. He reached into the inner pocket of his three-piece suit and handed me his business card. "Here." he said. "Contact me directly on my private phone if you need me. Anything at all."

Two weeks later, after considering other distinguished law firms such as Paul, Weiss, and Cleary, Gottlieb, I chose Oswald's firm. They offered everything for free. I was desperate to add the heft and clout of a prestigious big Wall Street firm to my case. I arrived at this decision based on what I had read about Oswald's qualifications. I did not stop to consider his stubbornness, or his competitiveness. Nor did I at the time perceive his disloyalty to the cause and his cunning. I was told by one of his law partners that Oswald had an obsession with playing "King of the Mountain". He had fooled Dean Redlich with his mock sincerity.

At first, Oswald was helpful, willing to take a supportive role as "second chair."I made it clear to all of the lawyers that I brought in to the Wallenberg case that I was "Captain of the ship" and would make all final decisions. But soon he began his well-planned effort to take over the case. He was there to sabotage rather than cooperate. He was a control freak. Beware of Greeks bearing gifts.

One secretary at his law firm, who completed the translation of the complaint, warned me "be careful" nodding towards Oswald. This was on a Sunday afternoon in New York at the law firm two weeks before I filed the complaint in both Russian and English as required by the *Foreign Sovereign Immunities Act*. The secretary, fluent in Russian and German, had an IBM Cyrillic typewriter. I should have listened to her. Her parents were Holocaust survivors who had managed to escape Germany in 1938, the year of *Kristalnacht.*

The case was moving in the right direction and I had a deadline to file the case. What was my deadline? My rendezvous with Raoul Wallenberg and bringing him home.

February 3 & 4, 1984
Washington, DC

The day before filing the complaint I checked into the Hay Adams Hotel—a small hotel across the park from the White House. I wanted a quiet place to fine tune the complaint and get ready for my appearance with Jane Pauley and Bryant Gumbel on the NBC Today Show at 7:15 AM. Guy Von Dardel thrilled me by making the effort to fly in from Stockholm. "I almost missed my SAS flight. I had left my passport on the bureau at home and then had to race back to get it." We had dinner at the hotel and the next morning he walked with my wife and me, and two hundred other supporters from around the world—all Wallenberg survivors—up the courthouse steps.

My PR team put me through a rigorous "training and quiz" session to help me prepare for the Today Show appearance on NBC. Ken Rice, a superb public relations man from Kalish and Rice of Philadelphia prepped me for this once in a lifetime opportunity. I hoped the exposure would bring forward more survivors, or even former Russian prisoners or prison guards, in response to the program. The feed was picked up by BBC and broadcast around the world. Twenty-five million viewers in the United States; many more in foreign countries—all part of an effort to shine a flashlight into the darkened cell. Murray Levin, the first volunteer lawyer on the case, played Bryant Gumbel. My wife Debby played Jane Pauley.

At dinner that night, Guy regaled me with stories about Raoul.

"When Raoul was still in grade school in Sweden at about age eight," he said, "we began to notice he had an unusual trait: he liked to take risks. When he played football, which you call soccer, we noticed he liked to take the ball directly at the opponent, rather than finesse a two-shot strategy around him. Sometimes it paid off, and sometimes it met with disaster. But he was always a good sport. He played hard. He was emotional and feisty."

"Did those traits stay with him as he grew up?" I asked.

"Yes," said Guy. "Later on, when he was shut out of the family banking business, he also reacted in an emotional way. He wanted to get even. He wanted to prove they were wrong. That is one of the reasons he seized on the opportunity to go to Hungary, to prove to everyone that he was a leader and that he could accomplish big things. When he got to Budapest it was not enough to observe and report. He wanted to be a hero. So he took action, and he took risks. He even wrote home to tell us that he enjoyed the sense of risk and danger. We lived his experience vicariously through his letters. He wrote once a week to our mother, no matter how busy he was. One of his last letters was his promise to be home for Christmas. But he postponed, said he would be home in January. It was a promise he never kept."

Whatever Happened to Raoul Wallenberg?

For the rest of dinner we spoke of happier things, but when the meal was over, Guy and I continued our conversation about Raoul on a long walk. We passed the White House, where lights were still on, and the Rose Garden, where President Reagan had honored Wallenberg in August, 1981. "I was there," Guy noted. "The President promised my sister Nina and me he would get Raoul freed if it were the last thing he did. Well, he never came through. We were later told that secret efforts behind the scenes had actually identified the prison location. Again, some heated talk of a swap. This time it would be between America and Russia, not Sweden. But we were then told that some snafu of communication within the White House staff and State Department staff put a kibosh on the idea."

Guy and I walked together through a light snow from the Hay Adams, then across to the White House and the Rose Garden and finally past the reflecting pools out to the well-lit Lincoln Memorial. Guy spoke of his brother Raoul's motivations for going to Hungary, and his letters home asking about his girlfriends. His infatuation for Viveca Lindfors continued through his six months in Hungary.

We swapped stories about family and got to know each other. Up until then it had just been phone calls and letters. This was our first time together and I enjoyed his company. He was easy to talk to and had a good sense of humor. As we approached the hotel at the end of our walk, Guy clasped my arm.

"There is something very important you must know."

The warmth of the hotel enveloped us as we walked in. The mahogany parquet floors were shined and buffed for the next day, and the overstuffed sofas and chairs beckoned. In the quiet of the lobby, Guy drew me aside.

"It is not by chance that I am the only relative of Raoul's here tonight. The others—the rich side of the family—have refused to come. They have contempt for what he did in Hungary. They also made big money from World War II by selling Swedish steel for the making of German tanks which took American lives"

We sat on one of the plush sofas in the lobby.

"Let me shed some light on some of the reasons for Raoul's continued detention," he said in a low voice. "Money," he said. "The Russians know that Raoul came from one of the wealthiest family in Sweden. And it's true. The industrialists and bankers of the Wallenberg Empire have money and assets."

"Our branch of the family was not wealthy. My mother, Maj Von Dardel, did her best raising Raoul, my sister Nina and me in the shadow of this wealthy empire."

"Shortly after the Russians took control of Budapest, the other diplomats began coming home one by one. The Russians held Raoul in captivity while they intimated to our Swedish foreign ministry that just a few million could quickly secure the release of this member of the prominent and fabulously wealthy Wallenberg family. So during the last week of January 1945 my mother went to Marcus Wallenberg. He was the richest member and self-appointed 'king' of our family. She pleaded with him and begged him, 'Buy Raoul's freedom. Pay the Russians whatever they want. Otherwise, we may never see him again.' Marcus and the others would not listen. Marcus offered an amount much smaller than what the Russians were demanding."

Marcus was afraid, Guy told me, that Raoul would reveal the truth about his business relationships. I was confused. Guy began to elaborate.

"We knew that before, during, and after the war the Swedish bankers were in league with the German bankers and with the Russian banks."

Then Guy showed me a book he had brought along with him. He translated the title from Swedish for me, *Sweden: the Middle Way,* by Marquis Childs. It has just been published in Sweden. Guy began translating from Swedish, taking time out to explain and comment on the text.

He read to me that by early August of 1944, when Raoul had only been in Budapest for about a month, that there were many top Nazi officials who could see that the war was lost. It was time to regroup and preserve for a later day the international finances of the *Wehrmacht* war machine.

The second most powerful man in the Reich, Hitler's deputy, Martin Borman, was not so incapacitated. On August 10, 1944, he called together German business leaders and Nazi party officials. The purpose of the meeting was to take steps to prepare for a post-war commercial campaign that would in time ensure the economic resurgence of Germany. These 'steps' came to be known as 'Operation Eagle Flight,' or *'Aktion Alderflug.'* It was nothing less than the perpetuation of Nazism through the massive flight of money, gold, stocks, bonds, patents, copyrights, and even technical specialists from Germany. As part of the plan, Borman, aided by the central Deutsche Bank, and the powerful I.G. Farben Company, created 750 foreign front corporations—214 in Switzerland, 58 in Portugal, 112 in Spain, 35 in Turkey, 98 in Argentina, and 233 in Sweden, the most in any country. And Guy told me that the front companies were being coordinated by the Wallenberg's *Enskilda Bank.*

Marcus Wallenberg, Raoul's uncle coordinated the flight of money out of Germany and into Swedish banks for safe keeping. He was the Nazis' 'family banker' in Sweden. Raoul, who had been preparing to enter the family business, was well aware of the close business connections between his family and the Nazis. Thus, it became impossible for Marcus to bribe the Soviets. He was entrusted with a large part of a national fortune, and the owners of that fortune happened to be bitter enemies of the Soviets.

Now some of the foot-dragging by the Wallenberg family which I had read about began to make sense.

Guy reminded me of facts documented by former *New York Times* writer Charles Higham, that Borman's efforts were substantially helped by close connections with foreign banks and businesses begun long before the war.

Whatever Happened to Raoul Wallenberg?

America's International Telephone & Telegraph Corporation, or ITT, sold Germany communications and war materials, including as many as 50,000 artillery fuses per month; this was more than three years after Pearl Harbor. ITT's German chairman, Gerhardt Westrick, was a close associate of John Foster Dulles, who later became Secretary of State under President Dwight Eisenhower. Westrick was also a private business partner of Dr. Heinrich Albert, head of Ford Motor Company in Germany until 1945. Two other German-born ITT directors were Kurt von Schroeder and Walter Schellenberg, head of counterintelligence for the Nazi Gestapo.

Throughout the war, the Chase Manhattan Bank maintained its financial connection with the Nazis through its Paris branch. I.G. Farben CEO Herman Schmitz served as a Chase Manhattan president for seven years prior to the war, and eventually held as much stock in Standard Oil of New Jersey as the Rockefellers.

I stopped Guy's narration to point out that the Chase Manhattan Bank was unfortunately a major client of Oswald's law firm. I advised Von Dardel that Oswald clearly had an undisclosed conflict of interest. I had investigated the firm's client list and discovered that the Oswald's law firm had several Soviet clients, including AMTORG, the major Soviet Trade Company that purchased all the wheat for Russia when the severe storms and early frost killed the home product.

I planned to enjoin those wheat sales as part of my strategy. I was troubled. What if Oswald might try to derail or sabotage my Wallenberg law suit as an economic favor to AMTORG or one of his other Soviet law firm's corporate clients. I tucked the idea and my concern away for later. It might be a coincidence, or more likely an undisclosed conflict of interest.

"Watch carefully where the money goes," Guy said. "It controls outcomes. Money from various evil regimes circulates internationally, with no scent or odor, through the world's major banks."

"Oswald had boasted: 'The USSR is one of the Chase Bank's main clients.' Chase is now financing the wheat deals from Iowa and the heartland to Russia. They are a sacred cow client of my law firm."

"Now perhaps you can understand my concern," said Guy. "One day the Russian money might be in Chase, the next day in *Enskilda Bank* under Wallenberg control. If the law firm ever has a conflict between rescuing Wallenberg and the financial interests of the bank—like not embarrassing Russia with a lawsuit or a judgment, we know where its loyalties will lie."

It was getting close to eleven. Tomorrow morning was going to be a full day, starting with the Today Show at seven, filing the lawsuit at nine and a press conference on Capitol Hill at eleven.

"Trust no one," Guy said softly.

With that we said goodnight. We shook hands at the elevator, and then hugged for a moment. Back in my room I tried to sleep. It was futile. The next day we planned to make history.

The 5 A.M. wake-up call dashed any hopes that I would be well rested. I was operating on pure adrenaline. As I looked into the camera at NBC's Washington, DC studio, I was told that as many as 25 million people were tuned in to watch. Anchors, Bryant Gumbel and Jane Pauley, were in New York, and interviewed Tom Lantos and me by satellite. I told Raoul Wallenberg's story and the story of the lawsuit to my largest audience ever. I told viewers that Wallenberg was alive, and that I was tasked with the fight for his freedom.

We left the NBC studio at 8:25 A.M., eager to be at the courthouse the moment it opened at nine. We climbed into the limousine outside the studio for a quick trip to the courthouse. With the American flag flying from the car's antenna, we received a police escort through Rock Creek Park Way to the federal courthouse at 4th and D Streets in downtown Washington, DC. Lantos told me it was he who had arranged the special treatment, to create some excitement at the courthouse. We arrived in ten minutes—a trip that normally takes half an hour in busy morning traffic. A huge crowd was gathering to welcome us and make the symbolic walk together with us up the courthouse steps.

I was reminded of similar scenes at the Federal District Courthouse in Montgomery, Alabama over 20 years earlier, when I filed civil rights lawsuits for black people in the Voting Rights cases during Freedom Summer in 1963.

Tom Lantos, Guy Von Dardel and I were also joined by the presidents of thirteen of the "Save Raoul Wallenberg" committees from around the world: Argentina, Australia, Belgium, Canada, Denmark, France, Israel, Jamaica, Mexico, the Netherlands, Sweden, the United Kingdom, and the US. Many of them were survivors Wallenberg had personally saved in Budapest. In the crowd of nearly 400 people, many were holding large homemade placards: *"Free Wallenberg," "39 years of hell is enough," "Reagan: Bring Him Home," "Long Live Raoul!" "Wallenberg: a hero for our times; a hero for all times."*

Some people were wearing large buttons with blue printing and an Israeli flag. I looked closer and read the printing on some of the buttons. Each carried a handwritten first name: "Paula," "Michael," "Ludwig," "Malka." Under each first name was printed, *"I am A Wallenberg Survivor, saved by Raoul."* I shook hands with the survivors. "We are here for you", one said.

I could feel the energy of the event shifting from solemn quiet into a loud and joyful celebration, as a group of children from the local Abraham Heschel Jewish Day School of Washington, DC started singing, *It's going to be a bright, bright sun shining day.* Then another group sang *Hatikvah,* the national anthem of Israel. I joined in as someone started singing *We Shall Overcome.*

We walked through the glass doors under the large sign: *Equal Justice under the Law.* In the clerk's office we filed three copies of the "Complaint and

Points of Law in Support of Jurisdiction. We got back one stamped copy and left. The case of *Wallenberg vs. USSR* was now officially on the record.

Later we would get a trial date and an assigned judge—hopefully "the right judge." But now we had to hurry over to the House Caucus Room on Capitol Hill, where the press conference was to be held. It was time to speak to the world.

We left the courthouse in high spirits. Buttoning our overcoats against the cold wind, we began the brief one-mile march up to Capitol Hill, where newspapers and TV stations from around the world were waiting. Hundreds followed as Lantos, Von Dardel and I, our arms interlocked, marched the half mile up to the Hill. Accompanying us, the brigade of volunteers sang and bantered in good spirits as we surged forward toward the white dome of the Capitol.

It brought back so many memories. As we approached 11th and Constitution, I remembered a street corner debate I had had there with a young black preacher in June of 1963. I was trying to explain the importance of what would become the 1964 Voting Rights Law, which we were then working on. He was unconvinced. He believed that the law was just a product of the corrupt political structure and that his people needed to help themselves. He shook his head at my ideals of changing the laws to ensure no one's rights were violated. He told me that the time had passed for turning the other cheek. It was time to turn to the Constitution, the Second Amendment, to be precise. He was quite calm, and his words were not contentious. And yet he spoke of the need for rifles and shotguns.

"There will come a time for violence. The white man cannot change things through laws". I tried to argue for non-violence, for the power of the vote, for the power of the law to effect change. But Malcolm X, this young preacher, holding the Bible and the Koran, stood his ground. We apparently respected each other's views, even if we could not agree and I could not endorse armed violence. The ways of achieving justice are varied.

Just as then, I was now at the start of another lawsuit looking to the courts for justice. As we reached the Capitol entrance, the guards were taken aback by the size of our crowd, numbering in the hundreds. Those of us at the front passed through security. The crowd stayed outside while 35 of their number were selected to accompany us. Once everyone was inside, we were ushered into the House Caucus Room on the first floor.

I looked around the Caucus room. Stacked neatly on a long table were 100 copies of the press kits prepared by Kalish and Rice, our PR firm. Harold Rice and Arlene Lieb were working the table, handing out kits to all the members of the press now filing into the room for this massive press conference. There were journalists and TV reporters from 83 countries and from 45 cities across America, all here to cover the action.

I sat down with Tom Lantos and Guy Von Dardel behind a huge array of microphones. While waiting, I quietly counted the mics—48 in all, including NBC, CBS, ABC, CNN, C-Span, Canal Plus from France, BBC from England, and Pravda from Russia.

The press conference was scheduled to start precisely at eleven. At 10:50, the bright television klieg lights came on, temporarily blinding us. I was aware of someone getting up from the third row and walking over to my right. Soon I heard noise and activity at the press kit table. Shielding my eyes with my hand, I looked over to see what was happening. There were still about 25 press kits left. But Oswald had now planted himself there. Strangely, he was rifling through the stack, pulling out and scattering papers on the floor. I got up and approached the table.

"What are you doing?" I asked.

"Going through the press kits," he replied, attacking another one and ripping it apart.

"Why are you destroying the press kits?"

"I want to remove your picture. Only Wallenberg's picture should be here." He ripped up ten of the photos and stuffed them in his pocket.

"Who do you think is in charge?"

"You are Morris."

I kept my cool, realizing that no one should witness this squabble between me and my hired subordinate.

It turned out that Oswald did not like his supporting role as second chair. He was jealous of my getting star billing in the press kit along with Wallenberg. I tried to calm him down.

I told him: "David, the idea of linking me and Raoul as a team is the brainchild of Kalish and Rice, our public relations firm. They feel that is the best way to feature both the past and the present for news media. Please do not interfere with their plan. They are the professionals." I pinched the nerves of his elbow, to stop his destruction, and guided him firmly back to his seat, reminding him that I was in charge as the captain of the ship, the lawyer retained by the family, and he was my assistant.

I realized that we now had a small mutiny within the law team. Jerome Schneider, Oswald's senior partner came over and told him "sit down and stop interfering with this important moment." Chastened, Oswald returned to his seat and folded his arms. Oswald was making trouble at the worst time and in public.

Oswald was not part of the public relations team. That was for Kalish and Rice exclusively. As the leading PR firm in Philadelphia, they knew their business. They had created a campaign that would most effectively "sell" our story to the media. K and R had decided on the theme: "Wallenberg is our man. We, the United States sent him into danger. It is our duty to rescue and bring him home."

The thrust of their campaign was to create a link between myself as the human rights lawyer and Wallenberg, the human rights warrior. They wanted both photos to appear in the newspapers and on the news wires—Wolff and Wallenberg, the past connected to the present; the active voice for justice in the public law forum pleading the case for the silent hero. Major media from all over the world were in attendance. This was proof that K and R's approach was effective. Ninety-three different newspapers from all over the United States and the world were present including but not limited to The Miami Herald, Washington Post and New York Times. Despite Oswald's bizarre conduct, the press kit was not about me. It was about visibility for Wallenberg's case.

The press conference went forward with an outward calm, and no other incidents. It lasted for 45 minutes of Q & A, focusing on what US courts could do to force the Russians either to release Wallenberg or make a new report on his status. We were educating the public on the value of using United States federal courts to force foreign governments to stop the illegal incarceration of Raoul Wallenberg and other innocent diplomats.

I tried to shake off the unease I felt about Oswald's strange behavior. Today was meant to be a day for celebration. Oswald was already sabotaging our chance to succeed.

March 1984
Wilmington, Delaware

As the Sterling Professor of International Law at Widener University's Delaware Law School, a position I held from 1979 to 1985, I arranged for guest speakers for our Celebrity Forum. It was a chance for our law students to hear from nationally known legal celebrities. Attendance was voluntary, and the Q & A period was often better than the speeches themselves.

In addition to Supreme Court Chief Justice William Rehnquist, we had my law partner Governor Harold Stassen of Minnesota and several distinguished lawyers from Philadelphia, Washington, DC and New York. As our final speaker, I decided to invite a legal figure whose fall from grace and the top echelons of government could serve as a cautionary example for these young attorneys-to-be.

I learned that John Ehrlichman was available as a speaker. From 1969 to 1973 he had been one of the most powerful men in the White House. John Ehrlichman, the convicted White House Nixon aide knew exactly why America in the 1970's did nothing to rescue Raoul Wallenberg. Nixon was compromised. The CIA told him in clear words "raise no question about Breznev's behavior with regard to Wallenberg during the S.A.L.T. (Strategic Arms Limitation Treaty) talks." Ehrlichman said "we're dealing with high level stuff; nuclear arsenals of the major nations were involved". As Special Counsel to President Nixon, Ehrlichman, along with H.R. Haldeman, was one of Nixon's two top advisers. After the attempted cover-up of the Watergate burglary was revealed, Ehrlichman resigned from his White House post in April 1973. Two years later he was convicted of obstruction of justice, conspiracy and perjury, and sentenced to serve 18 months in a federal prison in Arizona. He served the whole sentence.

I got his phone number from one of my law professor colleagues, gave him a call, and invited him to talk the following month. He needed the money. I was glad he accepted; the subject, "Ethics in Government," was one he was uniquely qualified to discuss.

When I first met him, I wasn't sure what to expect. At the pinnacle of power, Ehrlichman had a reputation as a pompous and arrogant man. I marveled at how different he seemed now. He was calmer, and less intense. Goateed, with a new career as an artist, selling his paintings on weekends, he had come to terms with his past and could speak about it with detachment and refreshing honesty. He was no longer selling ideas and important national policy matters to President Nixon, He had been reduced to selling his oil paintings at Saturday morning flea markets and other venues where he might earn a few dollars. Compared to Chuck Colson, a born again Christian, Ehrlichman was almost a pauper. The arrogance was gone and a softness and vulnerability had taken its place. He was likable, and seemed as if he wasn't trying to impress anyone. Prison and time alone had changed him. He let his hair grow long and looked like a hippy gone to seed.

The students were also taken with his candor and openness. He talked about legal and government ethics, about investigative journalism, and about what he would have done differently if he had a chance to do it all over again, beginning with staying in private practice. He told some stories about the 1972 re-election campaign, and CREEP, the Committee to Re-elect the President. And he confirmed what we wanted to know—President Nixon knew everything and was the mastermind of the Watergate break-in, the cover-up and all the dirty tricks. He admitted that he, Ehrlichman, had stood by and even helped.

"I completely forgot the things I had learned at my mother's knee and in law school," he said.

After the lecture I invited him to join me for dinner. Ehrlichman replied politely "I have time, I'm staying overnight in Wilmington at the Dupont Hotel before driving home to Virginia." We drove to the hotel together in Wilmington, just fifteen minutes from the law school. As we sat down, John Ehrlichman smiled, and ordered a dry martini with three green olives and three white onions.

"I like to straddle my tastes," he said. "A martini and Gibson combined."

One-on-one, I found John Ehrlichman easy to talk with. He lost any remaining stiffness as the martinis set in. As one of the most powerful men in the White House, he had ruled imperiously over a huge staff, making all major domestic policy decisions and submitting them to the President, who signed either "Accepted" or "Rejected." Ehrlichman was known to be impatient, brusque and angry.

"The anger," he confessed, "came from my childhood. Nothing was ever good enough for either of my parents. I would strive and strive for their affection but it never came. When I met Richard Nixon, I thought he might be the father figure or the source of approval I had never had. That is why I worked so hard for him and yearned for his approval. I trusted him. I was wrong. I tried to protect him from the scandal and I was willing to lie and destroy documents, knowing it was the wrong thing to do. I stupidly walked through fire and took a bullet for him. In prison I came to my senses, but it was too late."

I was struck by Ehrlichman's self-awareness, his candor, and his personal transformation. Yet I had another reason for inviting him to dinner. I thought he might have some useful insight on why the US government negotiations that might have brought Wallenberg to freedom were dramatically aborted during the Nixon Administration. Perhaps he could help me unwrap some of the mystery surrounding why Kissinger's effort to gain release for Wallenberg at my request was met with such a frigid and stiff response by the president.

After chatting for a while about his life after prison, I brought up the question I'd been waiting to pose.

"John, did you have any knowledge of my effort in tandem with Kissinger to rescue Raoul Wallenberg during your tenure at the White House?"

"I was familiar with the ardent lobbying by the Wallenberg family," Ehrlichman responded, "and all the national Free Wallenberg Committees from around the world. The man had an incredible following of survivors supporting this effort. They even got Henry Kissinger to take up their cause at one point. After all, Henry was a Jewish child of the Holocaust. His parents got out of Austria with young Henry, age seven or eight, in 1938—just in time. Adding fuel to the fire was a report circulating at State and at CIA that Wallenberg was alive. There were credible reports from eyewitnesses who had bunked with him in the Russian Gulag in Siberia or seen him at Lubyanka in Moscow."

"You would think all that public support would provide enough impetus to get the ball rolling," I said.

"Yes, it would seem so. But actually there was great embarrassment and fear at the State Department and on Nixon's part that Wallenberg's being alive would get out through *The Washington Post* to the general public. You have to keep in mind the state of global tensions at the time, especially our relations with the USSR. Through careful efforts and negotiations, US/Soviet relations had warmed up considerably by this point. *Detente* had begun to take on real meaning. Nixon was a master at foreign policy. He was planning his upcoming trip to Moscow, scheduled for May of 1972, to get the ABM and SALT I treaties signed, to limit the arms race and reduce the number of nuclear weapons. There was an era of good feeling just beginning. Nixon was getting ready to order three new Lincoln Continental limousines to be sent to Moscow. Brezhnev loved cars, and Nixon knew it."

"Amid this tense environment, in which no one wanted to disturb the uneasy calm, Kissinger, Secretary of State, went to see the President about the Wallenberg issue. On the plus side, Nixon had appointed Henry Secretary of State. He respected Henry's judgment, and was also a friend and confidante of Kissinger's. Nixon leaned on his expertise in all foreign policy matters."

Ehrlichman continued: "While I was still in the room, Kissinger encouraged Nixon to make a strong effort to negotiate the release of Wallenberg. He presented it as a win-win situation: If the Soviets free Wallenberg, Brezhnev will look like a hero. Relations would continue to warm between the two countries and no one gets embarrassed."

"What did the President say?" I asked Ehrlichman.

"He stared at Henry for a moment in disbelief, then he said loudly and menacingly, 'No way, Henry! Are you out of your mind? Do you have any idea what this would do to the warming up of Soviet relations? Do you have any idea how deeply this would embarrass Brezhnev?'"

"Henry looked like he had seen a ghost. He was startled by Nixon's reaction. I could see the President was about to explode with anger at Kissinger."

Whatever Happened to Raoul Wallenberg?

"Clear the room, John," he told me. "I want to be with Henry alone." I left as ordered. A few minutes later the door to the Oval Office slammed opened and Henry came running out. He didn't make eye contact with me. He just hurried forward down the hallway, as if running to get out of harm's way. He stuffed his papers in a brown leather case. His limo was waiting. He left the White House in a hurry. I had never before witnessed such a quick exit by the Secretary of State. I will never forget Nixon's anger of that day. He was pure Nixon. The glower, the fear, the droplets of sweat on the upper lip, his finger pointing in the air, stomping around the Oval Office, and finally getting down on his knees and waving his arms like an umpire signaling 'safe' on a close throw to home plate. He had totally lost it—waving his arms as if he were actually nuts He just kept muttering over and over, *No way, no way,* two of Nixon's favorite words."

"What was he so afraid of?" I asked.

Ehrlichman continued, "It had something to do with a secret CIA report to which Henry was not privy. Dick Helms, head of the CIA had a top-secret file—'President's Eyes Only'—. He brought it to the President. Helms had shown the report just to Nixon, detailing the startling involvement of Brezhnev in stealing the diamonds from Raoul Wallenberg in Budapest. The Helms report indicated that the Brezhnev theft had actually occurred in January of 1945 twenty-seven years before the effort to thaw relations in 1972. The scandal occurred much earlier than the period of detente."

Ehrlichman: "In 1945, Brezhnev was an ambitious, 39-year-old Soviet army officer. The 18th Red Army in January had just pushed the Germans out of Budapest and taken over the city. Brezhnev was involved in Wallenberg's kidnapping as the arresting officer. Not only that," Ehrlichman continued, "Brezhnev was a common burglar, and a greedy thief."

"According to the CIA file, after Brezhnev detained Wallenberg at the 18th Red Army Headquarters in Debrecen, he drove back to Budapest that same afternoon and took an axe and broke the lock on Wallenberg's office door. He cracked the safe open with the help of two other men. He stole all the gold, jewelry and diamonds he found inside, filling the pockets of his coat. These were valuables that the fleeing Hungarian Jews had entrusted to Wallenberg at his office. Wallenberg had stored them in his large safe for safe keeping just behind a clock near his desk pending their return."

"If Wallenberg had been released, even decades later, he would have fingered Brezhnev as his kidnapper. He also would have asked some very difficult questions, like the whereabouts of the diamonds and other valuables. The disclosure of Brezhnev's behavior would have disrupted diplomatic relations. Revealing the robbery would have destroyed Nixon's political career, which was already in jeopardy due to Watergate. It would have been more than embarrassing for a man who had become a world leader of Brezhnev's stature. It would have become a major international scandal." Ehrlichman finished his account and

120

reached into his coat pocket for a white handkerchief. He was perspiring profusely. "Sweating is one of my habits," he apologized. "Your effort to rescue Wallenberg is not an easy assignment. Too many Soviet scoundrels have played a part in blocking his release. Men like Brezhnev, Beria, Gromyko and Molotov. The path is littered by the bodies of thugs and bullies who all have something to fear if Wallenberg is located, cleaned up and released."

Ehrlichman's account of the involvement by Brezhnev was confirmed to me in a subsequent conversation on August 5, 1988, in Tel Aviv, Israel. I met there with a former Soviet soldier, Efrem Moshinsky, a Jew, who was with Brezhnev on the break-in of the Wallenberg office that cold day in January 1945 as a soldier in the 18th Red Army. Moshinsky is a little man about 5'4" and he is quite enthusiastic and dynamic. He speaks from certainty. He lives now in Tel Aviv, Israel. Moshinsky's report was further confirmed in my discussion that same day in Israel with Abraham Schiffrin, former Soviet Deputy Minister of Defense with Brezhnev.

Ehrlichman continued, "Brezhnev is a 'greedy bastard.' That is what Nixon told me, after Henry left. But Nixon then added, 'Brezhnev and I are now strange bedfellows. He is my new soon to be ally and friend. I can never raise this embarrassing theft issue with him. And Henry is not ever to know why.'"

Ehrlichman went on without interruption, "This is what Nixon told me to my face during a brief walk in the White House Rose Garden the day after Henry brought up his suggestion. Henry, as a good Jew and being politically savvy, knew the Wallenberg cause was important to Nixon's ability to attract money and Jewish voters. Nixon was all about votes. Nothing more and nothing less. Nixon did not like Jews but he loved their money. Henry wanted Nixon to include Wallenberg as a talking point on the Nixon-Brezhnev SALT talks in Moscow. Henry is clueless on the Wallenberg matter even up until today."

Ehrlichman pushed his chair away from the table, and took out a cigar.

"I connected the dots on this strange Brezhnev theft of diamonds, as revealed by the CIA and Nixon's angry response to Henry's effort to raise the Wallenberg freedom issue," he concluded.

"What about Kissinger, then?" I asked. "Did he make any other efforts, officially or unofficially, on Wallenberg's behalf?"

"Henry was stopped cold by Nixon's vitriolic reaction. Henry had his own pride. He did not want to risk being shot down so emphatically again. After that, he did not mention Wallenberg again ever; he did not want to take any action that would upset the *status quo*."

July 1984
Chicago, Illinois

In March and April, as the cherry blossoms bloomed again on the banks of the Potomac, I waited patiently for word that the seeds of Wallenberg's freedom would be planted in Moscow's Red Square. When would our Wallenberg complaint, sent by diplomatic pouch of the State Department, be served on the Soviets through our embassy in Moscow?

On May 1, 1984, word came from David Evans, at the Moscow Embassy, that *service of process* in the Wallenberg case had been achieved at the Kremlin. The lawsuit was now officially joined. David Evans, by a stroke of great luck, had been my classmate at the Germantown Friends School in Philadelphia. I now had a resource, on the inside of the government, who was willing to fight against Abe Sofaer, Fairbanks and the other oppositional figures. Now we were wired into the latest information concerning our case.

How ironic that it should be May Day, a day of celebration of freedom for workers who struggled against the Czar and overthrew the monarchy for the rights of free speech, decent wages and autonomy; a breaking of the oppressive chains binding the working class and serfs of Russia. Would this May Day help at last break Wallenberg's chains?

I met with Tony D'Amato again, this time in Chicago at the summer convention of the American Bar Association.

I was attending the ABA convention as the newly appointed dean of the Nevada School of Law, seeking official accreditation of my new law school so students could learn to use the law to help a client heal rather than continue suffering. I had also gone out from my home in Philadelphia to try to rescue the law school and its students who risked graduating from an unaccredited school. I got them accreditation so they could graduate and practice law in California and Nevada. I salvaged their careers.

We formed the Raoul Wallenberg Institute for Altruistic Studies, funded by John Flanagan, Sidney Stern and Warren Nelson, three trustees of the young law school. Wallenberg became a permanent role model for our students. I accepted the Deanship on one condition: We would mold and educate a new breed of lawyers who were altruistic by nature and who cared about people and rescuing lives. We studied and discussed informally in small group seminars just how lawyers, emulating Wallenberg, might offer to do good things for total strangers.

It was an idealistic educational venture starting from ground zero, and endorsed by the board of trustees. I wanted to create a different kind of lawyer— one who would truly seek injustice and aid the poor, and not just go to Wall Street to become an investment banker. At the Wallenberg Institute we worked to improve the negative image that lawyers had earned in America. Our new school, for a short while, became the bright beacon to the world sending a message that change was possible. It was a bright shining place, amidst the glitz of Reno, recalling the maxim impressed on me during my Quaker education at Germantown Friends School: "It is better to light a candle than to curse the darkness."

Tony was eager to see me after the American Bar Association convention. He said he had some new legal theories for me. We had been working together over the 15 months since March 1983, speaking once a week by phone up through this summer of 1984.

We agreed to meet at an outdoor cafe. We had things to be proud of. My complaint had been written and filed with the District Court. And service of process on the USSR had been accomplished on May Day. The Soviet Justice Ministry had my law complaint in their lap. They analyzed it and they quickly retained Wolf Popper (no relation), a New York law firm famous for representing Soviet interests, to tell them what to do.

Together Tony and I laughed trying to picture the Russian Minister of Foreign Affairs receiving our US complaint in Moscow, served by diplomatic pouch and delivered to him on May Day no less. D'Amato theorized that their silence since May first indicated that the Russians were disturbed by the case and couldn't decide what to do—whether to appear in court and answer or ignore it and hope it went away. Or, go to the US State Department and ask the State department to "dismiss" it—something they did try to do behind my back but without success. Some of his sources at the State Department had told D'Amato that the Russians were deeply offended by the lawsuit and my demand for 39 million dollars in damages. They were asking the US government to squash it. The Russians at first thought the lawsuit was a government initiative not a private citizen action. They then concluded it was a hostile government action, intended to embarrass them.

"Did you hear whether the State Department responded?" I asked.

"I did." D'Amato said. "In short, they said our hands are tied, no dice. Our government will not intervene. The Russians will have to face us in court." They told the Russians: "We have no control over the courts when private citizens like Morris Wolff file complaints."

"Under the US Constitution, federal courts are an entirely independent branch of government. Judges are appointed for life—free and clear from political interference."

The Russians in the Wallenberg case refused to accept the jurisdiction of the court. They had defended their legal interests without asserting sovereign immunity nine times in the previous three years in American courts, when they had been sued for breach of contract in commercial cases brought by private citizens. And there had been a personal injury case when an American tourist was killed, falling down the elevator shaft of a Russian government-owned tourist hotel. The family sued the Russian government in an American federal court and won a $12 million damage claim in their wrongful death action.

"Malfunctioning elevators that caused people to fall down empty elevator shafts to their death are not abnormal experiences for Russian people," D'Amato said, "just a normal symptom of a malfunctioning economy. The average Russian who waits in long lines to buy two strips of bacon and two potatoes would find the American expectation of elevator safety and reliability almost comical. Fortunately the American jury didn't think it was funny. They held the Soviets liable for $12 million and the Soviets paid as ordered by the federal court. So we have a good precedent to rely on" he continued. "If they fail to defend their interests in Wallenberg, they do so at their peril. We may win a 39 million dollar default judgment. I had already framed in my mind a plan to ask the judge for one million dollars in damages for each year of captivity. Then we will quickly enforce the judgment by attaching airplanes on the runway at Dulles and bank accounts at the Chase Bank. We will squeeze and crush their balls in a vise until they scream, 'pay up', and let Wallenberg come home to a tickertape parade down Fifth Avenue."

D'Amato hunched over the table getting closer to me, although there was no other table within 25 feet of us.

"The Russians have told the State Department that they consider the Wallenberg complaint a hostile and unfriendly act. They are planning retaliatory action in the event the State Department fails to liquidate the case. I suggest that you start being very careful. They may choose to liquidate you as well. Do not go to public places alone. Don't discuss the case with strangers. Stay between the lines. The Russians have a consulate here in Chicago, and a big delegation of KGB spies in New York at the United Nations. Half their personnel at both places are KGB. They are here to spy and collect data. They will spy on you and possibly intimidate, visit, and harass you. Actual physical harm may occur. They play rough."

Tony paused for effect.

"Morris, you have just been designated for trouble, harassment, and special recognition. I don't think you're going to want this 'award.' You have been listed officially this week as *persona non grata* by the Soviet Foreign Ministry. You are no longer welcome in Russia. You have created new complications in your life."

"That comes as news to me," I replied. "But I'm not totally surprised. They know they have a hot potato human rights lawsuit to defend. They never defend on the merits. They usually play dirty and tough. They go behind the back and ask someone to go after the lawyer."

He looked at me over the coffee cup.

"We will know in ten days whether they will defend, or duck and run."

A week later the Russians retained the New York law firm they had used for decades—ironically named, Wolf Popper. The Russians kept them on a fat retainer to do their work in American courts and behind the scenes whenever possible. Wolf Popper was instrumental in arranging the spy swap of Soviet agent Ivan Abel for airman Gary Powers who was shot down over Russia in his U2 spy plane in 1961. I was later told by one of Wolf and Popper's shrewd lawyers that they had advised the Soviets not to touch the case, and not to frame an answer for the complaint, because they would lose it. They advised the Russians to let it go to default judgment and force us to try to attach the Soviet bank accounts and aircraft in the USA, and in the meantime to use their political power behind the scenes.

Ten days later we would get the Russians' answer....or rather their non-answer. Refusing to file an appearance was their first step in a strategy of cowardice and deceit.

August 4, 1984
Washington, DC Federal Court

"Oyez! Oyez! Oyez!" intoned the bald-headed bailiff, rising to his feet and hitching up his baggy black pants. "All rise!"

The door at the back of the courtroom opened and Judge Barrington Parker Jr. of the Federal District Court walked very slowly, with a pronounced limp, toward the raised dark mahogany bench of the courtroom. He was a tall and courtly well-mannered African American gentleman with white hair. Everyone stood as he bunched his black robe in his right hand and painfully and deliberately made his way step by step up the three stairs.

We had been lucky in our draw of a judge. It was a 12 to 1 shot, and we won the right judge. "There is a God," I whispered to my team. "And that God has clearly sent us Barrington Parker, the only judge on this panel who will understand what I am trying to say, and be willing to do the right thing."

Judges are assigned to cases by the Court Clerk at random. Parker had served as judge in the case of *Letelier v. Chile,* finding the government of Chile liable for the car bombing death of former Ambassador Letelier at DuPont Circle right in our nation's capital. He ordered the US Marshal to issue writs of attachment for two Chilean airplanes right after the verdict. These two planes were quickly sold and reduced to cash, and the Letelier family received 11.4 million dollars in damages

Parker was a judge who believed the US courts had a broad reach and jurisdictional power to find foreign governments liable, even the big bad ones, and thus serve the cause of justice.

He had a history of compassion and an ability to feel other people's pain. He had known injustice first-hand picking cotton in the Mississippi Delta. Parker was the proud grandson of a slave, someone who deeply appreciated the importance of freedom and abhorred tyranny. He had been the first in his family to receive a law education. His son is now a US District Court judge in New York City, following in his father's footsteps.

"Please be seated," Judge Parker said gruffly, but in a mellow soft voice, as if welcoming friends into the parlor of his home. He completed the last few steps to his elevated seat on the bench. He grimaced from pain in his left leg, on which he had had an unsuccessful operation only three weeks earlier. A freak auto accident had threatened to end his great career on the bench.

"Is counsel for all parties present?" he asked the bailiff.

"Your Honor, may it please the court, we have plaintiff's counsel, Mr. Morris Wolff, here for Raoul Wallenberg, but the Russians have failed to appear."

The judge looked up at the clock at the back of the courtroom. Ten o'clock on the button. "I'm ready. It's time to begin."

He motioned to the clerk.

"We will begin the hearing now! The Russians know the drill. They know to be here on time. I telephoned their embassy yesterday afternoon to remind the Legal Attaché that this hearing would begin promptly at ten this morning. I know this is a very important case and I have taken special steps to inform them. For the record, there is no excuse for their behavior in failing to show up. It borders on contempt, and they know better. They have appeared in cases in my courtroom before, and they know well the ten minute taxi ride from their embassy to this courtroom. I find their present behavior to be both rude and arrogant."

Some of the people in the front row began to laugh at the judge's caustic remarks. The Judge raised his eyebrows and his dark brown eyes above his half-glasses and looked down at the folks—all Wallenberg saved survivors—behind me on the front row. That was all that was needed to restore silence in the courtroom.

I had rehearsed the case many times with other members of my legal team. We were ready to go. The judge looked down at his handwritten notes for a moment, then up at the clock. Perhaps he was hoping the Russians might simply be late and not completely flout the dignity of his court. He seemed to consider the international and the political ramifications of holding them in contempt for failing to appear, and waited a few minutes before starting. To give the lawyers for the USSR a little more time to arrive, Judge Parker reviewed the highlights of our case, making it clear that he believed that what had happened to Wallenberg was an egregious crime.

Parker placed his glasses up on his forehead and leaned forward to engage me in conversation:

"Mr. Wolff, I have carefully read your brief and I am inclined to assert jurisdiction in this case. The laws you have carefully cited in your brief are proper and relevant. They beg an answer from the other side, an effort by the USSR to explain the legality of their behavior. We will wait a few minutes for them to appear."

Parker continued:

"The main question, of course, is whether I have the power to hear the case, to take jurisdiction over this sensitive matter and rule on a matter involving the arrest and detention thirty-nine years ago of a Swedish diplomat-citizen working on Hungarian soil and kidnapped by the Russian government, in 1945, no less. I realize it is a case involving a great hero, but large or small, rich or poor, all men who are illegally detained have a right to be heard, a basic right to *habeas corpus*—to be tried for a crime or set free. The Russians have held this man for 39 years without a trial. That is simply not fair. I intend to rule on this matter. We have waited long enough."

"Mr. Wolff will you please begin your oral argument."

127

Whatever Happened to Raoul Wallenberg?

In the courtroom were many Wallenberg survivors—rich and poor—as well as active members of Raoul Wallenberg Committees from Israel, Sweden, Argentina, Mexico, France, Italy, Canada, Australia, and New Zealand. They had all come a long way; they had all paid their own way to be here. Many of the delegations had arrived just in time for the hearing. The room became unusually quiet as I began my oral argument on the court's power to hear the case. A judgment ordering the Russians to immediately release Wallenberg and to pay 39 million dollars in damages was my clear goal. But this would only be possible if I could first persuade Judge Parker that he had the power to hear and rule on the matter.

I rose to my feet, walked to the podium in front of the Court bench and placed my hand gently on the podium. I began my oral argument. At the podium the green light was on, indicating I had thirty minutes to present my points. I cleared my throat and began;

"Raoul Wallenberg has been kidnapped and tortured in solitude. He has been away from his family in the USSR and unable to see anyone for four decades. This detention is in violation of Russia's own criminal law, in violation of the *Alien Tort Claims Act* and in violation of public international law, your honor, as outlined in my brief."

"I have carefully read your brief, Counselor. Please proceed."

"Yes, I will, your Honor."

"The USSR has violated Wallenberg's right to *habeas corpus* and to a speedy trial. There are many violations of law and human decency involved in their behavior over the past thirty-nine years that legal codes alone do not fully embrace the enormity of their violation."

"The Soviet government has violated Wallenberg's right to a speedy trial and to a preliminary hearing. They have trampled upon his basic right to freedom over the past thirty nine years. He has never done anything wrong; As a humanitarian, he has rescued 100,000 frightened and endangered Jews. Is that a crime?"

"The USSR has violated international treaties which guarantee the protection of diplomats while on official duty, including the *Vienna Convention for the Protection of Diplomats,* signed by the USSR as an original signatory. Under your guidance, Judge Parker, this court has the jurisdiction to rule and to hold the Soviets liable for kidnapping a diplomat. The power and the duty to hear this case exists under two federal statutes."

I cleared my throat and glanced up at the clock on the wall above the head of the grey haired juror. "First, the *Alien Tort Claims Act* of 1789. Second, the *Foreign Sovereign Non-Immunity Act of 1976.* Wallenberg was our *de facto* diplomat. We hired him, we paid him, and we sent him into danger in Hungary, to save the dwindling Jewish population. Under the *Alien Tort Claims Act* Wallenberg's brother is an "alien", a Swede. There has been a "tort", a violation of diplomatic immunity and today we make a claim that all three parts of the *Tort Claims Act* are met.

The only significant Jewish population saved from destruction in Europe was the approximately 100,000 Jews in Budapest. Our government promised to protect him from harm and to rescue him from danger at the end of the war. We let him down. We actually abandoned him. To our eternal shame, we did nothing.

A few years ago, we made him a super level citizen of the United States. You may ask why a super citizen? And the answer, your honor, is that he is one of only three human beings granted *gold key* citizenship in the United States. The other two are Winston Churchill and the Marquis de Lafayette. It is my goal to breathe new life into the *Alien Tort Claims Act* in our federal courts, and at the same time to rescue diplomat Wallenberg.

For these reasons we bring this case in your court. It is fitting that we are here in this federal court, Judge Parker, as you, with great courage, decided in the *Letelier* case, there is a similar problem of violation of diplomatic immunity. Similar principles are involved here. Both cases involve harm to an innocent diplomat. Both involve criminal acts by a foreign government. I hope, your honor, that you will use the *Letelier* case decision as a jumping off place…a place on which to base your consideration of the injustices visited upon Raoul Wallenberg. Please help us gain his release by finding the Soviets liable, imposing a substantial fine of $39 million in your courtroom, and ordering the USSR to set him free."

I gathered my papers and started back towards counsel table. I stopped and turned around to face the Court.

Judge Parker stood up for a minute, giving his injured leg a chance to stretch. He rested his arms on the back of the large judicial chair. He looked down towards me.

"Are you saying Mr. Wolff that this *Alien Tort Claims Act of 1789* is still good law? It sounds to me to be rather old and outdated."

"It is still good law, your Honor. It has not been used often but has been enforced in other federal court cases. These include cases as ancient as *Santissima* and *Ortega*, involving the caning of a foreign diplomat in Philadelphia in 1823, and as recent as the *Filartiga* case, decided by Judge Kauffman in New York and your decision in the *Letelier* case…which I believe without any doubt was decided correctly. The *Alien Tort Law* is like a giant sequoia tree in California. It is venerable and strong and has dignity. It is good law. It has never been repealed."

"In addition, your honor, in the recent case of *Siderman de Blake vs. Republic of Argentina* in the Federal District Court for the Central District of California, the court held that the Republic of Argentina was civilly liable for the torture of a Jewish businessman Jose Siderman, who was living at all times in Argentina. Siderman was captured by the local military police without a warrant, tortured and beaten. They left him for dead in the street. The Argentine military government looted his family property and assets then valued at twenty-five million dollars. Mr. Siderman, despite very serious and brutal injuries, came to the United States and sued in the federal court in California. The District Court opinion in favor of the foreigner was handed down on March 12, 1984, just three months ago. The court entered a default judgment on the torture claims awarding Jose Siderman damages and expenses totaling 2.6 million dollars. And this man did not spend thirty-nine years experiencing constant torture and incommunicado anxiety as in the case of my client, Wallenberg. Wallenberg has had the strength to survive and be ready for release. The years have not dimmed his acuity. He has even invented a twenty four-letter vocabulary for communicating with fellow prisoners. We are asking this Court to enter default judgment as soon as possible in favor of plaintiff Wallenberg in the amount of thirty nine million dollars—one million for each year of illegal detention. The Siderman case and this lawsuit are quite similar. Like Siderman we want our client to live and to come home to his family. In both cases the District Court Judge found and took jurisdiction; found there had been a specific and egregious violation of both the *Foreign Sovereign Immunities Act* and the *Alien Tort Statute*."

"Our courts allow foreigners, whose family members have been abused and tortured by foreign governments, to reclaim money damages and gain their freedom. We ask you to enter judgment in favor my client Raoul Wallenberg as soon as possible. This will hasten the day when Raoul Wallenberg will rejoin his family and live in freedom. He is 72 years old. He deserves the right to spend his last years in peace and serenity."

Judge Parker had already read my brief. He was familiar with the research that led me to the 1789 law and the reasoning behind the 39 million dollars in damages, which I was requesting – one million for each year of illegal detention.

"That figure sounds reasonable," the judge said, "considering the malicious and criminal level of governmental misbehavior. I will take your case and your damages request under advisement. Too bad the Russians are not here to explain and defend their actions or to answer the reasonableness of your request."

The room was silent for a moment. Then there was an outburst of cheering, as if a dam of pent up emotions gave way. People were rushing up to congratulate me, thinking the case was won. The Judge tolerated the cheering. He knew these were victims of the Holocaust letting out at long last their deep sorrow and feelings of injustice. Their cause had been championed in court. And they were proud to be here to see the first step in getting human rights enforced and Wallenberg released. Two women dressed in black began to cry. They were both survivors. After a few minutes the people calmed down and returned to their seats.

"What makes you think your client is still alive?" Judge Parker asked.

"What makes this hearing anything but an exercise in futility—a show trial?"

"Your Honor, we have evidence that Raoul Wallenberg at age 72 is still very much alive and in good health, or else we wouldn't be here."

Judge Parker asked about other international treaties. "I have reviewed the protection accorded to diplomats under *The International Convention for the Protection of Diplomats,* signed by the USSR, Sweden and the United States, among other countries." Judge Parker said "I will follow that law."

Judge Parker began walking slowly off the stage towards his chambers. At the last moment he turned and with a gleam in his eye, "Attorney Wolff," he said. "Perhaps I can use the international treaties to grant you the relief you are seeking. We shall see." He stood perfectly still for a moment. "I have a lot to consider, including the pressure that will be brought to bear on me if I rule your way. I am concerned about the ethics of our State Department. The State Department lawyers should have been here today on your side with an *amicus puriae* brief. I smell trouble. I think they will be coming to my chambers in those dark pin stripe suits begging me not to make a decision against the Soviets. I can almost hear the footsteps in my corridor already. They will pressure me to duck the case and avoid an international confrontation." He then walked away muttering, "We shall see."

I felt in my gut that I had persuasively made the case, and had laid out the law for a winning decision. Judge Parker was buying into it. He seemed ready to help our cause, especially since the Russians had refused to appear. I had provided him with the treaties and the laws needed to sustain a positive legal decision and judgment for the plaintiff.

I gave him another legal leg for his decision, the *Foreign Sovereign Immunities Act,* which when taken in combination with the protection accorded diplomats was all he needed to avoid reversal.

"I don't mind sticking my neck out and making new law," the judge said, "but I hate being reversed."

Everyone inside the courtroom seemed to fill with elation as they sensed victory. Even the judge seemed relieved that the argument was over and that the USSR had chosen not to appear. They took a gamble that the court would refuse to find jurisdiction and to hear or decide the case, and they lost! They should have put in a special appearance to contest jurisdiction, and to present preliminary objections and show due respect for the court, as they had done in the past when they found themselves as defendant in a US Federal Court. No excuse for their arrogant absence had been offered. They were risking a default judgment in Wallenberg's' favor. They were gambling that the judgment would never be enforced in any meaningful way. We would cross that bridge when we came to it.

Justice for the moment had been served. The courtroom glowed with the smiling faces of the Wallenberg survivors, beaming with joy. The brilliant blue sky poured its light through the window. Was Wallenberg in an interior cell at this moment, or did he have a window? Was he looking up at the sky just now? Could he possibly feel the elation and energy coming from this courtroom? I prayed that Raoul Wallenberg's freedom was coming.

June 1985
Philadelphia

I began to wonder whether our lawsuit had been politically crushed by the intervention of the White House and the State Department. More than a year passed since the oral argument and we still had no decision. Wallenberg was not getting any younger. I carried his life like a burden on my shoulders. I wanted relief—a court decision and ability to go to the next step—whatever the next step might be. Certain cases merit priority and this was one. The United States and its Judiciary owed Wallenberg a swift rescue and freedom in 1945. Failing that, they now owed him the right to be heard and to be set free. The writ of *Habeas Corpus*—the great writ as it is called—was the best guarantor of rights. No one was to be allowed to remain in custody for even 72 hours without being brought before a magistrate for hearing.

"But this is America. And not the USSR," I thought to myself. "You will simply have to be patient. I know it's hard. But you ain't got any choice."

I called the Judge's chambers seeking to know why the year's delay—a daring thing to do that could lead to criticism and being hauled before the Ethics Committee of the Federal Bar Association in Washington, DC. It was worth it. His clerk was friendly—turned out to be a Yale Law graduate, just like the Judge. There was a spirit of camaraderie but still no decision in the case. The Judge's clerk gave me words of encouragement.

"He wants to rule your way, but this involves new law. He will be making history if he rules your way and you will too. He talks with other Judges. No one has seen a case holding the USSR liable in a US Court for what amounts to political behavior. Some of the Judges are telling him to declare it a 'political question' and send it back over to the White House."

"That's the worst thing he can do," I replied. "The White House will deep-six it and send it to the State Department and State will send me a nice courtesy letter thanking me for my interest and telling me they are doing everything possible to get him released. Lip service. That's all they give anyone who inquires about Wallenberg, just la-ti-da lip service."

I was frustrated. I could see the Judge was under pressure to buck the case to the White House and allow the Commander in Chief to kill it while preaching about his love for Wallenberg and the trees at Yad Vashem.

The clerk paused, and then continued:

"Cool your jets. The Judge wants to do the right thing. He just needs time to collect all the pertinent law and make an airtight decision. He is getting an inordinate amount of phone calls and flak from Abe Sofaer the Jewish State

Department lawyer that should be on our side. Sofaer is pressuring the White House to lay off the case and dismiss it as a political question."

"I did not realize the Judge might listen to behind the scenes *ex parte* pleas and interventions?"

"Don't worry; he has a ramrod back of steel. He wants this case to be his *magnum opus*, his big decision. Relax. I will stay in touch."

I hung up and thought to myself:

"Justice grinds slowly towards the outcome I want. State Department was meddling? Were the fragile politics of 1985, plus the frigid cold winter months of the Cold War, all adding up to delay?"

I learned from his law clerk that the pinstripe anti-Semites from our State department made 'a courtesy visit' and a 'straight pitch' to the Judge without me present as counsel for the plaintiff present. Highly irregular and unethical, but then again the State Department and the White House had little respect for ethics or the separation of powers. I knew that.

Was it possible that Judge Parker was taking his time to make sure he had a non-reversible decision? Who knows? In the meantime, I was still deeply involved with many other initiatives related to keeping Wallenberg alive.

June 1985

Margate Jewish Community Center, Margate, New Jersey

I was invited to the Margate Jewish Community Center in nearby Margate, New Jersey to address a Sunday evening Five Star Forum group and to receive an award for Wallenberg and his work. The invitation was from Esther Weiss, who I had met through the Frank Ford radio show. I accepted without hesitation. I loved talking to synagogue groups about the case. The elderly survivors I met each time galvanized me to keep working on the case. At the synagogue event I was presented with a small plaque marked

"Margate Jewish Community Center,

June 1985,

In Honor of Raoul Wallenberg, and his

selfless and valiant work. And in honor of

Morris Wolff, with gratitude for his

courageous initiative as Wallenberg's

guardian, lawyer and advocate for justice."

Rabbi Goldman stood up to introduce me at the pulpit. He beckoned me near and he put his hands on my shoulder and looked into my eyes. "Thank you, Morris, for your work to rescue our hero. You will meet three new friends here this evening who were actually saved by Wallenberg. They are grateful that you remind the world not to forget Raoul Wallenberg. We welcome you as our Atlantic seashore neighbor, and we are pleased that you have a summer place nearby at Stone Harbor. We hope you will visit with us on many occasions and will know our door is always wide open for you."

I spoke briefly about my legal efforts and then took some questions. In answering whether the Swedes and Americans had done enough to rescue Wallenberg, I read aloud from Harvey Rosenfeld's biography, *"Raoul Wallenberg: Angel of Rescue."* I simply opened the book to page 181 and began reading the following quote:

"Stig Bergling, a former Swedish Defense Ministry employee, was convicted as a KGB agent and sentenced to life imprisonment in November 1979. Bergling was later offered to the Soviets for Wallenberg."

"In secret negotiations between the Swedish Foreign Ministry and the Soviet Foreign Ministry, Wallenberg was offered by the Russians as trade bait in exchange for Stig Bergling, a Swedish national caught in Stockholm passing state secrets to the Russians. Bergling was arrested, tried, and sentenced. He was confined to jail in Stockholm where the Russians initiated the discussions. The trade failed when the Swedish government demanded a two for one swap. A one for one swap would have brought freedom in 1965 for Raoul Wallenberg."

The audience of survivors was up in arms, arguing and shaking their fists in disbelief, calling for Wallenberg's freedom. I was able to calm them down and the evening ended with a clarion call for new action by the survivors.

The next day I went to the Germantown Cricket Club in Philadelphia for my weekly tennis game with Ted Heisler, a friend from Amherst College. Both Ted and his Swedish wife, Lisbeth, had a strong interest in the Wallenberg case.

"Boy, you sure have started a ruckus," Ted said when he met me. "You are all over the front page of the *Inquirer* and on the morning TV news. What did you do?"

"I don't know what you're talking about."

Ted pulled out a copy of the *Philadelphia Inquirer* and showed me the front page. "Wallenberg lawyer claims Sweden failed to rescue their hero. Bungled spy swap in 1965 sealed Wallenberg's fate, claims Philadelphia attorney Morris Wolff."

"Well, Ted, that's simply true, and I was not the first to report it. Rosenfeld wrote his book a number of years ago. I just read and quoted directly from it in my remarks last night."

The paper apparently had responded to my remarks and had tried to create "news" where there was none. From my quoting aloud a small portion of a three-year-old published book, the paper had created a sensationalized, tantalizing "news" story—one with international implications. Undoubtedly this story went out on the AP newswire around the world. I could only imagine what the reaction might be in Sweden. Much ado about nothing new.

The reaction was swift and strong. The AP wire carried the Swedish response in papers throughout Europe, in *The New York Times* and *Washington Post,* and was broadcast on all the local TV stations in Philadelphia and as a national news story on CBS and NBC. Other media outlets around the world also picked up the developing story of how I had single-handedly embarrassed and humiliated the Swedish government by "meddling with top secret matters" and "divulging" their failure to execute a timely swap of Wallenberg for Bergling. They knew better. They just wanted to shift the responsibility to me for their tepid inaction. It was the Swedish government that created the sensationalism by suggesting I was divulging state secrets when all I had done was to read from a book. And I suppose the *Philadelphia Inquirer* and other papers wanted to find a way to sell more newspapers on a slow Saturday.

Their accusation of 'divulging' sounded vaguely like I was being accused of espionage. I tried to remember the last time someone was treated like a spy for reading publicly from a published book dealing with events from 20 years earlier. Besides, all this uproar would be good for the case—it kept Wallenberg in the public spotlight and consciousness. This was the kind of publicity we needed. I wondered what other ramifications might follow. I soon got my answer.

A few hours later, Guy Von Dardel called me on the telephone. At first, I was glad to hear from him. Guy still had a habit of calling me every Saturday, which was our normal day for communication and updating the case. Often he would call to talk even if there was no legal business that needed our attention. I got the feeling he was a very lonely man looking for kinship, and cut off from the rest of his family because of his devotion to the cause. Today, he sounded different. His voice was heavy, tired and sad.

"Morris, I have just now received a personal phone call here at home from the Swedish Foreign Minister."

"Yes?" I replied. I tried to sound positive as always, but I felt something ominous might be about to happen.

"The Minister is opposed to your comments in this morning's front page article in the *Svenska Dagbladet.*"

"I'm sorry to hear that," I said. "But my comments are accurate and true. We know that the Swedish Ministry in 1965 tried to swap Bergling for Wallenberg, and it is already written in a published book. This is not late breaking news worthy of front-page coverage. In fact it is not news at all. It is just one more effort by the Swedish Foreign Minister in cahoots with the bad branch of the Wallenberg family to silence and stymie my efforts. "

I told Guy about my speech at the synagogue, and the award they had given to me and to Raoul in absentia. "I answered a question afterward by quoting from Rosenfeld's book," I said. "It was all public knowledge already available. The Bergling affair is not brand new. It is not breaking news, let alone top secret information. You and I have known about it for a long time. If the shoe fits, then Sweden should put it on. They know they have failed Wallenberg for many years."

"It's not that easy," Guy replied. "The government not only feels embarrassed—they also fear diplomatic or economic, or even military retaliation from the Russians. They may capture one of our submarines. I know it's irrational, but that's just the way the Russians operate. You are now the focus, the scapegoat. I know the pressure should be on the Russians, not on you."

He paused and then began to cry.

He whispered, "I have been pressured by my family and arm twisted by my government to ask you to resign from the case."

"I can't resign. I will not resign. I have accepted full responsibility as captain of the ship. And you and your sister, and his legal guardian Sven Hagstromer have all signed on for the voyage. That is our agreement. I am working for Raoul and not for your corrupt government."

I felt dizzy and doubled over. Then I found a chair and sat down. I caught my breath and collected my thoughts.

"Why should I even consider resigning?" I said. "I have done nothing wrong. I simply told the truth. How would your brother have wanted me to handle the question I was asked at the synagogue?"

Guy sighed.

"The Swedish government has hinted that there will be repercussions against our family's commercial interests if you are not removed," he continued. "I want to do this quietly and without a fuss."

"Well there will be a fuss. I am going forward. We will win this case and hopefully spring your brother from jail. This case is not just about you, or even your family. It is about Raoul. And that is whom I represent"

"I'm surprised at you, Guy," I said. "Would you desert your brother's cause because the *Enskilda Bank* might lose some greedy state business? Would you back down for money?"

There was a pause. I could hear him mumbling, "I don't know what to do."

"Yes, Guy, in your heart of hearts, you know exactly what to do. Do not abandon your brother. As for me, I am not resigning. The Swedes have sold him out, and you know it. And now you too? The Swedes are putting pressure on you. The Russians need a fall guy but I'm not it"

"My family owned *Enskilda Bank* will be removed and deleted from the government's favored banking list," he said.

"So what? What does that mean?" I asked.

"No more new housing loans. No more bank financing of Swedish exports. Our bank will be wiped out within weeks."

They were just playing dirty pool, and I told him so. He didn't budge from his position, but I didn't either.

"Just tell Marcus Wallenberg, your uncle, that you have neither the power nor desire to fire me. There has been no failure to properly represent my client—if anything just the opposite. Tell the evil part of your family that under the federal rules of the District Court for the District of Columbia, that you and they do not have this power. It is as simple as that. If you need any more legal justification, I will guide you through a detailed legal response that will satisfy the authorities."

Guy seemed to brighten a bit, now that he had an answer to give his greedy family and to the timid neutral government.

"I am grateful that you're not a quitter. I am grateful that you are willing to continue the fight for my brother."

"Hang in there, Guy, and do not be intimidated," I said. "There may be some rough sledding ahead, but I as captain of the ship will stay steady and on course."

"I will hang in with you," he said. "That must be an Americanism—hang in and not hang up!" he laughed. "I am ready to report this conversation to my family."

"Send them my love—especially your sister Nina. She must be suffering through all of this."

We shared a few final quiet and peaceful moments, reminiscing about our nocturnal walk in the snow to the Jefferson and Lincoln memorials, our walk up the steps of the Court House to file the lawsuit, and his story on forgetting his passport as he raced to take the plane from Stockholm to DC. We laughed and talked about our families and children and how they were doing in school. "Come visit us someday soon," I suggested. "We do miss you here."

"I will," he said. "I will."

Three days later I got another surprise phone call—this one quite positive and heartwarming. My favorite professor from the Yale Law School was calling with good news. Myres S. McDougal, known to his students as "Mac," had been my teacher for twenty-three years. When I first walked into his classroom I was struck by the unforgettable image of a large man with combed back white hair, starched white shirt, red suspenders, and a warm smile. On his high forehead and over his rimless eyeglasses he wore a wide green eyeshade to protect his weak eyes. He would often read using a magnifying glass. From the podium, Mac's deep Mississippi drawl would boom out to the large classroom.

I disagreed in maverick style with almost everything he said, and had the courage or stupidity to argue back in class. I felt that "McDougalese," his new system of language for international law was not necessary. I was wrong. Today he is revered as the leader in shaping a new approach and a new language for analyzing global international legal problems.

Mac liked the way I argued with him. "It's like a tennis match," he said. "You hit the ball back hard and I like it. It stimulates my mind."

Mac arranged for my interview with Bobby Kennedy at the Justice Department. I wanted to work there and would not have achieved that without his phone call. I was selected for the Attorney General's Honors Program in January 1963 and worked on the 5th floor just down the hall from Attorney General Kennedy as a member of the United States Department of Justice Office of Legal Counsel. Mac and I stayed in close touch over the years. We talked often about my work on the Wallenberg case. We discussed the different law theories I was putting forward in my complaint and brief, and he listened in advance to my oral argument before Judge Parker. I was happy to still be one of Mac's boys.

"Marse," he said, running his Mississippi drawl over the two syllables of my first name linking them together as always, "Marse, you must now begin to be patient like a Mississippi fisherman with a fly on the water, just waiting for the bass to jump on the Yazoo River. No more phone calls to Judge Parker's chambers. Not necessary. You may not know this, but Barrington Parker was another one of my boys, one of my favorite students here."

Mac continued:

"Barrington Parker was among the first blacks ever to enter Yale Law School. We are both proud to be from Mississippi, having escaped from Senator Bilbo and the Southern segregationists, and having come north."

Mac chuckled at the irony of it all. Living up north with more power than Bilbo ever had, leading the civil rights movement from his office in New Haven at the Yale Law School. The Yale Law School network was abuzz with the knowledge that the Wallenberg decision was soon coming down - and would mark the coming of a new legal era in human rights litigation. Professor McDougal had picked up the phone and called me to tell me the news. I felt honored.

"Judge Parker's present law clerk was also one of my students. He is writing the opinion for you, so be patient. He knows what to do and how to nail the Russians on the jurisdiction question. You are not about to lose this case."

"The decision will be out in a few months and it will be a good one. It will set new precedent. It will allow US Courts to hear all kinds of human rights cases never considered before. You will be a known as a legal trail blazer if you can keep your mouth shut for a brief while." He laughed again. "I know from the class room that is no easy matter!"

"The judge will rule your way," said Mac. "He will hold the Soviets liable for Wallenberg's kidnapping. He is also inclined to give you the $39 million in damages. Most important, he will issue an order demanding the Russians yield Wallenberg and bring him into his courtroom in Washington, DC within 60 days. Now that is some accomplishment!"

"Judge Parker and I talked several times about this knotty and tough question of jurisdiction," Mac continued. "Specifically, whether he has the power to act on a matter filled with dicey international law issues. I told him he must decide this case. He has the power to decide, which is all that jurisdiction is about anyway. It simply means: will I as judge use my power and my courage to act? The laws you argued are valid and good, even the one from 1789. The *Alien Tort Claims Act* and the *Vienna Convention on Diplomatic Relations and the Protection of Diplomats* should be enough."

"Parker told me that he is getting a ton of pressure from the White House and State Department to duck the issue and refuse jurisdiction, on the grounds that this is a "political question." The President wants to grab back the power from the courts. It's a struggle between the two branches: the Executive and the Judiciary, just as Montesquieu predicted—these two branches of government are fighting each other for the right to decide."

"Judge Parker will be all right in his decision. He will make history on this one—as big as any case he has ever decided. He's a civil rights man who wants justice, and he knows the only place Wallenberg can get it will be in the courts. I encouraged him to take an expansive view, an activist, result-oriented view. So sit tight," Mac concluded. "Don't kick the beehive and make the honeybees swarm."

I got off the phone feeling relieved and happy. I felt good about my work, and that Mac, my international law mentor, had taken an active interest. My faith in my work and the final outcome was reborn. Now, all I had to do was wait patiently for the verdict and the written opinion.

October 1985
Philadelphia

Autumn 1985 seemed to arrive early. Indian summer, which often lingered for the month of September, was over. The warm days were gone, cold nights bursting with Arctic air. I packed up my house and belongings in Reno and returned home to Philadelphia to be with my family. The Deanship at the Nevada College of Law was completed on a triumphal note—I had gained accreditation for the school in the courtroom. In a five to four decision, the human rights to study, learn and achieve was now established in Nevada. I had won the day by successfully arguing to a red-faced panel of nine judges "Any State that can support prostitution and casinos can certainly support and give accreditation to a law school and its students so that they may study and learn the law." Chief Judge Manookian lost his position on the court in the next election for supporting my position. My students could now sit for the Bar. They would become lawyers. "Thank you Dean Wolff."—That was the blue and white banner, which was hung across the front of the law school library for my going away party. I had answered the challenge but was leaving a lot behind—good memories of a great Board of Trustees, eager students working one or two jobs and pushing their way through law school. And the establishment of the Raoul Wallenberg Law Center for Altruistic Studies.

I helped to raise $6.2 million dollars for the new law building with the assistance of Senator Paul Laxalt, Reagan's close friend, and the rest of the distinguished Trustees.

I was on tenterhooks waiting for Judge Parker's decision to finally be handed down. The same clerk who had given a heads-up to Mac tipped me off that an early October decision was possible.

On the evening of the 17th of October, the phone rang. The caller introduced himself as Steve Coleman, from *The Washington Post.*

"I have been following your *Wallenberg v. USSR* case very closely," Coleman said. "I was at the original press conference in February last year, when you first filed the lawsuit. I am the bearer of very good news. You have won a complete victory, hands down. A total rout, total knockout. Everything you asked for has now been granted by the court. Judge Parker has found the Soviets liable for violating international law and for detaining your client illegally for thirty-nine years. The judge has awarded the $39 million in damages you asked for. Most important, Judge Parker says the Soviets must produce Wallenberg in his courtroom within 30 days."

"How did you hear all this?"

142

"Well, the official decision in your case will come out tomorrow, but I have a scoop, an early lead on the story. I have a friend in the Judge's chambers who tips me off in advance when important positive decisions are coming down."

"That's great news, whatever the source," I assured him.

"What is your next step? What exactly will you do now, Morris?"

"First, I will seek an immediate attachment of Soviet assets at the Chase Manhattan Bank in New York City. Then I will personally drive with the sheriff out to the Dulles Airport and slap an attachment on the fuselage of the Russian Aeroflot aircraft which I know tonight are sitting there on the ground. There is no time to lose. I will pressure the Soviets to release Wallenberg. I will use this magnificent judgment as a crowbar to obtain his freedom. This judgment is a major leverage to actually rescue Wallenberg. I am glad to find that the judge agrees with me that Wallenberg is alive."

"Good luck. I will be waiting to hear from you."

The court decision handed down on October 18, 1985 received national notice in the press. Front-page articles were carried in *The New York Times, The Washington Post, The Philadelphia Inquirer* and in papers across America. My phone rang often in the following days. Congratulations poured in from law professors, especially a warm approval from my mentor "Mac" McDougal, Sterling Professor of Law at Yale and Professor Louis Sohn, Bemis Professor of International Law at Harvard.

Sohn wrote "Congratulating you on your great achievement. You will open doors for other human rights cases."

I sat down in my office to read the key parts of the decision. I skipped to the conclusion and read:

"In many ways this lawsuit is unique and without precedent in the history of actions against foreign sovereigns. It involves actions, which the Soviet Union has already admitted is unlawful. It involves a gross violation of the personal immunity of a diplomat, one of the oldest and most recognized principles of universal law. Furthermore this action involves a deliberate default by the Soviet Union. No statute of limitations has begun to run against Wallenberg's claim for freedom. The Soviet Union's treatment is unlawful, even under its own laws. Ambassador Wallenberg's detention violated even the criminal code of the Russian Soviet Federated Socialist Republic. Wallenberg's arrest and detention continued to be illegal under principles of international law and international agreements, which were in force in 1945 and to which the USSR was a party. Moreover, the 1957 *Gromyko Note* acknowledged the

illegality of Wallenberg's detention and of the misinformation that made it possible.

The Soviet Union's treatment of Raoul Wallenberg is unlawful under any standard of applicable law. It has never argued otherwise; it has denied and disclaimed its actions, but it has never defended them. For all of these reasons, default judgment is entered against the defendant, with the order that he be produced, and that the Soviet Union, pay the amount of $39 million dollars be immediately paid to the family of Raoul Wallenberg, as well as attorneys fees and all court costs. "
(The rest of this opinion in the back of the book.)

For the first time I actually began to feel that we would rescue Wallenberg. With this federal court opinion as a cudgel and weapon, I would force the sale of thirty-nine million dollars of assets in American banks. I knew where the money was. It was in bank accounts at the Chase Manhattan Bank in New York City and it was in airplanes coming in daily to Dulles airfield outside Washington, DC. I felt the Russians would rather release Wallenberg than suffer the embarrassment of the monetary damages. I was even ready to go back in to court if the Russians released Wallenberg and negotiated away the thirty-nine million dollar judgment. I had no interest in the money. I only wanted to go to Moscow and bring Wallenberg home.

November 1985
New York City

NBC had interviewed me in 1984 the morning I filed my complaint. They indicated at that time their interest in doing a documentary on the life of Wallenberg and asked whether they could retain me as an advisor and consultant for their project. I agreed to do so. A year and a half later the documentary was finished and I had provided them with copies of interviews of survivors.

The three-part docudrama on Raoul Wallenberg produced by NBC, in which Richard Chamberlain played the hero was celebrated by a celebrity reception in New York City. In November of 1985, I attended the opening night preview of "Wallenberg: A Hero's Story" in New York for those involved in the production, hosted by NBC. The miniseries would later receive various awards. Chamberlain's work was honored with Golden Globe and Emmy "best actor" nominations.

A buffet dinner at the NBC headquarters' Rainbow Room at the Rockefeller Center was laid out with prime rib, lobster, and filet mignon. Besides the television executives, dignitaries attending included former New York City Mayor John Lindsay, New York's senator Alfonse D'Amato, Senator Claiborne Pell of Rhode Island, and Congressman Tom Lantos. There were also members of the Save Raoul Wallenberg Committee, as well as a few people who had known Wallenberg. The evening skyline was silhouetted by the reds and purples of the descending sun and the lights of the city.

I spoke with Richard Chamberlain, whom I had briefed on Wallenberg's life when the mini-series was in preparation. He guided me over to a large burgundy sofa. He wanted to know still more about the man he had portrayed on screen and how I came to be involved in representing him. He was particularly intrigued with how I had persuaded the court to listen to our human rights claim. Chamberlain came across as sincere with considerable charisma.

Nearby I recognized a tall man with a head of wavy white hair dressed in a pinstripe navy blue suit, white shirt, gold cuff links and a royal red tie. It was Per Anger, Wallenberg's compatriot at the Swedish Legation in Budapest. I beckoned him over to join us. He certainly knew a great deal about Wallenberg and could enlighten both Chamberlain and me. Chamberlain assessed Per Anger as he headed toward us.

"He could be from Central Casting," Chamberlain joked. "Just look at him. Every inch the picture and figure of a diplomat."

"Yes, he has the movements and the careful and concise language of a diplomat. I have learned a lot more about my client Wallenberg just from talking with him."

Whatever Happened to Raoul Wallenberg?

Per Anger sat down on the edge of the burgundy couch, took an unfiltered Gauloise cigarette from a silver case, and lit it with his silver Zippo lighter. He told us more about Wallenberg's arrival in Budapest, dressed in what seemed to be clothes for a camping trip in the Carpathians.

"Wallenberg was friendly and decent, with no arrogance. He had a zealous focus on his mission to save the Jews. We offered him a night on the town on his arrival, but he refused. Can you believe it? 'I want to get right to work,' he told us. 'There is no time to lose.'"

He spoke about Wallenberg's time in Budapest, revisiting the story of his showdown with Eichmann, and then, of course, puzzling, not for the first time, over his arrest and detention and why neither the Swedish government, nor the US government did anything to help Wallenberg. Per Anger turned toward me and raised his eyebrows. The wrinkles on his forehead seemed to raise his eyes and make them larger. "We may never know" Anger answered. "Morris, I want to share with you a personal letter from Wallenberg that I have kept secret up until today." He reached in his coat pocket, pulled out an envelope marked 'Top Secret' and read the letter inside.

Dear Per

It is important that you tell all of the Jewish people that come to my office that my mission is to save as many Jews as possible. I cannot deal or visit with each person who arrives on our doorstep or I could never get my work done. I must focus on my trips to the train station to stop the exportation of the Jewish families as they are being stuffed in to the boxcars inhumanely. My printing of the passports at night must go on un-interrupted. I will continue to buy property as 'safe houses' for the rescued families. It is on this large-scale effort that I must focus my attention. Please be my front man and diplomatically greet everyone who comes to my doorstep. They mean well and I appreciate their support but I simply do not have time to meet with each family and hear their complaints. Per, I appreciate your friendship ever since school days in Stockholm, and trust you will do everything possible to maintain our good diplomatic relations with the Jewish people of Budapest.

Yours faithfully
Raoul

Tears were flowing from Per's eyes as he finished reading this brief letter of instruction from Raoul. I could feel and sense the deep friendship these two men must have had from their early days in Stockholm and their later work together in Budapest. Anger turned towards me as he wiped his eyes and put a white handkerchief back into his vest pocket.

"Now, it is up to you, Morris, to keep up the pressure and to stimulate and rev up world opinion so that the politicians take action and bring him home. We have two prongs, this movie and your lawsuit. These will be pincers of constant pressure to force the doors of the Kremlin and Lubyanka prison to open, and to set our friend free. I hope so. All else has failed. Yet, I am sure he is alive."

The three of us sat together for a moment in silence. Then it was time to watch the movie. Richard Chamberlain took Per Anger by one arm and me by the other. Together we walked to the large theater screening room set up by NBC for the film showing. Other people dressed in tuxedos and evening gowns were sweeping through the doors. They stepped aside for Richard Chamberlain. Per Anger and I followed right behind.

We sat down on the plush red velvet seats in the third row. The lights in the theater dimmed. Elie Wiesel entered and took the seat next to mine. I was thrilled to meet Wiesel again, a Nobel Prize winner in Literature. We had met before at a conference on the Holocaust in New York. I was stimulated in my work by his best book, *Night*, the memoir set in his home village of Sighet, Hungary, from which almost all the Jews perished during the Holocaust. We shook hands and chatted before and after the movie.

The screening room went dark. The film started. The face of Richard Chamberlain as Wallenberg, coming into Budapest by train and seeing the refugees trapped in the boxcars going out of Budapest headed towards Auschwitz, going the other way. He sees tiny leaflets being dropped through the thin slats of the rail cars exiting Budapest. "Remember me," the cards said "Remember me, remember me." I looked over at Elie Wiesel. His lips were quivering and I heard him say, "Remember me, Remember us...Remember Raoul."

Immediately following the premiere, the NBC producers hosted another reception. There was a festive feeling in the air, a feeling of celebration that Wallenberg's life had been honored and portrayed for millions to see. None of the complexities of Wallenberg's work for the US government were included, though; the miniseries was quite sanitized of these complexities.

Everyone was dressed formally, creating the feel of a diplomatic event. I met Bruce Teicholz, a leader in the underground resistance in Budapest who had worked closely with Wallenberg and was portrayed in the movie. I spoke again with Per Anger. The only person missing from the event was Raoul Wallenberg himself. A pity, since by all accounts he liked parties.

One of the quieter guests was Lars Berg, another Budapest compatriot of Wallenberg's, also attached to the Swedish Legation. For some time he had stood quietly in the background smoking a cigarette. After a time he approached me. We had met before, as I was researching the lawsuit. After the war, Berg had continued working in the Swedish Foreign Service, finally retiring. Now, 40 years after Wallenberg's capture, over glasses of champagne, Berg shared with me some of his memories of Wallenberg. He spoke of how bold Wallenberg was, the way he would rush down to the Hagysholom train station when he heard Jews were about to be transported, and push soldiers aside to climb on the cattle cars, handing out Swedish passports to bewildered Jews.

"The Arrow Cross soldiers did not know whether to stop him or just get out of the way. Usually they stepped aside. He was a brave man, bluffing his way as the ambassador. If they had discovered his game they would have shot him on the spot. Diplomatic immunity would not have saved him then." Berg paused for a moment. "It did not save him later, either," he added.

"Well, that's what we're trying to correct," I replied.

"What makes you think he is still alive?" he asked.

I took a breath, reminded again that Berg's country still found it difficult to admit the possibility that Wallenberg was alive.

"Do *you* think he may still be alive?" I asked him.

"There is a chance," he said. "Certainly he was alive in 1965 when my government bungled a spy swap for him. The offer was on for five days, take it or leave it. It was kept a secret in our foreign office, until years later. That was twenty years ago, but I think he is still alive. We could still trade for him, but I don't know if the Wallenberg family really wants him home."

"Why not?" I asked, though I had heard the answer before. I was always curious to hear new explanations for their reasoning.

"If Raoul had any fault, it was his outspokenness. He attacked what he saw as injustice, no matter what the consequences. Perhaps his industrialist family members did not want their wartime involvement with the Nazis brought to light—let alone attacked in the media."

"Steel?" I asked.

"Yes," he said. "Steel sold to the Germans to make tanks at a time when we were supposed to be neutral. Wallenberg's uncle, our ambassador in Berlin, facilitated sales by extending good terms. Your lawsuit puts a good face on things, but they didn't expect you to prevail. They are in fact worried you might succeed. And there's much at stake should that happen."

"Such as?"

"I don't want to speculate."

"We ought to talk more," I said.

"I am at your disposal," he replied. He put his hand in his jacket flap pocket and pulled out a small silver card case: 'Lars Berg - Foreign Ministry of Sweden (Retired).' It included his phone number and home address.

"I will help if I can," said Berg. "I will find out if there is still a live trail on him. The Foreign Ministry will know."

A few weeks later I received a letter from Lars Berg. In it he again congratulated me on the court victory. He encouraged me to continue the search and not to give up. His sources in Sweden had told him that Wallenberg was still alive, that the Russians even continued to interrogate him, although infrequently, waiting for the Wallenberg family to pay the ransom. His note reminded me that what he wrote was delicate information and that if I made it public, the Swedish Foreign Ministry would deny it. Interestingly, he suggested I begin to work with the Israelis, who had, of course, a vested interest in Wallenberg, a nation founded by survivors of the Holocaust.

Later, I would act on his valuable advice.

December 1985

New York City

The Soviets had only sixty days in which to appeal their defeat: from October 18 to December 18, 1985. On December 19, I moved quickly forward with my plan to attach Soviet assets at the Chase Manhattan Bank in New York City. I prepared the petitions needed by the sheriffs to slap on the fuselages of the aircraft on the runways at Dulles and JFK. Under Rule 60b of the Federal Rules of Civil Procedure, the Russians had only 60 days to appeal, after which we could immediately file the petition to attach US based Russian assets and enforce the default judgment.

The day before the deadline, December 18, 1985, still nothing had been heard from the Russians. I got Oswald on the phone. I had to be firm because he had already shown signs of disobedience and rebellion.

"You know the deadline is tomorrow," I said.

"Yes, I know."

"And....?"

"Everything's fine," he assured me. "We're ready to attach assets and force their hand."

Something I couldn't pin down bothered me about the offhandedness in Oswald's glib response. I couldn't shake my doubts. I reminded him of the "attachment of assets petitions" which we needed to prepare, and how to get them served by the US Marshal.

"And you will attach the Russian bank accounts at the Chase Bank right there in your building, right?" I said.

"Morris, I can't do that right now," he replied.

"What do you mean, you can't do that? That's our exact plan. Immediate attachment. Grab the money now, grab them by the short hairs, before they have time to move the money out of New York."

"I need time to think it over," he said.

"Chase Bank is a whore. They'll do anything to make money, They have no morals and no scruples. We must stop them from moving the Russian bank account from New York Chase to Paris Chase. Let me remind you of history dating back to 1942. At that time the Chase bank was one of five American banks with branches in Paris when the Nazis conquered France. Carlos Niederman, the Chase branch manager urged that the Paris branch continued doing business with the Nazis. New German accounts were opened in the Paris branch of Chase Manhattan Bank and Niederman approved loans to finance German industry assisting the Nazi War machine. A report by the US Reserve Bank in April of 1945 concluded that Chase's New York headquarters was well aware of the activities taking place in the Paris branch and did nothing to stop them until late in

150

1942, well after the United States declared war on Germany on December 7, 1941."

"There is nothing, Mr. Oswald, for us to think over," I said vehemently. "We know exactly what to do. There is absolutely no time to waste." I began to realize that he was a turncoat, and was simply creating tactics of delay.

Two days later, my suspicions were confirmed. Oswald, without my permission as Chief Counsel, had filed something perverse and insubordinate. What he filed was not our agreed upon petition to enforce the judgment. Instead he filed a petition seeking more money. We did not need more money. We needed Wallenberg's freedom. Oswald did just the opposite of what I instructed him to do. I had told him and everyone else that I was "Captain of the Ship" and would have the final word on any steps to be taken in prosecuting the lawsuit. I should have fired him on the spot. He later claimed that his law firm forced him to seek the delay. I reminded him: "do not give the Chase Manhattan Bank any time to empty its Russian accounts and shift them to Europe."

Oswald, in a major breach of ethics, went behind my back and contacted and persuaded the Wallenberg family to go along with his strategy of delay. He had no authority to ever speak directly to the family. At that moment, evil spirits entered the case.

The Wallenberg family owned, and still owns, the *Enskilda Banken of Sweden*. The *Enskilda Banken* at that time owned twenty-five percent of the Chase Manhattan Bank worldwide. Therefore, the Wallenberg family's greedy interests, at that moment, overwhelmed Guy Von Dardel's altruistic interests in rescuing his brother. There was never any legitimate reason to delay the attachment of assets and to force the Russians to release Wallenberg. Oswald was now asking in a delay tactic for contempt penalties against the Russians. This maneuver might be useful in other monetary cases because it could ultimately result in more money, as the defendant would end up paying damages for being in contempt of court. But in our case, it could only mean more years in custody for Wallenberg, and a fleecing of the New York bank accounts of the Soviet Union by the home government. The case would be strung out over a much longer period of time—possibly as long as a year—as we waited for the decision on Russia's contempt of court. I opposed that motion vehemently. More time in the Gulag was the last thing Wallenberg needed. I let Oswald know this immediately.

I called Oswald again. "What the hell are you doing? You must take direct action now. Do not fool around with contempt penalties. That will result in more delay, and we do not need one more day of Wallenberg in prison."

"Put pressure on them now," I said. "Execute the judgment without delay. We already discussed and I rejected contempt penalties," I said. "What do you think you're doing?"

"My firm wants more money. It seems the best course for my Wall Street law firm."

151

"But Parker may retire soon. We can't afford to lose our favorite judge."

"Well, I think it's the best strategy," he countered.

"I'm coming up to New York tomorrow, and we'll discuss this in person," I told him.

Even as we spoke, I knew the matter was getting out of hand. There were bad vibes emanating from Oswald as he stood there. I had been betrayed. I now had to resolve this act of insubordination quickly. What Oswald had done was highly unethical. His going behind my back and contacting the family when I was "Captain of the Ship and Master of the Case" was unthinkable. This wrong course taken by one of my appointees was unacceptable. Before heading to New York, I made some calls to a few other New York law firms. It was time to move the case, line up some alternative law firms and relieve Oswald, the man with the strange Russian family ties, which may have been the basis for his defection. When I arrived in New York, I went straight to Oswald's office.

When I next met face to face with Oswald he was a completely different and shaken man. He seemed to be on drugs and spaced out. His face was an ashen gray. His hair was disheveled. He looked totally distracted, as though his mind was on something far away. I wondered if he had had a stroke. Though I was angry at him, I was also concerned by his sudden transformation.

"What's happening Oswald?"

"I don't know. I cannot take the action you need to take. The executive committee in my law firm will not let me. I am under a lot of pressure from my partners to sit on my hands—to do nothing on the case."

"Then turn it completely back to me. Resign as assistant counsel and I will take over completely again." Oswald had tried to play "King of the Hill" with a case takeover. I had been warned by one of his law firm partners of his tendency to do this in other cases.

Oswald had been working to undermine my leadership on the case from the very beginning—back stabbing. He had made a secret deal with the State Department and with certain members—other than Von Dardel—of the Wallenberg family to sabotage the case. He thought by going behind my back and talking to the family he could unseat me as counsel.

He knew he was merely an assistant, but in a moment of unethical behavior he violated both the rules of court and the code of ethics. In thirty-five years of law practice I had never seen an attorney try a stunt of this nature. What Oswald did was illegal and unethical. He had somehow slipped in between me and my clients, and done the case a major disservice. What a snake!

"This is very difficult."

"No it's not. Just get out of the way. You are hurting the case. It is not difficult for you to resign. We must move quickly to attach the Russian assets before they move them out of New York City banks. Your captive client at Chase Manhattan Bank right here in this very building is headquartered with millions of dollars of Russian assets. I want to attach them this afternoon. If you won't do it I will do it myself. We will work through this temporary delay. If your partners tie your hands, I will do it myself. We are so close to rescuing Wallenberg. We can't stop now. We are near the summit. I can see it. I want to see Raoul free more than anything."

"I know." he said lamely. "Me too!"

"Then act!"

"I can't."

"Then get out of the way. Oswald, your petition for contempt penalties can't help. It will only delay the case. Judge Parker's law clerk called me. The judge is ready to issue the order to go out to Dulles Airport and to attach two Aeroflot jets on the ground right away. In addition, there is more than $39 million in Russian accounts right here at Chase Bank—you know, the Russian Wheat Purchase and Trade accounts. If we don't do this right away, they'll move these assets out of the country. We know their tricks. They will remove money to a bank in Montreal and buy Canadian wheat instead. Our farmers will lose. Wallenberg will lose. I do not want that."

"Maybe they've already moved the money."

"No," I replied. "As of today that Russian trade account was listed at plus seventy-two million. That's enough to pay the Wallenberg judgment and still let them buy plenty of American wheat!"

"How did you get that classified information?"

"I get it my way," I replied. "I have an active intelligence network. I have used it for the past twenty-three years to serve my international clients. Wallenberg is my chief client now. Oswald, I insist that you resign and step aside gently. Simply resign. I thank you for your work and I wish you well. I will get another New York law firm to assist. The firm of Paul, Weiss, Rifkind and Garrison is ready and willing to help"

"They're a good firm. I will see what I can do to get my firm to resign," Oswald replied "I want you to win."

He walked me to the elevator and pushed the down button.

"I have always wanted to help Wallenberg," he said.

"You have helped him," I told him. "You have done a lot of good. You translated our complaint from English into Russian. You helped me to prepare and present the arguments for the court hearing. You have been valuable as a friend and colleague. But now you are conflicted and you are no longer an asset. Your work is over."

The case was now in a precarious position. I planned to enlist Paul Weiss or Coudert Freres for immediate enforcement of the judgment. Little did I suspect that there would be additional surprises in store.

Soon after my visit with Oswald I received a strange letter from Guy Von Dardel. In it, he stated that the family was applying severe pressure. They were asking him to ask me to relinquish voluntarily my duties as chief counsel and place the management of the case in the hands of Oswald's firm. Von Dardel told me that both the government of Sweden and the *Enskilda Bank* were pressuring him to ask for my resignation. "Under no circumstances will I ever resign from this case. I do not consider you my client."

I stared at the letter and realized that Von Dardel was no longer in charge of his own mind. "Once you brought the case to me, Raoul Wallenberg became my client and only he could release me. You have no power to relieve me and you can tell your family and the people at the bank that I will yield to no one and to no effort to force me out. Place the full blame on me if you like but I'm not moving."

I sat down and wrote him a letter and arranged for a return receipt request in order to insure that he personally received and read the letter. My letter went on to state:

"You are no longer my only client in this matter. I am the 'Captain of the Ship.'

I am in charge of this case as per my written agreement with you. Simply resist the pressure. Tell them to go to hell; it is out of your hands."

A week later I received an encouraging reply: "I will tell them that. Continue your good work Morris."

Von Dardel's greedy family was now trying to kill the case after all we had been through together. I worried about the health of this good man, who alone carried the banner for Wallenberg all these years—the one family member to fly to Washington, DC to walk up the courthouse steps to be by my side when I filed the case. So much pain suffered in one lifetime from searching for his brother and now this grief from his own family. Where was the once strong voice of the man who warned me to be wary of the Wall Street law firms and their avarice, manipulation and greed?

"It is only money for them," Guy had said during our walk to the Lincoln Memorial. "Don't trust them. Keep them out in front of you at all times, where you can see them. Watch their behavior." These words still rung in my ears.

I learned later that his family had pressured Guy Von Dardel, to write a letter seeking to thank and to release me as his attorney, and to place all authority in the hands of Oswald's law firm. It did not work, but it temporarily stalled an excellent effort to force the release of his brother.

The strategy did not benefit Wallenberg. To delay the attachment of assets under the misguided plan of seeking greater penalties was a tactical error. Going for more financial damages might be an additional punishment to the Russians, but I thought it was the wrong tactic.

Judge Parker was outraged. He wanted to help Wallenberg before he retired. This was to be his *magnum opus*, his swan song, and his big case at the end of a brilliant career. He wanted desperately to help free Wallenberg.

A few months later, a very rare thing in judicial behavior occurred which I had never seen before or since. It was a judicial scandal. The Executive Branch's power to interfere and meddle with the vital independence of the judiciary was about to take place. In an unheard of procedure, with no lawful basis, Parker's monumental decision was taken or stolen from his calendar and shifted laterally to the docket of Judge Robinson. Robinson blew out the case, as if it had never been. He had no permission from Judge Parker to act in this unconscionable manner. I was never notified. A few months later I connected the dots.

President Reagan secretly elevated Robinson to Chief Judge for his "work" in destroying the Wallenberg verdict. Never before in the history of the Court had one judge taken a case from a judge of equal jurisdiction and destroyed it. What was our justice system coming to? I consulted with the Honorable Arlin M. Adams, a dear friend and federal appellate judge on the 3rd Circuit Court of Appeals. He reviewed the procedural facts with me and stated:

"In my 20 years as a federal appellate court judge, I have never witnessed this kind of judicial misbehavior. It's like a catbird stealing the eggs from another nest. I have never seen such a raw political maneuver. It violates the *Separation of Powers Clause* of our United States Constitution. I am certain that the State Department was involved. You had a valid final judgment as handed down by Judge Parker. Your case never went up on appeal. They accepted the default judgment. You should have been paid your judgment money of thirty-nine million dollars years ago. I will try to find out what happened. This is unorthodox behavior and may even be illegal activity by Judge Robinson. The Soviets failed to appeal in the 60 days allotted and the case was closed."

"It sat for four whole years on Judge Parker's closed docket. Then some time in 1989 someone without judicial authority arranged for it to be moved to Judge Robinson's active calendar. I can only imagine a political reason—not judicial. There was nothing to clean up, change or review. This is a scary precedent of judicial misbehavior. The judiciary must remain independent and its integrity preserved. If someone from the White House or State Department can finagle this kind of thing, then it shakes the very foundation of the separation of powers which underlies our democracy."

I felt frustrated and stymied. But at least I had received the input from a federal appellate judge. The Hon. Arlin M. Adams is one of the most respected federal judges in America. I spoke with him about the case as recently as February 22, 2011. He still holds the same views that he had back in 1965 when I worked with him as an associate at the Philadelphia law firm of Schnader, Harrison, Segal and Lewis.

Arlin has encouraged me to seek a reversal of Judge Robinson's illegal behavior by filing a petition with the United States Supreme Court seeking a reinstatement of the Parker decision, the collection of the 39 million dollars with interest, and the possibility of still rescuing Raoul Wallenberg from the Soviet gulag at this late date.

On March 23, 2011, I flew to California to consult with Supreme Court experts who are professors at Chapman University School of Law. I also met with a group of eager law students who are interested in drafting, writing, and filing this petition in concert with me as co-counsel. It would be tough from a political standpoint to get a hearing before the Supreme Court because John Roberts still sits as Chief Justice today, and he may be embarrassed by being reminded of the name Wallenberg.

It is interesting to note that Article III, Section 2 of the United States Constitution specifically provides that "Cases involving ambassadors, public ministers and consuls can be brought directly to The United States Supreme Court which shall have original jurisdiction over such matters." Wallenberg qualifies as an ambassador or public minister or both and thus, Wallenberg's case can still be heard directly by the US Supreme Court via petition with Chief Justice John C. Roberts presiding. This will provide Chief Justice Roberts with an opportunity to correct his earlier error.

Judge Parker had previously commended me for my work. In a phone call soon after the verdict: "Go and get your man," he said. "Come into my court and ask for the attachment of assets." Judge Parker was the only judge with the power to act. For just three days I permitted the family disloyalty to disturb me. Then I reminded myself that it was only Wallenberg who was my client and that I had made a promise to him in that room in the Shoreham Hotel to never quit the case. And furthermore Judge Parker had summarily rejected any effort to remove me from the case.

Parker in his brief opinion stated: "Morris Wolff has done all the work. Why should I dismiss him? I would never do that. He has shown the finest qualities of an advocate for a good cause. The request is rejected." Oswald's ill-conceived delay tactic of seeking additional money damages was simply a disguise for sabotaging the case. Oswald completely fooled Von Dardel. The rest of the Wallenberg family was delighted to simply stand by and do nothing.

Maybe Oswald was planted in my way at the beginning of the case when I first spoke of my plans to sue the Soviets at the NYU Law forum on December 11, 1983. Perhaps he climbed three flights of library steps just to begin the process of derailing the case. Piecing it all together now I wonder why he was so quick to volunteer on the first night. In Martindale Hubbell's book listing lawyers and their pertinent information, his mother's maiden name was Tolstoy. Was this a coincidence? Were there some existing undisclosed ties to Mother Russia from the very outset?

Oswald, in his moment of gross subordination, sold out the case for the benefit of his law firm and its major client the Chase Bank—the bank that gave his law firm three full rent free floors of space on Wall Street, and the bank that held the Soviet assets for its chief client the USSR. Chase Bank did not want those assets disturbed or diminished by any legal attachment of assets. Oswald had an unethical and obvious conflict of interest. He failed to reveal this conflict and step aside. He could not represent Chase Bank and assist me in the prosecution of the Wallenberg case at the same time. He had a major conflict of interest between representing Chase Bank and trying to represent Wallenberg.

Years later I found out from a key executive at the Chase Bank that the deal had been fully "wired." There was an actual effort to wipe out the Wallenberg district court decision in exchange for undisclosed Soviet political favors. It was an agreement reached between the US State Department, the White House, the Oswald law firm and its major client, the Chase Manhattan Bank. I later learned he had the temerity to file fraudulent papers suggesting that I had resigned from the case. Nothing could have been further from the truth. He had actually signed my name in a moment of forgery and submitted the document to the court. The joinder of the Oswald law firm, the Chase Bank, and key members of the White House working together to shake the foundations of an independent judiciary has bothered me and other scholars. This was an effort to corrupt the judiciary, the major protector of our fundamental freedoms. A constitutional crisis was almost precipitated. We lost our best chance for complete victory. Governmental pressure was applied, a terrible under handed deal was made, and Wallenberg was left to suffer further in prison.

I was deeply disappointed by the family's lack of support and ingratitude. Von Dardel had assured me that my interests and my family would be protected by his setting aside three hundred thousand dollars in his will to pay for all of the work that I had done. I had never demanded or even requested a fee. I had the pleasure and satisfaction of creating an historic law decision beneficial to their brother. The decision not only advanced the progression of human rights, it was also a positive lever to obtain Raoul's release. Was the evil branch of the family so ashamed of their behavior sitting on their hands for thirty-nine years that they wanted to kill the messenger of success?

Winter 1985
Florida

The case dragged on, stalled by Oswald's strategy of delay. I should have fired him.

Meanwhile, my personal life was deeply challenged. In my deep commitment to the case, I had neglected my family. I had allowed my relationship with my wife to deteriorate. In November of 1985, my wife Debby and I decided to divorce. We would go our separate ways while having joint custody of our children. I was living alone in a small apartment in nearby Mount Airy. I put my energy into my private law practice work. It all tasted like ashes. I was alone in a city where I had lived most of my adult life, bumping into friends on the street asking me, "How are you and Debby? How are your daughters getting on?" I felt ashamed to admit that the marriage had failed. I wanted to get away. I wanted to be in a new place and start over again.

Fortunately, that opportunity came to me the following month in the form of a friend who invited me to Palm Beach for the winter. After just a few weeks in Florida I was interviewed by *Florida Trends,* a magazine distributed across the state. They wrote about my work as an international lawyer, my work in foreign countries on business deals, and my fluency in three languages. They also wrote up the Wallenberg case. A few days after the article appeared, I received a phone call from Fred Harris, chairman of the Board of Directors and owner of the new World Trade Center of Fort Lauderdale. He asked me to consider serving as the new executive director of his World Trade Center. Honored and flattered, I accepted the offer.

In my capacity as executive director, I traveled to China to promote Florida and its new technology. I entered negotiations with the China National Ministry for Medical Equipment for the sale of Florida-based medical products to Chinese hospitals. Our most-in-demand product was a mobile medical unit with mammography and other new equipment to examine women in the work place.

My plan to rescue Wallenberg had to shift to a new level. I turned to the Israelis for help as Swedish diplomat Lars Berg had earlier suggested at the Chamberlain reception. Berg knew that the Israeli's were the only government willing to truly help rescue Wallenberg. I made a decision to go to Israel and to enlist the Mossad Intelligence Agency in a daring effort to enter Russia, find Wallenberg and bring him home. The original plan was to use helicopters to fly into the compound where Wallenberg was held hostage. Oswald's law firm continued to block my efforts to attach Soviet assets within the United States. Their ties to the Chase Manhattan Bank trumped their *pro bono* work on Wallenberg's behalf. The evil one, Marcus Wallenberg, who sold steel to the Nazis during the war, worked with the law firm to try without success to get me dismissed. I am still the attorney of record in the case and the only one appointed by the family.

I pondered also what other factors might be conspiring to hold Wallenberg prisoner. I kept recalling the meeting I had with Ehrlichman in March before I argued the case. What behind the scenes political factors with the Brezhnev Diamonds caused Nixon to back off? What similar pressures were being applied by the US government to cover up the Wallenberg case scandal this time?

Spring 1986
New York City

In the spring of 1986 the New York City chapter of the *Save Wallenberg Committee* hosted a black tie benefit dinner to help fund programs to educate school children about Wallenberg. I was happy to attend. The chapter was dedicated to preserving the positive memory of Raoul Wallenberg and his good deeds.

As I entered the Waldorf Astoria ballroom, however, I received a rude shock. There on the dais, next to Isaac Stern, was Henry Kissinger, now being honored as a spokesman for the cause of rescuing Wallenberg. While others may have been unaware of the irony, I was fuming at the hypocrisy of the situation. Kissinger's efforts were stymied by Nixon. I met with him after the dinner and he explained the whole story.

Kissinger: "I wanted to see Wallenberg freed. I did not realize that a secret CIA report had been handed to President Nixon indicating that Brezhnev was a thief. It was revealed to me later that Brezhnev had broken into the Wallenberg safe to steal the diamonds. At the time, in 1972, when the President met with Brezhnev there was nothing more I could do. Nixon was emphatic about never bringing up the Wallenberg question as long as Brezhnev was in power. My hands were tied."

The dinner did yield one pleasant surprise. I spotted Bruce Teicholz, whom I had met the previous month. Teicholz was a short, tough bull of a man in his early seventies. He had been a freedom fighter and valuable compatriot of Wallenberg in Budapest. Teicholz graciously offered me a seat at his table. Toward the end of the evening we agreed to meet again at his home in New York.

A few months later I returned to New York to talk with Bruce Teicholz. Traveling with me was John Guenther, a Pulitzer Prize winning investigative reporter for the *Philadelphia Inquirer*. I had invited John along to get Teicholz's story for his newspaper. As the train left Philadelphia's Center City we could see the young college students rowing their sleek craft up the Schuylkill River.

When we arrived at the Teicholz apartment at 57th and First Avenue, Teicholz answered the door.

"Come in," he said. "You are just in time for morning coffee."

"How did you come to know Wallenberg?" was my first question.

"I was born a Jew in Poland in 1912, the same year Wallenberg was born in Sweden. I too was in the import-export business with customers in Hungary. And like Wallenberg I had many occasions to visit and do business in Hungary before the war. I first fought the Nazis in Warsaw. I was just a teenager, but I was a young freedom fighter. The schools were closed. There was nothing else to do. Fight and be killed or just sit at home hiding and be killed. There were no other choices. We were surrounded. They choked off our food supply. We held out against the Nazis for 41 days and killed 550 of them with our few handguns and rifles, with our bare hands, with rocks, with shovels, anything we could get our hands on. We were the very first resistance."

He told us how he had entered Hungary in 1942, when the men he commanded on the Polish-Hungarian border were betrayed by anti-Semitic Polish underground fighters. He too, was captured by the Nazis, given a 20-minute trial, and condemned to death—but he escaped, digging his way out through a 35-foot tunnel. He hid out in the Carpathian Mountains and foraged for food. When he arrived in Budapest, later that same year, he helped form a Jewish underground resistance; 'soldiers' who smuggled Jews into Romania and built secret bunkers where Jews could survive. They also forged Christian baptismal certificates for these Jews, converting them instantly into *'marranos'*—overtly Christians, but still Jews at heart.

Teicholz' underground operations included the counterfeiting of documents and official papers from foreign countries, especially neutral ones. Of course, the value of the passes depended on how much the Hungarian and German authorities respected the neutral countries and their diplomats, so he preferred counterfeiting Swedish passports. Since Wallenberg was persuasive and respected, his passes were worth the most.

At first Wallenberg's focus was on saving those who could show 'significant business connections with Sweden' or had 'close members of the immediate family living in Sweden,' but only a handful could be saved with that approach. Teicholz convinced him the passes weren't fair. What about the poor and uneducated Jews, those without connections? To Wallenberg's credit, Teicholz told us, he was the first to admit that his passes were undemocratic. By the end of 1944 Wallenberg had improved the policy and redressed the basic inequality of the protective passes.

"How did you distribute the passes?" I asked.

"Very cleverly," he said. "I dressed my blond Jewish fighters in the green uniforms of the Hungarian Arrow Cross fascists. My bogus storm troopers then burst into the Jewish soup kitchens and raced up and down along side the rough wooden tables, thrusting passes into the hands of every diner who wanted one. They quickly handed passes to poor Jews who had never done business with Sweden, never traveled outside of Budapest, and even those who did not know where Stockholm was."

Teicholz went on to describe how he and Wallenberg strategized every week. They would meet each Wednesday morning at Gerbaud's Coffeehouse just off Veresmarty Square. It was an elegant setting. Waiters in black tie balanced pots of coffee on silver trays. Stout blonde ladies in starched aprons rolled pastry carts of strudel and poppy seed buns and cream cakes between tables. Until March of 1944 Budapest's Christian aristocracy and the Jewish merchant class had jammed these tables at midmorning to conclude deals, make plans for the evening, and enjoy the coffee and sweets.

Teicholz was a gracious host. The warmth of his apartment and the aroma of coffee and pastries he was serving made me feel at home.

"Quite a different life here now, wouldn't you say?" asked Teicholz. He lifted the silver pot of coffee and refilled our mugs. Teicholz had been the major underground partner of Wallenberg during his sojourn in Budapest. After the war he wanted to forget. In New York he had lived without fanfare or interviews, intent only on starting a new life. He had turned his brain and ambition and his 15-hour workdays to buying real estate in midtown Manhattan, quietly becoming a wealthy man. Teicholz died a few years ago. We were friends up until the time of his passing.

Teicholz continued his story.

He said Wallenberg's code word was *"Glick,"* the Yiddish word for luck. When he wanted to contact Wallenberg, to coordinate a safe passage of Jews through the underground, he would call his secretary Judith Yaron and let her know 'Glick' would move 20 people that night. And whenever Wallenberg needed Teicholz, a messenger would arrive at his cellar hiding place on the small street behind the main synagogue, near the trolley central station. The messenger always had brief handwritten notes from Raoul. He would say, *'Hagysholoam* main train station at 7 A.M. They are shipping fish tomorrow. They are going out at daylight. The fish stink.' That was Teicholz's cue to either come and kill the Arrow Cross soldiers or to bomb the railroad tracks.

According to Teicholz, Wallenberg got his information on 'fish shipments' directly from the Iron Cross soldiers themselves. He simply bribed them, paying them in US dollars. He had over $150,000 in cash—American dollars—in his safe, along with millions in gold, diamonds, rubies and emeralds. These jewels and lots of valuable antique jewelry were given to him at the last minute by Jews boarding trains for the death camps. So he could trade in money or gold.

The Nazis and the Hungarian Arrow Cross never figured out who the guerillas were. Most of Teicholz's fighters were very young, in their teens. They later migrated to Israel after the War and became members of the *Irgun*—the early Israeli terrorists who bombed out the King David Hotel, killing the British officers and persuading the British to get out of Palestine just before Israel became a state in 1948. Teicholz told me he had trained those men. They were his team.

"Wallenberg was my best friend," Teicholz said. "These were the best moments of my life. He walked with us, but sometimes I think his feet didn't even touch the ground. He just glided through each day. He moved so quietly with no huzzah that you didn't even know he was there. He would simply do the next thing, and move on. I hope somehow you find him. I believe he may still be alive. He used his wits and he definitely wanted to live."

Teicholz thanked us for the visit. We shook hands at the door, and he walked us to the elevator. I miss this man terribly. He and Tom Veres became the stalwart supporters of my case and were steadfast the whole way. They were my "life pillars" as I went through the twenty-seven years of rescue efforts in the courts and even thereafter.

Hungarian Jewish photographer Thomas Veres, (right) standing in the doorway of his camera shop and photo studio in Budapest.

Thomas Veres (1923-2002), Hungarian Jewish photographer who during the final months of the German occupation of Budapest in World War II, served as the official photographer of Swedish diplomatic rescuer, Raoul Wallenberg.

Hungarian Jews who were rescued from deportation by Raoul Wallenberg at the railroad station in the Jozsefstadt on November 28, 1944, walk along a street in Budapest on their way back to the 'international ghetto'. This photo (below) was taken by Thomas Veres from Wallenberg's car as they drove past the group.

Hungarian Jews and non-Jews walk along the Jozsef Korut [Ring] in Budapest. Many are holding shopping baskets.

Photographer Thomas Veres claimed in the 1990s that this image depicts Jews who were rescued from deportation by Raoul Wallenberg on their way back to the ghetto, but none are wearing the yellow star and many carry shopping baskets and appear to be waiting in line to enter a public market.

[Probably, elderly Jews being transferred to the newly formed central ghetto in Budapest.] On November 13, 1944 the Arrow Cross ordered the establishment of a ghetto, and by December 2 most of Budapest's unprotected Jewish population had been moved within its borders.

A crowd of Jews waits outside a branch of the Swiss legation located in the Glass House on Vadasz Street hoping to obtain Schutzbriefe that would protect them from deportation. Carl Lutz took the photograph from an upstairs window of the Glass House. Charles (Carl) Lutz (1895-1975), the Swiss Vice Consul in Budapest who is credited with saving more than 62,000 Jews who were living in Budapest between 1942 and 1945.

Raoul Wallenberg is present at the Jozsefvaros train station in Budapest where Jews who have been rounded-up for deportation, wait on the platform. Wallenberg stands on the right with his hands clasped. On one side of him is an officer of the Hungarian Arrow Cross, named Lullay; on the other side is a Jew holding a Swedish Schutzpass [protective pass].

Police attempt to control the crowd of Jews, who are waiting outside a branch of the Swiss legation located in the Glass House on Vadasz Street hoping to obtain Schutzbriefe that would protect them from deportation. In the foreground is the car used by Vice Consul Carl Lutz.

Jews await deportation at the Jozsefvaros train station in Budapest. The man in the black hat and coat in the center in the background may be Raoul Wallenberg.

Budapest Jews waiting in front of the Swedish legation main office in hopes of obtaining Swedish passes.

Monument to Raoul Wallenberg. The Communist government the night before its scheduled unveiling in Budapest's Szent Istvan removed the monument, consisting of a sculpture on a tall pedestal park. It was later reinstalled at a pharmaceutical factory in Debrecen, without the inscription referring to Wallenberg. The sculpture is the work of Imre Vargo. The portrait in the base of the monument was done by Paul Patzay after a photograph by Thomas Veres.

Part III: A New Front

Whatever Happened to Raoul Wallenberg?

1989

Switzerland & France

I won the lawsuit for Wallenberg on October 18, 1985. I won on each and every point; liability of the Russians for his kidnapping, complete jurisdiction of the matter taken by Judge Parker, and $39 million in punitive money damages. I truly believed that the Russians would surrender, put up a white flag, and release Wallenberg back to his family. I was preparing to go to Moscow for that purpose, and to bring him home. After all he was my client. Little did I know what evil losers the Russians could be. They turned out to be evil; they drew into their web of evil our own State Department and the previously distinguished law firm of Baker & McKenzie, a law firm apparently willing to do anything for money. The lawsuit was a major victory and did advance the cause of human rights. Since that time, in over one hundred and forty three cases lawyers have cited my Wallenberg case when prosecuting foreign nations engaged in torture and abuse. Before my lawsuit, suing a foreign enemy in a US court was virtually unheard of.

Winning was unbelievable. Would the verdict stick? Would we collect a judgment and receive thirty nine million dollars. Would Wallenberg be released and enjoy a sweet, mellow freedom again? Tragically, enforcement of the judgment was stymied. The State Department hired the American law firm of Baker and McKenzie to not only kill the judgment but to kill the case as well. That effort cost US taxpayers two hundred thousand dollars in misappropriated legal fees paid in effect, to keep Wallenberg in prison. My efforts to enforce the judgment and attach Soviet bank assets came to a halt. Our US government, which had hired and paid Wallenberg, actually filed a "Statement of Interest" with the US Federal District Court opposing the case. That was the cruelest cut of all. How ironic it was to set up a hero and then not only abandon him but make sure that he remains deep sixed for the balance of his life. It was a scandal. The US government, at the request of the Russians, moved to kill my case. Here's what happened.

Judge Parker, for health reasons, retired. The pain in his legs, which I had observed in person at the hearing in court in July of 1985 became too much to bear.

I wrote him a personal note of thanks and he wrote back: "Keep fighting. Don't let the bastards get you down. You will eventually bring Wallenberg to his home in Sweden, where he can sit alone by the birch trees and a lake and contemplate in peace his great achievements."

While still seeking relief in federal court, I decided to pursue Wallenberg's release from the Gulag through other means. I enlisted the Mossad in Israel on a dangerous rescue mission. I knew the head of the Mossad from my days of working for General Moshe Dayan in Israel in the summer of 1963. Both of our careers advanced over the next twenty-two years in separate countries. I was reintroduced to him in 1985 in Israel by my friend Mordecai Virshubsky, an important swing member of the Knesset. I presented my request in person to Moshe Dayan: "Please intervene with the Mossad. Ask them to help find our man and bring him home. Use the Entebbe strategy to go in, get him and get out."

The court case remained dormant on Judge Parker's docket for a period of four years. Then it mysteriously appeared up on Judge Aubrey Robinson's docket. Amazing and miraculous how the case developed a renewed life! It was as if Wallenberg's own energy was still driving the case. Judge Aubrey Robinson, my former colleague from Public Defender days in The District of Columbia somehow was awarded the case and received it on his docket.

Wow, what a strange coincidence, from Parker to Robinson. From the best judge to the worst. Was this a coincidence?

Robinson was a known wheeler-dealer with no international law knowledge or decent experience. He had no genuine feel for jurisdiction or for human rights. He was up for sale and the price he demanded was the chief judge-ship of the US District Federal Courts for the District of Columbia. His "flexibility" was obvious in his handling of the *Korean Airlines* case. The plane had strayed into USSR territory, was shot down by negligence of the Russians and reckless behavior of the Koreans in flying close to Soviet air space. The Soviets went alongside the commercial flight, saw it was commercial and still shot it down summarily—no chance to land anywhere. It was a commercial civilian plane with no military aspect to it. Robinson refused to allow any compensation to US citizen victims. There were no death action claim recoveries for any of the surviving US families who sued in federal district court. Liability was clear, but he turned a deaf ear. Here was a man willing to reward sovereign misbehavior of the Soviet Union over the needs of US widows and orphans.

Our State department knew he was just the right unfeeling foreign government oriented man to "blow out" the Parker decision of the Wallenberg case, four full years after it had been properly decided!

I remembered Robinson's bravado antics as a flashy and ambitious politico of limited intelligence. His apple polishing tactics were obvious even in the modest confines of the Public Defender's office. What was he doing on the federal district court? How did he get there? Whose ass had he kissed for his appointment? New and stranger developments were yet to unfold.

In 1989, the US State Department, which had originally pledged itself to Wallenberg's protection in Budapest and safe return after the War, filed a highly unusual and damaging "Statement of Interest" against the case, asking for dismissal, alleging a so-called "lack of jurisdiction." I was amazed. That issue was litigated and decided four years ago and never appealed. Jurisdiction had already been clearly and decisively considered on the record and decided in our favor by Judge Parker in 1985. Nothing had changed since that time. There were no new facts. Time for Appeal had expired. This was not even an appeal. It was an illegal effort to re-open the case at the same level—an effort to second guess Parker's decision.

The so-called "Statement of Interest" was bought and paid for out of its New York Chase bank account by the Russians. It was filed by Eugene Theroux of the Washington law firm Baker and McKenzie, one of the largest international law firms in the world. This was a strange, behind the scenes development. I called Mr. Theroux and had lunch with him at a classy white table clothed restaurant directly across the street from his 806 Connecticut Avenue, DC law office. Once lunch was over I asked him:

"What are you doing bringing this law case four years after a final decision? Who hired you? What was their reason? Who stirred up the hornets' nest? And specifically what have you been asked to do?"

Theroux was polite but close to the chest cryptic:

"We're hired guns. The client pays in advance. I then go to court. The merits don't matter! Our law firm handles many different matters, even the effort by some White Russians to recover principal and interest on Russian government bonds dating back to the Tsar Alexander in 1917; bonds purchased in good faith by Russian and foreign investors prior to World War One. We have offices all over the World. We work on a fee basis. I earn over $500,000 a year. I work for money. I am just a hired gun." That was his cryptic answer.

In 2007, still curious about Theroux's cryptic answer, and why and how his firm was enlisted to oppose my case—four years late—I called and invited him to be my guest for lunch. He accepted. We dined at the same restaurant. By this time I had a prestigious position, which he respected. I had been appointed by Congressman Lee Hamilton to be a Senior Policy Analyst with the Woodrow Wilson International Center for Scholars. My job involved doing research for this book. I was given two brilliant research assistants—both fluent in Russian—to help me write my book on the Wallenberg lawsuit and to analyze secret KGB documents in an effort to find out what the Russian prison system had done with Raoul Wallenberg. Documents we uncovered showed Wallenberg to be still alive. One document written in Russian actually discussed his status and concluded:

"It would be extremely foolish to release Wallenberg at this time or at any time in the near future. Such an action would be a propaganda disaster since the prisoner Wallenberg would undoubtedly tell everything he has learned about Russian prison conditions, and be offered a lecture tour for this purpose."

At the lunch Theroux brought a beautiful leather bound volume that contained the full record of the case. I was able to leaf through and read my original complaint dated February 2, 1984, and some very damaging documents including a letter from the Soviet Minister of Justice asking our State Department to find a US law firm to re-open the case. There was also a letter from the State Department to Judge Robinson asking him to take the case from Parker's closed calendar and re-open it. Unheard of behavior and interference was recorded in the volume. Then followed the cryptic opinion of Judge Robinson "blowing out" my victory opinion. The volume was well organized. It included the docket entries, including the date when my complaint was served on the Soviets on May 1, 1984 by diplomatic pouch of the US State Department. Then followed the Soviet refusal to answer, and a strange note written in Russian and in English asking the US State Department to argue the case against me on the Soviet's behalf and to claim sovereign immunity. Nowhere was there any suggestion that Wallenberg was not held captive.

The volume also contained the infamous State Department Statement of Interest supporting the Russians signed by Abe Sofaer, the Jewish Legal Adviser, whose family ironically had been rescued by Wallenberg.

Two weeks after he gifted me with the bound volume I received a call from Theroux's secretary. "Mr. Theroux wants to lunch with you again. Please bring the bound volume. He will give you an exact duplicate. He wants to keep the original in our library."

I should not have listened. I had already told him at our first meeting that I was writing a book on the Wallenberg case. He now promised to give me a full copy of the papers but wanted the hardbound first copy back. Naively, I agreed to meet for lunch and then go to his office afterwards across the street for the exchange of documents. It was a trap. When I innocently offered him the hardbound copy, as a gentleman, for the soft cloth copy three of his partners appeared in the conference room and demanded that I leave. One grabbed me by the arm and shoved me towards the door, supported by the other two. Theroux refused to keep his promise. In forty-four years of law practice I have never had anything similar happen to me. Fortunately, I had already made a full copy of my own.

In April 1989, the National Council of Christians and Jews presented me with its annual human rights award. The notation read: "For 25 years of dedication and work for human rights in the drafting of the Civil Rights Act of 1964 and for skilled efforts on behalf of Raoul Wallenberg." It felt good. I was being honored by other people and humbled not only by being selected, but because the other recipient on the podium with me that day was none other than Rosa Parks. She said very little as she sat there next to me but in the few words she did share I could sense her grit and determination. I could just imagine her determination that day in 1955 when she told the bus driver, "I ain't moving. My feet are tired."

A few months later at the historic 17th century Old Swedes Church in Philadelphia, the city hosted a dinner for the opening of a photographic exhibit of Raoul Wallenberg. I donated some of the photos given me by Tom Veres that appear in the pages of this book. The exhibit extolled and honored the achievements of Raoul and his heroic feats in Budapest. As an invited speaker, I talked briefly about the lawsuit—its high points and low points, including the shabby and backstabbing treatment the State Department was giving it. I would not let up. Every chance given I called on my own government to account for its two faced behavior.

Wallenberg's sister, Nina Lagergren, who was there to cut the ribbon for the exhibit, conspicuously avoided talking with me, although she had been peaches and cream when I first filed the lawsuit. For some reason, she was cold and downright rude. I had publicly questioned why the Wallenberg family had sat on their hands and not been more outspoken during the thirty-nine lean years between his capture and my lawsuit. I specifically questioned why her husband Nils Lagergren, an esteemed member of the International Court of Justice at The Hague had not used his substantial judicial clout and been pro-active in seeking Wallenberg's release through his Russian colleagues on the court. She refused to sit next to me at her designated place at the table of honor. The master of ceremonies at the dinner was my friend Judge William C. "Bill" Lederer of the Philadelphia Common Pleas Court. He sat next to me and fumed:

"That woman tried to have you deleted and removed as our keynote speaker tonight! And that is after you helped me and other Philadelphians put this exhibit together. You are our advocate for Wallenberg. You are our connection to Raoul Wallenberg here in Philadelphia."

When he got up to introduce me Bill Lederer recounted:

"My esteemed friend, Morris Wolff, honors us by being here this evening as our keynote speaker. Morris became Chief Assistant District Attorney of Philadelphia in January of 1965 and headed up the Family Court Division. It was not enough for Morris to prosecute. He wanted to rehabilitate. With his interest in the needs of children, he and his devoted wife Debby, a teacher of history at the Overbrook High School, started the innovative Take-A Brother Program, a volunteer effort matching 150 exemplary high school boys with kids in trouble with the law. Morris was not paid for this work. He did it as a labor of love just as he has done the Wallenberg litigation. He is an extraordinary public servant. Morris was a volunteer, working on weekends with delinquent kids referred to his program by the court. That program won the 1968 White House Points of Light Award for volunteer initiatives. My brother, Chief of County Detectives, Franny Lederer, and the staff at the DA's office in May of 1965, as a surprise wedding gift arranged for Morris and his bride, Debby, to have the honeymoon bridal suite at the Holiday Inn at 13th and Walnut as a gift from the DA's office. Morris Wolff is a brave lawyer and a good man. He is Philadelphia's contribution to the Wallenberg case. It gives me pleasure to introduce to you the Philadelphia lawyer with the guts to sue the Soviets for Raoul Wallenberg and to win the case in court." There was a wonderful standing ovation from my hometown crowd and I thanked Bill Lederer. Words of praise and moments like this one make all the quiet hours of research and hard work well worth it.

The rest of the dinner went smoothly. I got up, went to the podium, and made some brief remarks about Wallenberg and his bravery, and our continuing effort to rescue him despite the temporary setback in court. I thanked Bill for his gracious introduction and the support of his family and others present.

In June, I left for Switzerland to teach a course in international law at the American College of Switzerland in Leysin. I looked forward to a relaxing summer. There was one unresolved piece of business I needed to handle. Guy Von Dardel was continuing his quiet work at Vevey, Switzerland as a scientist at CERN (The Center for Nuclear Research). He had worked there since we filed the lawsuit. I needed to know if he really knew about the Swedish government's effort to run me off the case, and the mysterious lateral shift of the case to Robinson's calendar. It was time to clear up the hijacking of the case, and the efforts to shove me aside. I thought a quiet walk, and an outdoors lunch by the lake might help.

I arrived at the gates of the Research Center; Guy came down to meet me at the security guard's office. He noticed my reaction to the high level of security.

"This place has a military, top secret feel to it," he said, as we walked toward his office, "but I am a pacifist. All of my work is for the use of nuclear energy for peace."

He smiled at me, his quick impish grin that I had come to know in our days together in Washington, DC in 1984 when I filed the case in court. I had not seen Guy since then.

Guy showed me into his office. After a few pleasantries, I pushed to the heart of the matter.

"What happened to your faithful support, and your promise to see this thing through to the bitter end? Why did you, of all people, quit, give up and go south on me just at the moment when we had full victory in sight? We were near the summit and the case suddenly disappeared."

I watched him closely. Body English is important in quiet moments. He could not look me in the eye. I stared at him for a few minutes. There was just a very awkward silence and I stared out the window at the white swans swimming placidly on the lake, beneath the white-capped mountains beyond. I waited. Silence. He fiddled with his gold pocket watch and looked down at his hands. He cleared his throat a few times. His hands shook. He was afraid to speak. He looked up at me with sad apologetic eyes.

I continued: "Some strong political pressure must have been applied to you Guy by the Swedish government. I have heard that a deal was made behind my back at both the White House and the State Department to appease the Russians by killing my lawsuit. There was an exchange of scientific information from space missions and an agreement to limit the number of missiles. I understand other things of value like nuclear missile information and Star Wars data was exchanged as a price for killing the case. Were you privy to any of that?"

He took a long draw on his un-filtered cigarette, which he had placed in a silver cigarette holder. I had never seen him smoke before. Perhaps this was his nervous habit in times of stress. I watched his performance, but I kept my eyes on his face—a lawyer in cross-examination. He frowned and looked away, avoiding my constant stare. He sighed and looked out the window.

"I don't know the full story," he said. "All I know is that just after your victory in court I was severely chastised by the banking arm of the family. They own the *Enskilda Bank* and the Soviet Treasury is a major client. Our family bank has cordial and very strong relations with the Chase Manhattan Bank in New York. When you started speaking about attaching assets at the Chase Bank they simply went ballistic. They pressured me to try to force you off the case and I at first, adamantly refused. I said no way—this man has helped us!"

"I begged them. I told them you were our only hope for Raoul's freedom, and they laughed at me. They threatened me with the loss of my job here in Switzerland. They have long arms and international power. They said it was the bank; something about the close relationship of our family bank with the Chase Manhattan."

"They warned me not to ever write or call or contact you in any manner as our legal counsel. They tried to put me in a doghouse. They said that the international banking community, including our family *Enskilda Bank*, was embarrassed and frightened by your plan to attach Soviet accounts in the New York Chase bank. That bank happens to be the *Enskilda's* major banking partner in the United States. Banks are strange creatures. It is as if they run themselves without a conscience and interfere in human rights and politics. Then they— Oswald and his law firm—forged papers saying you wanted to withdraw. Why would they ever consider presenting such an idea? I know of your passion for bringing Raoul home to us and I thank you for it. Then Oswald made a special trip to Sweden. He tried to force me to sign papers saying that I wanted you to withdraw. I told him I would die before signing such documents. I learned later that he forged my name to a document and submitted it to the federal court in Washington, DC."

What followed was a moment of silence as I stared at Von Dardel in disbelief. I replied, "My God! They went so far as to forge my name."

"So that's it. That explains everything. You were threatened. You were not allowed to speak for yourself. You were frightened by your own family. The greed factor has dominated everything. Follow the money. Oswald's law firm does all the Chase Bank's dirty work—they even have free rent from them for three floors of offices in the choicest building in Manhattan. They're all in bed— *Enskilda Bank*, Chase Bank and Oswald's law firm. No different than when the 'neutral' *Enskilda Bank* funded the Nazis purchase of Swedish steel. The Nazis and *Enskilda* were chummy and in bed together getting rich during World War II."

Guy sat silently looking out on Lake Geneva and the white sails of the graceful white sailboats sliding silently by in the early morning sunlight. Guy answered:

"They actually forged my name on a letter asking you to resign. I was fighting for you not to resign. I am glad you refused to resign. You are the lawyer I appointed, and no one else. Period. These other people do not have my brother's best interest at heart. Please continue to serve Raoul. That is the important thing. There is no quit in you. Thank God."

Von Dardel walked over to his desk, took out a sheaf of letters that his brother had mailed to him during his term of service in Hungary. "I want you to have these letters Morris, as a reminder of my brother and your tenacity. I also want you to know that in my will, I have made provisions for you to be paid for all of the work you have done in helping to resurrect my brother's good name. When I die, I will instruct my daughter to be sure that you are paid. You have served beyond the call of duty, even though you took the case *pro bono*. I want at least two hundred thousand dollars to go to your children from my estate."

He took a white handkerchief from his pocket and blew his nose. "Those bastards. They said I would be fired and never again work for CERN or anyone else."

I had planned to stay for lunch but I felt empty and sick to my stomach. I wanted to be alone; to absorb this terrible confirmation of what I had long suspected, but had somehow hoped was not true. Behind my back, the bad Wallenberg branch of the family had sold steel to the Nazis, financed loans to the Nazi government, and failed to bribe the Russians for Raoul's release. Then by extending their arms across the water they conspired with the Russians and our State Department to file "A Statement of Interest." Raoul Wallenberg was no longer of any importance to any of them. He was simply a forgotten chess piece— a pawn or a knight—no longer in play.

Von Dardel had been shoved aside by powerful influences including the US government, the government of Sweden and the mercantile section of the Wallenberg family. I headed my car out the gravel driveway of the CERN and started driving back to the American College of Switzerland at Leysin. The snowcapped mountains seemed to cradle my rocking self as I drove home singing "Climb Every Mountain" and "Happy Talk" from South Pacific, and other songs from "The Sound of Music."

The feeling of anguish, anger, disappointment and frustration stayed with me long after my visit creating for me a dark undertone to my teaching sojourn in the beauty of the Swiss countryside. I thought of all the work I had done to create the legal arguments for holding the Russians liable, fashioning new theories of jurisdiction, winning a verdict that most of my colleagues said was impossible, and creating new human rights law to hold nations accountable for criminal misbehavior involving innocent diplomats.

Yet, I could not let the anger win. I was determined to take a new and different tack. I started to push the envelope in a new direction. I wanted to secure Wallenberg's freedom, but it had to be by efforts akin to terrorism rather than through the law courts. My best legal efforts so far had not borne real fruit. Other ideas began to take shape. Reports had filtered to me through certain valued contacts in Washington that Wallenberg was alive and being held in a comfortable dacha—a high wall surrounding a Château—45 minutes outside Moscow.

I planned to track down the reality underlying these reports. After my teaching stint was completed I took a trip to France to visit my friend Professor Robert Malfait in Saint-Remy de Provence in the south of France—the place where Van Gogh painted his wild and beautiful "Starry Night."

Driving from Geneva to Aix-en-Provence, I saw a road sign that read, "Avignon - 3.5 km." The words from the song I had learned as a child came flooding back: *Sur le pont d'Avignon, on y danse, on y danse...*(On the bridge at Avignon, we are dancing, we are dancing). I wanted to see the famous half-bridge and have lunch. I was so close; I simply had to visit and perhaps even dance on this world famous 12th century stone bridge.

I drove to the parking area, got out and walked up onto the remains of the Avignon bridge jutting out halfway across the Saone River. A group of teenage college girls were on the bridge singing and dancing. One tall and beautiful raven-haired girl wore a blue sweatshirt with "Brandeis" written in bold white letters.

"Do you study at Brandeis?" I asked.

"Yes, I do. I am a happy Political Science major." She giggled and swept back the hair from her face.

"And as you can see," she pirouetted, "I am quite obviously a college student," she giggled, "and what do you do kind and inquisitive sir?"

She was very beautiful. A brunette version of Julia Roberts, brown eyes sparkling, white teeth, a playful and teasing young lady. We fell into a flirtatious conversation.

"I just speak a bunch of languages and practice law in broken English. I used to work in Switzerland, in Geneva. I was president of the AIESEC exchange program. This summer I am a college professor. I teach international law and things like that," I replied.

"Is there really an international law that governs mankind?" the girl asked. "Or is it all politics and power struggle. How can you have an international law when you can't enforce it? I think there is international politics, but there is no law."

"Funny you should mention that," I answered. "I was just thinking and wondering about the very same thing. Maybe there is no international law, just mayhem, anarchy, international political power and dirty politics."

"But, you have to believe in the possibility that one day there will actually be an enforceable international law or else you would just give up what you are doing, right?"

"Well, I hope to create some enforceable international law. There is a need for a basic enforceable international human rights law."

"How do you get there?"

"By bringing test cases in court. By getting students like you willing to go to law school and do *pro bono* work. And then by drawing attention to the inhuman treatment of others by bringing specific cases and testing the waters in court."

She replied: "I plan to go to law school. My aunt in Israel is a lawyer. She bugs me to become one, too. What kind of cases do you bring?"

I replied: "Right now I have a case involving a Swedish diplomat who is in prison in Russia after rescuing the Jews of Budapest during World War II. I sued the Soviets for his release and I won the lawsuit. But we are still working on getting him released."

There was a silence and the girl in the blue Brandeis sweatshirt narrowed her eyes at me.

"Did you say Swedish diplomat? Budapest? And from World War II?"

"Yes."

"Are you speaking of Raoul Wallenberg?"

"Yes, how did you know?"

The girl took a breath.

"Wallenberg is a very real part of my family. My family is Jewish from Budapest. We survived the war. My aunt, Judith Yaron, was his private secretary in Budapest. She was just 19, but as soon as she met Mr. Wallenberg she devoted her life to his work. She worshipped him. She typed all his letters from the Swedish Embassy in Budapest. She taught him all the Jewish holidays and got him to go to synagogue in Budapest on Rosh Hashanah. She was his eyes and ears in the streets of Budapest. She translated for him. She told him when the Arrow Cross troopers were coming. She was madly in love with him. She worshipped the ground he walked on."

"Yes, I know of your aunt, I said. "I had heard of her from a radio talk show caller a few years ago in Philadelphia."

"Is she still alive?" I asked. The coincidence of our meeting on the bridge took my breath away. Judith Yaron was not someone who had come forward as a survivor during the course of the litigation, much as I hoped it might happen as word of the case spread around the world. Teicholz must have known her and Harry Spitz. I had met them in New York and Arizona. They worked in the Wallenberg office.

"Yes, alive and well."

"My aunt also deeply believes that Raoul is still alive. She still feels deeply connected to him."

"Where does she live?"

"Israel."

"Can I meet her?"

"I can try to arrange it. I'll call her and ask if she'll receive you."

"Let's call her now!" We made the phone call from a phone booth, calling collect.

Three days later I was on a plane flying from Geneva to Tel Aviv.

My mission: Meet first with the beautiful Judith Yaron. And then after that? Meet with the Mossad and plan a rescue of Raoul Wallenberg

July 1989

Israel – Part I

Could Judith Yaron help me find the answers to some of the questions I had about Wallenberg? I wanted to know what he was like as a human being. Was he short tempered? Did he get angry? Did he have a good sense of humor? Was he kind and gentle with other people? Did he focus just on the big picture? Or was he interested in the "little man" as well? Judith was an experienced lawyer. She was well connected. Could she introduce me to her contacts at Mossad? She had been a curvaceous and attractive spy in Budapest; was she possibly now a patriotic spy for Mossad?

This was the summer of 1989. Twenty-six years earlier, in the year 1963, I was privileged to work for the Ministry of Agriculture in Tel Aviv as a water resources attorney. As a gift to a visiting American law student, they placed my office next door to Israel's war hero General Moshe Dayan. I worked that summer as an international lawyer with Mordecai Virshubski, the Water Law Advisor who was later elected to the Knesset. Dayan was a brave general. He was "parked" temporarily at the Ministry of Agriculture between wars. Four years after my tour of duty in 1963, Dayan saved Israel from extinction by leading his troops to decisive victory in the 1967 Six-Day War with Egypt, Jordan and Syria. When I returned in July of 1989, my first priority was to meet with Dayan and to persuade him to lead a rescue mission of Wallenberg. I had learned a lot about Israel and its intelligence service from Dayan. Maybe there was a way for me to reach Israeli intelligence through Dayan and to persuade them to do a rescue mission of Wallenberg.

But even before meeting Dayan, I had to first meet the curvaceous Judith, and learn more about her love life with Raoul, and how she "tamed him," according to her niece. My brief dance "sur le pont d'Avignon" had a good ending. I wanted to know more about Wallenberg as a human being. Was he kind to her? Was he basically considerate and loving of other people? Or did he have that arrogant "noblesse oblige," that imperious quality of other members of the family.

I had heard from Esther Weiss on the Frank Ford show: "He is a kind and gentle man, but can throw a temper fit when people fail to do their work."

Was he a spy, doing double duty? Was it more than just saving Jews? Was he acting for the American government on a separate agenda as a secret agent?

On the plane from Geneva to Tel Aviv I sat next to Avril Stein, a Hungarian survivor who ran a catering business in Ranana, a suburb populated by Hungarian and Romanian Jews near Tel Aviv. When she heard I was coming to search for Wallenberg survivors, she immediately took over my plans.

"You will stay at my home. You're not going to a hotel. You are family my dear." Her eyes twinkled and her 5'2" body quivered. "I will bring the survivors to you. It will be a great honor for me to have you stay with my family, and for my children to learn about your Wallenberg work. I can drive you wherever you want to go. And feed you too," she said with a twinkle in her eye. "I am a good cook—the best in Ranana!"

And I did stay with her and her three sons and two daughters, enjoying their hospitality in Ranana for an entire month, in lieu of staying at a hotel, as I had planned. Ranana was a new town built for refugees. In fact, there were so many Jewish survivors from Budapest living there that the town was nicknamed "Wallenberg City." It was a mix of "old refugees" from the Holocaust—Hungary, Germany and France—and the "new refugees" fleeing the new threats and pogroms and upheavals in South Africa, Ethiopia and Russia.

Avril, even following a double mastectomy, had incredible energy. She was a human dynamo, always on the move, always a new idea on how to meet survivors. We drove everywhere during the day, including Masada and the Dead Sea, visiting and interviewing many survivors personally saved by, as she put it: "your friend Mr. Wallenberg." We were busy from sun up to sun down. Her pace wore me out.

I called Judith Yaron. When she answered, her voice was tender and sensuous. I understood immediately why her niece had emphasized to me that her aunt was sexy and seductive. She sounded like a velvet-voiced Marlene Dietrich with an Eartha Kitt purring overtone.

"Meet me at the public swimming pool," she purred. "I go there every day. It is on top of the tallest building at the seaside in Tel Aviv. You cannot miss it. I will see you there tomorrow at ten. I will be wearing a one-piece yellow bathing suit, with dark brown hair and sunglasses. My Rita Hayworth look!" She laughed at herself.

The next morning I drove to the tallest and most modern building on the seaside. It was easy to spot. Waiting for me next to the swimming pool on the roof was a statuesque and stunningly beautiful brunette in a one-piece yellow bathing suit. Her brown hair was pulled back with a scarf. She was a body double of Rita Hayworth, my favorite movie star!

"Miss Judith Yaron?" I asked, with a smile.

"Yes, one and the same" she answered, extending her hand and pulling me down towards the chaise lounge chair next to hers. She lowered her sunglasses and stared at me. Beautiful blue eyes hid beneath the protective shades. At 62, she was still attractive with an excellent figure. When she took the scarf down, her brown hair fell to shoulder length. She looked like a blend of Jane Russell in "The Outlaw" and Rita Hayworth in "Gilda." She pulled her chair closer to mine and rested her hand on my arm.

Whatever Happened to Raoul Wallenberg?

"Now tell me," she whispered. "What is a nice Jewish boy like you doing getting involved and wrapped up in a mystery like this? You could get hurt you know. Especially if you step on the wrong toes or push the wrong buttons. This is no game for neophytes."

"It is my mission plain and simple. I've been on this trail for five years. I am obsessed with finding Raoul."

We chatted about family for a while, and then moved to a table near the pool. She brought with her an old brown, worn-out leather attaché case with papers in it.

"I haven't discussed my beloved Raoul with anyone in many years," she said. "I had to bury him psychologically for my own sanity—put him away, out of my memory. And yet on many nights I can still hear his voice. He says, 'Rescue me. Find me, Judith. I am here. I am still alive.' It torments me."

She looked at me. Her body tensed with the recollection. I was astonished.

I shared with her the time when I saw his face in the mirror in the room at the Shoreham Hotel. "I also feel he is alive. I have moments when I actually sense his presence with me, prodding me to do more!"

"That means for me that he is alive," she said. "I know he is alive. We must find him." She began to cry. She collected herself and continued. "I have kept some special mementos that he shared with me," she said. She snapped open the combination lock of the attaché case. Two blue-and-yellow dog-eared Swedish passports fell out on the glass table, along with a small pile of papers. *Shutzpassen.*

"These were the last two Swedish passports he made. His loyal driver, Vilmos Langfelder, came to get him at our office on the last morning we shared together—the morning of January 17, 1945. People think he went to see the Russians voluntarily, that he simply took a car trip 80 miles north to Debrecen. It is not true. He was 'escorted' and brusquely taken there against his will. He knew he was not coming back, but he went like a courageous hero. He did not want to alarm any of us, so he just said, in an offhand way, 'I am going for awhile. I'll be back soon.' He knew better. He was no dummy. He knew the stakes were high and that he was at great risk. Brezhnev was in Debrecen. Brezhnev knew that Wallenberg could not be left loose to report things like rape which the Russian soldiers had already done to Jewish women in the ghetto."

Judith and I spent several happy hours together beside the pool. She spoke and I listened. Her stories were simple stories, anecdotes of courage. I received a glimpse into the human side of the man I was seeking to rescue.

Judith stretched out on the chaise lounge:

"Raoul and I would smoke and drink gin and tonics together after hours at the office. It was his way to relax. He was a shy and gentle man. All day long he would keep up this stern face for the public—the mask: a persona of the fearless leader making plans and taking steps to save the Jews. But after the last applicant had gone home, he was able to relax, even laugh and become playful, or sometimes very sad. He was a great mimic, a great actor. He would impersonate different people who had come to the office that day. He loved to impersonate Eichmann and Churchill. I laughed when he 'performed' Eichmann pacing the floor of our headquarters, stiff legs and arms shooting out, and with the beast threatening him: 'No more passports; no more protecting these Jews. They are mine.' Raoul could perfectly mimic Eichmann's ugly accent and his menacing ways. Somehow the laughter and the poking fun—it made it bearable. He kept us all laughing somehow, right in the middle of our serious work."

She told me of a young couple who were about to be married. Their name was Behrend. Wallenberg's office had actually arranged for their passage out of Hungary by train for Sweden. They were rich Jews; their parents were merchants. They owned a textile company. They could pay extra. The extra was passed through to the Hungarian Arrow Cross as cash bribes to guarantee safe passage. They were scheduled to leave in the first week of December, while the Nazis still controlled Budapest; just three weeks before the Russians came. They never made it. Signals were crossed up. The bribe money did not get paid into the right hands. Someone simply stole it. The Nazis dragged the members of the family from their home in a little town seven miles from Budapest, burned the home—valuable paintings, tapestries—took their jewels, and shot them in the town square. They never used the passports. Judith told me she still kept the passports, "as a memory."

"Raoul made everyone believe in the value of the fake Swedish passports, and the importance of appearing to be Swedish citizens in order to achieve survival for the Jews. He could persuade the Jews, and the Hungarians, and Germans. He was a super salesman wherever his passion for saving human life was involved."

"I helped him to get "*shutzpassen*" passports into the hands of families. I knew Budapest well, like the back of my hand. I knew the streets and the secret passages between houses."

Judith and Raoul created 'stories' that saved families. And the 'story' would often change to fit the circumstance. Such as "Christianize" the names to avoid suspicion. Both the Arrow Cross of Hungary, and the German Gestapo were very document oriented, and would usually accept the documents at face value. If the documents were not persuasive, then bribe money made up the difference.

By noon the heat by the swimming pool in Tel Aviv was becoming intense and we took a break from the stories to swim in the pool. I got in the blue water and swam up next to her.

"What was he like to be with—what was he like as a person?" I asked her, when we were drying off.

"That we will save for tomorrow," she said.

The next day we convened at the same time and she answered my question of the day before.

"He was patient most of the time," she said. "But he had a temper too, especially when someone messed up a passport or failed to deliver documents. He knew that each day counted, that each day another train of boxcars left the station for the death camps. 'Every death is my failure,' he would say. He tortured himself, as if he could single-handedly stop what was happening around him."

"Raoul confronted the Nazi leadership. On one occasion he 'ordered' Eichmann to appear at his office. Amazingly, Eichmann came. He closed the doors of the office and clicked the golden brass heavy lock."

"'Herr Eichmann,' he barked. 'The killings must stop. The train rides to death camps will stop. Walking men into the Danube River with a bullet in the back of their heads must stop. If you do not stop now, then I will testify in person at your war crimes trial in front of the American and British Tribunal. That tribunal has already been formed.' I watched the confrontation as they were nose to nose, just three inches away by this time. Wallenberg continued his harangue. 'Herr Eichmann, plans are being made in London as we speak to convene a special war crimes tribunal. This war is virtually over for you Nazis. The Russians are advancing from the east. You have no more than two weeks left in Budapest.'"

"As his private secretary, I was the only one present during the delivery of this ultimatum. It worked! The killings stopped. The train rides stopped. The death marches stopped. The shootings in the head of men tied together at night to float down the Danube before morning—it all stopped."

I told Judith: "I often have had a strange feeling that Wallenberg was constantly with me as I was writing the complaint. This image of a 'no-nonsense get it done now or else' Raoul Wallenberg is quintessential in my feelings of respect and admiration for him. These are his qualities that I have emulated and modeled in my own life for my own habits. Copying his behavior has made me a happy man. I have very strong feelings and memories of him. When I worked at my desk at home in Chestnut Hill there were times I could feel him leaning over my shoulder in the evening directing me in the drafting of the brief—choosing and deleting words with his own pen."

"What about your personal relationship to him?" I asked.

"If you mean were we 'special', the answer is yes. He tried to avoid it— said we have no time for this, we must stay with our program to save the Jews. It took time. We both could see it coming. One night he simply came over and put his arms around my neck as I was working at my desk. Everyone else was gone. He leaned down and kissed my cheek and I took his hand—held it to my cheek. He simply said, "Let's go home. We did and we were lovers every day after that first night together. It was an immediate attraction for me—love at first sight. He was a handsome man, very refined and cultured. He spoke well, with a large vocabulary. He gave instructions in a kind and decent fashion. No one was too small or unimportant. Everyone was his equal or his superior. He looked down on no one. His door was always open to anyone who wanted to see him. It was only closed when the Jews came to entrust him with their diamonds, rubies, emeralds, and other jewels. He put them meticulously in the large office safe, and he gave each family an itemized receipt. 'They will be here for you when you return to Budapest,' he assured them. 'No one will touch them.' And no one did touch them until Brezhnev and the 18th Red Army broke into the office in late January of 1945 and stole the diamonds and the jewels."

I was amazed. Ehrlichman was right about Brezhnev. Judith squared the circle and confirmed the daylight heist of jewels that financed Brezhnev's rise to the top of the heap—Premier of the Soviet Union, financed by the Wallenberg diamonds.

Judith continued: "In the midst of the hubbub and with people constantly swirling around him Wallenberg was ironically a very lonely man. He had many acquaintances, but only one or two friends—Teicholz and Spitz, whom he saved from the Danube. Wallenberg began to come to my family home on the Danube for Sunday dinner. He enjoyed listening to classical music" Beethoven, Brahms, Mozart—all the music of the cultured Germans. He loved Viennese waltzes. Sometimes he would even get up and we would dance spontaneously, or he would take me by the hand and waltz gently around the living room. He was an excellent dancer."

"My parents loved him, approved of him, and admired the work he was doing."

"He was no spy. His work was simple. Save the Jews and go home. He never received a chance to return to his home."

"Wallenberg and I worked closely together, day in day out. I opened the office, the first to come and the last to leave. Raoul would scold me, 'Go home. Get out. It is late, and well past your bedtime. Your parents will worry.'"

"I can take care of myself," I told him.

She showed me an old photograph of the two of them together, sitting on a blanket in a park.

"We fell in love. It was maybe an accident, maybe a necessity. We had no intentions, it just happened. Sometimes when he dictated a letter, or a memo for the office staff, he would say to me, 'You know, Judith, just what I want to say. Just write it and say it in my words.' I could do that. It got easier and easier."

"Did Raoul have other women? Did he use his charm to work his way into the political structure? Did he have an affair with the influential Baroness Kameny?" I was eager to know and wanted to put it as diplomatically as possible.

She replied: "It is possible. I was never sure. He used Baroness Kameny to help save the Jews. Beyond that I do not know. The Baroness was very caring for the plight of the Jews. She worked against the Iron Cross regime, and against Hitler. She did not like the sadistic bullying and brutality of the Nazis. 'They are heathens,' she once said to me. She was daring. She actually hid Jewish families in the basement of her home for many months."

"The Baron was shot by a firing squad soon after the war ended but the Baroness Kameny was able to escape. We do not know where she may be. Maybe America? I have heard that, but it may just be a rumor. The Baroness had been born Elizabeth Fuchs, of Jewish descent and had worked for a Jewish book company before the Nazi takeover of Hungary. Raoul went to see the baroness on many occasions. Her husband, Baron Gabor Kemeny, was the Foreign Minister, the second in command. Raoul persuaded both the baron and baroness to side with his cause. The baroness helped to hide Jews. The baron was later tried as a war criminal by the new Hungarian government and shot before a firing squad soon after the end of the war in 1945. That was another injustice," Judith said.

She opened a brown leather book; its cover embossed in gold and the words "Diary-1944" were written in gold letters. She read to me from the August 1944 entries in her diary, the first and only time, so far as I know, that she had let another person "see" her diary.

"On August 3, 1944, Raoul met with Lieutenant Ferenczy, the chief of the Hungarian gendarmes and the man who helped Eichmann arrange the deportation to death of the provincial Jews, those in the districts outside Budapest."

She paused from her reading, diverted by more stories she wanted to share with me. "During his meetings with Ferenczy and Horthy, and also with the Hungarian Arrow Cross police," Judith told me "Raoul exploited their fears that they would be tried as war criminals. He threatened them with trials and pretended that he had the authority to grant exemptions. He acted like the Pope granting absolution. He completely outfoxed them. He acted as if the war was over and he was the victor's Hungarian representative. He exploited the uncertainty, the double and triple loyalties of the Hungarian officials during that period. He was so confident and energetic; his manner so intimidating that when he first strode into the office of the Jewish Counsel, its members took him to be a senior Gestapo officer."

"By the middle of August," according to Judith, "Raoul had succeeded in transforming his protective passes into respected legal documents. The Hungarian Ministry gave him permission to distribute 4500 passes on condition that the holders renounce their Hungarian citizenship and acquire the status of Swedish citizens visiting Budapest on a temporary basis. They had to report 'as Swedes' each week to the government agency in charge of supervising aliens. He also went to the Germans and persuaded them to honor the passes. The Germans had a reflexive respect for any official looking document, and the passes were a cheap way of satisfying their conscience."

"To distribute the passes, Raoul created his own organization within the Swedish legation, Section C. Within less than a month after his arrival, he hired me along with a Jewish staff of 40 and divided it into sections responsible for reception, registration, archives, correspondence, housing, and transport. I was his personal assistant. I kept his schedule and screened his appointments. I was in charge of all written correspondence, and accepted responsibilities as assigned by him."

"Raoul expanded his operations into houses bordering the legation, procured a fleet of automobiles from wealthy Jews anxious to have them under Swedish protection, and organized an equitable system for distributing the passes. He borrowed chairs, purchased desks and file cabinets, had three telephone lines installed and printed thousands of application forms for passports at a time when allied bombs were disrupting Budapest's normal commercial life. At one point, the original office staff of 40 grew to be 400, as he expanded his offices to five other outposts within Budapest."

I told Judith that Raoul had financed his extensive rescue operations with money entrusted to him by wealthy Jews and Jewish organizations in Budapest, as well as $100,000 paid by the US government before he left Stockholm. I told her how after the war approximately half of the $100,000 was returned to the War Refugee Board in the United States. We adjourned for another day.

Judith said, "We will meet again tomorrow: same place and same time. I will make a picnic. I will include some *frikadella* and a few special things Raoul loved."

She gathered her things and walked towards the changing room – tall and elegant. She must have once been quite the beauty. She still was.

We were lucky in the weather for our picnic together. The humidity had disappeared. It was another blue sky summer day by the sea in Tel Aviv.

"I brought you something special I made at home. It's called *frikadella,* a Swedish delicacy that Raoul loved." She opened a clear plastic container.

"They look like gefilte fish," I said.

"These are made of ground meat."

She took out a red and white checkered table cloth and laid it over the glass table top, setting up for our morning picnic.

We ate silently, looking out at the sea and the wind surfers bobbing in the waves, their red, orange and yellow sails filled with sunlight. After we finished eating she took out a handful of letters from her leather attaché case. She sorted them out on the table in chronological order. They were copies of the letters Raoul wrote to his mother. Judith had saved them.

I lifted the first letter from the table. It had turned tan to brown, and was weathered by years of safekeeping. The words were still legible and in good condition.

Whatever Happened to Raoul Wallenberg?

The small blue typewriter print was clear:

Dear Mother,

I have just spent the most interesting three weeks of my life. Everywhere you see tragedies of the greatest proportions. But the days and nights are so full of work that one seldom has time to react. I have set up a large office with forty employees. We rented houses on either side of the Legation and the organization grows every day. I will try to write more often.

> *My love to Nina and to Guy.*
> *Your son,*
> *Raoul Wallenberg*

"He always signed his full name even to his mother. He didn't write to her often enough," Judith said. She showed me other letters. There was one to the US War Refugee Board, written in September, 1944. "The Nazis and the Russians knew about the letters," Judith said. "Even though they were sent by diplomatic pouch, they were often opened anyway." It was a strange arrangement; Raoul writing to a foreign government. No doubt this caused suspicion.

The letter read:

The Honorable Iver Olsen
American War Refugee Board
Stockholm, Sweden

Dear Mr. Olsen,

When I look back on the three months I have spent here I can only say that it has been a most interesting experience and I believe, not without results. When I arrived, the situation of the Jews was very bad indeed. The development of military events and a natural psychological reaction among the Hungarian people have changed many things. We at the Swedish Legation, have been an instrument to convert this outside influence into action in the various government offices. I have taken quite a strong line in this respect, although, of course, I have had to keep within the limits assigned to me as a neutral. It has been my object all the time to try to help all Jews. This, however, could only be achieved by helping a whole group of Jews to get rid of their stars. I have worked on the

190

hypothesis that those who were no longer under the obligation to wear the star would help their fellow sufferers.

Also I have carried out a great deal of 'enlightenment' work among the key men in charge of the Hungarian government's "Jewish extermination program" here. I am sure that our activity is responsible for the freeing of many endangered Jews.

Mr. Olsen, believe me, your donation on behalf of the Hungarian Jews has done an enormous amount of good. I think they will have every reason to thank you for having initiated the Jewish action in the way you have in such a splendid manner.

/ S/ Raoul Wallenberg
Secretary of the Swedish Legation

"One day Raoul literally danced into the office and swept me up in his arms. He was glowing with pride, talking about how he had accomplished something the wealthy Wallenbergs had denied him. He was saying that he had proven himself worthy of the family name. The day before when he had gone to the train station, the train was already moving. He had stopped the train dead in its tracks. He had gotten everyone off, bribed the guards and saved 300 people. It was the high moment of his work in Budapest. That morning he fulfilled himself."

Judith and I walked to the edge of the retaining wall by the pool and looked down on the Mediterranean Sea. The beach was filled with people, many of whom had survived the Holocaust, or were children of survivors.

"Raoul cared deeply for the Jewish people of Budapest. 'It is my duty and my mission to save each one of them. That is why I go to the train station to bribe the Arrow Cross guards.' He read the Talmud with me. He kept an English version in his desk. And on his desk, for all to see, as a motto were the lines from the Talmud:

'He who saves one life, saves the world.'

"The Jews, for their part, cared deeply for Raoul. On the eve of Rosh Hashanah, one of the two holiest days of the year, celebrated by the Jews, I dragged Raoul from his desk to the synagogue."

"I told him: 'The Jewish families need to see you tonight in the synagogue; they want you to pray with them. You will allay their fears by being there. Rosh Hashanah is a very important night.' At the synagogue, as Raoul walked down the aisle to find a seat near the front, the people touched his suit with their prayer books, kissing the books after they had touched him. And where he

191

walked there was the last ray of sunshine coming through the stain glass window and showering him with light. It was like Jesus had come to the synagogue."

As an observant Jew, I knew what reverence this was. Such action is normally reserved for touching the Holy Book of the Torah as it is carried down the aisle. But here people were honoring the "savior" Raoul Wallenberg in the same way.

Judith told me how Raoul struggled with the issue of choosing whom to save, knowing it could not be everyone, how he might walk the streets at night, looking at the homes, wondering who would be spared and who would not. One day he simply told Judith that he would leave it to God.

At two o'clock, on our third day, after we had been talking and reading letters for four hours, Judith finally rose to leave.

"You remind me of Raoul," she said. "Same determination, same drive, same dry sense of humor, and the same curiosity about life and people." She got up to leave and to gather her papers. She turned and looked back at me and smiled. "Tomorrow we will take a drive up to Haifa. I want to show you the spot where Raoul first saw the poor Jews of Europe getting off the boats with their burlap bags of family possessions. They were given one rotten bag for all they held dear."

The next morning Judith Yaron arrived at Avril Stein's house in Ranana just after 9:30 in a brand-new royal blue Ford Escort. She had more papers.

"Here, you drive," she said, handing me the keys. "I can read some things to you as we drive up the coast."

We took the shore road, driving along the edge of the Mediterranean on a narrow two-lane highway.

When we reached Netanya, the seaside homes got larger. The jacaranda trees in bloom, red and violet bougainvillea spilling over the walls. "Some rich Hungarian Jews live there," Judith told me. "Some who got out just before the war and others who bought their way out in the last days of the war, making special deals with the Nazis and the Hungarian Arrow Cross."

Many of the people who received the Swedish passports during the summer and early autumn of 1944 belonged to Budapest's wealthiest and most prominent Jewish families, those most likely to have friends abroad who did business transactions with Sweden.

The entire Manfred Weiss family—some thirty-nine persons—was permitted to leave Hungary, staying for a month in Vienna, then continuing on to Lisbon. The Weiss cement factory was simply handed over to the Gestapo for payment of $400,000 for twenty-five years. Judith pointed out their house in Netanya and said: "At least they had the brains to get out and not hold on to their property, their business in Budapest. They would have died running the cement factory at the estate."

Many of those whom Raoul chose to be his closest aides were also members of this Jewish business elite like Manfred Weiss. Hugo Wohl, for example, was one of Raoul's most trusted aides. Wohl had been the director of the large and dominant Orion Radio Company. Men like Wohl had the training and experience necessary to administer the huge relief organization Raoul was creating.

"Wohl escaped three days after Raoul was captured. He knew Raoul was not coming back at the moment he left," Judith said. "I can just feel it," he told her. "There is something terribly wrong."

Judith took up again the topic of Raoul's tough task of distributing the passports in a fair manner. He did everything to make the allocation fair and to maximize the effect of the available 4500 passes. He limited each family to a single pass. He insisted that each pass be allocated on a first-come, first-serve basis. No one could move a friend or relative to the top of the pile of applications. He dismissed two aides he suspected of accepting bribes to process applications out of order and made a report to the Swedish Ministry.

I thought also of Bruce Teicholz and his report on working with Raoul to insure fairness in the distribution of passes.

"But the long lines outside the Legation were so heartbreaking that Raoul could not resist breaking his own rules from time to time," Judith told me. "At the end of one day he emerged from the Minerva Street office, one of the several Section C offices, for a breath of air to find a young mother collapsed against the metal fence of the Legation sobbing. She held a baby in her one arm; a small boy stood next to her silently. As Raoul comforted her she explained that the line was so long she was afraid she would not get to the front before the curfew. She had been coming every day for a week. Raoul told her to wait. Fifteen minutes later he returned and handed her a pass."

"I often wondered what happened to the little boy," Judith said. "Two years ago I received a letter, with a postmark—Toronto, Canada. The mother had remembered me. She had learned I moved here to Israel after the war. I was on a Canadian Broadcasting System of Canada Public Radio program about Raoul. She heard my voice and remembered me. She recalled that I was with Raoul when he gave her the pass. These two photos came with the letter. This is the little boy. He has a family of his own now. That is his wife, his mother, and his sister."

I was sorry that I had not met Judith earlier. She would have been excellent at my side during the Congressional hearings. She was a showstopper. Members of Congress would have listened to her and passed any resolution she requested!

We stopped at Netanya, which Judith claimed was the best beach in all of Israel and Judith insisted we swim, a command not hard to comply with. Her company was so bright and gay, so filled with laughter and positive energy— always.

Later we returned to a more sober matter. She had recovered a special letter to show me from her scrapbooks. She opened a pink envelope and took out a handwritten letter—dark blue ink on matching pink paper.

"This letter is precious to me. It is from a friend who worked in our humanitarian section."

August; 1944. Budapest, Hungary

Dear Judith,

Remember me. I leave in the morning to save Jews elsewhere. I will not be here long. Raoul gave us courage. He was so courageous that he made the rest of us ashamed to be afraid. Because of him we all became more optimistic. He also shocked us by his relaxed and easy manner. He was a man who didn't believe we Jews were vile and despicable. He socialized with us. He reminded us there was nothing wrong with whom we are, no matter what the Nazis in the street were saying. This I found to be amazing.

After a while it became impossible for us to consider him to be a normal human being. We didn't ask ourselves the normal objective questions about his background. In fact, we didn't even know that he was a member of the famous Wallenberg family. Instead we came to see him as super human; someone who had come to Budapest to save us, our Messiah."

Hanna Elbert

Judith carefully folded the letter and put it back in the envelope. Tears welled up in her eyes. She continued: "Hanna Elbert was my best friend in the office. She died in front of a firing squad for refusing sex with a Nazi officer. We shared so much together—so much laughter and so many tears. She was shot in front of my eyes in the last week of the war. Her family had their protective passport; they were scheduled to leave for Sweden. But she volunteered to go back into the office to help two families get the passports that Raoul had prepared. As she came out the door that morning she was grabbed by two Arrow Cross storm troopers. They took her away thinking they had a "fish;" a rich Jew who would command a large reward as ransom bait. We could not find where they had taken her. When there was no money, they decided to rape her. She fought furiously, kicking one officer to death with her pointed shoes. Her family was frantic. The husband would have paid anything. But the ransom demand never could be delivered. The next morning her body was discovered with the bullets from the firing squad. She was floating in the Danube, tied with ropes at the wrist to two other Jewish women, also from wealthy families. They never found the two soldiers. They just disappeared into the woodwork, back into the army and were reassigned out of Budapest to avoid a scandal. Killing innocent women in the streets of Budapest was no longer tolerated near the end of the war. What a terrible waste."

We sat down together in the warm noonday sun. We ate our picnic lunch, setting up a blue and yellow tablecloth on the beach. Later we drove to Haifa, the site, as Judith had told me, where Raoul had first seen Jews getting off the refugee ships with burlap bags on their backs containing the family possessions. This sight first seen by Wallenberg in 1936 inspired him to help the Jews.

The last story Judith told me was about Raoul's birthday. In her diary she had noted that he was now 32 years old—young in life but old in wisdom and the ways of the world. "At times when he is tired he looks 50," she wrote. "For his birthday the staff chipped in and purchased for him a new tie and a light blue shirt to match the dark blue suit he wore. And also a brand new prayer shawl with blue braids and a yellow Star of David, and a yarmulke or skull cap for his head. He had become through his compassion an honorary Jew."

She showed me an old photograph, brown now with years of touching and holding on the edges.

"This is how I want to always remember him - the day of his birthday, surrounded by friends and members of the Jewish Counsel who loved and revered him. Most of us would have done anything he asked, knowing it was always decent, always aimed towards saving lives. We revered the ground he walked on—this decent, humble, warm and wonderful man. In the face of derision and humiliation—people spitting on us and reviling us as less than animals—he gave us all dignity. He made us feel human. He restored to us a sense of self-respect."

Judith put away her personal remembrances; her memories, her diary, her letters, and her links to Wallenberg.

"Let's take a walk," she said. This ended my visit with Judith but not my friendship, nor my fond memories. She transferred her love for Raoul Wallenberg over to me and she told me so.

"You are the new warrior." she said. "You must carry the torch in the night, and find the terrible cell of loneliness in which Wallenberg is hidden and bring him home to me, to be loved and cared for in his final days."

We stayed in touch by letter and met during my subsequent visits to Israel. She died in 2009. I still think of Judith. I fell head over heels in love with her, just as my hero once did. But mine was platonic. It was a different kind of love. She was much older, yet we were on the same wavelength. A different time. A different place. And yet the same close connection of the heart.

July 1989
Israel – Part II

I journeyed to Israel to learn more about Wallenberg and to listen to the poignant stories of people he had saved. I also came in order to help the Mossad prepare a daring rescue effort. We all worked together at headquarters to prepare the mission. I wanted him released and rescued. It was almost an obsession. We developed a methodical and careful rescue plan. Moshe Landau would help me develop the argument defending our mission to Russia.

As Chief Judge of the Israeli Supreme Court, Landau had created the theory of universal jurisdiction. This theory gave Israel the legal power to prosecute Adolf Eichmann and put him to death in 1961. Landau, at 6'4" was a "tall drink of water," while his little wife Leah stood only five feet tall. She was the guardian of his time, and she brusquely let us know that. We would only have an hour, she decreed. The hour expanded to three and a half, though, and I stayed for lunch.

"I knew Wallenberg very well as a close friend. We met soon after he started working in Haifa in 1936," said Landau, smiling at the memories. "He worked at the Hapoalim Bank learning money and credit financing of big ship deals. He became an expert in international finance and import-export laws and practice. He loved horse-trading and negotiations."

"Working in the Haifa Bank was a training program for him. He was preparing to re-enter Sweden and to work in the family's *Enskilda Bank*. But he soon discovered the evil practices of the family bank and was repulsed. They were up to their armpits financing the Nazi war movement in the 1930s, just when Raoul and I met here on the docks of Haifa."

"That bank, and the Wallenberg family, did evil things. They funded the sale of Swedish steel to the Nazis. Raoul was the idealistic exception. He would not support evil. He had no sense of greed."

"He cursed his uncles, burned his bridges and went to Budapest because he was disgusted with their Nazi sympathies. Now, that same powerful *Enskilda Bank* finances oil operations in Saudi Arabia, and works closely with financing countries that boycott Israel."

Landau told me: "Raoul had a great humanitarian drive. He loved adventure and being center stage. He liked having people looking up above the foot lights to find him. He had a keen sense of the dramatic and a flair for acting. It led him into trouble in Hungary, especially his trying to tell Soviet soldiers what to do near to the end of his stay."

Landau told me how he and Raoul would walk over to the docks in Haifa sometimes and watch the ships off loading the bedraggled Jewish refugees. One day they watched the homeless Jews get off the boats and wearily walk up the steep gangplanks, hunched over with overloaded burlap bags on their backs—their life's possessions in one large satchel. Raoul saw firsthand the suffering of the Jews, and he knew from his grandfather's letters that they were being displaced from Europe. According to Landau, Raoul decided then and there that he would work to rescue the Jews if the opportunity ever presented itself. He found his calling in his savior like mission to Hungary.

Leah came in and looked at her watch.

"It's time for your nap," she said.

"Just a minute," said the Judge. "Morris, I want you to come back and see me tomorrow. I want to give you a book I wrote, as presiding Justice, on the Eichmann trial. I can also introduce you to some very special Hungarian survivors. I also will put you in touch with the top operative at the Mossad."

I promised to return on the following day. When I called to confirm I was told that Justice Landau was sick. He suggested we re-schedule for August 5th, when all of Israel celebrated Raoul Wallenberg's birthday.

Before I met with Landau again, I was fortunate enough to meet with two others who had known Wallenberg. The first was Abraham Schifrin, the top ranking Jew in Stalin's pre-war and post-war cabinet. Stalin used Jews for their brains and discarded them to the labor camps when they challenged his opinions. As Solzenitzyn makes clear in his book *The First Circle*, this often led to short political careers, and long prison terms of twenty years, while being constantly shifted between rural prison camps and city prisons.

After World War II, Schifrin, serving as Stalin's Defense Minister, became the USSR's top ranking Jew. Then he was quickly purged. He spent years in the gulag.

The tan sandstone edifice of the Jerusalem Hilton sits prominently on a hill near Mount Scopus. A circular drive on dark pavement stones leads to the front door where a liveried doorman opened our car door. I recognized Schifrin from the description given to us. He was unusually tall for a Russian Jew, and he reeked of cigarettes. He was well dressed in a blue shirt and a brown three-piece suit with a gold watch fob across his vest. He spoke five languages, including French, Chinese, Russian and German. "And some Polish," he added, as we sat down on the tan leather couch under a crystal chandelier in the lobby. His gray hair was combed back, and he had a habit of running his left hand through his hair unconsciously as he became animated and nervous during our conversation.

Schifrin carefully looked around the lobby as he spoke, as if searching out the corners of the room. He reached under the long black marble coffee table in front of the couch, scrambling his fingers along the under surface, feeling for bugs.

"It's clean. No one is listening. We can talk here."

"When were you first sent to the camps?" I asked.

Whatever Happened to Raoul Wallenberg?

"It was in May of 1947. I had been elevated to the status of a general, but Stalin was bent on purging the military of all Jews. I was the highest ranking Jew in the whole Army. Stalin was nervous and insecure about my loyalty. He wanted to smear me, make an example of me. I had done nothing wrong. I became the showcase Jew for punishment. Just ship him out. Put a chill in the Jewish population of Moscow not to want to leave for Israel."

"The Iron Curtain was already in place. Russia had pulled Latvia, Lithuania, and Estonia back into their circle of influence. My job was to make sure that these three fiercely independent peoples' republics remained as part of the Union of Soviet Socialist Republics. I was detailed to Tailin in Estonia. From there I had command of the Russian security forces, to make sure that the peasants in the three enslaved Baltic Republics didn't revolt."

He shifted one knee onto the tan sofa, took several puffs of a cigarette, and exhaled. "It turns out I was sent there to get me out of the struggle for political power in the Politburo. It seems I was making too many controversial suggestions at Politburo meetings regarding expansion to the East. So while I was out there on assignment, Molotov and Beria persuaded Stalin that I was a troublemaker and an 'enemy of the state.' I went from high-ranking officer to prisoner in an instant. I was exiled to the labor camps, first to Mordvinia, a favorite place where Stalin parked political prisoners in internal exile. Later I was sent to the bitter cold of Siberia, at Wrangel Island in the Arctic Circle. It was there that I met Raoul Wallenberg."

"How much did you see of him there?" I asked.

"We would talk together during exercise period, when he would lead the men in push-ups, sit-ups and stretching exercises that remind me now of yoga. We actually became good friends. He had guts and humor and stayed in shape. He built a sauna at the camp and had the men rolling in the snow and hooting, and then going into a sweat lodge to warm up. We had great heated discussions in the lodge about how to stay alive and beat the system. Wallenberg was an inspiration and a leader even in those terrible conditions. We were there from 1947 to 1962. He was very healthy and in good spirits when I left. We shook hands on my final morning and said goodbye. His last words to me were, 'I will meet you on the other side.' I never knew what that meant, whether he meant here on earth or later on upstairs. When I was released, I received an exit visa stamped "*Jew*," in big bold black letters. It was as if I were permanently marked as a Jew and not as a Russian military hero. I received a one-way air ticket to Israel and about $500 worth of rubles to begin a new life. And here I am, happy to be in Israel."

"You know he wasn't only keeping the Jews safe," Schifrin said.
"What do you mean?" I asked.
"He was also keeping their precious jewelry safe for their return."
"Yes, I know that."

"Yes," he said, "but here is something you may not know."

Abraham Schifrin told me the story of exactly how the jewels entrusted to Wallenberg were stolen.

"I went to Raoul Wallenberg's office with Leonid Brezhnev, my 18th Red Army Commanding officer. Leonid Brezhnev was the greediest booty hunter of the Soviet 18th Red Army. We could hear Soviet tanks and troops approaching just outside of Wallenberg's office, which had been locked shut before our arrival. Brezhnev located Wallenberg's safe, and then drew the shades."

Brezhnev told Schifrin that a Jewish informant had advised him of the cache of diamonds, and other valuable jewels in the safe; jewels they could sell, now that Wallenberg was out of the way.

Brezhnev took a sledgehammer and swung it repeatedly at the safe until it opened. The safe indeed was filled with gems, the ones the Jews had entrusted to Wallenberg for safekeeping. As Schifrin watched, Brezhnev opened his coat and scooped up the gems into secret pockets on the inside lining of his jacket.

I had previously learned of Brezhnev's thievery from Judith Yaron, and from John Ehrlichman, the assistant to President Nixon, and from Abraham Teicholz. All three men verified the 'theft of the diamonds' report which later played a major role in US politics and Nixon's inability to demand the release of Wallenberg once he knew Brezhnev had stolen the Wallenberg diamonds. This was the fourth confirmation of an amazing and scandalous international story, nailing the Premier for theft and grand larceny. Shifrin's account was shocking. Now, face to face with the witness to the crime, I was chilled anew—struck by the egregious unfairness of it all. I shook my head in disgust.

"This pig stuffed his pockets with the precious jewels of the fleeing Jewish families of Budapest. I couldn't believe how beautiful they looked. I'm sure they came in very handy over the years. There's a lot of influence that kind of wealth can buy."

Schifrin stood up and looked around the lobby again. "The big nations of Sweden, the USA and Russia haven't managed to free Wallenberg. He simply disappeared, and things went on without him. In a way that is comfortable for them. Then you come along and upset the apple cart by raising the whole issue in their face again. You are asking 'What has happened to Wallenberg? What have you done with him? Only one country can possibly care—Israel, where the people he saved reside.'" Schifrin looked at me intensely. "You must work with the Mossad," he said. "They have many Russian nationals working in their program. Some of these people may have met Wallenberg. Some might have an idea of a concrete action that could be taken. And all are probably just itching to poke a finger in the eyes of the Russian Bear."

I thanked Schifrin and left the Hilton. I felt stimulated by the meeting. It not only helped me get to know Wallenberg better, but gave me renewed hope that Wallenberg had the incredible strength, humor and perseverance needed to survive the gulag. I prayed he could hold on until he could be freed.

The next day I met another Russian Jew with a different, more adversarial sort of contact with Wallenberg. Not everyone who survived was his admirer or friend.

In the summer of 1962 I was privileged to work in Israel as an assistant to Moshe Dayan, the famous Israeli General, but serving between wars as the Minister of Agriculture. At the time I rented a room at 22 Hanarkiseem Street in Ramat Gan, a small suburb of Tel Aviv. The owner was Zehava Vompinsky. She had been deserted two years earlier, she said, by her husband Isaac, a doctor who left Israel for New York's Bellevue Hospital, where the pay was better.

Now back in Israel in the summer of 1989, I sought out Mrs. Vompinsky. We had dinner together and I told her about my Wallenberg work. She told me an amazing story about her nephew, a man who had known Wallenberg as perhaps no other Jew had ever known him—as his Russian interrogator.

Zehava said, "My nephew, David, arrived on my doorstep from Russia several months earlier. He told me he had been forced to join the KGB as a Jewish interrogator of Wallenberg, along with another Jew—Yacov Walinski." The Russians had played this cruel trick on Wallenberg—the rescuer of the Jews—to try to intimidate him. Now her nephew had been purged from the KGB and permitted to leave for Israel, along with many other Jews.

When I arrived this time in 1989, sitting next to Zehava on a blue painted wooden chair I met her nephew, an athletic bald headed gentleman in his sixties. The heat and humidity of the day had subsided, but the air was still warm. On the table next to him was a notebook filled with photos. Next to it was pink lemonade in a glass, with droplets on the glass still perspiring.

She introduced us and I sat down.

"Tell the story, David," she said. "You have nothing to hide and nothing now to be ashamed of. You were doing what the authorities ordered you to do. That's all."

David Vompinsky looked at me for a moment, and then began:

"It was 1945. I lived in Moscow, a Jew in the wrong place. I was fluent in Russian, Hebrew, Swedish and English. I was just 22 at the time. I'd never done anything like this. I signed up with the KGB and was assigned to watch Jewish dissidents. For my first assignment I was ordered to interrogate a new prisoner. At first I did not know he was famous or that he had helped the Jews in Budapest. At first he said nothing, just mumbled, 'I don't belong here.' He stonewalled me. He wouldn't even say hello; no words. He was grilled for up to 20 hours a day during the first week. He was known as 'prisoner 7'. This went on for days. At first, he just sat like in a catatonic trance. He only repeated his name and title,

Raoul Wallenberg, Secretary of the Swedish Legation. Then he confronted me. 'I want to know why I am being held,' he said. 'I want to know if you plan to charge me with any crime or plan to let me go.' He was smart. He knew they wanted to know why he, Wallenberg, the rich Swede, had come to save the Jews. The KGB wanted to find out what he was doing in Hungary, what was his real mission. The lot fell to me, David Vompinsky, to interrogate this good man."

"Wallenberg was placed in cell 123 in Lubyanka, beginning in January 1945. It was a clean cell on the fifth floor, above the KGB office on the first three floors of the building reserved for VIPs. At first, he was not alone. For the first two months, Gustav Richter, a former police attaché at the German legation in Budapest, and an Austrian lieutenant named Willi Roedel shared the cell. All three were suspected of being spies for the Americans."

Vompinsky had to interrogate Wallenberg every day for the first three weeks in sessions lasting between sixty and ninety minutes.

Vompinsky would say, "You are very well known to us. You are a member of the wealthy Wallenberg family. Your capitalist family helped finance the Nazis."

"I accused Wallenberg of spying for the United States, but he did not flinch or even blink an eye. He would just repeat that I, David Vompinsky, had it all wrong. Wallenberg was angry and frustrated. He claimed his detention was a mistake and a violation of diplomatic immunity. His friends Lars Berg and Per Anger were also detained briefly, about a month or so, but then were released. When Wallenberg learned of their release, and that they were on the way home, he mumbled something about being punished for doing good things. His reward was solitary at Lubyanka. He was given more mistreatment at Mordivinia."

"Vompinsky was re-assigned, but he would see Wallenberg from time to time working out in the exercise yard, taking off his brown prison shirt and scooping newly fallen snow onto his body to increase circulation. Wallenberg was a true physical fitness person," Vompinsky said. "He was always optimistic, and immune to the interrogator's brow-beating efforts. Wallenberg never gave anything but name and diplomatic status. And he demanded to see the prison director."

"At one point, he asked me for paper and a pen. I got it for him, even though prisoners were not supposed to keep pens. He sat down in his cell, with the paper on a board on his knees, and wrote three drafts and a final copy of a letter to the director of the prison, asking for an audience. He said his incarceration violated international law because he had diplomatic immunity. But because no one from the Swedish Embassy even tried to visit him, that made the Russians think he was not truly a Swedish diplomat. Wallenberg was a model prisoner, but he always maintained his innocence. 'It is wrong that I am here,' he would say. 'There is some mistake.'"

Whatever Happened to Raoul Wallenberg?

After he resettled from Russia to Israel, Vompinsky chose to live the life of a recluse in total obscurity. On December 17, 1991, the *London Telegraph,* in a front-page article disclosed for the first time that Wallenberg ironically had a Jewish interrogator during his first two years at Lubyanka from 1945 to 1947. The newspaper in effect "outed" Vompinsky. This made Vompinsky move over night to a different location in Israel to hide from possible retribution by survivors now living in Ranana, a suburb of Tel Aviv. In my interview with him, and in the later newspaper account, he maintained that Wallenberg was strong and determined, impossible to break, and he insisted that Wallenberg was still alive.

August 1989
Israel Part III
The Mossad

As previously arranged, on August 5, I drove with Judge Landau up to attend a celebration for Wallenberg's 77th birthday. On the way I shared with him some of what I had learned from Schifrin. He confirmed Schifrin as a reliable source.

When we arrived at the Russian legation, a large group of survivors and other supporters had already gathered. They were there not only to celebrate Wallenberg's birthday, but to protest his detention. People paraded with handmade signs begging the Soviets to release Wallenberg and to allow him to come to Israel.

Landau surveyed the crowd. He pointed out a short little bantam cock of a man about 5' tall. "There is Efrem Moshinsky, a veteran of the 18th Soviet Red Army. He may be short, but he doesn't take orders—he gives them. He claims he was with Wallenberg on the day he was kidnapped. He knows all the shenanigans of the Russians, both during and after the war. He was a good military officer. But since he was Jewish, Stalin didn't trust him. And if Stalin had the least suspicion about anyone, he put them 'out to pasture.' So Moshinsky, like Schifrin, was sent to Wrangel Island in 1952. He spent a year there, where he first met Wallenberg. Back in the army again, Moshinsky the Jew was never accepted as an insider. He was easy prey when it came time to look for a scapegoat. They shipped him for a second term to Wrangel Island in 1956. Again he spent time with Wallenberg, and they became friends. He came out of Russia just a few years ago, migrated here, and wrote a book about his experiences. As a result, little Efrem has become the major voice for Wallenberg in all of Israel. Come, let me introduce you."

We edged our way through the crowd, now tightly gathered around the Russian legation. A Russian official was scheduled to come out and take part in the Wallenberg birthday celebration. They had prepared a cake for the people.

Judge Landau introduced us, and we shook hands.

"What the Russians are doing here is just propaganda," Moshinsky told me. "I know how much they love ceremonies. Today they are honoring Wallenberg, pretending he's dead, but I know better. I bet he is alive. I knew him first hand. That man has one singular purpose—to stay alive, come out of Russia and tell his story."

Moshinsky was called away by someone. After he left, I turned to Landau. "There was something else Schifrin said that intrigued me."

"Yes?"

I lowered my voice. "He suggested getting in touch with the Mossad."

203

Landau's eyes glistened. "That is perfect," he said. "If anyone can help you, it is the Mossad. Tomorrow I can take you personally to meet one of them, Tommy Lapid. He was a leader of the Hungarian underground. He's now the new editor of one of our major newspapers. Most of his readers are survivors, and some are new Russian immigrants. They may have knowledge of where Wallenberg is today."

By a stroke of luck Landau already had an appointment with Tommy for nine the next morning. He suggested I come with him and make my own pitch right then. Tommy might be able to both give me some publicity to reach more people and take me personally to the Mossad.

It was hard to sleep that night. I lay awake trying to imagine meeting Landau's contact in the Mossad the next morning. And he was just one of many such trained and dedicated Israelis who might be willing to risk their lives for a man who had rescued them or their parents or grandparents.

I met Tommy Lapid, editor of *Maariv,* a popular daily newspaper. Tommy is a barrel-chested man approximately 5'3" tall. He looked like David Ben-Gurion, the former leader of Israel, with bright twinkling blue eyes and fringes of gray hair around the sides of his otherwise bald head.

He greeted Landau with a bow and a wink and called him "Your Lordship." He then walked me over to where the printing presses were humming. He went to the daily's desk and picked up an early proof of the next day's morning edition.

The front-page headline was "Wallenberg Lawyer Seeking Budapest and Russian Survivors." It described my visit to Israel to reopen the search for Wallenberg, and my search for recent Russian émigrés with possible knowledge of Wallenberg's whereabouts in the Gulag.

"How do you like the article? Does it suit your needs?"

I scanned the article. "It is perfect," I said.

Lapid looked at his watch.

"It is time to go. I will personally introduce you to the leaders of the Mossad Intelligence Agency. A plan of rescue will be developed based on your knowledge and what they gather from their resources. The leaders will review with you the preliminary strategies they have devised and their options. We have some recent information regarding Wallenberg's whereabouts from Jewish emigrés who left Russia only two months ago."

We got into Lapid's car and drove to a restaurant on Dizengoff Circle. There we changed cars and headed off again toward a small yellow building at the university. On the way Lapid told me that I would be meeting a number of people with the Mossad.

"In fact," he said, "if you're lucky, you may even get to meet Chaim Herzog."

"I've already had the pleasure," I told him.

Lapid was surprised and taken aback.

My first visit to Israel was during the summer of 1962, as already reported. I was still a law student at the Yale Law School at that time. I was grateful to be a returning Jew "coming home" for the first time to Eretz, Israel. I had flown over from New York City where I had been working with a Wall Street law firm—Casey, Lane and Mittendorf. My two-month assignment in Tel Aviv was to work with the government of Israel as a Deputy Legal Advisor to the Ministry of Agriculture, specializing in Water Law. I took up the task of writing a brief for argument in the World Court to support Israel's position on the sharing of upper riparian water rights of the Jordan River and its tributary, the Yarkon River.

The sensitive position of heading the new water source development in Israel, necessitated by the massive Jewish immigration at the time, was handed to General Moshe Dayan, a courageous and brilliant military tactician who had led Israel against Egypt in the 1956 Suez Crisis in which Egypt had nationalized the Suez Canal and closed it to Israeli shipping. No one knew it then but he was between wars; the next would come in 1967. He was "parked" at the ministry at that time, a safe place to house this warhorse between conflicts with the Arabs. Dayan was also a farmer, so his assignment to the ministry of agriculture met, not only his needs, but the needs of the nation as well. He had great skill in the area of turning deserts into fertile valleys. And agricultural development, of course, was intimately connected with issues of water rights.

I was ushered into Moshe Dayan's office soon after my arrival in late June.

"I am glad that you're here," he said. "We need all the help we can get." He had a quick smile and was at ease with himself thus making it easy for me to relax in his presence. "I have been to the wheat fields in Kansas and made a special to the Tennessee Valley Authority project, your nations first effort to bring water to poor farmers under a federal program. FDR, your president, was a visionary similar to the men who first developed farms here in Israel. Your work on the Yarkon River project is critical to the future of Israel, and the possibility of peace with our neighbors. When can you get started?" He said. "Right away," I answered. "I can get started this afternoon."

Mosha Dayan moved over to a table within his office and opened a map of Israel showing the Yarkon river valley with Jordan next store. "We must find a way to share. The theory of good neighbors *"sic utero laedes"* is a crucial law of sharing according to ones needs that you must adopt as the centerpiece of the Yarkon River Treaty.

Mosha Dayan was a clean-cut bald headed man about 5' 7." A black eye-patch covered his right eye. That eye had been destroyed by an explosion during the War of Independence in 1948.

"I intend to make the Negev a place of peace," he said. "We will turn the desert into a garden of blooming flowers and vegetables. We will siphon some of the waters of the Jordan and Yarkon rivers to build new communities, schools, and kibbutzim."

"We will build our nation and its defense system by scattering villages throughout the country. We will share our technology with our neighbors and live in peace. You are here to help this vision come true," he told me. "We need a lawyer to prepare and present the arguments for shared ownership in international rivers. No nation that finds itself twenty or thirty miles upstream should be permitted to divert waters away from downstream nations. But that is what the Jordanians are trying to do and we cannot permit this. It seems as though each of our neighboring nations wants to extinguish Israel but I will not let this happen."

I discussed the theory of *"sic utero laedes"*—that each user of water, whether rancher, farmer or even a nation, could only use water with due regard for the needs of its downstream neighbor.

"Formulate that for me," he said. "We will be meeting with the Jordanians in just two weeks. I want them to share the vision that they get back more by sharing than taking. That is, we will give them our technology in exchange for a fair share of the precious water. Thus we can all live together peacefully."

A few days later I walked into his office with a ten page memorandum. Sitting with him was General Chaim Herzog, who along with Moshe Dayan, was a hero of the Israeli people. This shrewd man had planned the strategy of the 1948 War and the one in 1957. I was introduced to Herzog, whose peacetime position was chief of Israeli military intelligence. Herzog was a big man, with a full head of hair graying at the temples, and bushy eyebrows. I could feel his bone-crushing strength as he shook my hand.

Born in Belfast, Ireland in 1918, Herzog, as a thirty year old was placed in charge of Israel's Seventh Brigade as Operations Officer. He and Dayan loved to recount their adventures as soldiers. So at their invitation, I put aside my briefing materials for the moment, and sat down and listened to their war stories.

Herzog was a great storyteller. He had already risked his life three different times for his country and would be mentally prepared to lead his troops into a defensive war again in 1967 before becoming the first military governor of the occupied West Bank in 1967.

I shared my ideas and research on water law with Chaim Herzog and Moshe Dayan. They both had many questions and a very different approach. Herzog wanted to have the whole picture and decide for himself the best strategy. Dayan, on the other hand, wanted me to present the bottom line. He was like a civil engineer with a blueprint. He thought linear; he wanted to know how to get from point to point to point with the least effort and abrasion. He saw the goal—

get the water Israel needs and, at the same time to, have Jordan feel that they got a good deal.

I stayed in touch with Chaim Herzog after he became Ambassador to the United Nations for Israel from 1975 to 1978. I corresponded with him after reading his books *The Arab-Israeli Wars,* published in 1982, and his 1989 book, *Heroes of Israel.*

Tommy Lapid was fascinated by my account of having worked with both Mosha Dayan and Chaim Herzog. He was about to ask me more, but just then we arrived at a beautiful mansion near the university. Lapid got out and was met by an army officer. Lapid told me I was going into the meeting with the MOSSAD alone. He didn't want to know the details, the fewer people who did the better.

I was ushered into a room with grey walls and was greeted by a small group of four men and one slender woman. This was the team that would go into Russia to try and get Raoul and bring him to Israel. I also met their leader, Abram Ber, and visited with head of Mossad, Chaim Herzog, once again. I was sworn to secrecy. I then told the Mossad that I fully supported their effort to rescue Wallenberg. "Because of the publicity you are raising," they told me, "we are moving up the date for our rescue effort. We already have an idea where they are holding him."

They pin pointed Wallenberg's location on a map. He was now located in a country dacha in deep woods, forty-five minutes east of Moscow. One of his former guards had revealed his location for cash. It was a small country estate, dating back to the time of the Czar in 1912, which the Russians now used to entertain and house visiting diplomats. Herzog took me aside for a brief chat. He fidgeted, rubbing his thumbs and his first fingers together.

"I have arthritis and my bones are old. Vestiges of the wars I fought when I should have been farming." He opened his hands to show me their shriveled and warped condition. "Souvenirs of the wars," he said. "They last longer than the medals. War takes its toll sooner or later. And war captures innocent people like Wallenberg in its awful grip, and sadly, does not let go. But I will rescue your client for you."

I loved his positive and gung ho attitude.

Herzog remained quiet for a moment. I could almost see the military computer in his head plotting out the rescue plan—just as he had once planned in 1947 the building of the secret "Burma Road" to lead to the rescue of the besieged people of Jerusalem.

Herzog masterminded the Wallenberg mission, code-named "Operation Brother's Keeper." The blueprints for this heroic mission were kept in storage at the Mossad headquarters in Israel for many years.

Herzog carefully handpicked the agents to go into Moscow for Wallenberg. They were brave and physically fit—recent Russian émigrés to

Israel. Some of them were former KGB officials and interrogators. A few of them knew the forests around Moscow and the country road leading to the estate in the woods where Wallenberg was held in isolation. Some of the team had undergone facial plastic surgery, been given Russian tattoos, and new identities. Soon they would be smuggled back into Russia. The team included Hungarian Jewish survivors from Tel Aviv and Jerusalem. Wallenberg had saved them and this was payback time.

Herzog arranged to have two trucks "acquired" in Moscow. He measured and timed the distance from Moscow to the country dacha. He studied the Russian terrain and had obtained the most recent maps of the roads. He learned the timing of the changing of the guard at the dacha's two entrances and he studied the routines, distractions, and lax behavior of the guards assigned to watch Wallenberg. He knew the 4:00 P.M. to 4:45 P.M. window of opportunity for attack and entry—the precious forty-five minute exercise period granted to Wallenberg, the solitary prisoner. He gave the members of the mission their specific duties, instructions, and suicide pills in case they were caught.

I was told the raid would take place in a few weeks. Since my work in Israel was completed, and my main mission accomplished it was time to return home. My teaching of international law and human rights back at Stockton State College in New Jersey was scheduled to begin soon. I booked a flight on El Al, and returned home. Abram Ber, Herzog's main deputy, promised to call and let me know the outcome of Herzog's mission to Moscow as soon as it was accomplished. Herzog's last words before I left were, "We will accomplish this mission. This is an important moment for redemption for the State of Israel."

I returned to the United States and resumed my life. I was waiting for a miracle and working on a dream.

October 1989
Atlantic City

It took two months for something to happen. The mission to the château compound, forty-five minutes outside of Moscow was delayed several times due to the KGB's frantic efforts to move Wallenberg from prison to prison. They had somehow caught wind that the Israelis were mounting a rescue effort. They were fully familiar with the effectiveness of a Mossad air strike, having read about the successful raid on Entebbe in Uganda where the Mossad miraculously rescued Israeli citizens on an El Al flight, being held hostage by Idi Amin, the dictator of Uganda.

Finally, in early October, I received the phone call from Abram Ber, the leader of the Mossad brigade into Moscow.

"We drove down a long forest road and quietly entered the compound with two trucks, exactly as planned. The guards had been paid off big time, bribed to look the other way. The secret location was a château. It was heavily guarded with tall outer and inner walls but no moat. Wallenberg was being held and hidden in a country estate of the former Tsar's family. Our afternoon timing was perfect. We got through the gate, based on the food goods we were carrying 'for delivery.' We quickly captured and knocked out the guards. No shots, no deaths. Just chloroform over their faces as they sat there dozing off on the job. They will remember nothing. We checked out all the buildings of the compound and found some interesting things. We got there exactly at what would normally have been the beginning of Wallenberg's exercise hour."

My heart pounded. "Tell me, tell me he's healthy, and tell me he's free at last."

Ber hesitated, cleared his throat and continued, "The good news is that we found where he last stayed. We know for a fact that he is still alive."

"At 4 P.M. the team of five Mossad agents left their carefully camouflaged trucks in the courtyard of the dacha. The château compound was surrounded by tall woods. We advanced quietly on foot towards the dacha. Two of my crack commandos guarded the perimeter, the other three moved into the dacha. The German shepherd guard dogs were sleeping, a result of drugged 'sweet meat' steaks given to them. This was a very well-planned job."

"Two agents crept up behind the outside guard, knocked him out with a 2x4, used chloroform in a handkerchief, and took his keys. With no one guarding the outer perimeter of the house, the three commandos walked in the front. No one was guarding the inside of the dacha either. The commandos made a thorough search of every room. In one of the bedrooms of the dacha they found something no Westerner had seen for over 40 years: Wallenberg's bedroom. Some of

Wallenberg's papers, books, notes and personal possessions were in the room. There were books in both Russian and English, indicating that he was learning Russian while in custody. The bed was unmade, with coffee cups and cigarette butts nearby waiting to be cleaned up."

"One of the commandoes spotted a black and white photograph on top of a pile of books on a night table. It was slightly curled up, an amateur photo such as the kind taken by a Kodak Instamatic camera. The photo showed an older face of Wallenberg, sitting and having coffee next to two of his guards. It was definitely Wallenberg. She showed the photos to the others and then stuffed them into her pocket. Wallenberg had recently been there. They looked under the bed and everywhere else in the room, but found it empty. They continued the search in the adjoining rooms of the dacha."

"We know he was there," Ber said, "because of the photo the agent brought back. Back in Tel Aviv our photo analyst compared it with the younger face of the 32-year-old Wallenberg. The eyes, the bone structure—everything matched."

"But" he continued, "We did not find our man there. He had been moved moments or perhaps hours before we arrived. Someone tipped off the Russian Intel—we don't know who, but we will find out. Possibly one of our five Mossad agents, but I doubt it. This was a loyal group. We vetted them carefully. Perhaps Wallenberg knows we came to save him. Maybe that will give him the stamina to live for the next effort. I am sorry to bring you this frustrating report."

"The effort is what counts," I said. "The hope continues and the dream will never die. We will find him. Your brave and fearless Mossad people have done something very special. They have done a brave thing, risking their lives for a good man. Abe, you did everything possible. Maybe another chance will come. Then this will have been like a dress rehearsal."

Ber replied, "It is a chess game with the Russians. Every time they move him we will follow. It will be harder now, but we will not quit. One day, when least expected, we will bring him home. Someone on the inside will be brave and help us." I thanked him for the brave and daring effort and hung up the phone.

"So close, So close," I muttered to myself. I wondered if Wallenberg might have sensed our effort to rescue him."

The Mossad wanted to make the effort again. The brave effort by this team of Mossad agents has gone unmentioned and unheralded until now. It could not be told earlier or it would have yielded retaliation and repercussions against Israel. But now the truth can be told. Israel cared. Israel took action. In Israel the true soul and spirit of Wallenberg continues to live. There the true family of Wallenberg resides, the true "children" and "grandchildren" of people Raoul saved. Raoul Wallenberg, who never had his own chance to build a family, has a family. And this caring will be remembered through future generations. *They shall speak of it in their houses, and mark it upon the doorposts of their homes.*

They will share the story with those for whom stories of true heroes are handed down from generation to generation and never die. Twenty-one years later, on April 30, 2011, the Mossad rescue plan was resurrected and basically copied in the assassination of Osama bin Laden in Abbottabad, Pakistan. The Mossad, directly helped the CIA locate and extinguish Bin Laden. And thus the Wallenberg rescue effort lives on in the success of the Navy Seal Team Six.

Shutzpasse issued by the Swiss consulate to Tihamer Pal.

Ivan Pal (now Yehuda Egri) is the son of Tihamer Pal (b. April 4, 1896) and Margit Rosenthal Pal (b. July 9, 1896). He was born on April 4, 1932 in the city of Berehovo in Transcarpathia, and he grew up in Budapest where his father owned a store. In 1939, in accordance with anti-Jewish laws, Tihamer officially no longer could own his store. He therefore asked a non-Jewish employee whom he thought he could trust to serve as the titular owner, while he continued to run the business. On March 19, 1944, German troops occupied Budapest and life quickly changed for the Pal family. On April 3, the day before Ivan's twelfth birthday, Jewish residents were ordered to wear the yellow star. Meanwhile, the man to whom Tihamer had entrusted his store turned out to be a member of the Arrow Cross who prohibited Tihamer from entering his own business. In order to support the family, Ivan's father took a job in a shoe factory. However, on the first day of work a machine fell on his hand and broke it. Consequently Tihamer was temporarily excused from being sent to a labor camp until later that summer. He was allowed to return home for occasional visits. On October 15, after President Horthy tried to negotiate a separate armistice, the Germans orchestrated a coup d'etat and installed the radically anti-Semitic Ferenc Szalasi as the new head of state. Tihamer's brigade was sent by foot towards the Austrian border. When they arrived in the town of Hegyeshalom someone appeared from the Swiss Consulate and offered a Shutzpass to anyone who wanted one. Tihamer's commander respected these documents and allowed the entire unit to return to Budapest. Tihamer deserted his unit and returned home to rejoin Ivan, Margit and Ivan's

212

grandfather. The apartment had been specially designated for Jews, and a large yellow star hung on the entrance.

Ivan's mother and grandfather also obtained Shutzpasses, and the family moved to a safe house. However, in November 1944 the Arrow Cross ordered the remaining Jews of Budapest into a ghetto. The Pal family remained in the ghetto until January 18, 1945 when they were liberated by Soviet forces. Since there was a post-war food shortage in Budapest, Ivan spent several months in a Zionist camp in Szeged where food was more plentiful. In June 1949 Ivan escaped from Hungary to Czechoslovakia. From there he went to Italy where he boarded the Atzmaut bound for Israel. After arriving in Israel Ivan joined the Israeli army and later became an engineer. His mother joined him in Israel in August 1949, while his father remained in Hungary.

October 1989
Washington, DC

In October, the Wallenberg case was mysteriously back on the active calendar of the US federal district court. It no longer belonged to Judge Parker. It had been mysteriously moved laterally from the calendar of Judge Parker to Judge Robinson, two judges of equal jurisdiction! The case was never appealed! I will ask the United States Supreme Court to correct this unethical and illegal action in a *writ of certiorari*, which I plan to file later in 2011. It is an example of judicial misconduct and must be corrected in order to preserve the independence of the Federal Judiciary.

Although Judge Parker, after painstaking research and deliberation, wrote an eleven page finding of jurisdiction, Judge Robinson somehow stole the case. He voided my victory—and thus prevented Wallenberg's release even at that late date. In a curt, short and spineless decision he simply "blew out the case," obviously at the request of the White House, as we later in fact learned.

Federal courts lost their independence at that moment. Article III courts cannot be pressured or tampered with by the President under our basic separation of powers doctrine. This was a dangerous example of interference. The Parker decision was the right decision. It was principled and based on law. The second Wallenberg decision was a power grab. It was illegal and expedient. But why would the Russians seek to tamper with a final court decision four years later? Why did they hire a Washington law firm to re-open the case? Did the Russians instigate it? The case had been dormant for years.

There were several factors lending a sense of mystery to this action. For one thing, while Robinson's decisions always tended to be lengthy, this one consisted of a terse, one-paragraph opinion. Furthermore, though opinions were normally published, this one was unpublished and issued very quietly. No one notified me. I only learned about this behind the scenes shenanigans in a phone call from the judge's clerk. This action was remarkable in a legal sense because it was entirely unprecedented—a judge of equal standing grabbing a case off a fellow judge's closed calendar and attempting to void and countermand another judge's decision.

It felt like a double whammy—first learning of the Mossad's failed attempt to free Wallenberg, and then watching Wallenberg's victory in court overturned.

In this moment of despair, I called Earl Silbert, Watergate prosecutor and my longtime friend and one of the original members of the Wallenberg legal team, to ask for his help. Earl is an outstanding lawyer. I needed another reliable point of view.

"I am absolutely dumbfounded and amazed," he said. "It is like judicial theft. There is just no precedent for this judicial misbehavior in the history of our US Federal District Court. Someone outside the judicial system must have put some real pressure on that judge to initiate special action. There's a big risk if Robinson is asked to explain what he has done. That could become a very big scandal."

Earl Silbert had seen his share of 'dirty tricks' in the dirty details of Watergate. He had prosecuted Ehrlichman and other key figures of that scandal.

"Earl, can you find out who put out the word to kill this case?" I said. "I want to know who is on our side and who is against us."

"I will get back to you in just a few days," he said, and hung up the phone. A few days later he called. "Morris, I have news for you and it ain't pretty. I think you may want to back off this case. This is not a game of tennis. There are some pretty strong forces working against you, including the FBI, the CIA and other forces at high levels of our government. They will use any means to derail your effort including stealing closed cases off of another judge's docket. They don't want to see our federal courts used as forums for the advocacy of human rights or as arenas for human rights litigation. They want to kill your case, and they don't care whether you personally get hurt in the process. If I find out anything further, I'll let you know"

I was reminded again of Tony D'Amato's warning that there could be danger involved in taking the case and in prosecuting Russia. But I had always intended to see this case through, and from that goal nothing would deter me. I have never felt fear in this matter. I have always felt God's gentle hand on my shoulder and the admonition coming from the 23rd Psalm: "Yea, though I walk through the valley of the shadow of death I shall fear no evil for thou art with me."

October 1989
Moscow

As I was receiving the discouraging legal news and report of the foiled rescue, Russia was putting on a major propaganda effort to whitewash its behavior in the Wallenberg case.

In June 1989 the Soviet government for the first time permitted a mention of Raoul Wallenberg's name on the radio and apologized for the kidnapping of Wallenberg. Then in October the Russian Ministry of Foreign Affairs manipulated the innocent arm of the Wallenberg family. The Russian government in Moscow gave a ceremonial dinner for Nina Lagergren, Guy Von Dardel, Per Anger, and Sonya Sonnenfeld from the Swedish Raoul Wallenberg Committee. They were invited to this black tie state dinner ostensibly to honor Raoul Wallenberg as a hero. I advised them firmly not to go unless the Soviets were ready to answer a list of specific questions I prepared. The family once again was about to be used as a shuttlecock of phony diplomacy between Sweden and Russia.

Guy called me several weeks before the dinner to tell me about it and I counseled him against attending. Guy was determined to be there. Alternatively, I offered to be present, but the Russians threatened to cancel the ceremony if I appeared as legal counsel for Wallenberg at the dinner.

Von Dardel called: "Morris, the Russians are emphatic. You are a good man and a great lawyer. But the Russians fear your being present. They fear you will turn it around and accuse them of misbehavior."

I replied: "Then take another lawyer. I will prepare and send the questions to him. Take advantage of the dinner to find your brother and get him released."

Here was one of the effects of my having been declared *persona non grata* by the Russians a few years earlier.

The dinner was held in Moscow and the family was manipulated for propaganda purposes. The Wallenberg family members feasted on the finest delicacies, and Raoul received a champagne toast *in absentia*. It was a mockery, a pathetic moment in the history of the case. The only fly in the soup, of course, was that Raoul was mentioned only in the past tense, and yet the fact was that he was still alive as 'prisoner 7'.

After dinner, there was a gruesome ceremonial moment, which Guy later described to me, "They gave me a brown cardboard box marked "Lubyanka Prison." I opened it and I pulled out my brother's dark blue pants, his alligator skin wallet, some change in Hungarian money, his official diplomatic passport and some *shutzpasses*. It was a ghoulish moment touching his possessions after 40 years."

216

Guy looked for an autopsy report, death certificate, or other proof of death; there was nothing. He asked for proof that his brother was dead. To which the Russian Foreign Minister answered, "We have no proof. We just know he is no longer with us."

Guy asked for the gulag to be searched, but he was told that official state policy was that his brother was dead and "has been dead on many occasions for quite some time." Guy laughed grimly at the Soviet minister's clumsy yet ironic choice of words in broken English. Meanwhile, Nina was given a statement written in Russian, and was pressured to sign it. When Sonya Sonnenfeld pointed out that the paper stated that Russia was being absolved of responsibility for Wallenberg, Nina refused to sign.

After leaving the "party," Guy called me the next day from Moscow, reported the details of the sham ceremony, and said, "I wish you could have been there. We needed you to ask legal questions. We needed your backbone and bloodhound instincts. Morris, I asked them, now that we had the pants and passport, whether you would be allowed to come here, to make a full investigation of the matter. But they refused my request outright. All they wanted was a public relations ceremony to put a good face on their bad deeds. We were badly used, and poorly treated like stupid children and I now regret it."

May 1991
Washington, DC

Almost a year and a half later, I got a call from Nicholas Zumas, a Washington, DC attorney interested in helping me on the case.

"I found some information pertinent to the blowout of your case," he said. "You had asked me to find who put out the word to kill the case, and who reached Robinson, and why."

Nick continued: "You were stabbed in the back by evil forces. Abe Sofaer, the Chief Legal Adviser at State sold your client out to the Russians. Ironically Sofaer is a Jew. His relatives were saved by Wallenberg. This man Sofaer worked closely with Oswald to develop the infamous *"Statement of Interest"* and the strategy to derail the case. Oswald obviously was working both sides of the street—while pretending to work with you; he had already crossed over to work with Sofaer. They developed the infamous *"Statement of Interest"* and the strategy to derail your case. It was the evil one—Theroux, a former State Department Law Adviser—who provided the link between State and The White House. Theroux was now making millions in private practice. His firm Baker and McKenzie got a fat $400,000 retainer from the taxpayers of the United States just to fight you and to get your courtroom victory destroyed"

Theroux admitted to me at lunch that he had written the *Statement of Interest*, but it had been ghost written by a team of lawyers at The State Department. Zumas said, "It was truly a 'Statement of Interest' against the citizens of the United States and Wallenberg." On the surface it was a strategy to re-argue the issue of jurisdiction. But its real purpose was to refrigerate Wallenberg for the rest of his life.

"Your friend Abe Sofaer, the Jewish Legal Adviser at the State Department," Nick told me, "That bright Yid, is a clever turn coat with plenty of *chutzpah* and selfish ambition. He was selected to do the hatchet job. He slammed the door on your client. You are lucky you got as far as the judgment from Judge Parker. You should have grabbed the Russians by the balls right then and there and made them cough up Wallenberg. My friend at CIA confirms that Wallenberg was definitely alive when you won your verdict. Damn shame how things turned out. You were on the right road. Oswald, in his delay tactic, acted directly against your client's interests. I don't know if Oswald was just a stubborn fool, or sold out to the State Department in exchange for new business in the future. Either way he messed up big time."

Nick continued, "I went over to the clerk's office at the District Court. I examined the docket entries. I found the entry of October 18, 1985, marking your courtroom victory. Judgment for you and your client is $39 million. This $39 million fine was to have been paid by the Soviets within 60 days, plus an obligation to produce Wallenberg in the same time period."

"The next entry surprised me. Without your permission your subordinate Mr. Oswald, filed a petition for a contempt citation against the Russians for failing to appear, rather than filing for immediate enforcement of the $39 million judgment. I think the Chase Bank and his Wall Street law firm pressured Oswald. They must have told him point blank, 'get rid of this nasty judgment or you are gone. Our bank client-the Russian government-doesn't want to cough up the money.'"

"It starts to get weird at this point," Nick said. "The docket shows a series of postponements and delays—all by Oswald and his law firm. Your name is not mentioned except when you filed on February 2, 1984, and when you argued in July of 1985, and then won the case on October 15, 1985. Now after four years of delay the docket shows the US State Department filing a *"Statement of Interest"* through the Washington, DC law firm Baker & McKenzie, against your client, and asking for a re-hearing. What was there to re-hear? The case had been quiet for four years. And just after that notation there is written in ink—not typed— 'Counsel for the State Department requests that the case be re-assigned to Judge Aubrey Robinson.' Where was Judge Parker?"

"Officially he didn't retire until early February of 1990," I said. "He should have been the judge to hear this request, not Robinson. They knew Parker would slam them and ask why they hadn't rescued Wallenberg by now. This was a behind the back deal to steal it from Parker and put it on Robinson's docket—a most illegal and unethical move."

"Finally, we have Robinson's one-paragraph decision—a blowout of the case. They don't call it that. They just call it 'Judgment Reversed.' None of the clerks I talked with has ever seen any other example of a case stolen from one judge's docket and given to another of equal jurisdiction. Besides that, they're puzzled; they say it's not like Robinson to write curt, laconic and brief opinions. They smell a scandal coming from cahoots of the State Department's Legal Office, the White House and the Russian government. Our own government must have been offered vital scientific information, or a major political commitment from the Russians to disarm a few of their missiles aimed at the United States and nearby Turkey, our NATO ally. This whole thing stinks. Something is rotten in the State of Denmark according to Hamlet and something stinks in the State of Sweden too."

I replied to Nick's famous quote, "So now you're quoting Shakespeare? That's what Hamlet said to his mother, the Queen, when he discovers his uncle has killed his father, the King of Denmark, and married his recently widowed mother. That move by the uncle ranks high along with this one! That was a chutzpah move too!"

Whatever Happened to Raoul Wallenberg?

"Obviously a cover-up and political pressure coming from someone high up, perhaps at the White House or at National Security. It would seem that doing secret deals with the Russians is the top, if not the only priority."

"I plan to re-open the case. By publishing my book I hope new evidence will arrive from the international readers. I believe this case can be revived, even at this late date, in the United States Supreme Court because there has been a serious judicial misbehavior by a federal judge, which must be corrected and possibly punished. The Supreme Court has original jurisdiction over cases involving ambassadors and diplomats specifically under Article III, Section 2."

My conversation with Nick Zumas confirmed that a re-instatement of the case was in order. We would also re-double our effort to rescue Wallenberg by asking the Mossad to renew its effort to bring our world citizen home. I remained Wallenberg's personal representative and lawyer even if his family had quit on him. The new route towards rescue was the right one—gather clues on Wallenberg's constantly shifting whereabouts, re-double my efforts to save Wallenberg in my capacity as the son of a survivor and private citizen, not as a court room lawyer.

I soon after met with Abe Sofaer, the State Department lawyer responsible for trying to kill the lawsuit. He was now in private practice at Hughes, Hubbard and Reed on Wall Street. He had come down by Metroliner from New York to Philadelphia to serve on a panel with me at the Penn Law School. The subject was International Law. He had no awareness that I knew what I knew. I spied him sitting on the couch speaking to some students after the lecture.

"I need to ask you something, Abe," I said. "Is it true what I heard about you and the 'Wallenberg sell out?'"

His face reddened. "What are you talking about? I handled hundreds of cases as Legal Adviser."

"You know about this one. My friend, Nick Zumas, the famous lawyer who represents David Cone of the New York Mets in arbitration, tells me you helped the Russians shop for a law firm in DC to help them file a "*Statement of Interest*" against my Wallenberg case against the Soviets. Then you came in on the Russians' side and asked the court to set aside my verdict. Is that how you purchased your new partnership at Hughes, Hubbard and Reed?"

"Is that how lawyers play the lobby game, a revolving door between State Department to Wall Street, a shuttle back and forth from government to rich plums in private practice?"

"I can't talk about that case. It's still under investigation."

"What investigation? Are you kidding me? This case is under destruction, not investigation. It is being destroyed by you. How ironic. Wallenberg saves your parents in Hungary. You come here and go to law school so you can do this kind of legal work?   Shame on you!" I began to walk away and turned back.

"Come on Abe. You are in private practice now. Help me out. Help me get rid of this *"Statement of Interest"*. File a brief. Come in on my side. Tell your pin stripe boys in the State Department to come in on my side, not the Russians. Your tongue is not tied by the State Department."

He abruptly got up and walked away.

I followed him out the door and asked again, "What about Wallenberg?"

"I told you, I am not allowed to talk about that," he said. "Now leave me alone!" He actually began to run. "I have to make a train," he said. "I have no time for this."

Nick had warned me.   There was too much power working against us. We needed to wait for a new administration, one that cared about human rights.

Sooner than I knew, I would get my chance to re-invigorate the search for Wallenberg.

That opportunity started when William Jefferson Clinton, of the Yale Law School '73 was elected President in 1992. He had graduated ten years after me. Bill Clinton is an avid reader of everything including important federal cases. He had read Judge Parker's opinion when it first came down in 1985.

"I always wanted to meet the lawyer who started that case," Clinton whispered. I was actually seated between the President and First Lady, Hillary Clinton, and with other Yale Law School friends at the funeral of Marc Richman in Philadelphia on January 17, 1992. Next to me was seated one of my favorite law professors, Dean Guido Calabrese of Yale Law. We discussed Wallenberg and my desire to have the President intervene with the Russians. Every chance I got I took up the rescue of Wallenberg issue, and especially with people with power. Marc Richman was important to the Clintons, as the very first finance director and fundraiser for Clinton when he ran for governor of Arkansas. He became Bill's first national finance chairman.

Marc and I both practiced law in Philadelphia; he as a partner at Blank, Rome and I as managing partner at Stassen and Kostos. He died tragically in a car accident just a few days after the 1992 Presidential inauguration. Hillary, dressed in a dark pants suit with a white orchid, nudged me, "You now have access to the White House. We will re-open the matter through new diplomatic channels. We will get to the bottom of this. We will find out what really happened amidst all this corruption. We will see if he is still alive."

I was exhilarated. *"Hope springs eternal in the human breast,"* I muttered to myself and I bowed my head in prayer as the rabbi started to chant the mourners' Kadish for Marc Richman and all of the Jewish dead of the Holocaust.

The Wallenberg case was now back in play. Access to the Oval Office, was mind. And two of the most powerful people in the world, the President and the First Lady were now available. They were ready and willing to fight and to do the right thing.

November 22, 1993
The White House

I drove up to the front gate of the White House, showed my pass and was directed to the Executive Office parking lot. I got out, took my brief case and headed towards the West Wing. I walked through to the White House with Neal Wolin, Deputy National Security Adviser, down the long corridor and entered the President's office. It felt good to come in from the brisk November air to the warmth of the Oval office of the White House.

I had been in the Oval Office several times before with President John F. Kennedy to brief the President as an emissary from Bobby Kennedy as recently as April 12, 1963, just five months before his assassination. On that date I briefed him on the Civil Rights legislation being prepared and written for the Congress from the Justice Department's Office of Legal Counsel where I worked as a lawyer, on the fifth floor down the hall from Bobby Kennedy.

I was an attorney with the Office of Legal Counsel helping to write and then brief the President with the progress we were making in writing the Civil Rights Act of 1964. This was April of 1963. The President was seated in his rocking chair when I was ushered into the office by his secretary Evelyn Lincoln. Her desk was directly outside the door of the Oval Office. She was his cheerful and watchful gatekeeper.

The President rose with a grimace; he was in pain due to his bad back. But he stood tall and came across the room to greet me, and shake my hand as if nothing else was going on in the world.

"Good to have you here, Mr. Wolff. I asked Bobby to send you over to explain to me the plans for the new *1964 Civil Rights Act* to me. I have a delegation of black ministers coming in later this morning, and I need to tell them where we stand. I need to know what will be your strategy for the foundation of the new law. Are you basing its legality on the Article One 'commerce clause' or the 14th amendment Equal Protection Clause? I know it is both a political and a legal question. I need to know what the thinking over there at Justice happens to be as of today on this issue. What is your strategy for getting it passed? What is the constitutional basis of the proposed new law?"

I responded, "We are debating placing it on both Article One Section Eight Clause Three of the Commerce Clause, and the 14th Amendment Equal Protection Clause. There is a split of opinion, in the Department of Justice. John Doar of the Justice Department Civil Rights division wants it placed on the 14th Amendment Due Process and Equal Protection clauses. Harold Reis and Sol Lindeman of my Office of Legal Counsel suggest the Commerce Clause."

President Kennedy replied, "What do you see as the strengths of both arguments? I don't want to see this law overturned by the Supreme Court. There would be riots in the streets. Black people have waited 240 years for this law since 1720. What route is safest? Which one is best?"

"The best, in my opinion, is the commerce clause, Article One, Section Eight, Clause Three. There is more history and usage there. Congress has plenary power to regulate commerce. That section specifically provides that 'Congress shall have power to regulate all commerce between the states and foreign nations.' That has been used before in social legislation. It was used to allow Congress to regulate against child labor in *Hammer v. Dagenhart* in 1937. It can be used by the Congress to regulate against unlawful racial discrimination and segregation in the year 1963. We feel that if the Supreme Court accepted that piece of social legislation, as a basis for prohibiting child labor that we can pragmatically use the same commerce clause for allowing black people to move freely in commerce as they choose to eat in restaurants and sleep in hotels along the highways of interstate commerce."

"In other words, people are like goods in interstate commerce when they travel?" asked the President.

"That is right. People have the equal right as citizens to travel, stop for a meal, sleep in a hotel with no interference. Discrimination is now considered to be a 'burden' on the Interstate Commerce Clause and is thus illegal. The southern states and their senators may oppose the new law. So we have found a precedent like *Hammer v Dagenhart* that paves the way. The Supreme Court wants precedent to rely on. They feel more comfortable if the path is already laid. Precedent is important. The Equal Protection Clause sounds better cosmetically— the clear idea that all human beings have the same rights—but your brother and his advisors think we are safer against being overturned in the Supreme Court if we place the new Civil Rights law on the solid and well established foundation of the commerce clause."

"Then, let's do that. Let us not risk a chance of reversal by the Supreme Court on any basis. If that law is reversed there will be a terrible reaction. The Negroes will claim that they are being sold out once again by the white majority. It will be tough enough to get sixty-seven votes for cloture and the cutoff of senatorial debate. I want to move this matter quickly to a vote on the bill. Those southern senators—John Stennis of Mississippi, Spessard Holland of Florida, Ellender of Louisiana, even high falutin' William J. Fulbright of Arkansas—they will stand up in the Senate, and for home consumption will make a long winded big filibuster. As it is, I will have a battle on my hands. It will be a tough and close vote."

He looked out the window at the Rose Garden. "This is important work you are doing. How does it feel just being out of law school and doing important work, knowing that you might be guessing right or wrong on the choice of law, knowing that whatever you decide you will be involved in an historic debate and you will be walking in the corridors of history." He smiled and sat down to rock in his rocking chair, relieving the awful pain in his back. He looked tired and gray, the pain making crow's feet markings near his eyes. Maybe he had too much of his medication for Addison's disease. The public only got to see the well-tanned and robust John F. Kennedy. Sitting next to him on the couch next to the rocking chair, I could see him as he was; a man in constant pain as a result of his PT 109 boat injuries during World War II when he spent several hours in the water fighting off sharks and waiting to be rescued. This was a man who knew about the dilemma of rescue first hand. He was not feeling well but he soldiered on. There was a lot on his platter that morning.

"I love my work. This is the most exciting work a lawyer can do. I love working for social change and justice. Many of my classmates went directly to Wall Street, and are making tons of money. But I like this chance to work on vital issues concerning our nation. This is why I went to law school. The men at the Justice Department are bright and caring. They have so much experience. They have taught me a lot. I have some great mentors over there—Nathan Siegel, Harold Reis, Sol Lindenbaum and of course your brother the Attorney General."

"Do you enjoy working with Bobby?"

"Yes sir, I enjoy working with your brother very much."

"He's a tough nut, hard driver but he is the best. He's feisty and very intense at times. He likes to argue, very impatient at times. He even argues with me," said the President.

Kennedy got up from the blue rocking chair and walked stiffly over to his desk. He opened the top middle drawer and reached in his desk. He took out a small box, wrapped in white paper and a silver ribbon.

"Here, this is for you. A token of appreciation for what you are doing."

I opened it and thanked him. It was a tie clip, with ships on it, symbolizing the Cuban Missile Crisis, an event in history where America was inches from going to war. This all happened before I came from the Yale Law School to Washington, DC in January of 1963.

I returned from my reverie about the gallant, young John F. Kennedy to consider my upcoming meeting with President Clinton.

Now it was November 22, 1993, thirty years later, and again I was coming to the White House to brief a President. Ironically my visit was to occur exactly thirty years since the death of John F. Kennedy. President Clinton and I both shared a deep affection and admiration for President Kennedy. We had talked about it on October 18, 1993, just a few months earlier when I met President Clinton at the unveiling of his large portrait at the Yale Law School. He had invited me to the White House to discuss Wallenberg. "Wallenberg is my hero too," he reminded me. "You must come to Washington and tell me what you are trying to do. I will help you if I can."

I was anticipating a warm welcome from President Clinton and was not disappointed.

I mentioned the terrible irony of my coming to see him on the twenty second of November, exactly thirty years to the day. We shared a moment of silence together with his aide Neal S. Wolin.

When I met with the President at Yale in October of 1993, Dean Guido Calabrese organized a private meeting for just the three of us. Guido emphasized the importance of the Wallenberg case as a human rights matter and as an important new aspect of international law. Judge Guido Calabrese is now a highly esteemed member of the Federal Court of Appeals for the Second Circuit. He has always supported my work.

Judge Calabrese had opened the discussion:

"Mr. President you have an important policy matter here where you can help rescue Wallenberg and advance the cause human rights."

"Wallenberg is my hero too," the President responded. "I have read a lot about him. He is a very unusual and good man. Morris, when you come to the White House we will work out a plan where I can contact the Russians— President to president at the highest level and get some movement on this matter towards finding out whatever happened to Raoul Wallenberg. You and I will discuss this with the Secretary of State, and my National Security Adviser. I have a trip to Russia coming up in a few months. I will make some contact with Yeltsin and his people before I go. I will do some quiet pre-work. I can take a note to Premier Boris Yeltsin to ask him personally to re-open the matter. Sure. Why not? We owe Wallenberg everything for his work in Budapest."

Then on November 22 President Clinton entered the Oval Office. He beckoned me from the couch to sit on the chair next to his—a seat normally reserved for heads of state.

"I appreciate your visit, Morris. As I told you in our visit at Yale, Raoul Wallenberg is my hero, too. I first read about him in high school and the story of his heroic work has stuck. I have every intention to follow up and get the Russians to support a new investigation. They have nothing to lose. It'll be part of Glasnost, their new policy of openness and transparency."

"Mr. President, I appreciate your good intentions," I said. "But there are some major impediments to Wallenberg's freedom that you should know about. And unfortunately, they're caused by a handful of unfriendly lawyers in the State Department."

I told him of the behavior of the US State Department in stimulating and encouraging the Russians to file a "Statement of Interest" against my case. I also told him about my experience with private gun lawyer Theroux and his conspiring with lawyers at the State Department to sabotage my original Wallenberg verdict. I outlined how the "*Statement of Interest*" action was instigated by State. The President stared at me in disbelief.

"You mean we helped the Russians bring an action to reverse your verdict and Judge Parker's opinion?"

"Exactly, and I fear there will be more such internal attempts at sabotage, including an effort to abort your planned initiative with Premier Boris Yeltsin, since some of the same people are still in power at State."

"I will be sure to work with the right people at State," he said "Most important, Brezhnev, Gromyko and Kosygin have been dead for over ten years. The old Soviet Union disintegrated almost two years ago. Besides, Boris Yeltsin seems like a different breed of Russian leader. I am scheduled to meet with him soon. I will discuss Wallenberg with him and ask him to make a full new search of the prisons. We will try our best to find him." President Clinton promised to speak with Yeltsin directly about Wallenberg at their upcoming meeting.

It was time for the President's next appointment. Thanksgiving was around the corner, and there was much to be thankful for. And now there was good reason to hope that a new light would open on the case. "Never give up, never give up, and never give up." I said these words of Winston Churchill to the President as we shook hands, thanked him for the visit, and left the Oval Office.

November 30, 1993
New York City
My Birthday Present

November 30th was my 57th birthday, a day of celebration that I share with Mark Twain and Winston Churchill, two men I deeply admire. Both men permeate my personality—one with the indomitable perseverance and courage of Churchill; the other with the puckish sense of humor, and satire of Mark Twain, and Twain's love of adventure and travel.

I had just returned to my law firm in New York City buoyed by my visit. The President had promise to carry the Wallenberg rescue issue directly to Premier Boris Yeltsin in Moscow.

The President and First Lady took a deep interest in the injustice perpetrated on Wallenberg. The rescue strategy was again gathering steam and legs. An investigation was underway in Russia. I tried to find a Soviet lawyer to work with me from within the country, and to locate Wallenberg.

But on this day I set those matters aside and took a birthday walk in Central Park.

I was about to receive a completely unexpected birthday gift—yet another lift to my spirit and my efforts. I walked out of my Manhattan apartment on West 57th Street and headed towards my favorite entrance to Central Park. My normal routine was a brisk walk through the park to my office on the East Side. Though I normally walked the 30 minutes alone, that day I walked with a friend.

As we reached the east side of Central Park—where we would normally exit near the Hotel Pierre on Fifth Avenue-my friend tugged suddenly on my arm and pointed to a beautiful young woman dressed in a tan camel hair coat coming out from under one of the arched stone bridges in Central Park. She was scuffling the leaves in front of her causing them to go up in the air and down again in the early autumn sunlight. She seemed like a young college girl, playful and immersed in her own thoughts. She was beautiful—a young looking brunette dressed in a tan camel hair coat, with royal blue earmuffs and white mittens.

"That looks like Jackie Kennedy," he said.

The woman came closer. It certainly was. After her second husband Aristotle Onassis' death, Jackie had settled in an apartment on 5th Avenue in New York, where she was now a book editor at Doubleday. My friend headed off to his office and I looked again at the woman approaching me on the curved asphalt path. She was now about 10 yards away. I decided it was time for my birthday gift. I moved in front of her. She stopped and looked up at me and smiled at my flirtatious behavior. She could have been a Mount Holyoke student, and I could have been an amorous Amherst College student. It was indeed Jackie Kennedy.

"And who are you?" she asked, with a twinkle in her eyes.

"I am the birthday boy," I replied, not knowing anything better to say. "But even better, I wanted to tell you how proud I was to be an American when you were our First Lady." She liked that. She stopped and smiled back at me. "I also once worked in Washington at The Justice Department with your brother-in-law Bobby." That gave our whole conversation a sense of familiarity. These were moments of remembrance we both could share.

"Oh," she replied, looking at me with new interest. "Bobby was my favorite of all the boys. We were very close. He always took an interest in me, good times and bad. I could always confide in him. He was by my side during all the difficult times, especially after the President's death."

She asked me what work I had done for Bobby and I described my work on the Civil Rights Act of 1964, and how I had briefed the President during my time in the Office of Legal Counsel at the Justice Department. "I was right on the fifth floor. Just down the hall from Bobby."

"And what are you doing now? Anything exciting?" she asked.

"I am working here in the city with a law firm. And I am writing a book on Raoul Wallenberg. It involves my case in the federal court to try to force the Russians to release him."

"Sounds very interesting. I'd like to read it. When you are ready will you bring me a draft, or just a few chapters of your book? In my work at Doubleday I get a chance to select new books to publish."

"That would be wonderful," I replied. "I will definitely bring you the draft and have you take a look at it."

She looked at her watch and whispered, "I have to go. I have enjoyed this visit with you and hope you will come by to see me at Doubleday. I would love to read your chapters." She smiled back at me and extended her hand. We shook hands and I wanted to kiss her on the cheek, but wisely refrained.

A Secret Service man now appeared and he ushered Mrs. Kennedy gently along the walk and out of Central Park. He opened the door of a green Mercedes. He had been watching and listening to our conversation the whole time. I was glad to know they were keeping an eye out for her.

I sent some chapters to Jackie. She marked them and sent them back. "We want to publish your book," she wrote. "Hurry up and finish it!"

Less than six months later Jackie died, and with her demise, Doubleday's interest in my book evaporated. I shelved my efforts on the book for a little while. It was just as well, for more twists and turns in the story were yet to unfold.

When I met Jackie in the park, she was already suffering from the cancer that would end her life. She did not show it and she did not talk about it. She was a very brave woman. I admired her stoicism, a characteristic she shared with Wallenberg.

Jackie Kennedy breathed a new spirit into me, her soft purring voice told me to sustain and to fight and to continue not only my book writing, but my effort to get Raoul free from the Soviet dungeon where he languished alone.

At times my energy wavered, but my brief meeting with her reminded me what it meant to be a 'Kennedy' and to fight the good fight, no matter what tragedy or heart ache came along to block one's path.

Here she was, the indomitable and brave Jacqueline Kennedy, soldiering on in her new life as an editor at Doubleday, fighting cancer without a whimper. In her memory the least I could do was to get up off the canvas and continue the good fight, despite the lack of support, and the harsh opposition of my own government in a cause they should have championed.

I decided that day in Central Park to continue to be the banner carrier and to move the battle forward, even if at times I marched alone. Jackie renewed that fighting spirit in me. Even if only one voice of conscience would be heard, it would be my voice. I did not realize how much energy I had set in motion by filing the lawsuit, and then the second effort in going to Israel to work with the Mossad. The carefully planned blue prints of the Mossad raid to rescue Wallenberg, which I helped to develop in 1989 during a visit to Tel Aviv, were gathering dust in a closed Mossad file in Tel Aviv. Twenty-two years later they would become valuable once again. They were loaned to the CIA and FBI for a new raid. Little did I know how much life they would regain in May of 2011.

December 1993
New York & Washington, DC

Henry Kissinger seemed perturbed. "Nothing could be further from the truth," he declared.

I had arranged to meet Henry Kissinger on December 11, 1993 at his *Kissinger and Associates* offices on Fifth Avenue to discuss Wallenberg's plight and what he might do to help.

When I questioned his commitment to Wallenberg's cause, he suddenly became defensive.

He told me that he had done everything possible. He had wanted to re-open the Wallenberg matter, but the CIA had kept him in the dark on the Brezhnev diamonds theft. As long as Brezhnev or Gromyko remained in power, there was nothing the US could do, in his opinion. But he disagreed with me about US responsibility for Wallenberg's present plight. Kissinger said it was the Swedes and the Russians, never the US, who opposed Wallenberg's release, and thus we had no responsibility; though he agreed with me that we had the power to do something and did not use it. Wallenberg was in an odd position given the fact that we sent him there.

"Well, the question now becomes what do we do now?" I said. "Gromyko is dead. Brezhnev is dead. Wallenberg is still alive. No more embarrassment for the Russians. Now we have *glasnost* and *perestroika* and a new Russian government in place of the Soviets. What about you heading up a blue ribbon panel of international investigators to go to Russia and get the answers?"

Kissinger liked the idea. He even suggested that I work as chief counsel and he could serve and suggest names and personally contact top diplomats from Russia and Sweden. I found Kissinger warm, intelligent, and genuinely interested in Wallenberg. Henry served tea on bone china. Everything about him that day seemed very classy as befitting a diplomat. He was on time for our 5 P.M. appointment, courteous and refined. Yet I felt unrewarded and unfulfilled by the visit. A blue-ribbon commission could never find Wallenberg. I wanted to take another path and to re-activate the Mossad. Soon after my meeting with Kissinger, I received a phone call from President Clinton's secretary.

"Mr. Wolff? Will you hold the line for the President?"

I had no idea he would get back to me in person.

President Clinton got on the line, "Morris, I spoke directly and candidly on this Wallenberg matter with Premier Yeltsin during my visit. Yeltsin claims effusively that Wallenberg is dead. Or more precisely, Yeltsin said there was no actual proof of death, but the Russians simply couldn't find Wallenberg anywhere."

"Confidentially, he has been lost in the gulag somewhere," Yeltsin told me.

"Did you ask Yeltsin for proof of death, for a state autopsy report, or a death certificate? Did you ask when and where and how he died?"

"Yes, I asked all that. Dotted every "i" and crossed each "t".

"They have nothing; No autopsy, no proof of death, no evidence that he even died."

Clinton assured me he had pushed Yeltsin hard, as any good lawyer would do.

"I told him that Wallenberg is our mutual hero," Clinton said, "I told him about your work and that people in the United States want a decent answer."

"Yeltsin seemed to want to help," Clinton told me, "but the Russian President does not know where to turn. The KGB is fighting against Yeltsin. They do not like him. He drinks a great deal and is tough to protect from harm. The KGB does not want the Wallenberg matter reopened. Yeltsin called in his KGB chief while I was there. The KGB chief would not flat out say that Wallenberg was dead. He just said 'we have no proof or records that indicate that he's still alive.'"

"The best I could do was to get Yeltsin to agree to your idea of a joint Swedish-Russian committee of inquiry regarding Wallenberg."

I thanked the President for his phone call and his efforts on Wallenberg's behalf.

"No problem," he said. "Call on me if I can be of further help. After all we are both Yale Law. Professor McDougal has called me on this Wallenberg matter as well. It seems like you have lit up a lot of circuits of appeal on this."

True to his word, the President gave the impetus to the formation of a new US-Sweden-USSR blue ribbon commission, which was convened from 2000 to 2010—a commission of inquiry. I thought they might succeed where other diplomatic efforts for Wallenberg's rescue had failed but they came up with nothing.

December 1993
Meeting the Dalai Lama

I was to meet yet another spiritually interesting individual before the year was out. Because of my human rights work, especially the Wallenberg case, I was honored by being given a private audience with the Dalai Lama in the nave of a church on East Fifty-Seventh Street in New York. We sat on pink pillows beneath the stained glass windows with the afternoon sun shining a radiant spectrum of blue, red and yellow—a rainbow of colors—through the Rosetta stained glass windows.

The Dalai Lama was considering human rights litigation against China. He wanted my advice on how he might present a human rights claim on behalf of his people from of the International Court of Justice at the Hague. He wanted to plead his own case to the world court. During our meeting, the Dalai Lama seemed to be smiling through the pain. His large horned-rimmed glasses were perched at the end of his nose. He had a perennial smile on his face, and although it was cold and snowing, he was only wearing his red and yellow Tibetan prayer robe and sandals. For some reason he just kept smiling, exuding a sense of bliss, as if he had not a care in the world.

He was followed by film actor Richard Gere, a Dalai Lama devotee. I admire Richard Gere's dedication to the Dalai Lama and the Tibetan cause. There were only the three of us. The Dalai Lama came over, put his large arms around me, and gave me a big hug.

"You are a human rights lawyer, Mr. Wolff," he said. "I am glad to meet you here today."

He motioned for me to sit back down against the pillows. The lights in the room were dimmed. He asked me more questions about my work.

"I understand it is quite unique and creative—out of the box, as you Americans say."

I answered: "I believe that somehow, your holiness, we are all connected," I said. "Your ancestors, my ancestors, we all knew each other as friends and family at one time during times of peace and harmony in the past. Our souls are all inter-connected. So I believe that my human rights litigation for one man like Wallenberg is actually human rights law work for all. I believe that no matter the amount of evil, that the spirit of God prevails in the courtroom of human rights at the final moment."

The Dalai Lama chuckled and asked if I could help to free the innocent people of Tibet, and help to regain their homeland, and to be free to pray—free just to be.

"Yes, simply to be!" We chatted for about forty-five minutes and the Dalai Lama continued: "Being is a sacred right. It comes before doing. We have many monks who simply want to be. They want to live and to pray to the Great Buddha."

Then he stood up, again smiling. He pulled back the sleeves of his crimson and tan robe, showing his tan arms. He was sweating a bit, even on this cold day.

Suddenly he shouted "Free Tibet!" "We must free Tibet!" He chanted "Free Tibet" quietly to himself, meditating on the word for a few minutes. Then he turned to me.

"What can you do to help us? Will you go into federal court like you did for Ambassador Wallenberg and ask for freedom for my people?"

I said that I could certainly give it a try, but that it was a better case for the World Court at The Hague. But then a state like India would have to start it. The Dalai Lama invited me to sit next to him and outline my plan. He asked me to represent the people of Tibet, but I had to decline. I was going broke on *pro bono* work. Also my plan was to travel to India in just a few weeks in February of 1994.

I was invited to India by Guru Risharshi Muniji, a holy man in an ancient temple near to the sacred city of Kaya Varohan, north of Bombay. I had promised to study Talmud with him, as well as the Bagavad-Gita and the Koran. I was leaving for India in just a few weeks, and planned to be gone for at least a month. I promised to help find other lawyers for them in New York.

I asked the Dalai Lama if he felt that Wallenberg might still be alive.

"Most definitely yes," he replied. "I can feel his spirit and his soul vibrating near to us in this place."

I felt relieved and encouraged. A week later, I was a pilgrim on my way to India.

February 1994

Kayavarohan, India & New York City

I was drained from my ten years fighting for the freedom of Wallenberg. All the blind alleys I pursued brought no results, time spent drafting the complaint, time spent lobbying the members of Congress, time spent asking Congress for the joint resolution. I had actually visited twenty-seven congressmen—a very time consuming experience. Then there was time preparing and presenting the case in court—finally, winning the victory. The elation and euphoria and sense of hope were soon to be dashed—all dashed, as the judgment was reversed four years later. There seemed to be nothing positive now to show for all my efforts.

Wallenberg was still a captive.

I went to India to renew myself—to search for meaning through religion or spiritual channels—to try to understand my life—where I had been and where I was going.

Every morning in my white or saffron robe, with my clean-shaven head, I walked the dusty roads around the village of Kayavarohan in a spirit of meditation. Not far away, I could see the temples on either side of the road - white marble monuments with ornate ivory carvings of the gods.

The women of the village were also up early, working on the bank of the muddy stream washing clothes and slapping the white cotton sheets against the black rocks. Inside me a quiet voice whispered, "What about me? What about me? You are so busy with all the needs of others. When will you find time for me?" I was so tired. I looked at my hands, searching for the source of the quiet voice coming from within me asking for time for myself

Late one afternoon as I was meeting with my teacher he said, "You have paid a big ticket not just in money but in spirit in your coming all the way to India," he chuckled. "You have come up into the quiet hills of little Kayavarohan, to sleep on thin mats and take cold showers every morning, only to learn that your knowledge, your source, is waiting for you back home. It is not in the Koran or Gita, it is in your own Judaism, in your own upbringing, in the energy of your own roots and in the mystical writings of Spinoza, Maimonides, and the mystics of the Kaballah. You have unfinished business. You must make another effort to find Raoul Wallenberg. He is waiting for your rescue. I can feel it, even here. He is alive. He is waiting for you. Renew and return."

I was ready. I had regained my energy and my fighting spirit. My grief had passed and there was more human rights work to be done.

I flew home from Bombay to JFK.

I was met at JFK by my friends Bert Manning and Barbara Lazarus. "Well, look at you!" she screamed.

Whatever Happened to Raoul Wallenberg?

Still in a spiritual mindset, I had worn my Indian garb on the plane—white robe, sandalwood mandala, and of course my shaved head. I was holding on to my quiet life in India as long as possible.

"Where is the nice Jewish boy we sent to India?" Barbara chided.

"I am still here!" I replied. "Just a bit older, hopefully a little bit wiser. I had a great time."

I swept up my white robe and proceeded to the car, enjoying every moment of the uproar over my appearance. It was good to be home with friends again.

We drove to Bert's home in Larchmont, in the suburbs of New York. As president of the world-famous J. Walter Thompson advertising agency, he commanded a top salary and lived very well.

After I washed and sat down with the rest of the guests for a glass of red wine, we began the Passover Seder prayers.

After dinner was over, Bert drew me into his study.

"I have located for you a man by the name of Tom Veres," Bert said.

"Tom Veres?" I said. "You must be joking. He was Wallenberg's photographer in Budapest. But he died there at the end of the war. There are even theories that he was taken away with Wallenberg and his driver."

"No, Tom Veres is alive."

"Amazing! Is he still in Budapest?"

"No."

"Where?"

Bert smiled ever so slightly and announced, "He works in my office in downtown Manhattan"

"What!"

Bert laughed. "It's true," he said. "He's been working for me for three years, but I only found out yesterday who he really was. He shows up for work every day just like everyone else. He is a gifted photographer, taking shots of celebrities like Marilyn Monroe, Tony Bennett, Louis Armstrong, Carol Channing and many others. He never talks about the war."

"Then how did you find out?" I asked.

"Yesterday a man came in and Tom and he started speaking Hungarian. I asked Tom where he learned it. Then he told me about Budapest and his work with Wallenberg. I assume you know the story."

"Yes, of course."

"Then I told him about you, who sued the Soviets for Wallenberg's release. His eyes lit up and he smiled for the first time I can remember. He said he wants to meet you. Come downtown to my office tomorrow and I'll introduce you."

The evening wrapped up early, as everyone was tired. I made my way back to the city. Another part of Wallenberg's past seemed to be reaching out to reveal itself to me.

The next day Bert took me to see Tom Veres in his "photography studio" inside the agency. Tom was eager to show me his shots of well-known entertainers: Louie Armstrong, Carol Channing, Tony Curtis and George Burns.

"Now this was a lady," Tom Veres said, showing me a picture of Carol Channing. "What a fox, and so intelligent." She wanted to know all about me, where I came from, and what I did in the war. I told her I had been Wallenberg's private photographer, that I followed him around all over Budapest, shooting pictures of him as he bargained to get the Jews off the boxcars. Some days just to relieve him of stress we went for walks alone along the Danube River. I caught him in every mood and in every situation." Carol Channing was fascinated with all that. She also lost people in the Holocaust. "Sometimes I had to hide my camera under my sweater so the Nazis could not see that I was recording their behavior. The Nazis and Arrow Cross would often destroy my film, when they heard the camera clipping."

"Raoul would buy me new film and a new camera. 'I want it all recorded,' he told me. 'There will be people who say it never happened. Get all of the suffering down in pictures. In Black and White. The war will end one day, and without the photos and the pictures no one will believe what happened.'"

"I followed him day and night, everywhere he went. I was only 19 years old. I was too young to know better. I could have been shot. I did not care. I was headstrong and brave, taking vital photographs for posterity. My parents were taken away in a truck one night and never returned. They died at Auschwitz. My savior, Raoul Wallenberg, did everything possible to try to recover them. He was a saint and a gutsy fighter, all at the same time."

Veres opened one of his desk drawers. There were the original photos of his time with Wallenberg. There was Wallenberg as a young man, one of him standing in a three-piece gray suit at his desk in the office in Budapest—a picture you will see on the cover of this book—another on the phone, sitting confidently signing papers, surrounded by his colleagues—influential Jewish bankers, former industrialists and lawyers who helped him run the office.

Veres had one other prize possession—a picture of Wallenberg negotiating with German and Hungarian officials to win the release of a trainload of Jews bound for the death camps. Wallenberg is on the outside of the crowd, with his back to us, quietly negotiating and bribing the soldiers.

"He created miraculous luck," Veres said. "There is no other explanation. The Germans tried to kill him almost once a week. They shot at him, tried to run him down with cars and trucks in the street, threw bombs into our offices. He would just shrug it off and move to another location. It was scary following him around and taking pictures. He would just move the back of his hand when he wanted a picture taken. I would hide the camera under a scarf or some garment as I took pictures. I was arrested twice with him, and the film taken and dumped on the ground when they realized what I was doing."

Per Anger had introduced Wallenberg to Veres, who was the streetwise son of a well-known society photographer. Young Veres had learned from his father, taking pictures of children of the Swedish diplomats. A Jewish convert to Christianity, he signed on as Wallenberg's photographer in exchange for Swedish protection. He did not really know what he was getting into.

But as he observed Wallenberg move through the city, dealing fearlessly with Nazi thugs, Veres also overcame his fear. He devised a technique of wrapping his camera in a scarf, then shooting through a hole in the scarf. He would then develop the pictures in his darkroom and Wallenberg would send them to Stockholm in the diplomatic pouch. "Wallenberg always behaved," Veres said, "as though nothing was impossible."

Once, Wallenberg scribbled a note to Veres to meet him at the Jozsefvarosi Railroad Station, which had been a freight-loading yard. Grain and other foodstuffs from Budapest and the provinces were loaded onto freight trains, to be shipped to Vienna from this out-of-the-way station in eastern Pest. In the last few months of the war though, Jews, on the way to forced labor in the Third Reich, replaced the cargo. When Veres arrived the next morning, Wallenberg, flanked by heavily armed gendarmes, was waiting. The station itself was entirely ringed by gendarmes. Wallenberg's newly acquired Studebaker, driver behind the wheel, was parked a few feet from the platform. An endless mass of men, some carrying bedrolls, others with suitcases, some still wearing business suits and hats, stood waiting.

Wallenberg and the head of the gendarmes, Laszlo Ferenczy, were bent over a long table on the platform. "My people get in line here," Wallenberg called out.

Then several hundred of "his" people were allowed to begin their walk home. By contrast, no one else appeared at the yard to claim the Swiss or the Portuguese passport holders.

While Wallenberg engaged the gendarmes in animated conversation, Veres took advantage of the chaos and slipped around the side of a rail car filled with people, which had not yet been padlocked, though it was shut from the outside. He opened the door. Hundreds of startled people poured out, running for their lives.

A short distance from Wallenberg, a gray-uniformed SS officer, who until that moment had stayed in the background, now stepped forward. It was Hauptsturmführer Theodor Dannecker.

Dannecker shouted at Wallenberg and Veres to stop. A vigilant gendarme picked up the cue. He slowly lowered the barrel of his automatic rifle until the Swede was centered in his gun sight. Wallenberg ignored the gun. He bounded across the platform to the other side of the train and into his waiting car. He pulled Veres in next to him, while his driver barreled the Studebaker out of the station.

Dannecker, one of Eichmann's closest henchmen, was furious. He made no secret of his plan to even the score with Wallenberg. Later, when the protection afforded by diplomatic license plates became meaningless, Dannecker ordered Wallenberg's car smashed by a German armored personnel carrier. Luckily, Wallenberg was not in it.

Veres' photographs also served another purpose—blackmail. In the middle of the death marches, Wallenberg paid a call on Ferenc Fiala, spokesman for the Nazi-backed Szalasi government. Wallenberg tossed a packet of fifty Veres photographs on the desk of this former Hungarian fencer of little note. The shots showed Hungarian Nazis rounding up Jews from safe houses that were flying the official Swedish flag. Wallenberg threatened to send them immediately to Stockholm, which would create outrage and destroy the Szalasi regime's chances of being recognized by Sweden.

Fiala objected vehemently to Wallenberg's power play. Nevertheless, he promised to give the Arrow Cross an unambiguous order: the Swedish houses were to be off limits. There was a problem, though. Wallenberg knew that the Arrow Cross often did not pay much attention to their leaders. But at least this commitment now offered Wallenberg a nominal legal leg on which to stand. He packed his things up and started to leave, with the pictures. Fiala objected again, but Wallenberg said he'd keep the photos.

At Wallenberg's suggestion, Veres began disguising himself in the tall black boots and riding pants of the Arrow Cross. One night as Veres approached Vorosmarty Square, his pocket's bulging with the day's film, which he planned to develop in his darkroom overnight, he was blinded by a light shining in his eyes. All he could see was a pair of black boots much like his own in front of him.

"Long live Szalasi!" Veres shouted automatically, flinging his right arm straight out, in his best imitation Nazi salute. The Arrow Cross patrol lowered his searchlight and returned the salute.

After this incident Wallenberg shipped the undeveloped film straight to Stockholm.

"I stayed with him until the very end," said Veres. "I wanted to go with him on that last day, the day he drove up to Debrecen from Budapest to meet the Russians. He thought he was going to be placed in charge of urban redevelopment of Budapest. After all, he had the architect's degree from the University of Michigan. He was very proud of that—and of his ties to America. And the man was immune to fear or anything else that stood in the way of fulfilling his mission."

After the war, Veres immigrated to the United States. By then a skilled photographer, he was still suffering from the effects of the war. At times, he said, he would sink into moments of deep melancholia and depression.

Veres and I became good friends over time. We shared a common hero. When he retired from J. Walter Thompson, he retired to a chicken farm in upstate New York. Yet he never forgot Wallenberg. "I am haunted by his absence," he once told me, "but I feel his presence. I feel he is still alive." Veres died a few years ago—penniless, or close to it.

In his final years the movie star Tony Curtis helped to cover Tom's expenses. Curtis, a Hungarian Jew also helped to finance the rebuilding of the main synagogue in Budapest where a plaque to that effect stands today. Tony Curtis, an unsung hero and a quiet philanthropist died recently in the year 2010.

April 1995
Budapest

In the spring of 1995, I led a delegation of Wharton Business School students from the University of Pennsylvania on a ten-day business study trip to Budapest. I was thrilled at the chance to see Wallenberg's office and get a feel for Buda and Pest as Wallenberg had seen the divided city 50 years earlier in 1944 and 1945.

On my first afternoon, I went to the Great Synagogue in the center of Pest, the part of the city where most churches and business firms are located. I opened the heavy door to the synagogue and walked in. I sat in one of the wooden pews with red cushions and began to pray for all the Jews who had worshiped here and who would never return. As I sat there, quietly, I began to daydream:

In my dream, I see Judith Yaron and a young Raoul Wallenberg coming in the door to attend services. The place was filled with people singing and praying.

"Hurry, Hurry Raoul. We are late. The services are starting. It is Rosh Hashonah. The Jewish families are dressed in their best clothes. They are waiting for you. They want you there at the beginning of the service."

I dream that I see Judith in a lovely white dress and Wallenberg in a gray three-piece business suit, blue shirt and red tie. They walk in arm in arm together up the main aisle as if they are about to be married. The grateful people reach out and touch him gently with the edge of their prayer books as he walks down the wide isle to his reserved seat. There is a bright light from the menorah shining on his face giving him a glow and aura that no one else possesses. His path is bathed in light.

I shake myself awake. I am in the great synagogue. I feel Wallenberg's presence for the third time in my life. It seems as though he is there with me, just a few pews away. This is the synagogue where Judith Yaron took Raoul every Friday night—so that he could connect with the Jews he was helping, and to learn more about the history of the Jewish people. It is on the eastern side of the Danube River. Budapest is divided down the middle by the Danube. The synagogue was partially destroyed during the war. Film actor, Tony Curtis, quietly paid to have it rebuilt. A plaque on the synagogue wall proudly says so. "Restored through the kindness and generosity of Film Actor Tony Curtis (born Tony Schwartz). Our grateful congregation thanks him."

I met Tony Curtis on my return and briefed him on my work for Wallenberg. He was ecstatic. "That is so great," he said. "I am glad you saw the beautiful new synagogue. I am proud of it." We stayed in touch. I remember his dark bright eyes, curly black hair and a very sweet smile. I will not forget his wild sense of humor. He cared deeply for the Hungarian people of Budapest. He loved Raoul Wallenberg.

Going up the Danube River north towards Germany, Buda is on the western bank, built on hillsides, with rich private residences and clean fresh air at the top of the hill. That is where the Swedish legation was located in 1944 and 1945. This was the safer side. On the eastern side of the river was Pest, where Wallenberg had his four office locations.

On the second morning, I woke up early and decided to walk through the city. I arrived at the Budapest City Museum. There, in a small case was a handwritten letter addressed to Joseph Stalin, and dated November 17, 1947.

November 17, 1947

Generalissimo Stalin
Moscow, USSR

Dear Mr. Stalin:
        As an old Jew I appeal to you to do everything possible to find and send back to his country the Swede Raoul Wallenberg, who was one of the very few who, during the bad years of Nazi persecution on his own accord and risking his own life, worked to rescue thousands of my unhappy Jewish people.
                Yours very respectfully,

                        Albert Einstein.

Dear Mr. Stalin:

As an old Jew I appeal to you to do everything possible to find and send back to his country the Swede Raoul Wallenberg, who was one of the very few who, during the bad years of Nazi persecution on his own accord and risking his own life, worked to rescue thousands of my unhappy Jewish people.
Yours very respectfully,

Albert Einstein

When I returned to the hotel and asked the concierge where I could find Wallenberg's central headquarters, his face lit up and he became enthusiastic.

242

There was not enough he could do. He insisted I wait for him to get off his shift in five minutes. He assured me I would never find it alone, as there were no signs, no notices. He knew. He was a Jew.

We left the hotel together and walked the empty cobblestone streets, passing the flower shop owners and small bakeries and meat and sausage stores as they opened their small shops for Saturday morning business. One or two stores with the words "Kosher" in Hebrew above the door stayed closed and shuttered in observance of the Sabbath.

Along the way he told me his story:

"I was there at headquarters many times with my parents, as a young boy. I was a messenger. My family was taken out of our home by Wallenberg the night before the last roundup of Jews in December of 1944. Wallenberg came to our home and gave my father the famous "Wallenberg passport." I still have my family passport at my home. It is in a frame above our fireplace with the young faces of my two parents. Wallenberg saved me, my two sisters and both my parents."

The concierge and I wound our way down the irregular cobblestone streets. The smell of fresh bread and cakes sweetened the damp cold air. After fifteen minutes we arrived.

"Here it is," he said. "There are no signs directing people to this famous office—it is only 'famous' for us as Jews. The rest of Budapest today is happy to forget the whole period."

There was a Jewish family living in the upstairs who acted as caretakers. The concierge got the key from them, for which favor I gave them five dollars. The heavy brown wooden door with its clean brass knocker opened outward to the street. Two well-worn marble steps led up to the front door. The sun over my shoulder threw shafts of light onto a dark wooden floor covered by Persian rugs, gifts it turned out from Wallenberg committees from around the world— especially from Australia, Canada and Israel, from where many of the survivor families have emigrated.

As I entered 43 Tatra Ulloi there was a large waiting room with chairs around the side. Large windows opened to the street. The caretaker switched on the fluorescent lights. Beyond the waiting room was Wallenberg's private office. First, there was a large outer office, where Judith Yaron had worked. The caretaker showed me examples of the passport applications, yellowed parchment pages with blanks where the names of families and children were provided and a spot for a family photo.

Beyond the first office was a second, smaller one with Wallenberg's desk, a two-tiered in-and-out box and a green shaded lamp on his desk. There was an old leather chair on a swivel. I sat for a moment in the chair seeking to find and to feel the energy of the man who sat here from June of 1944 through January of 1945.

Whatever Happened to Raoul Wallenberg?

"I want to be alone for a few moments," I told the others.

They closed the door behind them. I passed my hands over the dark mahogany desk, donated for Wallenberg's use by a Jewish family. Everything had a second-hand feel to it. The green glass lamp still worked. The old Wallenberg blotter with the calendar reading "January, 1945" was still there with markings, notes written by Raoul Wallenberg in each daily square up to January 17, 1945. On that date it said "Leaving this morning for a meeting with the Eighteenth Red Army in Debrecen." That was the last entry.

On the blotter, I read the earlier entries leading up to January 17th— Wallenberg's to-do list: "Go to train station at 8 A.M., Major out shipment of Jews—Major death march by foot to Hungarian border scheduled for January 12th." "On January 14th: last desperate efforts of the Germans to bomb the Jewish ghetto; intervene with Schmidthuber and Eichmann. Threaten war crimes trial if they fail to abandon the idea."

All the notations were in pen, in a small, meticulous hand. All the "t"s were crossed, the "i"s dotted—the work of a careful, measured man, a man with purpose and vision, who knew that saving lives required daily detail and organization. For ten minutes I sat there alone, thinking of him. As I left I read again the small plaque on the front door that the delegation of the Wallenberg Committee of Budapest had placed there: "This was the office of Raoul Wallenberg during the final days of World War II. From this location Wallenberg and the Jewish Counsel of Budapest worked to save the last remnant of Jews from Hitler's executioners. Brave Man. Brave Work. May he be at peace wherever he may be."

April 1996
Washington, DC

I first met William Colby in early 1996 in Philadelphia. A heroic and daring World War II paratrooper behind enemy lines for the Office of Strategic Services, which evolved into the CIA, Colby spent most of his professional life in "The Agency," rising to become the director from 1973 to 1976 under Presidents Nixon and Ford. Colby had unique access to some of the darkest secrets of our government's involvement in covert operations in other countries. He still had up to date working contacts with high-level KGB retirees.

Now out of government, Colby was allowing his conscience, rather than money, to direct his actions. Though it angered many in the corridors of power in Washington, DC, Colby had "come clean" about certain controversial CIA programs, and was now devoting his energy to the causes of justice and human rights.

The LANARC (Lawyers Alliance for Nuclear Arms Regulation and Control) meeting we both attended was for lawyers interested in controlling nuclear arms proliferation. On hearing about my work on Wallenberg, Colby stepped forward.

"I have a good network of contacts who are now retired former officials of the KGB," he volunteered to me. "Perhaps they can help us."

Indeed, he was highly encouraging and supportive of my efforts. He suggested a luncheon meeting at Zaberer's, an elegant Washington, DC restaurant, as he had something to show me.

I arrived a few minutes before twelve for our scheduled luncheon. The restaurant was bustling with people in suits—serious faces standing behind the red velvet rope of the waiting line. When I said I was there to meet William Colby for lunch, the headwaiter escorted me past a long line of small tables, all with white tablecloths and small vases of red and white roses. He pulled out a small square table, nodding his head for me to sit on the leather bank of seats looking out on the room.

I spotted various prominent patrons. New York Senator Daniel Patrick Moynihan, seated at the next table with David Broder of the *Washington Post,* was talking nonstop, gesturing with his hands to make a point.

My former boss, Pennsylvania Senator Arlen Specter, sat nearby at another table, speaking in hushed tones with two of his legislative aides. He smiled and waved a brief hello and returned to his conversation.

At 12:15 the headwaiter brought Colby to the table and seated him next to me, so that together we looked out on the room. He was dressed in a dark blue suit, white shirt, and a tie with little embossed figures of Minutemen in red, white and blue. He carried a slim black case.

Whatever Happened to Raoul Wallenberg?

No sooner had he said hello than Colby reached his hands under the table, as if to sweep away the underbrush.

"Sorry about that," he said. "It's a habit—a quick sweep just to make sure there are no bugs planted to intercept our conversation. I can't afford to have others listening. This is my favorite table. These two marble pillars next to us make it harder for people to listen in."

Colby nodded toward the far corner of the room, indicating two military types in dark suits with crew cuts, who looked away, as we both looked at them.

"They're Russians. Two KGB agents from the Soviet Embassy. I recognize them and they know it! We have whole large cells of KGB here in Washington, DC, pretending to be military attachés. Between the United Nations in New York City and here in Washington, DC, there are approximately 280 KGB agents in the USA and they are free to travel anywhere, including nuclear installations. I'm sure they'd love to hear our conversation."

"Are they still interested in you?" I asked. "You've been out of the CIA, out of the loop, for almost ten years."

"A former CIA Chief is never out of the loop. They also know I am trying to solve a few things."

"Well, I certainly appreciate your offer to help me solve the Wallenberg mystery."

We ate lunch before getting down to business, waiting for the Russians, who were ahead of us in their meal, to leave.

We talked about tennis, canoeing and other sports. Finally, the two Russian agents finished eating. On the way out they passed our table. There was a momentary pause as they stared at Colby, then moved on. As soon as they were out of earshot, we leaned over to talk to each other.

"They know I am networking, reaching out to connect with a team of retired KGB people on some peace projects. They are not happy with this potential peaceful involvement of the USA and KGB," Colby said. "They also know I am working with you to try and get some inside info on where they are storing Wallenberg. KGB knows he is alive. They take care of his feeding. For some reason unknown to me they seem to want to still keep him alive. It is as if he has some current value. Now let's get down to the business at hand."

From the black case he pulled out a file, the only item inside. On the front in black magic marker he had written, "Confidential: Wolff / Wallenberg file."

"This contains all of my work for you. It lists the different places the KGB has been housing Wallenberg in the last five years. Apparently he is well cared for and still alive. This is for your review, and your eyes only. It is the preliminary material I have received from my KGB counterpart Stopatkin. Read it here, in front of me and then hand it back."

The two-page memo outlined the places Wallenberg had been over the past ten years—Lubyanka, Lefortovo, Mordvinia, Wrangel Island and Kazan—

shuttled back and forth every three or four months. Elinor Lester had showed me a similar document, but this one was updated, even showing that Wallenberg had been moved away from a dacha near Moscow just prior to the Mossad raid.

"The Russians are absolutely correct when they say that 'Wallenberg' is dead."

"What do you mean?"

"Wallenberg is no longer called 'Wallenberg,' but instead has been given two new Scandinavian names for "shipping" purposes—'Andersen' and 'Pedersen.' So while the prisoner known as 'Wallenberg' is officially dead, the man himself lives on under these two aliases."

I breathed a sigh of relief as Colby continued.

"We know he is still alive and is normally moved on a regular basis between some of these sites. He is in decent health, takes exercise on a daily basis, and is in good spirits. Most of his time is spent alone, under the watchful eyes of guards who tend to his needs."

I finished reading the memo, put it back in the folder, and returned it to Colby.

"The next time we meet, I will have some more information for you," Colby said. "It will be new material from a 'mystery guest.'"

"Who might that be?" I asked.

"His name is Viktor Cherkashin, a cold war warrior and my other former KGB counterpart and nemesis at the chess table of intelligence and counter-intelligence. He was head of KGB when I was head of CIA. He is an expert on Beria and the hench men of the late 40s and 50s. He claims that the Gromyko letter in '57 suggesting that Wallenberg was dead in 1947 was a complete hoax, an effort to lull the USA into a state of indifference and inaction."

"He knows where all the bones are buried. He was their superstar and they have treated him like dirt. Helping me on Wallenberg is part of his quiet revenge to the system that failed to honor and reward him. Exposing Wallenberg as alive will embarrass a lot of people and that is what he wants to do—embarrass the top brass. What do we care? He has his motives. I have mine—as long as we come together for the same result. I want to find out what they did with Wallenberg. I have the same desire you have, and that is to yank him loose."

At 2 P.M., after a very pleasant lunch together, Colby abruptly said, "I have to go. See you next week on Tuesday at my office. I guarantee you it will be worth your time."

When I arrived at Colby's office on the following Tuesday I was disappointed. He was not there and my heart dropped. I sensed foul play; somehow I knew there was something desperately wrong. The receptionist simply said: "I am very sorry we were not able to reach you in time. We had a call this morning from his wife Sally. Mr. Colby did not return home from his Sunday canoe trip. He has been missing for the last few days. We are all concerned."

"But I just spoke to him on Friday."

"We know. I took your phone call and passed you through to him."

"Then what happened?"

"We do not know as yet. He is reported as missing."

From the conference room at Colby's office I called his wife Sally. She told me his canoe had been found downstream, but that he had never returned from his canoe outing of the past Sunday afternoon. Something was wrong.

Several days later, Colby's body was discovered lying face down on the marshy riverbank. Someone suggested that he had fallen out of his canoe and drowned. An autopsy found he had been suffering from hardening of the arteries. The cover up cause of death given was drowning and hypothermia, and it was ruled accidental. There were no blood clots found, though any such clots could have dissolved during the weeklong search for his body, according to the medical examiner.

There were a few strange details that left many people wondering. I scoffed at the idea of "death by canoeing error," and I doubted a heart attack.

First of all, Colby was a skilled canoeist and in excellent health, according to his wife Sally. Second, the location where his body was found had been thoroughly searched before. How could his body have mysteriously beached itself after more than a week? Finally, Colby's body was discovered without the life jacket he always wore, and without his shoes. None of these items were ever found. Had Colby this one time decided to throw caution, and his life jacket and shoes, to the wind?

The truth? According to one member of the Green Berets, a crack marine commando unit: "Bill Colby was whacked," a Green Beret term for murdered. He knew too much and was moving in a direction dangerous to others. He knew too many Cold War secrets and planned to expose people.

I suspected the Russians. He was taken forcibly from his canoe, injected with chemicals drowned, put back in the canoe, and set afloat. This information was recently uncovered in secret Green Beret reports. The CIA confirmed the fact: "whacked" or "taken out."

Colby was planning to give me materials from the KGB showing precisely where Wallenberg was located as of April 1996. It was my plan to forward that information to Abraham Ber at the Mossad. Ber and his team were in the early stages of planning a second Moscow rescue effort. This new KGB report was to have become the basis for their new plan of rescue. The Russian KGB asset whom I was to meet with Colby was a double agent working for the Russians and the USA. I agree with those who believe that Bill Colby was murdered—taken off the playing field as the man who knew too much.

Summer 1998
Phoenix

Fifteen years after first speaking with Esther Weiss, I met another tough and charming survivor, Harry Spitz. I visited and interviewed this eighty-three year old gentleman at his home in Phoenix during the very hot summer of 1998, when I was there on business and had been introduced to him at the Synagogue.

This is his story:

Harry had been working as a volunteer with Raoul Wallenberg since the day Wallenberg arrived in 1944. By late December 1944, the war was almost over. Harry had a sense of foreboding. They were expecting the Russian invasion any day now. The Nazis knew their days were numbered and that the war was lost. Despite all that, they continued frantically killing Jews.

One day Wallenberg closed the office early, sending everyone home and counseling them to hide. It was to be a night of terror—of horror—the last night-massacre and roundup of Jews by the Nazis. Bruce Teicholz, Harry's underground counterpart; had gotten word that the Nazis were planning to evacuate the city. The Russian troops were moving in on Budapest and had pitched camp only 30 miles from the city limits.

Harry was the last to leave the office at 4:30. It was already getting dark. He began walking down the cobblestone street toward his home only a block away when he heard three quick rifle shots fired over his head. *"Halt, juden gehen sie nicht weiter!!"* ("Stop there, Jew. Go no farther.")

He froze in his tracks. Three Gestapo in long gray coats came up behind him. One slammed his rifle butt between his shoulder blades while the other two hit his ribs. He fell to the ground. They continued to beat him.

Then he was ordered to get up, put his hands behind his neck, and march. He did as he was told. The three Gestapo marched behind him. They ordered Harry to turn towards the river, saying that he was going for a little swim in the Danube. Harry began to pray quietly as they marched along the cobblestones, past the tall bright windows of the pastry shop, Napoleons in the window. There was a girl with a white hat on her head standing behind the counter. She froze and stood dead still as the men walked by.

By the river, there was a group of twelve men, all Jews, all friends, volunteers from the Wallenberg headquarters. Someone had squealed. Wallenberg was nowhere in sight.

The German soldiers took pieces of rope and tied the men's wrists together behind their backs. Then they took longer pieces of rope and tied the men together, three to a group, each man one foot apart. They were then marched in threes to the edge of the river. The first group was lined up on the bank. One single rifle shot in the back of the middleman's head caused him to topple forward, pulling the other two men in with him. Fifteen minutes later the next group of three was lined up and the process repeated. Harry was in the next group. Fifteen minutes left to live. It was getting dark. The lights above the bridges over the Danube near to the Grand Hotel could be seen flickering on.

When the time came it was mercifully dark. Harry began to work the rope, making efforts to loosen his hands. He was on one of the ends of his group. He would not be shot, but the weight of the other two men would pull him under. "I made my peace with God"

Harry was just 5'6", but strong and tough, in good physical condition and mentally ready. He walked with his head held high, his back erect, and his eyes straight ahead. He looked for the reeds on the other side of the river.

As a young boy, his brother David and he would come and swim in the river, near the same spot. David and he would play in the bulrushes, and go under water and breathe air through the hollow cylinders of the reeds, pretending they were dead.

A bullet whizzed just behind Harry's ears and killed the man next to him. The man on the other end began to scream, so they shot him, too. The three were pushed into the icy waters of the Danube, and began to float away from Budapest, southward toward the sea.

Harry pretended to be dead, holding his breath and staying face down, fearing another bullet from the water's edge by an impatient gunman. He felt the weight of the other two men, the dead weight of the man in the middle and the lighter weight of the man on the other end, who miraculously survived the head wound and was thrashing in the water, gasping for air. After a few moments, the thrashing on the other end stopped. Harry started swimming, carrying the dead weight of his two companions. The current carried them away from the city and the soldiers. When he was out of sight, Harry swam up quietly to the muddy riverbank on the opposite side of the river, pulling his companions with him. With a sharp stone he cut the rope and freed himself. The other men's bodies floated away.

Harry stayed on the riverbank throughout the night. Every time he heard voices, Harry slipped back into the cold water, using a hollow reed from the bulrushes to breathe.

At first light he climbed out of the river and walked along the road until he came to a farmhouse. There was a small blue and gold Swedish flag "growing" out of a red geranium pot in the front window. He was seven miles south of Budapest. He knew he was safe.

He stayed at the farmhouse for one month, until January 27, 1945. A few weeks after his detainment, Budapest was liberated. Wallenberg was captured and never seen again.

When I met Harry, he told me he believed that Wallenberg was still alive.

"I feel his energy. I feel connected to his life energy. I know he is a survivor like me," Harry Spitz said.

After the war, Harry was moved to Vienna, Austria with many other Jewish survivors—all assisted by the American Joint Distribution Committee. In Vienna, he met and married his wife, another survivor from Budapest, and together they chose America as their future home.

In 1946, they moved, looking for a quiet place of retreat in the desert. Harry's life had seen enough turbulence by that time. They settled in Phoenix in the early days of its development. Phoenix was a quiet small town then. Harry went into real estate and began to buy properties. He was cunning and shrewd, two talents which he learned from Wallenberg and from being a survivor. He became a multi-millionaire and donated most of his fortune to The Holocaust Studies program at Arizona State University in Tempe near Phoenix. His career had started in the 1950's, before air conditioning and the land boom. He worked twelve hours a day for 50 years. When I met him he was retired, living quietly with his wife in a small and unpretentious house. He stayed home and took care of his garden. He is a self-professed health nut and he exercises every day. His children live nearby with his three grandchildren.

He said, "I owe Raoul Wallenberg my life, and the life I have been able to build here."

August 1998

Sacramento

I flew to Sacramento to attend the wedding of my favorite nephew Landy, named for my father Leo. I woke about seven, showered and dressed in my room at the Hyatt.

When I opened my hotel room door, planning to head down to breakfast, I saw at my feet the morning' paper, the August 12th edition of the *Sacramento Bee*. The headline shouted up at me: *Raoul Wallenberg Could Be Alive in the Gulag.*

The article, a reprint of one that had originally appeared eight days earlier in *The Times,* London's respected newspaper, carried the byline of Giles Whittell, a correspondent whose writing on international espionage I had read before.

"A Swedish diplomat who saved up to 100,000 Jews from Nazi concentration camps could still be alive, a top official has admitted after the discovery of a Hungarian prisoner of war in a Russian mental hospital 55 years after he was captured on the Eastern Front." I read on. "The recent discovery of Andras Tamas, 75, in a psychiatric hospital 300 miles east of Moscow has again raised the possibility that Raoul Wallenberg is alive. Some research suggests that the two men may have been held in the same hospital in Kazan."

What research? I wondered. Who is doing the sleuthing now? Why the renewed interest in Wallenberg's fate? And the mention of Kazan—that was one of the places listed in the memorandum Colby had shown me.

Whittell indicated the findings resulted from an investigation by a Swedish-Russian commission of inquiry, the same bilateral commission President Clinton had promised me he would champion in his upcoming meeting with Yeltsin. I knew the commission had been established. But this was the first I heard of their doing anything of significance. It's taken them a long time to act, I thought, but perhaps it's been worth the wait.

"The commission's report offers evidence that Wallenberg did not die, as earlier reported by the Russians."

Well, that's nothing new, I thought.

"The commission's report offers evidence that Wallenberg was moved around the gulag system, with stays in Kazan and Vologda."

I was excited but frustrated. Those were only two of the seventeen places where he has been sighted. Had the commissioners explored other leads? Did they have the clout—or the will—to actually find him? To rescue him?

This was merely a confirmation of what I had long insisted to be true. But surely this commission, after all these years, had learned something new. Giles Whittell's August 12, 1998 article ended on a cryptic and ironic note:

252

"Mr. Tamas' history only surfaced when doctors tried to have him removed in order to alleviate the hospital's overcrowded conditions."

The following Monday, I called David Evans at the US State Department. We had been friends ever since our years together as classmates at The Germantown Friends School in Philadelphia. We were both members of the class of 1954. We were also co-editors of the school's underground newspaper, *The Rebel*. David had quietly supported the Wallenberg cause even when his superiors at The State Department turned their backs on it. David had already read the same news article and was ready to act. He promised to contact the US embassy in Budapest.

"I have one bone to pick with you, Morris"

"I am listening, David. Tell me about it."

"Your big bossiness on the soccer field. You were always telling me what to do and how to play and where to position myself."

"You were always coaching me."

"That hasn't changed much."

"What do you mean?"

"I'm feeling bossy again. I want you to find Wallenberg."

True to his word, and with the assistance of Ambassador Peter Tufo, my Yale Law School classmate, who was now US Ambassador to Hungary, David traveled to Hungary and visited Tamas in a Budapest hospital. He spoke with him directly and discovered that Tamas had been held in the gulag all those many years, not because he was mentally ill, but because he spoke an indecipherable Hungarian dialect that the officials could not understand.

"He was not crazy, just misunderstood. He had great strength. He told me he spent time with Wallenberg at one of the hospitals along the Volga. He said it was Kazan."

David continued: "Tamas, through a translator, told me he had spoken with Wallenberg in a Russian hospital on several occasions. He was called the 'Swede from Budapest' who had rescued the Jews in 1944 and 1945. He was well respected, a celebrity, a good man among the prisoners."

"Tamas speaks no standard Hungarian, only a rare dialect," David said. "That's why the Russians captured him in 1945. Since he couldn't make himself understood to any one at that time in any language familiar to them, they thought he was talking gibberish or crazy talk and they simply locked him up as a mental case."

Through a translator, David learned that Tamas had been drugged into a comatose state for decades. Only recently, when the medication was stopped, did he make sense to his fellow mental hospital patient Wallenberg, who knowing Hungarian happened to understand his dialect.

"The Russians," David confirmed, "only released Tamas because of overcrowding at the hospital. When they needed additional space, they were suddenly eager to send him home. From his hospital bed, Tamas recalled Wallenberg, known as 'the Swede from Budapest,' as one of his fellow prisoners at the Kazan facility, 500 miles east of Moscow on the Volga River. According to Tamas, 'there was an older man, a cultured, intelligent gentleman...a quiet man...very withdrawn but alive and awake. He had a good sense of humor. I think once he mentioned his name was Wallenberg, and we were able to converse in my Hungarian dialect.'" David Evans added, "The Swedes are very conservative. Their commission would not have issued that report unless there was a basis for it."

"Could it be that simple, David?"

"Can Wallenberg be alive in the Kazan hospital on the Volga River?"

As recently as three years earlier, CIA reports had indicated Wallenberg had indeed been in a mental hospital, perhaps under his name Wallenberg, or under the name Sven Andersen. Could Tamas's "cultured gentleman" be Raoul Wallenberg?

"Can you send one of your Moscow people out to Kazan right away?" I urged.

"I could do that. But better yet, I will go myself." David answered.

Kazan is a gray seaport town on the banks of the Volga River, 500 miles east of Moscow. It is basically known for its gymnastics and athletic prowess. The black mountains there form a prison-like overwhelming backdrop, a reminder that few are ever released from its granite prison-hospital. Until 1997 it had been off-limits to Western visitors, who were still not welcome.

"I will try to find him," he said. "I'll let you know."

David showed great personal courage in his decision to go to Kazan. It could have cost him his life, or just his highly paid State Department job, and his government pension. "I am going against US policy, but I know it's the right thing to do," David related. It was already quite clear that the US government was choosing to do nothing to rescue Wallenberg. In fact, the "*Statement of Interest*" filed against our case was concrete proof of my government's concerted effort to destroy our victory, and to sabotage the outcome. As the Economic Affairs Officer at the Moscow Embassy, David Evans was fluent in Russian, French and Swedish. He was a close friend of Anatol Dobrinyn, the respected Soviet Ambassador to the United States during the Nixon years. David also had many friends in the US Congress, having served as the State Department representative to the Helsinki Accords. Evans, a brilliant linguist spoke several dialects of both Russian and Hungarian. He had graduated from Germantown Friends School and Harvard University where he obtained a PhD in Russian Studies and had been a career diplomat for thirty-five years. He called me after his return from Kazan.

"I made my way to Kazan by train. I found the hospital—a big, sprawling complex, and walked in easily by using my diplomatic pass. I decided to pass *incognito*, so I went to a closet, found and donned a white lab coat and stethoscope and checked in at the front desk. I spoke Russian, and since I look Russian, they thought I was a staff doctor. I met with the hospital's deputy administrator, who gave me a plastic "Visitor-Doctor pass" This gave me literally a free rein to roam."

David continued:

"I searched the patient roster for Swedish-sounding names and visited all the wards. The patient list contained no such name as Wallenberg, so I began to ask among the staff if there was an aging patient who spoke Swedish and Russian. They knew who I was talking about and pointed towards the stairs leading to the second floor of the hospital. An old man, mainly bald with a few strands of gray hair was sitting alone by the window watching the sunset. It was about 4:30 P.M. The sun begins to set early there. The trees are bare, but there is a great view of the Volga River and the mountains. A blue blanket covered his lap and his legs."

David stopped for a moment and said, "I need to look at my notes." Then he continued:

"I walked quietly up to this gentle man. He was sitting in a wheel chair with old rubber wheels, hunched over staring out the window, not moving, just staring. This man, according to the nurse, would just sit and gaze out the window across the flat desert of Kazan toward the distant mountains, as if looking for home. In the afternoons, he had been seen motioning with his open arms toward the setting sun, as if beckoning."

"The old man suddenly sat up as I approached him."

I interrupted David's report, "What did you do first? Did you talk to him? What name did the nurse use for him? What was his name?"

"Oddly, they gave him no name at all," said David. "Only a number and a notation. The tag on his chair said 'Swede from Budapest.' I read that in Russian and was amazed. Someone on the staff had put that nametag there. He spoke English. I think he spoke Russian too, but we chatted in English. The nurse said that his hospital records showed he had been transferred to Kazan from Mordvinia Prison. She related that he was in good health when he arrived. He was still in good health, quite alert, but recently he had a stroke. He still speaks clearly. I could understand him though he spoke to me in a whisper."

"Did you speak with him at all?"

"I asked him how he was feeling and whether he wanted to converse in English or Swedish. He chose English, and yet I spoke to him in both Swedish and English for approximately one half hour. There was a quick start to his body and a light glint in his eyes when I mentioned Budapest and saving the Jews."

"Yes?" I asked hopefully. "And then?"

Whatever Happened to Raoul Wallenberg?

"I told him an effort was underway by an American lawyer to secure his freedom. I told him of your work in court to rescue and bring him home. I spoke to him of your perseverance. He reached out and took my hand as if he could hear me better that way. We held hands for five minutes and he began to cry. I told him gently of your dedication to rescuing him. He smiled and was quite pleased."

"What did he say?"

"He beckoned me to come close and to listen to him. I leaned closer. He thanked me, and then said, 'I am the Swede from Budapest. I am Wallenberg.' And then he said mysteriously 'Turn your face to God, and God will turn his face towards you.'"

"He held my hand. I smiled up at him and we shared a moment of quiet time together." David's relaying this encounter with Wallenberg brought new hope to me.

"What happened next David?"

"I saw the orderlies coming towards me with a bad look on their face and I decided it was time to leave. I did not want to risk being arrested, or all the embarrassment this would create."

Then David slipped away, went downstairs, and left. Mission accomplished! No one had suspected his true identity. No one seemed to care.

I was thrilled with the news from David Evans. He became the latest and most courageous volunteer in the rescue effort. My hope was renewed. At last we would bring Wallenberg home to live his last years in peace.

The next day I called the White House: "May I speak to President Clinton?"

"President Clinton is in conference. I will give you Neal Wolin, his deputy security adviser." I spoke to Neal Wolin, the deputy security adviser for Russia and related matters.

"Neal, I have great news. News from an ambassador to Russia that Wallenberg has been located alive. Please re-activate the contact with Yeltsin and the Russians. We have a chance to bring him home."

I took the time to give Neal the details of my conversation with David Evans.

"Great news" was his response. "I will mention it to the President. We will follow up with you and decide the next step together."

I learned later from Neal Wolin that President Clinton received and read my report of the Evans hospital visit and my final plea for rescue. I also learned that the President referred the matter for action to The State Department. Unfortunately, I never heard back from President Clinton or from The State Department. Who put down the roadblock this time? Was it coming from the State Department? Was someone still there, a holdover from the Reagan days, a graduate of the Justice Roberts' school of "Let's dodge the issue?" Who still wanted the Wallenberg investigation to disappear? Who had something to lose from the re-opening of the effort to rescue Wallenberg and get to the truth? President Clinton said it was 'high priority,' and yet the matter was apparently buried once again by the State Department in the final days of the Clinton administration. This was the most disappointing and frustrating moment in my twenty-seven year effort to rescue Wallenberg.

At the end of my chat with David Evans we had returned to discussing school day memories. We recalled ironically how our underground school newspaper was actually christened with two names. The first was *The Rebel* because we took on all the schools policies. The second was "Samiztat," the name of the Soviet underground newspaper.

The long effort to locate and rescue Wallenberg had its best moments with David Evans' heroic visit. In our phone call after his visit with Wallenberg, David reminded me of the key pages in our senior yearbook—the Blue and White.

David had been the editor-in-chief and wrote the captions under peoples names. We all predicted he would become a diplomat and we were right. He was the smartest in our class. David went to Harvard and the Fletcher School of Diplomacy. Then he spent forty years in the diplomatic corps. He was fluent in Russian and French and spent his career as a Russian political affairs expert.

"In later years," he said, "I often recalled your urging me to play harder, run fast, not be so pokey on the soccer field, get to the ball faster. I think your words inspired me, although you kinda bugged me at the time. And do you remember, Morris, what I chose to place under your name in the senior yearbook? Take it down and read it someday. I took the quote from Lord Shallcross when he was honoring the gustiness of Winston Churchill. Look it up. It is poignant and prescient—both at the same time. I chose it after watching your masterful performance of Marc Antony in 'Julius Caesar.'"

"Hold the line, David, I'm going upstairs to get my copy of the Blue and White." I came downstairs, and thumbed through the yearbook.

"OK, I got it."

David had a copy of the yearbook in front of him too.

"You see. It's from Lord Shallcross, a member of parliament during World War Two with Churchill during the darkest hours. Shallcross said: 'He [Churchill] sees the right and he pursues it too.' Those words Shallcross uttered in support of Churchill's effort to wage war against great odds. They apply to you too."

I thanked David for the compliment. And I thanked him for his heroic and daring visit.

"Keep in touch, Morris. We have not seen the end of this."

And yet, unfortunately, we had.

257

Whatever Happened to Raoul Wallenberg?

David Evans, my highs school classmate, and a distinguished US official in Russia, died a few months later. He was given a state funeral with full honors at the Washington Cathedral in Washington, DC in October of 2000—two years after his heroic adventure for Wallenberg. He died on October 4, 2000 of prostate cancer after 32 years of distinguished diplomatic service, mainly in Eastern Europe and in Russia as our Ambassador. Soviet Ambassador Anatol Dobrynin attended and gave a eulogy, and spoke of David's courage. I think Dobrynin, the Soviet Master Spy, knew somehow about David's mission. I think he knew about Colby, too. Members of the diplomatic corps came from all over the world to pay homage.

David was a great diplomat and a beloved friend. He was a friend of Wallenberg and remains to this day one of my unsung heroes.

It would be years after David's visit with Wallenberg when I finally connected the dots concerning Wallenberg's terse message.

Wallenberg had again been very strategic and clever. He had only a few minutes to talk to Ambassador Evans and to send a message to the West. His message was lifted directly from the Jewish Priestly Blessing, or Three-Fold Benediction.

In the hospital ward, near to the end of the day, Wallenberg turned to David, took his hand and gave him a blessing. He also gave David a message to carry back home.

"Turn your face towards God and God will turn his face towards you."

Wallenberg knew that Evans had broken into the hospital to find Wallenberg, to talk to him, and to encourage him. His mission was to encourage Wallenberg to stay alive and to let Wallenberg know that help was on its way, even though terribly late in the year 1998.

Wallenberg, ever alert and clever, realized that Ambassador Evans mission/visit was against the rules. He knew that this mission of mercy and encouragement would be brief. He had only a few moments to send a message to his family in Sweden. So he encoded one within a blessing

On June 3, 2011, thirteen years after Ambassador Evans heroic mission to Kazan the meaning of the riddle of words finally dawned on me. I realized the sub text translation of Wallenberg's terse words. Wallenberg was known by Judith Yaron to read the Old Testament and the Talmud. Wallenberg loved the history of the Jewish people. He had time in prison to become religious. It was one way to survive.

"I pray each day in order to stay alive," he told Evans. "It is one of many daily rituals. I count my blessings. And I bless you for coming to see me."

Prayer had become a major part of his survival strategy. He might even consider himself to be a self converted Jew. That day in 1998 with David Evans, he was quoting not just the Bible but the Naso portion from the Talmud, a section of the Holy Book normally studied only by Rabbis and Yeshiva students.

The blessing from the Bible reads:

'May God bless you and keep you.'
'May God cause his face to shine upon you and be gracious to you.'
'May God turn his face towards you and grant you peace.'

"Wallenberg was at peace," David had said. "He was quietly just sitting there in his wheel chair looking out the window at sunset. He held hands with me. We were simply two foreign diplomats meeting for the first time. He was still blessing other people."

"He was hemmed in by the light blue knit blanket over his knees, and he was gazing out with a far away look in his eyes at the sunset. There was a slight tremor in his right hand."

"But he still was smiling and even laughing at times during our conversation."

"Who has tried to rescue me?'" he asked.

"Only your brother and your lawyer; they will come to bring you home."

That was 1998. There was still an opportunity of rescue.

January 2001
Stockholm

After nearly ten tepid years of stop-and-start progress, the joint Swedish-Russian commission finally released its report on "the alleged fate of Raoul Wallenberg" at a press conference on January 12, 2001. The commission's work was held up as a positive example of international cooperation, but according to inside sources it was "actually a whitewash". Even my friend, Swedish Ambassador Jan Eliasson, later President of the UN General Assembly objected to the closure of the effort to get at the truth. He fought valiantly to keep the investigation open. He told the commission "You cannot close the investigation without hearing the testimony of Morris Wolff. He has information which we must hear." The commission brushed his request aside.

Ambassador Eliasson told me later in the office of Congressman Tom Lantos, "It was a white-wash—strictly a superficial PR job. No one had the courage to tread on the toes of the Soviets. There was no true investigation. The effort to put a lid on the bubbling and boiling Wallenberg scandal was all that mattered. Wallenberg was again used as a pawn to restart Swedish-CIS Soviet trade relations. They specifically chose not to call you as a witness, because they knew you had contradictory evidence which would have forced them to make a search of Kazan, and the other prisons in the gulag which you detailed to them as places of Wallenberg custody."

Sweden admitted that it had failed to trade Raoul Wallenberg when it had a chance during Stalin's reign, and later in 1965 during the Stig Bergling spy swap opportunity.

Russia, for its part created a new fiction by reinventing for the third time the lie about the "murder" of both Wallenberg and his driver, Vilmos Langfelder in a KGB prison. This statement, simply the latest in a pattern of lies about Wallenberg since 1945, perpetuated a cynical practice and a supreme irony—Russia "admitting" to a crime that it said it had never committed!

Nevertheless, ostensibly in an attempt at reconciliation, the Russian statement claimed that both Wallenberg and Langfelder would be posthumously "rehabilitated," and cleared of having committed crimes. Thank you very much! What crimes?

The commission's final report, oddly, yet perhaps predictably, arrived at two contradictory conclusions; First the Russians stated Wallenberg was dead, and they claimed responsibility for his death. The Swedish delegation stated there was no proof of his death and maintained that he was still alive; the inherent implication and truth. Despite spending millions of dollars in a fruitless search neither the Russians nor the Swedes made any serious effort to find Wallenberg. Wallenberg may well still be alive.

Whatever Happened to Raoul Wallenberg?

There is absolutely no proof that Wallenberg has ever died. The mystery continues, and so does the scandal of how three governments worked against his ultimate freedom.

Summer 2005
Geneva, Switzerland, and Washington, DC

I was in Geneva on international law business when I received a late afternoon phone call from E.J. Kessler, a journalist for the *Jewish Forward*.

"Morris, I am writing an article on John G. Roberts, on the occasion of his nomination to the United States Supreme Court. I have uncovered some information at the Reagan Library in California about Roberts's unusual involvement in the Wallenberg case and his role in the possible cover up. I thought you might like to hear what I have uncovered. It is a story of scandal and misbehavior by our own government in your Wallenberg case," he said.

Kessler continued in a voice of excitement: "Back on November 11, 1983 you wrote an incisive letter to President Reagan asking him to intervene in the rescue of Wallenberg, using his executive power under the *US Hostages Act of 1868*. Brilliant argument. Wallenberg was by 1983 a citizen of the United States you said, as declared by Act of Congress in 1981. I have a copy of your letter right here in front of me. I found it in the archives of the President marked 'secret material; not for distribution.' In your letter you reminded the President of his absolute executive duty and power to demand that the Russians release Diplomat Wallenberg. You urged him to take action leading to Wallenberg's immediate release from Soviet custody. You stated that the President's power was mandatory...and not discretionary. Apparently Supreme Court Chief Justice Roberts, who at the time was a White House staff lawyer, at first agreed with you. Roberts wrote a memo agreeing completely with your interpretation of the law. He even said you were correct. But he said, '*despite the Presidential power to demand Wallenberg's release, I suggest we dodge the issue.*'

Kessler continued: "This Roberts memo, has apparently been buried as 'secret' until now. It has just come to light during the confirmation hearing. Did you ever see the Roberts memo, Morris?"

"No, I never did. This is the first I heard of it."

"Would this have changed things had the President taken the action you recommended?"

"Why, absolutely, yes. Wallenberg could have been freed even before my lawsuit was filed, based on my letter demand. *There were nearly three months between the time my letter was hand delivered to the President and read by him on November 11, 1983 and my filing of the lawsuit on February 2, 1984. It would have changed my whole game plan. I could have had the power of the President backing my lawsuit. It would have been awesome. Reagan and I going after the Russians on a joint initiative—two branches of government, the Executive and the Judiciary, and his personal lawyer—all demanding Wallenberg's release from Russia at the same time.*"

"I did not file my Wallenberg lawsuit against the Soviet Union until February of 1984. Swift use of awesome power by the President in November of 1983 would have led to Wallenberg's release. It might have made the lawsuit unnecessary! The Russians would have realized this was the end of the game. And Wallenberg would be a free man today! The President had a duty to use his awesome legal power; this was not a discretionary choice. His legal counsel should have told him so. Reagan had an absolute duty to demand the immediate release of Wallenberg as a hostage held illegally, and without even the semblance of a trial by a foreign power. I am appalled by this information. I want to come home and ask Mr. Roberts face-to-face at his Senate confirmation hearing why he took this step in his memo to condone the kidnapping and to encourage a 'no action policy.'"

Kessler continued, "Do you think this failure on Roberts' part shows more than poor judgment?"

"Yes, much more than just poor judgment," I answered. "It goes to the very character of the man. It shows him to be indecisive and devious. He lacks guts. He failed to do his duty—and that was to advise his President to follow the law. As Assistant White House Counsel he had no choice. That's why he got paid. He was a coward on this decision. It might be indicative of a pattern of weak thought that might carry over to the Court. No guts, no glory. What if he's a coward on the Supreme Court? Is he going to duck the tough questions like *Brown v. Board of Education* and *Roe v. Wade*? I want to ask him a few questions."

I sat there in a state of shock in the sunlight of a small café in Zurich, Switzerland. I was on a work assignment and a holiday back in one of my favorite places of mountain beauty, where forty-five years earlier at age 24 in 1960, I worked for two years establishing the international office of the AIESEC exchange program, and extending it to universities in Nigeria, Ghana and Sierra Leone.

No wonder I never got an answer to my letter. It had been buried by Roberts and Fielding. A quiet cover up. All I got was a cryptic letter of appreciation thanking me for my interest in the Wallenberg case, and an assurance that President Reagan wanted me to know he was "interested" in Wallenberg's freedom as well.

The Roberts memo and my letter had been buried in the secret canyon of White House records. These "radio active records" like the Nixon tapes somehow found their way to the surface and they incriminate Supreme Court Justice Roberts. Later these documents were transferred to the Reagan Library to die a natural death. Kessler, an ambitious Jewish reporter had somehow dug them up and made them front page news. All things finally come to the surface of the lake. It was ironic, discovered by a Jewish reporter—Holocaust survivor—and it was as we say in Yiddish, "Bescharet," destiny and simply meant to be.

263

Whatever Happened to Raoul Wallenberg?

I had written a letter to President Reagan in early November 1983 asking him to use the 1868 *Hostages Act* as a basis for pressing for the release of Raoul Wallenberg. The law provides that the President of the United States has an obligation to "demand the release of any US citizen held hostage and in custody without a trial by a foreign government."

Faith Whittlesey, the President's assistant was entrusted with the fast and guaranteed delivery. "I will stand and watch him read the letter," she assured me. "I am totally in your corner on getting the President to act. It will be a good initiative and quite consistent with his signing the law for Wallenberg's full citizenship back on August 5, 1981. I attended that Rose Garden ceremony and celebration. I stood right behind the President when he announced: 'full citizenship for Wallenberg.' We must hasten his rescue and bring him to freedom." She later assured me that she hand delivered the letter directly to the President, and stood patiently by his desk as he read it carefully and grimaced.

The President said to her, "I want to make this demand on the Soviets, and I want to make it now! Faith, this is an important letter from Morris Wolff. I like this kind of opportunity to showcase an issue. We can do something good for human rights and for Ambassador Wallenberg. We can use this as a lever to gain Wallenberg's release."

The President instructed her to take the letter to White House Counsel Fred Fielding for immediate follow-up and fast action. He marked the letter "Yes, do this, and do it now" Ronald Reagan. That note and my letter were delivered to Fred Fielding. (That is the same Fred Fielding who 21 years later served as George W. Bush's White House Counsel from 2004 through 2008, and counseled that water boarding and torture were perfectly legal activities under US law.) Fielding assigned the drafting of an answer to my letter to the future Supreme Court Chief Justice John G. Roberts. John Roberts was at that time Assistant White House Counsel working for Fred Fielding.

Roberts, in a White House internal memo told Reagan he had the "duty to demand Wallenberg's release." He also noted that Reagan had the power to take immediate action; there was no need for Congressional approval. Roberts admitted in his memo "there has been strong pressure placed on me by State Department Counselor John McFarland to ask you to dodge the issue. Nonetheless, there is only one lawful action for the President to take." In the official White House memo to President Reagan, signed by both Roberts and Fielding—which was never brought to my attention until Roberts' confirmation hearing for the Supreme Court appointment in August of 2005—Roberts' craven language of "I suggest we dodge the issue" was incorporated in that infamous letter.

In other words, leave Wallenberg to rot despite my letter and the begging by the Wallenberg family to gain his release. Thus, no action was taken despite the President's initial impulse and desire to use his power as the Chief Executive under the 1868 *US Hostages Act* to demand release.

When I learned of Roberts' unprincipled action I was outraged. This man was now headed to the top of our Supreme Court with no interference in sight. It was a virtual honeymoon trip. I called my old friend and former boss Senator Arlen Specter, chair of the Senate Judiciary Committee, the senate committee entrusted with the Roberts' confirmation hearings. Arlen had been my friend. We played on the same softball team. He and Joan attended my wedding. He had sworn me in to the Court of Common Pleas in Philadelphia as an assistant District Attorney for the City of Philadelphia in 1965. The hearings were about to begin. I flew home to testify against the nomination, based on Roberts' behavior in the Wallenberg case and in some of his other ill-advised opinions, which also showed a lack of good judgment. I wanted a chance to raise questions before the Senate Judiciary Committee. Arlen trusted my honesty and integrity. He knew all about my years as Wallenberg's lawyer. I had briefed him individually and in private in his Senate office in June of 1983 when I testified before Congress on my plans to sue the Soviets. He supported my judgment then.

"What do you want to testify about?" Arlen asked me.

"I want to raise questions about his character and fitness to serve just like you questioned Judge Bork's wisdom on *Roe v. Wade* and his values and qualifications. You effectively blocked the Bork nomination. I want to ask Judge Roberts what he thinks now about his position on his handling of the Wallenberg case by the White House during the Reagan years."

"There is a disturbing memo with his name on it. In the memo he commends my recommended use of the US Hostages Act, but suggests that the President take no action to rescue Wallenberg. Between his two positions in the same memo there is a disconnect that needs explaining."

"Those questions need to be asked," Arlen said. "I'll see what I can do to get you on a panel to testify. It should be a rigorous hearing, just as with Judge Robert Bork, some years ago."

I was waiting for a follow up. I expected to be called as a witness before the panel of the Judiciary Committee. A few days later a surprise answer was delivered by phone. Arlen did not call back. Bork and John Roberts were two different moments in Arlen's political life. He disappointed me and lacked the courage to call me directly. Specter did not have the guts to challenge Roberts. His aide, David Brog, called. That was a bad sign. Arlen normally called me himself. I had made him look good as District Attorney with the Take a Brother program for kids and my good trial work.

In the phone call, his aide David Brog apologized, "We do not have any room for you to testify and ask questions. I suggest you might want to submit your questions in writing. No room can be made for you on the panel of witnesses to testify."

Whatever Happened to Raoul Wallenberg?

Arlen obviously wanted no embarrassment. He was now an obedient 'company man.' Now he was Orrin Hatch's boy on a leash. He had paid dearly for his position as Chairman of the Senate Judiciary, a post Hatch had also coveted.

Now Arlen, "Mr. Independent" was owned temporarily by his conservative Republican brethren, before bolting to the Democratic side of the Senate aisle when he was faced with losing the Republican senatorial primary in the spring of 2010. Unfortunately he lost that race as well, because he had lost touch with his own basic principles of integrity and carriage. It had been those principles, which had originally endeared him on a bi-partisan basis to the voters of Pennsylvania.

The hearings without my testimony were tepid, boring, non-controversial, rigged and banal. Roberts rode smoothly through a cream puff hearing with no one asking any of the tough questions. He was handled with kid gloves. The tough questioners were removed in advance and not invited to testify. *Potential troublemakers.* I submitted my questions in writing. They were completely ignored and never raised, nor was my written testimony as submitted, even included in the official record.

I wanted to learn why the Supreme Court nominee had taken such cowardly action? At the time when my Wallenberg letter was on his desk before he wrote the "let's duck the issue" memo why did he not argue the opposite result of my being right? This was no profile in courage. Not a stand-up guy. He could have been instrumental in the Wallenberg rescue. He could have counseled the President to use his full lawful powers and awesome political leverage to force the Russians to release Wallenberg in November of 1983, months before my lawsuit was filed on February 2, 1984. Wallenberg was alive at that time.

With full candor I told the *Jewish Forward* journalist Kessler, "I believe that Roberts' actions in the Wallenberg matter were cowardly and unprincipled. He acted in what amounted to an agreement, a small conspiracy with Fielding and Dan McGovern to kill Wallenberg's chances to see the light of day outside prison walls. His negative advisory memo impeded the release of Wallenberg. The White House under Reagan played a game of duplicity—claiming publicly an ardent desire to free Wallenberg, while in private burying his opportunity for freedom, and condemning him essentially to life imprisonment."

In Kessler's article, on the record, I called Roberts's behavior 'unprincipled and cowardly.' He wrote it up that way. Some of my colleagues have suggested that it may not be a wise thing for a trial lawyer who appears before the Supreme Court to criticize a sitting judge. But Roberts' actions were cowardly and unprincipled. He could have done better. He could have done the right thing. As the Renaissance poet Dante, in *The Inferno* once told us: "The hottest rim of hell is reserved for those who, in a moment of moral crisis, suspend judgment."

Roberts now sits as the most powerful Judge in the United States. No one has ever challenged him on his role in the Wallenberg matter. Maybe with the publication of this book some news hungry reporter will trek up the steps of the United States Supreme Court and ask him, "Mr. Roberts, what did you do to help rescue Mr. Wallenberg?"

His record stands as written. Like so many others, he could have helped. He could have played a pivotal role in obtaining freedom for Wallenberg. Instead he chose to duck out and leave the work for others to do. It is a disappointing coda to the quest I have been on for so many years.

In Reflection

The question 'Whatever Happened to Raoul Wallenberg?' remains unanswered to this day. There is the possibility that he is still in a Soviet prison or hospital, gazing out the window of his confinement.

I still, to this day, fantasize about the phone call that starts "Morris, we've found him. He's alive and he's on his way home." I know that I would be on the first plane to meet him. Would he know who I was? Would he remember being told about my efforts? All of this wouldn't matter. Just the fact that he had been freed would be enough payment for all of the years that I had spent working for his release. All of the hours thinking about his captivity and sorrow. All of the time spent traveling to meet new contacts and to plan new strategies. It would be a great victory for me, and of course, for Raoul.

I know that he is certainly not forgotten. The many people who I meet daily, remember him either as their savior, their family's savior or just one of the great saviors of mankind. They show me that my efforts, as small as they were in comparison to his, were not wasted. They help me to remember the good that is possible in this world and they encourage me to strive to make myself, and this world, a better place.

At times we must live with ambiguity. Yet, at other times, in the quiet of my room or when I am walking on the beach at sunrise, I sense his presence all over again, as I did that first night at the Shoreham hotel. These moments tell me that Wallenberg is still alive in the most meaningful way possible.

Letter of protection (Schutzpasse) issued by the Swedish legation in Budapest to the Hungarian Jewish Rabbi, Dr. Jozsef Katona.

Epilogue

Whatever Happened to Raoul Wallenberg?

June 2011
Washington, DC
Woodrow Wilson International Center for Scholars
Daytona Beach, Florida
Bethune-Cookman University

Was it all worth it? My students at Bethune-Cookman University here in Daytona Beach often ask me that question. They wonder why a lawyer, who could have earned approximately $600,000 in corporate legal fees would choose to do human rights legal work *pro bono* instead.

I tell them, "It's like a health insurance policy for me. It makes me feel good and keeps me sharp."

I encourage them to pursue careers in fields of professional activity where they have an opportunity to serve the true needs of mankind. I am happy in my new life as Professor of Human Rights Law and as a teacher of remedial composition and writing for students who have been "passed up the line" from elementary school through high school without learning how to read and write at a freshman college level. At Bethune-Cookman University I am able to help students who genuinely need to learn the basic skills of writing.

I still do legal work upon occasion as long as it is related to human rights. My students still push me back to the basic question of "was it all worth it?" Was my *pro bono* plunge into the rescue effort, the research and hours of sleuthing and advocacy worth it? My answer is yes.

The Wallenberg case gave me a chance to stay in close touch with my idealism, and put my ideals into action. By bringing this litigation, I have made good use of my education, and I have honored the ideals and lessons of my mother and my German Jewish immigrant father, who provided me with everything in life, including ideals, perseverance and an energy to do the right thing. The case gave me an unusual opportunity to meet some great people, including a host of survivors rescued by Wallenberg, an enchanting birthday visit in Central Park with Jackie Kennedy, and sharing a panel with Nobel Peace Prize winner Elie Wiesel. It also led to interesting National TV appearances with Tom Brokaw, George Will, Bryant Gumbel and Jane Pauley.

Very few people ever had the privilege to enter the White House. I have enjoyed meetings in the White House; in order to discuss plans for passing the Civil Rights Act of 1964, with President Kennedy in 1963 and with Bill and Hillary Clinton in 1993 to discuss the possible rescue of Raoul Wallenberg. I also enjoyed my an Israeli sojourn with the beautiful Judith Yaron, lunch and working sessions with Congressmen Lee Hamilton and Tom Lantos, Chair of the House

Whatever Happened to Raoul Wallenberg?

Foreign Affairs Committee, meetings with Wallenberg's family and with his official photographer, Tom Veres. I also was privileged to have lunch at Sardis with Tony Curtis and Carol Channing, and was gifted with a friendship with CIA Director Bill Colby and his charming wife Sally. There are also friendships with Harry Spitz of Arizona and Bruce Teicholz of New York, former underground leaders of the Wallenberg Rescue effort in Budapest, which I treasure.

Many survivors, with interesting and harrowing stories of great grit and courage assisted me in research. Their love sustained me through the quiet nights of writing the complaint and brief for the case and gave me strength and the will to write this book, which I hope you enjoyed reading. I will welcome your comments and criticisms at my blog found at:WallenbergBlog.EduPublisher.com.

I thank the Woodrow Wilson Center for the appointment to the post of Senior Policy Analyst. I learned a great deal from my several lunches at a round table of scholars with Director Lee Hamilton, former Congressman for 34 years from Indiana and author of the Baker-Hamilton report on Iraq and the Baker-Keane report focusing on the causes of the 9/11 attacks.

Lee Hamilton is thanked for his wisdom, guidance and generosity of time. I also thank the library staff, and my research assistants Munir Jawed and Robin Murphy, for providing key advice and for locating a key document in Russian. This secret document from the KGB stated: "Wallenberg will not be released during his lifetime. To release him now would be a public relations disaster for Russia that we will never live down. It is clear that Mr. Wallenberg will be pressed into a speaking tour, and will certainly disclose all the weaknesses of our political system. He might run for public office. This would be bad news for our country. For all these reasons he is detained." This was the only internal document pilfered from the KGB on Wallenberg. There must be plenty more.

Taking the lawsuit also gave me an opportunity to associate silently and *in absentia* for 27 years with Raoul Wallenberg, a great client and human being. I have felt his presence with me many times—including that first visit in my room at the Shoreham Hotel where I feel certain he came to visit with me and encouraged the filing of the lawsuit. I also felt his spirit on the day I walked up the steps of the courthouse, with Guy Von Dardel, the only Wallenberg to genuinely support my work. Late at night when I wrote the brief and legal arguments over and over again, I felt his spirit hovering over me. And one time, I felt his hand upon my shoulder, and when I meet the men and women he worked with in Budapest, I have a sense of him every day.

Every day I try to live by the ideals he portrayed in action: loving, caring, saving the lives of others, being in touch with God. This assignment gave me a chance to do something deeply worthwhile.

It gave me an opportunity to be a good citizen and a good lawyer. I have been invited to speak to law students at many law schools on "making a difference" and "on the law as an honorable profession."

It was my ticket to meeting very exciting and truly heroic down to earth and humble Wallenberg volunteers in forty-three countries, many saved by Wallenberg and so grateful and, of course, proud of his work.

It has also given me a chance to walk quietly in the corridors of history. One day my book will be on a dusty and forgotten shelf in a library somewhere, perhaps in New Orleans. A young lawyer, temporarily disillusioned, bored with the day-to-day practice, and looking for "a cause" will take it down, leaf through and read it and hopefully be suddenly inspired. It might be years from now. He or she may be inspired to do something major, something that benefits others, and that adds to the evolving and positive record of human rights. In that way I will live on through eternity and be admired for what I have done.

The Wallenberg case has created a new law of jurisdiction, an outreach tool in the field of human rights litigation. It has spawned many valuable cases for confronting acts of governmental torture and abuse. My case has given plaintiffs a basis for resisting and standing up against human rights abuses and governmental tyranny.

I have lived to see it used as one of the building blocks for a new generation of lawyers willing to question and then aggressively prosecute different nations for the human rights abuse created by unbridled power. The misbehavior of our own government at Guantanamo and Abu Gharib, and in shipping people to secret foreign prisons to be tortured, abused and water boarded has recently been scrutinized and condemned as illegal and inhumane. This began with Wallenberg. The law and the strategy I created in Wallenberg is now used in courtrooms as legal arguments for justice and fairness all over the world. Wallenberg litigation, in which an entire nation is called to account for criminal behavior, has led directly to the creation of the International Criminal Court in 1998. Not only did we make new law, we helped to create the International Criminal Court as a new institutional structure for human rights litigation.

Human rights activism and the use of litigation to achieve human rights are alive and healthy today. In Volume 15, Issue One (Fall 2007) on page one, the editor of the *Human Rights Brief,* published at the American University Washington College of Law, writes,

> *"Issuing reparations to victims of human rights abuses is gaining recognition in the international community as a practice both legally and morally essential...Reparations not only provide survivors of human rights violations with the resources to begin rebuilding their lives but also provide justice—an indispensable step in achieving peace."*

Whatever Happened to Raoul Wallenberg?

In the Wallenberg case, we started this vitally important process of holding nations accountable by our success in gaining jurisdiction over the Soviet Union, and successfully causing Judge Parker to hold the Russians accountable for the abuse of one human being's human rights. This was a team effort with a large and positive objective. It involved dedication and many hours of hard work. It was worth every unpaid penny. I do not regret one minute of the effort, even the discovery of lawyers like Roberts and State Department Legal Adviser Abe Sofaer, and the greedy and villainous Gene Theroux at Baker and McKenzie unwilling to see the larger picture.

At one point Mr. Theroux, thinking that I was merely a political analyst with the Woodrow Wilson International Center for Scholars, actually gave me the original volume of the full Wallenberg case record. When he learned that I was also the fighting litigious lawyer for Wallenberg, he asked for the original record back in exchange for a full copy of that record. When I went to his office in good faith for the purpose of that exchange, he took back the original which I gave him willingly and then he grabbed from me the copy which I was reading that he had offered to me to take home. Then three of his partners entered the conference room and threatened me with physical assault if I failed to leave the Baker and McKenzie office immediately.

With the publication of this book I hope to arouse and even provoke a community of discussion, dialog and interest. Hopefully support for doing the right thing will stimulate young members of the legal profession.

I also plan to re-open and set aside the illegal second Wallenberg opinion and expose the incredible meddling by the White House with my federal court judgments. If successful we will recoup the $39 million plus compounded interest. That brings the present value of the case to approximately $142 million since the first verdict.

We will work to reinstate Judge Parker's brilliant and historic opinion and devote all of the monies recovered to scholarships for high school and university and law school students who demonstrate in their young lives the positive traits of altruism, service and generosity which Wallenberg practiced during his brief six months of work in Budapest between his arrival on July 6, 1944 and the day of his kidnapping by his Soviets on January 17, 1945.

Judge Parker's order still stands: "the Russians must produce Wallenberg in my court room within sixty days or produce credible proof of his death." Justice is still important and is still available. Perhaps his son Federal District Court Judge Barrington Parker III of New York will help me to encourage Chief Justice John G. Roberts to order a rehearing. This will give Roberts a chance to redeem himself.

The so-called second Wallenberg opinion is illegal, outside the power of a federal district court judge to grant. Judge Robinson had no right to even hear the case much less decide it. That unlawful decision needs to be wiped from the judicial record. I believe the first opinion should be reinstated. The law team is forming. A brilliant group of young lawyers from Chapman University Law School and other law schools will be leading the effort. I will be serving as senior co-counsel. We will win. "It can be done," as my grandfather use to say. We can recover the dignity, integrity and truth of the first judgment.

We will form the Raoul Wallenberg Center for Altruistic Studies and contribute the funds of the lawsuit verdict to the center. This money will be spent on altruistic human rights projects to alleviate torture and pain in the world.

Guy Von Dardel was a good man. May he rest in peace. I was the only lawyer selected by the Wallenbergs to bring the case and carry out my duty. Recently, in May of 2011, his daughter contacted me to thank me for my service. She has promised me a fee for my twenty-seven years of service, which I will contribute to the Wallenberg Center. This makes me feel good after all of the pressure that was placed on Guy Von Dardel by the evil wing of his family to drop the case when we were so near to rescue.

I use the word duty, because I believe every lawyer has a duty to step forward and help solve the injustices of the world. As mentioned earlier, "suspended judgment in a time of moral crisis" is not a moral choice. It is not the choice that Wallenberg made when he accepted the mission to save one hundred thousand lives.

The government of Sweden in 1981 had an excellent chance to force the hand of the USSR with the capture of a Soviet submarine trapped in Swedish waters. This has been documented in the biography of Wallenberg by John Bierman. At that time the Swedish government was asked by Wallenberg committees from around the world: "Please detain and capture the submarine until Wallenberg is released." The Swedish government failed to do so. The submarine was set free. Wallenberg remained in jail. Leverage for his release was lost.

Certain members of the Wallenberg family, and many officials of the Soviet government, and even President Reagan, Justice Roberts and Fred Fielding failed Wallenberg at a critical moment when Wallenberg could have been rescued in good health. He was only seventy-two at that time. Reagan allowed his aides to talk him out of "demanding Wallenberg's release" following my letter in November 1983, which he read and failed to act upon!

The failure to recover Raoul Wallenberg was not for lack of effort. We had strong support from good people who cared deeply about his rescue and his freedom. Instead, it was the failure of those who had the awesome power to do right, but chose to do wrong, and who said, "Let us dodge the issue."

You may ask again, was my work and my effort worth it? Again a resounding yes! It was fully worth it because I can live at peace with myself, and with what I have accomplished. My family and friends are proud of what I have done and that is all that really matters.

Whatever Happened to Raoul Wallenberg?

Do I believe that Wallenberg is alive? Yes, I have a deep and abiding faith in this possibility. I sense his energy and believe him to be still in this world. We have no proof whatsoever of his passing. Ever since that night at the Shoreham Hotel in Washington DC when I felt his presence in my room, urging me to take the case and seek his rescue, it has been my accepted duty to seek his freedom. That night when he nodded his head up and down in silence, in the spring of 1983 I took up his cause and I accepted the case. I have never looked back. I remain "my brother's keeper." I have been blessed by good health, good friends and family, and the respect of many people, including strangers who have now become new friends, as a result of our *pro bono* efforts together. I have tried to follow Wallenberg's example. I sense that he and I and all of us are survivors.

My journey to universities and synagogues has introduced me and Wallenberg to thousands of people and organizations. By their coming to know him he lives on in their collective memory, and in this strange way he has gained a renewed life in freedom. I am always reminded of how many were touched by his life's work, and how his life is an example of the best in human kind. In that sense Raoul Wallenberg will never die. He will always be a role model for others in the years ahead. Particularly for young people, Raoul Wallenberg was a man of ideals, committed to a higher purpose. The lawsuits now based on "Wallenberg law" are brought in his name. His work will be an inspiration for young lawyers committed to human rights.

In three short and brutal months, from March 16 to June 6, 1944—just one month before Wallenberg's arrival—the Nazis and Arrow Cross deported nearly 400,00 Hungarian Jews to Auschwitz from the towns and villages outside of Budapest. At Auschwitz a special ramp was built, next to the train tracks, to take the Hungarian Jews directly from the trains into the "showers" and the crematoria. Raoul Wallenberg saved only the remaining remnant of Jews in Hungary during his brave six months of work. As a result there is a major colony of Hungarian Israeli Jews living freely today in Israel in a small village near to Ranana. Some Jews living there call the village 'Wallenberg'. I visited with them during my summer trip to Jerusalem in July 2011. They shared their stories with me of parents and grandparents saved by Wallenberg. The handful of old survivors were reticent to tell their stories. They burst into tears when I mentioned his name and the work I had done. They reached out to hold my hands in silence. After awhile they simply muttered, "Wallenberg, Raoul Wallenberg....he saved my life.

We must continue to have the courage to fight for creative uses of the law. Justice is the law's ultimate purpose. I will continue to teach my students to use the law for noble ends, to take daring and innovative "out of the box" steps in order to rescue people, to achieve justice and freedom, and to deter new tyrants from imposing degrading behavior, including the burning of people in crematoria, and other forms of abuse and torture. These young lawyers will follow the idealistic example set by Raoul Wallenberg in pursuing justice and fairness for all.

Raoul Wallenberg answered the call. He fought every day for what he believed was right. We must do the same. As the Talmud tells us: "He who saves one life, saves the world."

I am only one, but I am one. I cannot do everything, but I can do something. What I can do, I should do. And what I should do, by the grace of God, I simply will do.

- Edward Everett Hale

We will have to repent in this generation not merely for the hateful words and ghastly actions of the bad people, but for the appalling silence of the good people.

-Martin Luther King, Jr.

Whatever Happened to Raoul Wallenberg?

Exhibits

Whatever Happened to Raoul Wallenberg?

Remarks on Signing a Bill Proclaiming Honorary United States Citizenship for Raoul Wallenberg of Sweden
by President Ronald Reagan

October 5, 1981

THE PRESIDENT: Not only a distinguished gathering here on the platform, but a distinguished audience out here. Today we're here for--I'm signing the bill to make Raoul Wallenberg an honorary citizen of the United States. But in making him a United States citizen, I think we're the ones that are being honored.

Raoul Wallenberg is the Swedish savior of almost 100,000 Jewish men, women, and children. What he did, what he accomplished was of biblical proportions. Sir Winston Churchill, another man of force and fortitude, is the only other person who has received honorary United States citizenship. And as John F. Kennedy said at that signing ceremony, "Indifferent himself to danger, he wept over the sorrows of others."

That compassion also exemplifies the man we are gathered here for today. In 1944 the United States requested Sweden's cooperation in protecting the lives of Hungarian Jews facing extermination at the hands of the Nazis. In the months that followed, the United States supplied the funds and the directives, and Raoul Wallenberg supplied the courage and the passion. How can we comprehend the moral worth of a man who saved tens and tens of thousands of lives, including those of Congressman and Mrs. Lantos?

Whatever Happened to Raoul Wallenberg?

In 1945, in violation of diplomatic immunity and international law, he was seized by the Soviet Union. The Nazis were gone, and the Soviets had come in as an ally. And yet today, there is evidence that he is still imprisoned by the Soviets. Wherever he is, his humanity burns like a torch.

I heard someone say that a man has made at least a start on understanding the meaning of human life when he plants shade trees under which he knows he will never sit. Raoul Wallenberg is just such a man. He nurtured the lives of those he never knew at the risk of his own. And then just recently, I was told that in a special area behind the Holocaust Memorial in Israel, Hungarian Jews, now living in Sweden, planted 10,000 trees in Raoul's honor.

Mrs. Lagergren, Mr. Von Dardel, we're going to do everything in our power so that your brother can sit beneath the shade of those trees and enjoy the respect and love that so many hold for him.

Note: The President spoke at 2:35 p.m. at the signing ceremony in the Rose Garden at the White House. Participants in the ceremony included the Swedish Ambassdor and Mrs. Wilhelm Wachtmeister, members of the Senate and House of Representatives, representatives of the Jewish community, and Mr. Wallenberg's sister and brother, Nina Lagergren and Guy von Dardel, who came from Sweden for the ceremony. Also in attendance were Representative Tom Lantos of California, the principal sponsor of the resolution in the House of Representatives, and his wife. While a 16-year-old youth working for the Hungarian Underground, Representative Lantos was saved in Budapest by Mr. Wallenberg.

As enacted, S.J. Res. 65 is Public Law 97 - 54, approved October 5.

PHILA. LAWYER SEEKS JUSTICE IN THE WALLENBERG CASE

By Mary Jane Fine, Inquirer Staff Writer
Source: Philadelphia Inquirer, The (PA);

Published: 1984-02-02

Section: NATIONAL | Page A02 | Edition: FINAL | Memo: REPORT ON A LEGAL EFFORT

This morning, Chestnut Hill lawyer and law professor Morris Wolff, buoyed by his mission and confident of its timing, plans to sue the Soviet Union.

At 10 A.M., he will enter US District Court in Washington to file the suit on behalf of the family of Raoul Wallenberg, the Swedish diplomat credited with saving thousands of Hungarian Jews from extermination by the Nazis during World War II.

The suit seeks either Wallenberg's release from the Soviet Union—where he was taken under "protective custody" in 1945 and where the Soviets say he died that same year—or the return of his remains for a hero's burial. The suit also asks for a declaration of illegal action on the part of the Soviets, all pertinent information concerning Wallenberg's detention and a judgment of $39,000,000 - $1,000,000 for each year since his captivity.

"If possible, I want his freedom; if not, an honest accounting of his life," Wolff said last week, pacing the floor of the sun porch that serves as his office. "It's time now for the truth."

Having said that, Wolff and his colleagues—lawyers drawn from two prestigious law firms and three universities—are well aware that theirs may be an impossible mission.

The attorneys agree that the thorniest legal problem they face is jurisdiction - whether the court has the authority to adjudicate a case against a foreign government. At issue, Wolff explained, is the Act of State Doctrine, which holds that an US court cannot examine the merits of a case when it is alleged that a foreign government acted illegally within its own borders and under its own laws.

Wolff and his colleagues say they think their case falls outside the definition of the doctrine, because they believe that the Soviet action violated international law. Not only was Wallenberg protected by his diplomatic status, they contend, but at least part of the money that funded his humanitarian work came from the United States.

285

Whatever Happened to Raoul Wallenberg?

Two recent developments also have encouraged them to seize the moment: the honorary US citizenship bestowed upon Wallenberg by President Reagan in 1981 and the emergence of a letter written in 1957 by then-Soviet Deputy Foreign Minister Andrei A. Gromyko, acknowledging that Wallenberg's detention amounted to "criminal activity."

"This is a dynamite brief," Wolff said, slapping his palm with a copy of the rough draft. "We're saying (to Gromyko), 'You wrote this letter, you acknowledged you committed a crime. . . . Well, we'd like to ask you a few questions."

Until May, Wolff had not heard of Raoul Wallenberg.

That was hardly surprising because until 1979, when Wallenberg's sister visited the United States to organize a Wallenberg Committee, few Americans knew of the events that had long before become a cause celebre in Sweden.

The Raoul Wallenberg Committee of the United States, headed by Sens. Frank Church, Claiborne Pell, Daniel Patrick Moynihan and Rudy Boschwitz, soon embarked on a massive educational campaign designed, according to its literature, "to make the name of Raoul Wallenberg a household name."

Through documentaries, news programs and brochures, the story began to circulate.

Wallenberg was 32, the scion of an influential Swedish family, when he was dispatched by the Swedish government to Budapest. By the time he arrived, on July 9, 1944, all the Jews outside the capital—437,000 men, women and children - already had been deported to concentration camps. Wallenberg's mission was to save as many of the Jews of Budapest as he could.

The impetus for his assignment came from the War Refugee Board, established by President Franklin D. Roosevelt in the hope of saving Jews and others targeted by the Nazis. After the partial Nazi occupation of Hungary in June 1944, the board made Hungary its primary focus.

It approached Sweden, a neutral country with an embassy in Budapest, asking for someone to undertake the mission. That someone was Wallenberg.

Once in Budapest, he redesigned the Swedish protective passport, the "Schutzpass," into a more impressive and readily identifiable document; he established shelters, hospitals and soup kitchens, all flying the Swedish flag, and he and other volunteers even distributed blankets, food and clothing to Jews already marching toward death camps.

According to the lawsuit on his behalf, "From July 1944 until January 1945, Wallenberg is credited with having saved up to 100,000 lives."

In January 1945, the Soviet army liberated Budapest. On or about the 17th of that month, Wallenberg was taken into "protective custody" by Soviet secret police, transported to Moscow and placed in Lubyanka prison. The Soviet ambassador to Sweden notified Wallenberg's family of his arrival in Russia and assured them of his safe return.

In February 1957, the Soviet government informed the Swedish government that Wallenberg had died "in his cell . . . probably as a result of a heart attack" in July 1947 at the age of 35. His remains, the communique said, had been cremated.

Wolff says he has "an intuitive belief" that Wallenberg is alive. His belief, he says, goes beyond the family history of longevity, beyond the fact that "the man had a tremendous perseverance in life.

"One of my favorite poems is Emily Dickinson's," he said, "the one that goes, 'I never spoke with God, nor visited in Heaven, yet certain am I of the spot, as if the checks were given.'"

Wolff's introduction to Raoul Wallenberg came via a colleague, Northwestern University law professor Thomas D'Amato, who had been contacted by Wallenberg's half-brother, Guy Von Dardel.

Von Dardel had learned about D'Amato's success in suing the Soviet Union on behalf of a Chicago woman who, while on a student visa in 1981, married a Russian citizen, but the Soviets refused to let him leave the country and join her in the United States.

The case, Frolova vs. USSR. was resolved when the Soviets, presumably to avoid the publicity and hassle, released Lois Frolova's husband in June 1982, only two months after D'Amato filed suit.

Von Dardel asked D'Amato's advice regarding his half-brother, and D'Amato recommended Morris Wolff, a former assistant district attorney in Philadelphia and a teacher of international law at the Delaware Law School of Widener University.

Wolff immediately bought and read *Righteous Gentile*, a book by John Bierman, which includes recollections by Jews whom Wallenberg rescued and eyewitness accounts by others who say they met him in prison in the Soviet Union years after the time when the Soviets say he died.

Whatever Happened to Raoul Wallenberg?

D'Amato and Wolff discussed the case, talked strategy and decided to file suit, using Frolova vs. USSR for a model.

"The family is very realistic," Wolff said last week. "They realize (Wallenberg) may be dead, but they want the final chapter of his life written with dignity. They feel it is a political case in part, but they feel it must be heard in a court with a tradition of freedom."

As for the Soviets' response, Wolff mentions the possibility of a grand gesture, a prelude to peace talks, by the Soviets. If that does not happen, he said, he offers "two face-saving ways in which they can release him: they can say that their hospital system is so vast, he apparently was listed under another name, a bureaucratic oversight. Second, they can say that the man has been in such a condition . . . that he has been unable to communicate with them.

"They may even see it as a diplomatic accomplishment to locate and free him."

Murray Levin, of the Philadelphia law firm of Pepper, Hamilton & Scheetz, another lawyer attached to the Wallenberg case, also talked about the possibility of a "gesture."

"I think it's fair to say the odds are long," he said, "and, in the long run, an American court can't force the Russians to release him, but it can do things that are damaging."

The attorneys say they may ask the court for injunctions—perhaps more restrictions on Soviet air travel here and embassy bank accounts—aimed at forcing the Soviets' hand. The timing of the injunctions has not been determined, they say.

A State Department spokeswoman said she was not aware of the pending lawsuit and would be reluctant to comment even if she were familiar with it "for fear of prejudicing the case." She did say that it would be unlikely for a suit filed by an individual to affect US-Soviet relations because the Soviets would not view it as an official action.

A spokesman for the Soviet Embassy in Washington declined to comment, saying he was not familiar with the case.

Wolff talked about the one clear moment years ago when he knew what his future would be. He was 17, working on a high school project, sitting in a magistrate's court in Philadelphia absorbing the litany of complaints and miseries that unfolded there, when he decided he would be a lawyer.

288

"The law was to be for me an instrument for the accomplishment of social justice," he said, brandishing the papers from the Wallenberg lawsuit, "and this is the most wonderful privilege, to be the custodian of this man's human rights."

The New York Times

DIPLOMAT'S FAMILY SUES SOVIET

UPI
Published: February 3, 1984

WASHINGTON, Feb. 2—The family of Raoul Wallenberg, a Swedish diplomat who saved the lives of at least 100,000 Jews in World War II, filed a $39 million lawsuit against the Soviet Union today, demanding that the Russians tell what happened to him.

The suit was filed in Federal District Court by lawyers for Guy Von Dardel, the half brother of Mr. Wallenberg.

The diplomat was imprisoned by the Russians in 1945 after carrying out his life-saving mission in Nazi-occupied Hungary. The suit asks that the Soviet Union either release Mr. Wallenberg or supply definitive proof that he is dead, and in either case pay $39 million in damages to the family.
The Soviet Union said Mr. Wallenberg died in prison in 1947, but the diplomat's family believes he is alive.

The suit was filed under the *Foreign Sovereign Immunities Act of 1977*, which makes foreign governments liable to lawsuits in United States courts for wrongful acts, according to Mr. von Dardel's lawyer, Morris Wolff.

In 1944 the United States and Swedish Governments sent Mr. Wallenberg to Budapest to help save Jews still under occupation by Nazi Germany.

GUY VON DARDEL, on his own behalf and on behalf of his half brother, RAOUL WALLENBERG, and SVEN HAGSTROMER, Legal Guardian of RAOUL WALLENBERG, on Behalf of RAOUL WALLENBERG, Plaintiffs, v. UNION OF SOVIET SOCIALIST REPUBLICS, Defendant

Civil Action No. 84-0353

UNITED STATES DISTRICT COURT FOR THE DISTRICT OF COLUMBIA
623 F. Supp. 246; 1985 US Dist. LEXIS 14886

October 15, 1985

DISPOSITION: [**1] Default judgment is hereby entered against the defendant.

COUNSEL: Morris H. Wolff, Anthony D'Amato, Joseph W. Dellapenna, Jerome G. Snider, Murray S. Levin, for Plaintiff/Petitioner.

JUDGES: Barrington D. Parker, United States District Judge.

OPINION BY: PARKER

OPINION [*248] Barrington D. Parker, United States District Judge:

MEMORANDUM OPINION

In this proceeding declaratory and injunctive relief and damages are sought against the Union of Soviet Socialist Republics ("Soviet Union" or "USSR") for the unlawful seizure, imprisonment and possibly death of Raoul Wallenberg, a Swedish diplomat. The complaint is brought on behalf of Wallenberg by Guy Von Dardel, his half brother, and Sven Hagstromer his legal guardian. Guy Von Dardel and Sven Hagstromer are Swedish citizens. Hagstromer was appointed guardian of Wallenberg's legal interests by the District Court in Stockholm, Sweden.

The plaintiffs allege that in 1945, Raoul Wallenberg was arrested in Budapest, Hungary by representatives of the Soviet Union and that since then he has suffered imprisonment and possibly death. At the time of his arrest he was acting

291

at the initiation of the United States government [**2] in an attempt to save the Jewish population in the Budapest ghetto from deportation to Nazi extermination camps. If these allegations are true, they violated Wallenberg's diplomatic immunity, the laws and treaties of the Soviet Union and the United States, and the law of nations.

BACKGROUND

1

1 The facts in this proceeding are based on statements of USSR officials, official actions taken by the United States Congress, reports and resolutions of House and Senate Committees and official actions taken by the President. The plaintiffs have filed voluminous appendices in this proceeding.

During the course of World War II, the United States Government, in an effort to save from extermination by the German Nazis the thousands of Jews then domiciled in Hungary, sought the assistance of Sweden, a neutral nation. This was an effort that the United States could not undertake alone. Because the United States was at war with Hungary, its diplomatic presence was withdrawn. Raoul Wallenberg agreed to join the Swedish [**3] Legation in Budapest, and to otherwise cooperate with the efforts of Sweden and "to act at the behest of the United States." Joint Resolution of Congress declaring Raoul Wallenberg to be an honorary citizen of the United States, Pub. L. No. 97-54, 95 Stat.971 (1981) ("Joint Resolution").2

2 Mr. Wallenberg became the second person to be voted by Congress an honorary citizen. Winston Churchill was the first. Representative Thomas Lantos of California, a Hungarian Jewish refugee is credited with taking the initiative in making Wallenberg an honorary American citizen. New York Times, April 13, 1985, p. 9.

[*249] Granted full diplomatic status by Sweden, and funded by the United States, Wallenberg arrived in Budapest, Hungary, in July 1944. While stationed there, he served as Secretary of the Swedish Legation and was entitled to full diplomatic immunity. In the next six months, until his arrest by Soviet officials, Wallenberg saved the lives of nearly one hundred thousand Jewish persons providing them with [**4] funds and other means of support provided by the United States. While in Budapest he became the counterforce to the notorious German Nazi—Adolf Eichmann. His efforts to save Hungary's Jews from extermination were described in a Senate Report:

He printed and issued thousands of Swedish protective passports of his own design. He purchased and rented scores of houses in Budapest, declared them to be Swedish Embassy property and equipped them with Swedish flags, and protected and cared for the refugees he gathered within these safe houses. Risking his own life time and time again, Wallenberg followed the "Death Marches" and went daily to the deportation trains where he literally pulled people out of the clutches of the Nazis. And, when the Nazis decided to blow up the ghetto in Budapest and all its inhabitants with it, Wallenberg confronted the Nazi leaders (Adolf Eichmann), threatened to see to it personally that they were hanged as war criminals if they proceeded with their plan, and thus prevented its execution.

S. Rep. no. 97-169, 97th Cong., 1st Sess. at 2 (1981)
("Wallenberg Senate Report").

Hungary was later overrun by the Soviets and in early 1945, Wallenberg was [**5] arrested by their occupation forces in Budapest. From that time forward, his precise whereabouts and his status within the Soviet Union have not been ascertained. In a note dated August18, 1947 and delivered to the Swedish Embassy in Moscow by Soviet Foreign Minister, Andrei Ya Vyshinsky it was asserted that "as a result of a thorough investigation it has been established that Wallenberg is not in the Soviet Union and he is not known to us."

Ten years later, however, in response to renewed diplomatic inquiries based on the testimony of persons released from Soviet prisons that Wallenberg was still alive, Deputy Foreign Minister Andrei A. Gromyko admitted that Wallenberg had been a prisoner in the USSR. He further stated that while imprisoned, Wallenberg had died of natural causes on July 17, 1947.In a note dated February 6, 1957, delivered to the Swedish Embassy in Moscow, Gromyko described the detention of Wallenberg, and the misinformation which made the detention possible, as "criminal activity," and attempted to fasten the [**6] blame for it upon Viktor S. Abakumov, a former Minister of State Security who died in 1953.

Raoul Wallenberg was apparently among other persons detained in the area of the military operations of the Soviet forces. At the same time it may be considered indubitable that the subsequent detention of Wallenberg, and also the incorrect information about him which was given by certain former leaders of organs of state security to the Ministry of Foreign Affairs of the USSR over the course of a number of years, were the result of criminal activity of Abakumov. As is known, in connection with the grave crimes committed by him, Abakumov, acting in violation of the laws of the USSR and striving in every possible way to inflict harm on the Soviet Union, was condemned and shot by order of the Supreme Court of the USSR.

Whatever Happened to Raoul Wallenberg?

The Soviet Government sincerely regrets what has occurred and expresses its deep condolences to the Government of Sweden and also to the relatives of Raoul Wallenberg.

Wolff Affidavit, *supra*, Ex. F, pp. 2-3.

However, between 1954 and 1981, a steady flow of reports from former Soviet prisoners indicate that Wallenberg did not [*250] die as claimed in the [**7] Gromyko note. To the contrary, the reports suggest that Wallenberg remained alive and in the defendant's custody after 1947. Joint Resolution, *supra*.

There is insufficient evidence before the Court to support a definitive finding as to whether at this time, Wallenberg is dead or alive. While the USSR has continuously represented that Wallenberg died in 1947, those representations are inconsistent with and at odds with credible and uncontroverted evidence presented by the plaintiffs in this proceeding and they are rejected. On basis of the record here presented, the Court finds that the Soviet Union has always had knowledge and information about Wallenberg; that it has failed to disclose and has concealed that information; and that otherwise, defendant's representations are suspect and should be given little, if any, credit. If alive, Wallenberg would be 72 years of age and he would have been held in custody for nearly 40 years.

The complaint in this proceeding was filed with this Court in February 1984. A request for documents relevant to the issue of jurisdiction was filed along with the complaint. The summons, complaint and discovery request, together with a notice of suit [**8] and Russian translations of the documents, were regularly processed through the United States Department of State. The packet of documents was then delivered to and served upon the Soviet Ministry of Foreign Affairs in Moscow in accordance with the Foreign Sovereign Immunities Act ("FSIA" or "Act"), *28 USC. § 1608(a)(4).* On May 1, 1984, a certified copy of the diplomatic note evidencing service of the documents was filed by the Department of State with the Clerk of this Court.

The defendant's time to answer or otherwise respond to the complaint expired on June 1, 1984. The Soviet Union did not respond to either the complaint or the document request. On April 19, 1984, the Soviet Ministry of Foreign Affairs returned all of the documents to the United States Embassy in Moscow, together with a note asserting absolute sovereign immunity from suit in non-Soviet courts. Wolff Affidavit, *supra*, PP 4-6 and Ex. B.

Under the circumstances, it is appropriate to consider the plaintiff's application for a default judgment. In the discussion which follows, the Court will address first, the questions of jurisdiction, venue, and statute of limitations. It will then address the merits of [**9] the litigations and an analysis of the issues arising under the substantive law. This Court's factual findings are supported by a satisfactory, substantial, and well documented record.

JURISDICTION AND VENUE

Several sections of Title 28 United States Code allow this Court to exercise jurisdiction over this action. Under *Section 1330(b)* of the Foreign Sovereign Immunities Act, personal jurisdiction is present when the defendant may be found in the United States, through its agents and instrumentalities, and because defendant has been duly served with process pursuant to *28 USC. § 1608(a)(4)*(Wolff Aff., *supra*, P 3 and Ex. A). Because this is a civil action arising under the "laws, or treaties of the United States," subject matter jurisdiction under FSIA is appropriate pursuant to *Sections 1330(a)* and *1331.Letelier v. Republic of Chile, 502 F. Supp.259, 266(D.D.C. 1980).* Additional reasons to support this conclusion are discussed ante at p. 11. Finally, this Court may exercise subject matter jurisdiction over this proceeding under the Alien Tort Claims Act, *28 USC. §1350* because it is a "civil action by an alien for a tort only, committed in violation of [**10] the law of nations or a treaty of the United States." *Tel-Oren v. Libyan Arab Republic, 233 US App. D.C. 384, 726 F.2d 774, 813-14(D.C. Cir. 1984), cert. denied, 470 US 1003, 105 S. Ct.1354, 84 L. Ed. 2d 377 (1985),* opinion Bork, J.; *Letelier,502 F. Supp.at 266.*

Venue is appropriate in the United States District Court for the District of Columbia because the defendant is a foreign state, *28 USC. § 1391(f)(4).*

The Foreign Sovereign Immunities Act, *28 USC.§ 1602*

This Court has subject matter and personal jurisdiction under the Foreign Sovereign [*251] Immunities Act. Under the Act, a foreign state is generally immune from the jurisdiction of federal courts, *28 USC. § 1604*, subject to a number of exceptions and limitations set forth at *§§ 1604* and *1605. Section 1604*provides that the immunity afforded by the Act is "subject to existing international agreements to which the United States is a party at the time of enactment of [the] Act." *Section 1605(a)* sets forth several categorical exceptions to immunity, including situations in which the sovereign defendant has waived immunity, *§ 1605(a)(1)* situations involving certain commercial activity [**11] or property in the United States, *§ 1605(a)(2)-(4)*, and certain non-commercial torts committed by the foreign state or its agent, *§ 1605(a)(5).*

Whatever Happened to Raoul Wallenberg?

The Act provides the district courts with subject matter jurisdiction over civil cases against foreign governments where immunity is not appropriate under its terms. *28 USC. § 1330(a)*. Moreover, where the requirements of subject matter jurisdiction have been met and proper service has been made, the Act operates to create personal jurisdiction over the foreign government defendant. *28 USC. § 1330(b)*. 3 The absence of immunity thus establishes both subject matter and personal jurisdiction over a case against a foreign government. *See, e.g., Yessenin-Volpin v. Novosti Press Agency, 443 F. Supp. 849, 851 (S.D.N.Y. 1978)*. 4

3 A court's assertion of jurisdiction over a defendant pursuant to *§ 1330(b)* must also comport with minimum jurisdictional contacts and due process as required by *International Shoe Co. v. Washington, 326 US 310, 90 L. Ed. 95, 66S. Ct. 154 (1945).See World-Wide Volkswagen Corp. v. Woodson, 444 US 286, 292-93, 62 L.Ed. 2d 490, 100 S. Ct. 559 (1980); Kulko v.California Superior Court, 436 US 84, 92, 56 L.Ed.2d 132, 98 S. Ct. 1690 (1978); Hanson v.Denckla, 357 US 235, 253, 2 L. Ed. 2d 1283, 78S. Ct. 1228 (1958). See also Gilson v. Republic of Ireland, 221 US App. D.C. 73, 682 F.2d 1022, 1028 (D.C. Cir. 1982)*. These minimum requirements are clearly satisfied because the defendant maintains a substantial presence in this District. [**12]

4 As a threshold matter, it is noted that the Supreme Court has upheld the constitutionality of the FSIA's authorization of suits by foreign plaintiffs against foreign states. *Verlinden B.V. v. Central Bank of Nigeria, 461 US 480, 490, 76 L.Ed. 2d 81, 103 S. Ct. 1962 (1983)*.

In 1976, Congress had a twofold purpose for enacting the Foreign Sovereign Immunities Act: (1) to liberalize the law of immunity by adopting and codifying the doctrine of "restrictive" immunity, and (2) to assure consistent application of the law of sovereign immunity by eliminating the participation of the executive branch of the government so as to "assure litigants that . . .decisions are made on purely legal grounds and under procedures that insure due process." H.R. Rep. No.94-1487, 94th Cong., 2d Sess. 7 (1976), *reprinted in* 1976 US Code Cong. & Ad. News 6604, 6606 ("House Report"). To accomplish these objectives, the Act established a set of legal standards governing claims of immunity in civil actions against foreign states. These standards were explicitly intended to incorporate established principles [**13] of international law regarding the immunity of sovereigns. House Report, at14, 1976 US Code Cong. & Ad. News at 6613.

According to the drafters of the FSIA, "sovereign immunity is an affirmative defense which must especially pleaded, [and] the burden will remain on the foreign state to produce evidence in support of its claim of immunity." House Report, *supra*, at 17, 1976 US Code Cong. & Ad.News at 6616. Thus, the burden of demonstrating that immunity exists rests upon the foreign state. *See, e.g., Arango v. Guzman Travel Advisors Corp., 621 F.2d 1371, 1378 (5th Cir. 1980).* In the absence of an appearance by the defendant, however, the Court must make an independent determination that it has subject matter jurisdiction. *See, e.g., Letelier v. Republic of Chile, 488 F. Supp. 665, 667 (D.D.C. 1980).*

The plaintiff cites five independent reasons why the USSR should not enjoy immunity in this case. The Court has taken note of all these arguments but finds the first four far more compelling than the last. The reasons are as follows: First, by virtue of its decision to default, the USSR failed to raise the defense of sovereign immunity.[*252] Second, the FSIA [**14] incorporates preexisting standards of international law, under which a government is not immune for certain acts in clear623 F. Supp. 246, *250; 1985 US Dist. LEXIS 14886, **10 violation of the universally accepted law of nations. Third, the FSIA is limited by treaties to which the United States is a party; the USSR cannot claim immunity under the FSIA for acts which constitute violations of certain of those treaties, to which the USSR is also a party. Fourth, the USSR waived immunity in this action, and is therefore not entitled to raise it as a defense, pursuant to *28 USC. § 1605(a)(1)*. And, fifth, the actions of the USSR constitute non-commercial torts within the meaning of *28 USC. § 1605(a)(5)*; immunity for commission of such is therefore inappropriate under the Act. A fuller discussion of the first four is set out below.

A

Under the FSIA, sovereign immunity is an affirmative defense that must be pleaded and proved by the sovereign defendant. These obligations were made clear in the documents which were served upon the Soviet Union. Included among them was an explanatory notice of suit and the full text of the FSIA, both with Russian translation. The transmittal note from the United States Embassy accompanying the papers [**15] underscored the procedures:

Please note that under United States law and procedure, neither the Embassy nor the Department of State is in the position to comment on the present suit. Under the laws of the United States, any jurisdictional or other defense including claims of sovereign immunity must be addressed to the court before which the matter is pending, for which reason it inadvisable to consult an attorney in the United States. (Wolff Aff., Ex. A.)

Moreover, because of prior involvement in FSIA litigation, the procedure is one with which the Soviet Union is fully familiar. Indeed in several reported cases in which the USSR has been a defendant since the passage of the Act, it has appeared through counsel for the purpose of contesting jurisdiction. [5]*See Bland v. Union of Soviet Socialist Republics, 17 Av. Cas (CCH)17,530 (E.D. N.Y. 1982); Harris v. VAO Intourist, Moscow, 481 F. Supp. 1056 (E.D. N.Y. 1979); United Euram v. Union of Soviet Socialist Republics, 461 F.Supp. 609 (S.D. N.Y. 1978); cf. In re Estate of Petro Semeniw, 78 Ill. App. 3d 570, 397 N.E.2d 64, 33 Ill. Dec.731 (1st Dist. 1979); In re Estate of Bari Nabif, 69A.D.2d 904, [**16] 415 N.Y.S.2d 901 (2d Dept. 1979).* [6] However, in this proceeding, the USSR has chosen to default and to raise the issue of immunity not by a motion filed with the Court, but merely by a communication addressed to the United States Embassy in Moscow.

5 The Soviet Union defaulted without comment in *Frolova v. Union of Soviet Socialist Republics, 558 F. Supp. 358 (N.D. Ill. 1983), aff'd, 761 F.2d370 (7th Cir. 1985).*6 The instrumentalities of the Soviet Union have also appeared when sued under the Act. *See Houston v. Murmansk Shipping Co., 667 F.2d1151 (4th Cir. 1982); Yessenin-Volpin v. Novosti Press Agency, 443 F. Supp. 849 (S.D. N.Y. 1978).*

In *Letelier, supra, 488 F. Supp. 665, 669 n.4,* this Court raised the question of whether such a diplomatic assertion of immunity, in lieu of "a formal appearance or the filing of a pleading," could suffice to raise the defense of sovereign immunity. In that case, the foreign state defendant sent a diplomatic note to the Department of State challenging [**17] the jurisdiction of the Court. The Court declined to rule on the sufficiency of this method of raising the affirmative defense of immunity, because the Court found that it had subject matter jurisdiction "even assuming it has been pleaded properly." *Id. at 670 n.4.*

The degree to which a foreign state is entitled to immunity under the Act is necessarily determined by the procedures set forth by Congress. Congress explicitly intended that sovereign immunity remain an "affirmative defense which must be specially pleaded, the burden[remaining] on the foreign state to produce evidence in [*253] support of its claim of immunity." House Report, *supra,* at 17, 1976 US Code Cong. & Ad. News at 6616.This allocation of the burden of proof was, in fact, one of the bases for Congress' decision to structure the Act as a presumption of immunity subject to a group of exceptions. *Id.*

In the present case, defendant has not only failed to lead immunity as an affirmative defense, but has chosen to raise immunity in a manner explicitly precluded by the Act. Prior to passage of the FSIA, the defense of immunity could be raised by diplomatic approaches to the Department of State. [**18] *See, e.g.,* House Report, *supra,* at 17, 1976 US Code Cong. & Ad. News at 6605-06; *Ex Parte Muir, 254 US 522, 532-33, 65 L. Ed.623 F. Supp. 246, *252;* 1985 US Dist.

LEXIS 14886, **14*383, 41 S. Ct. 185 (1921)*. It was the express purpose of the FSIA to remove the executive branch from the determination of such issues. By raising the issue of sovereign immunity in a diplomatic note, the USSR has knowingly chosen a procedure that is no longer available under United States law. As such, it cannot be recognized as an adequate pleading of the defense of immunity. *ExParte Muir, supra, at 533.*

Having failed to raise immunity as an affirmative defense, or to provide even a bare allegation that its acts do not fall into one of the exceptions to the FSIA, defendant has deliberately chosen to forego whatever entitlement it might have had to immunity under the terms of the Act. [7]

7 This Court notes plaintiff's further argument that this Court should find subject matter jurisdiction as a sanction for failure to comply with its discovery order but does not find it as persuasive as the others they have offered for consideration.

[**19] **B**

The Foreign Sovereign Immunities Act, like every federal statute, should be interpreted in such a way as to be consistent with the law of nations. *See, e.g., MacLeod v. United States, 229 US 416, 434, 57 L. Ed. 1260, 33 S. Ct. 955 (1913)*. Congress explicitly anticipated such an interpretation, stating its intent that the Act"[incorporated] standards recognized under international law." House Report, *supra*, at 14, 1976 US Code Cong.& Ad. News at 6613.

Historically, when a nation has committed a clear and egregious violation of a well-established and universally recognized standard of international law, courts have recognized the need for an appropriate exercise of jurisdiction. In *Bernstein v. N. V. Nederlandsche Amerikaansche Stoomvaart-Maatschappij, 210 F.2d 375 (2d Cir. 1954)*,the court deferred to a press release issued by the Department of State in which the Department took the position that in cases seeking reparations for confiscations of property by Nazi officials, American courts should not be restrained by doctrines of international law that, under more routine circumstances, would require a court not to exercise jurisdiction or reach the merits [**20] of a claim. *210 F.2d at 375-76*. Moreover, the doctrine of sovereign immunity has historically been based on principles of "grace and comity." *Verlinden B.V. v. Central Bank of Nigeria, 461US 480, 486, 76 L. Ed. 2d 81, 103 S. Ct. 1962 (1983)*. As such, the doctrine is inherently limited and appropriately disallowed where the foreign state defendant has acted in clear violation of international law.

Whatever Happened to Raoul Wallenberg?

In *Banco Nacional de Cuba v. Sabbatino, 376 US398, 11 L. Ed. 2d 804, 84 S. Ct. 923 (1964)*, the Supreme Court held that the act of state doctrine barred consideration of the validity of a Cuban confiscation of property located in Cuba, basing its decision largely on the fact that there is some division in the international community regarding state expropriation of the property of aliens. ("There are few if any issues in international law today on which opinion seems to be so divided . . ."*376 US at 428*). In dissenting, Justice White urged that the act of state doctrine should not shield acts which are clearly violations of international law, even where (unlike the present case) such acts would otherwise be subject to the act of state doctrine:

[*254] The reasons [**21] for nonreview, based as they are on traditional concepts of territorial sovereignty, lose much of their force when the foreign act of state is shown to be a violation of international law. All legitimate exercises of sovereign power, whether territorial or otherwise, should be exercised consistently with rules of international law, including those rules which mark the bounds of lawful state action against aliens or their property located within the territorial confines of the foreign state.

376 US at 457.

The concept of extraordinary judicial jurisdiction over acts in violation of significant international standards has also been embodied in the principle of "universal" violations of international law. *See, e.g.*, Restatement of Foreign Relations Law of the United States (Revised) § 404 (Tent. Draft No. 2, 1981) ("A state may exercise jurisdiction to define and punish certain offenses recognized by the community of nations as of universal concern"). The concept of universal violations is not limited to criminal jurisdiction, but extends to the enforcement of civil law as well. *Id.* at Comment *b*.

Congress was fully aware of these doctrines of international law [**22] in 1976 when it adopted the FSIA, and meant to incorporate them into the statute. [8] The statute should be read, then, not to extend immunity to clear violations of universally recognized principles of international law.

8 The fact that the legislative history of the FSIA does not contain a specific reference to these doctrines is not surprising. Congress' primary concern was to codify jurisdictional standards relating to the burgeoning area of commercial litigation against foreign governments. House Report, *supra*, at 6, *reprinted in* 1976 US Code Cong. 7 Ad. News at 6605. The codification was necessary in order to ensure that these more routine cases did not take on undue political

significance through the sometimes inconsistent development of the common law, as influenced by the Executive. *See* discussion at pp. 10-11, *supra*.

The violation of the diplomatic immunity of Raoul Wallenberg is such a violation. The ancient and universal consensus on diplomatic immunity places it squarely within [**23] even the most restrictive interpretation of the coverage of the Alien Tort Claims Act, *28 USC. §1350. See* discussion at slip op. pp. 27-28, *infra*. As such, the Congress in 1789 opened the district courts of the United States to suits by aliens claiming tortuous violations of diplomatic immunity. Congress has also enacted statutes designed to protect internationally protected persons, including diplomats, *18 USC. §§1116* and *1201*, as to which a private remedy has been implied. *See* discussion slip op. at pp. 36-38, *infra*. If the FSIA was interpreted to bar suits against foreign governments under *§ 1350*, or to preempt the private rights created by *§§ 1116* and *1201*, it would act *protanto* to repeal these statutes. ⁹ Statutory interpretation that would affect such a repeal is not favored, *e.g., United States v. United Continental Tuna Corp., 425 US 164,168-69, 181, 47 L. Ed. 2d 653, 96 S. Ct. 1319 (1976)*, and is therefore rejected by this Court.

9 In a footnote appended to the end of the majority opinion in *Persinger v. Islamic Republic of Iran, 234 US App. D.C. 349, 729 F.2d 835(D.C. Cir. 1984)*, *cert. denied, 469 US 881, 105S. Ct. 247, 83 L. Ed. 2d 185 (1984)*, Judge Bork (with Judge Edwards dissenting) rejected plaintiffs' argument that United States courts had jurisdiction over claims for damages arising out of the seizure of the American Embassy in Iran, although this seizure constituted an international crime. *729 F.2d at 843 n.12 (D.C. Cir. 1984)*. Sofar as the opinion reveals, Judge Bork did not consider the intent of Congress in enacting the FSIA to preserve existing remedies for violations of international law, as described above, or the effect of *18 USC. §§ 1116* and *1201* or *28 USC.§ 1350*.

[**24] C

Section 1604 of the FSIA provides that immunity is "subject to" international agreements to which the United States was a party at the time of its enactment. Thus, where the substantive provisions of the Act would operate in a specific case to interfere with any such international agreement, such provisions must be preempted to the [*255] extent necessary to permit the full operation of such agreement.¹⁰ In this proceeding, both the United States and the Soviet Union are parties to two international agreements, the operation of which would be frustrated by any decision granting immunity to the Soviet Union: the Vienna Convention on Diplomatic Relations, April 18, 1961, and the 1973 Convention on Internationally Protected Persons.

10 The House Report would limit the immunity of a foreign state under the Act to cases of an express or manifest conflict between the provisions of the Act and those of an international agreement or treaty. House Report, *supra*, at 17*reprinted in* US Code Cong. & Ad. News at 6616.*See, e.g., Mashayekhi v. Iran, 515 F. Supp.41, 42 (D.D.C. 1981)*. Given the clear and unambiguous language of the statute, however, resort to the legislative history is in this instance unnecessary for interpretative purposes. *See, e.g.,Greyhound Corp. v. Mt. Hood Stages, Inc., 437US 322, 330, 57 L. Ed. 2d 239, 98 S. Ct. 2370(1978)*; *National Insulation Transportation Committee v. ICC, 221 US App.D.C. 192, 683F.2d 533, 537 (D.C. Cir. 1982)*. This reading of the clear language of § 1604 is given further support by the language of *28 USC. § 1330*, which gives the federal courts jurisdiction over actions against foreign states with respect to which the foreign state is "not entitled to immunity" under the FSIA "or any applicable 623 F. Supp. 246, *254; 1985 US Dist. LEXIS 14886, **21 international agreement."

[**25] The Vienna Convention and the 1973 Convention are both designed to protect diplomats from offenses against them. In order for the conventions to operate effectively, the perpetrators of such offenses must be subject to liability for their acts. To the extent that the FSIA would shield the Soviet Union from such liability, it is in conflict with the terms of the conventions and thwarts their effective operation. Under § 1604, the immunity granted by the FSIA must be limited so as to avoid such a result; in the present case, the Soviet Union must be denied immunity.

This result is particularly just since the Soviet Union is a party to both conventions. Under the Vienna Convention the USSR is pledged to protect the very rights it is violating. Under the 1973 Convention it is pledged to punish the very crimes it is committing. Moreover, the Soviet Union's unlawful treatment of Wallenberg was ongoing even as the Conventions were drafted and signed. Thus, it knowingly accepted the validity of legal standards that it knew at the time were being violated. Against such a backdrop, the denial of immunity against claims seeking relief for such violations does not seem unjust.

D

[**26] Under § 1605(a)(1) of the FSIA, foreign states may waive immunity "either explicitly or by implication." According to the House Report, an example of an explicit waiver under the FSIA might be found in the form of a treaty obligation under treaties of friendship, commerce, and navigation. Neither the statute nor the legislative history, however, makes clear how immunity can be implicitly waived. [11]

11 The House Report provides two illustrative examples of implied waivers—an appearance in court by the sovereign defendant, or an agreement by the sovereign defendant to arbitrate claims in another country. House Report, *supra*, at 18, 1976 US Code Cong. & Ad. News at 6617. These examples, however, are not exclusive.

The United States courts have not yet fully explored the proposition that by ratifying an international agreement a foreign state implicitly waives a defense of sovereign immunity against claims seeking compensation for acts which constitute violations of such agreements. In *Frolova v.* [**27] *Union of Soviet Socialist Republics, 558 F. Supp. 358, 363 n.3 (N.D. Ill. 1983), aff'd, 761 F.2d 370 (7th Cir. 1985)*, the court in dictum rejected plaintiff's argument that because the Soviet Union's refusal to permit plaintiff's husband to emigrate violated international and Soviet law, it had impliedly waived immunity. In *Siderman v. Republic of Argentina,*No. Civ. 82-1772-RMT (C.D. Cal. March 12, 1984), however, the court found jurisdiction over the Republic of Argentina for claims related to the torture of one of the plaintiffs "by applying the 'Law of Nations' concept." A number of legal scholars have examined this principle in the context of [*256] human rights violations, 12 and have concluded that a sovereign may implicitly waive its immunity for such violations when it ratifies human rights agreements. R. Lillich and F. Newman, *International Human Rights: Problems of Law and Policy* (1979); Comment, *The Foreign Sovereign Immunities Act and International Human Rights Agreements: How They Co-Exist*, 17 USF. L. Rev. 71(1982).

12 The importance of looking to the writing of legal scholars in this area of the law was explained by the Supreme Court in *The Paquete Habana, 175 US 677, 700, 44 L. Ed. 320, 20 S.Ct. 290 (1900). See also, e.g., Filartiga v. Pena-Irala, 630 F.2d 876, 879 n.4 (2d Cir. 1980).*

[**28] These conclusions are directly relevant to the present case, which involves violations not only of international human rights agreements but also of treaties codifying the fundamental principle of diplomatic immunity, which has been universally recognized as binding since before the times of Blackstone and deVattel. 13 By explicitly agreeing to be bound by the terms of those agreements, the USSR has implicitly waived its immunity in this action alleging their breach. As Lillich and Newman have noted with respect to the United Nations Charter, it would be most difficult to conclude that the Charter provisions on human rights cannot legitimately be given effect by the courts in appropriate cases. Indeed, it would be contrary to the letter and the spirit of the *supremacy clause of the Constitution* if the courts did not attempt to carry out a treaty provision to the fullest extent possible.

Whatever Happened to Raoul Wallenberg?

R. Lillich and F. Newman, *International Human Rights, supra*, at 76. Any other result would rob each of those agreements of substantive effect, and would render meaningless the act of the Soviet Union in signing them.

13 *Frolova v. Union of Soviet Socialist Republics, 558 F. Supp. 358 (N.D. Ill. 1983), aff'd, 761 F.2d 370 (7th Cir. 1985),* on the other hand, on one interpretation dealt with a legal right—the right to emigrate—on which there is not yet such universal agreement among nations. *Cf. Tel-Oren v. Libyan Arab Republic, 233 US App. D.C. 384, 726 F.2d 774, 813 (D.C. Cir. 1984)*(Bork, *J.* concurring).

[**29] **The Alien Tort Claims Act, 28 USC. §1350**

The Alien Tort Claims Act, *28 USC. § 1350,* was enacted in 1789 by the First Congress of the United States. The section provides that the "district courts shall have original jurisdiction of any civil action by an alien for a tort only, committed in violation of the law of nations or a treaty of the United States." The statute vests this Court with subject matter jurisdiction over this proceeding and the right to determine liability for injuries resulting from violations of the diplomatic immunity of Raoul Wallenberg.

The Court of Appeals for this Circuit recently considered the application of *§ 1350* in *Tel-Oren v. Libyan Arab Republic, 233 US App. D.C. 384, 726 F.2d 774 (D.C. Cir. 1984).* That case involved a terrorist attack on an Israeli bus by members of the Palestine Liberation Organization. Plaintiffs, survivors of the attack and representatives of some of those killed, asserted jurisdiction under *28 USC. §§ 1331* and *1350.* [14] The District Court dismissed the case for lack of jurisdiction, and plaintiffs appealed. The Court of Appeals issued three opinions which affirmed the decision of the District Court, but [**30] each opinion stated separate grounds for reaching that result.

14 The District Court held, and plaintiffs conceded, that with regard "to the role of the law of nations," the jurisdictional prerequisites of *§1331* were equivalent to those of *§ 1350.Tel-Oren v. Libyan Arab Republic, 517 F. Supp.542, 549 (D.D.C. 1981), aff'd, 233 US App. D.C.384, 726 F.2d 774, 800 (D.C. Cir. 1983).*

Judge Harry Edwards adopted the interpretation of *§1350* previously adopted by the Second Circuit in *Filartiga v. Pena-Irala, 630 F.2d 876 (2d Cir. 1980),* whereby proof of a tort in violation of international law as that law is currently understood establishes both a cause of action and jurisdiction in the District Court. Judge Robert Bork proposed a more narrow reading of the statute, arguing that the doctrine of [*257] separation of powers should be seen to limit the effect of the statute to those violations of international law that were recognized as actionable in 1789 or to those which, though more recently [**31] established, explicitly entail a private right of action. Judge Roger Robb concurred on the ground that the political question doctrine precluded judicial consideration of the claims raised by the plaintiffs because the legal issues surrounding terrorism are complex and imprecise. It is clear that even under the narrowest of these standards proposed in *Tel-Oren*, or adopted in other forums—*§ 1350* provides this Court with subject matter jurisdiction to determine the liability for the injury that has resulted from the violation of Raoul Wallenberg's diplomatic immunity.

A

In *Filartiga v. Pena-Irala, 630 F.2d 876 (2d Cir.1980)*, a former Paraguayan police official was sued by the father and sister of a young man whose death by torture he was alleged to have caused. The District Court dismissed the case, saying that although official torture violated emerging standards of international law, it was obliged by dicta in prior Second Circuit opinions to rule that *§ 1350* does not reach a state's behavior towards its own citizens.

On appeal, the Second Circuit reversed. Judge Kaufman wrote that the "law of nations," as used in the statute, is a developing body of principles [**32] which must be interpreted "not as it was in 1789, but as it has evolved and exists among the nations of the world today." *630 F.2d at 881.*[15] Looking to the sources of international law enumerated by the Supreme Court in *The Paquete Habana, 175 US 677, 700, 44 L. Ed. 320,20 S. Ct. 290 (1900))*—"executive or legislative act or judicial decision" and the works of expert "jurists and commentators," *630 F.2d at 880*—the court found that" the limitations on a state's power to torture persons held in its custody" constitute a principle on which the opinion of civilized nations is so united as to raise it to a norm of international law. *630 F.2d at 881.See also 630 F.2d at 887-89.* The court concluded that the cause of action "improperly brought in federal court." *630 F.2d at 887.*

15 This position was endorsed by the United States Government in an amicus brief submitted by the Departments of State and Justice (Amicus Br. at 4-5).

In *Tel-Oren*, Judge Edwards adopted the approach of the Second Circuit. [**33] He stated that *§ 1350* provides jurisdiction in federal district court where a plaintiff alleges a tortuous violation of a principle of international law on which the community of nations has reached a consensus. This is true even where no other basis of jurisdiction is present, and regardless of whether or not a "right to sue" on that violation is independently granted by international law. 726 F.2d at 772-82. Applying these standards to the facts in *Tel-Oren*, Judge Edwards found that, however reprehensible the actions of the defendants may have been, no consensus existed among nations sufficient to warrant an extension of the *Filartiga* approach to the law of nations to include disapproval of non-state acts of violence or terrorism. *726 F.2d at 791-96.*

The facts presented here easily satisfy the criteria set forth by Judge Edwards. An accredited diplomat has been detained and held incommunicado for more than 35 years; his whereabouts have been concealed; and the defendant may have caused his death. There can be no clearer violation of the law of nations. Under the analysis of Judge Edwards, this proceeding is appropriately before this Court.

B

Judge Bork concurred [**34] in dismissing *Tel-Oren* on the ground that plaintiffs had failed to meet a more stringent test than proposed by Judge Edwards and relied upon by the Second Circuit. Under Judge Bork's analysis, plaintiffs would have to show not only a violation of the law of nations, but also a source of a right to sue under federal or international law. *726 F.2d at 801,808.* Judge Bork stated that only by limiting *§ 1350* to cases in which [*258] the law of nations clearly envisions judicial involvement would the doctrine of separation of powers be properly served. In cases such as *Tel-Oren*, where the rule of decision under international law is insufficiently developed, he creates a presumption against jurisdiction which can only be overcome by showing that plaintiffs have been provided with a cause of action under federal or international law. 726 F.2d at 1808.

The facts and allegations of the present case appear to satisfy the requirements set forth by Judge Bork. First, in discussing the unsettled nature of international legal standards regarding terrorism, Judge Bork acknowledges that related areas have been the subject of international consensus through written conventions. *726* [**35] *F.2 dat 806-07.* Among the conventions he lists is the 1973 Convention on the Prevention and Punishment of Crimes Against Internationally Protected Persons, Including Diplomatic Agents. Diplomatic immunity is an area in which international legal standards have long been clearly stated, and the Convention complements preexisting international accords on the treatment of diplomats.

In the course of his analysis, Judge Bork notes that he is "guided" by the language of the Supreme Court in *Banco Nacional de Cuba supra*, slip op. p. 16, in which the Court established a sort of sliding scale with respect to judicial application of international law:

The greater the degree of codification or consensus concerning a particular area of international law, the more appropriate it is for the judiciary to render decisions regarding it, since the courts can then focus on the application of an agreed principle to circumstances of fact rather than on the sensitive task of establishing principle not inconsistent with the national interest or with international justice.

726 F.2d at 804. The rules of diplomatic immunity are so well established that judicial determination of a violation [**36] of diplomatic immunity poses little or no threat to the doctrine of separation of powers. It is, therefore, fully consistent with the rationale underlying Judge Bork's opinion to permit the federal courts to apply the law of diplomatic immunity.

However, even if his opinion is read to require inexplicit showing of a cause of action granted under international law in any case that may touch on foreign relations, plaintiffs' allegations fall within one of the areas that the opinion specifically places within the reach of *§ 1350.*

He stated that the statute is given its more appropriately limited meaning by looking to the "law of nations" as understood in 1789. At that time, the "law of nations" was limited to three primary offenses: "1.Violation of safe-conducts; 2.Infringement of the rights of ambassadors; and 3. Piracy," *726 F.2d at 813, quoting* 4 W. Blackstone, *Commentaries,* 68, 72, and Judge Bork concluded that "one might suppose that these were the kinds of offenses for which Congress wished to provide tort jurisdiction for suits by aliens in order to avoid conflicts with other nations." *233 US App.D.C. 384,726 F.2d 774, 813-14.* The American colonies, having[**37] adopted the common law of England, adopted a "private cause of action for which *section 1350* gave the necessary jurisdiction to federal courts" in these three types of cases. 726 F.2d at 1814 n.22.*See also Respublica v. De Longchamps, 1 US (1 Dall.) 111, 116,1 L. Ed. 59 (Pa. Ct. Oyer & Term. 1784).* Thus, the doctrine of diplomatic immunity is so firmly established as to fall within even the very limited interpretation of *§1350* favored by Judge Bork.

C

Judge Robb invoked the political question doctrine to dismiss *Tel-Oren,* based on arguments similar to those used by Judge Bork in defense of the separation of powers. The opinion cautions against judicial interference in a politically sensitive area where the rule of decision is not adequately defined. *726 F.2d at 827* and *passim.* However, international legal standards with regard to the treatment of diplomats have long been clearly established, and their application should therefore pose[*259] little risk of embarrassing the political branches. As Justice

Whatever Happened to Raoul Wallenberg?

White wrote in his dissent in *Banco Nacionalde Cuba*, while political matters in the realm of foreign affairs are within the exclusive domain[**38] of the Executive Branch . . . this is far from saying that the constitution vests in the executive exclusive absolute control of foreign affairs or that the validity of a foreign act of state is necessarily apolitical question. International law, as well as a treaty or executive agreement, see *United States v. Pink, 315 US 203, [86 L. Ed. 796, 62 S. Ct. 552]*, provides an ascertainable standard for adjudicating the validity of some foreign acts, and courts are competent to apply this body of law, notwithstanding that there may be some cases where comity dictates giving effect to the foreign act because it is not clearly condemned under generally accepted principles of international law.

376 US 398, 461-62, 84 S. Ct. 923, 11 L. Ed. 2d 804. The political question doctrine should therefore not defeat jurisdiction in this case.

D

Under any one of the three *Tel-Oren* opinions, *§1350* provides this Court with subject matter jurisdiction to consider this case. Plaintiffs are aliens; the causes of action they bring are in tort. There has, without question, been a violation of the law of nations, as defined by legal scholars, confirmed in international conventions [**39] to which the United States is a party, and codified in United States law. The requisites of the Edwards/Filartiga approach are thus satisfied.

The violations alleged involve an area of international law in which standards and norms have long been well-defined. The underlying rationale of the opinions of Judges Bork and Robb—a reluctance, where legal standards are uncertain, to permit the courts to enter politically sensitive areas—is therefore met.

Finally, this case satisfies the most stringent of the requirements set forth by Judge Bork. Well before 1789, the protection and well-being of diplomats were understood to be a part of the law of nations, and English (and then American) common law recognized a private cause of action where the law was violated. This right to sue has recently been reaffirmed by the Congress and this Court with respect to acts of violence against internationally protected persons.

STATUTE OF LIMITATIONS

Plaintiffs' claims against the USSR are not barred by any applicable statute of limitations. [16] Plaintiffs contend that Raoul Wallenberg is still alive, and that his unlawful detention is therefore a continuing violation of the laws of the [**40] United States, the laws and treaties of the USSR, and the law of nations. In such circumstances, the[*260] statute of limitations has not yet begun to run. The tortious conduct by the defendant is an ongoing violation which precludes the running of a limitations period.

16 The appropriate District of Columbia statutes are applicable to all of plaintiffs' claims, including not only those arising under federal law but also those arising under other sources of law. With respect to plaintiffs' federal law claims, where, as in the present case, Congress has not enacted a statute of limitations governing a particular claim, the courts will look to the statute of limitations of the forum where the district court sits. *E.g., Johnson v. Railway Express Agency, Inc., 421 US 454, 462, 44 L. Ed. 2d 295, 95 S. Ct. 1716(1975); Forrestal Village, Inc. v. Graham, 179 US App. D.C. 225, 551 F.2d 411, 413 (1977).*The forum statute of limitations to be applied is that which is applicable to the most closely analogous claim under the forum law, and that which best effectuates the federal policy involved. *E.g., McClam v. Barry, 225 US App.D.C. 124, 697 F.2d 366, 373-75 (D.C. Cir. 1983); Forrestal Village, Inc. v. Graham, at 413.*

With respect to plaintiffs' claims not arising under federal law, the statutes of limitations of the District of Columbia apply as the law of the forum. *E.g., Gilson v. Republic of Ireland, 221 US App. D.C. 73, 682 F.2d 1022, 1024-25 & n.7(D.C. Cir. 1982); Steorts v. American Airlines, Inc., 207 US App. D.C. 369, 647 F.2d 194, 197(D.C. Cir. 1981).*

The District of Columbia has several provisions which could arguably apply to one or more of plaintiffs' claims. The statute of limitations for "false arrest and false imprisonment," *D.C. Code Ann. § 12-301(4)(1981),* and for wrongful death, § 16-2702, are both one year. The D. C. Code also provides a three-year statute of limitations for claims which do not have "specially prescribed" limitations. *§12-301(8) (1981).*

[**41] In cases involving an ongoing tort, as here, the cause of action does not accrue for purposes of the running of the statute until the last act constituting the tort is complete. *See Page v. United States, 234 US App. D.C. 332, 729 F.2d 818, 821 (D.C. Cir. 1984)* (citing, *inter alia, Gross v. United States, 676 F.2d 295, 300 (8th Cir. 1982); Leonhard v. United States, 633 F.2d 599, 613(2d Cir. 1980), cert. denied, 451 US 908, 68 L. Ed. 2d295, 101 S. Ct. 1975 (1981)).*

Moreover, even if Raoul Wallenberg is no longer alive, defendant's concealment of the facts and circumstances surrounding Wallenberg's detention and possible death, since the 1957 Gromyko note, provides two further reasons for this Court to refrain from barring plaintiffs' claims. First, under the "discovery rule" of the District of Columbia, plaintiffs' claims have not yet accrued for statute of limitations purposes. Under this rule, a plaintiff's cause of action does not accrue until the plaintiff learns, or with reasonable diligence could have learned, that he has been injured, *see, e.g., Wilson v. Johns-Manville Sales Corp., 684 F.2d 111, 116-18 (D.C.Cir. 1982)*; *Grigsby v. Sterling Drug,* [**42] *Inc., 428F. Supp. 242, 243 (D.D.C. 1975), aff'd without opinion,177 US App. D.C. 270, 543 F.2d 417 (D.C. Cir. 1976),cert. denied, 431 US 967, 97 S. Ct. 2925, 53 L. Ed. 2d1063 (1977)*, and that his injury is due to wrongdoing on the part of the defendant, *see, e.g., Dawson v. Eli Lilly and Co., 543 F. Supp. 1330, 1333-34 (D.D.C. 1982).*[17]

17 Application of the discovery rule in the District of Columbia is not limited to any specific type of tortious injury. Rather, the rule inapplicable to any "tort claim in which the fact of injury may not be readily discernible." *Wilson v. Johns-Manville Sales Corp., 684 F.2d at 116. See Burns v. Bell, 409 A.2d 614, 615 (D.C. App.1979).* The Fifth Circuit in *Dubose v. Kansas City Southern Ry., 729 F.2d 1026 (5th Cir. 1984), cert. denied, 469 US 854, 105 S. Ct. 179, 83 L. Ed. 2d113 (1984)*, recently held that the discovery rule applies to all federal causes of action "whenever a plaintiff is not aware of and had no reasonable opportunity to discover the critical facts of his injury and its cause." *729 F.2d at 1030.*

[**43] In this proceeding, the plaintiffs have no way of knowing whether Wallenberg is dead, or if he is dead, the circumstances of his death and the identity of those responsible. The Gromyko note, in light of the weight of contradictory evidence, cannot provide a reasonable basis for holding that plaintiffs have learned that Wallenberg is no longer alive. Such information remains solely within the control of the USSR.

Second, when a defendant has fraudulently concealed facts giving rise to a cause of action, the statute of limitations is tolled until plaintiffs, employing due diligence, discover or should have discovered the facts giving rise to the claim— in this case, evidence that Wallenberg is indeed no longer alive and that defendant was involved in his death. *Richards v. Mileski, 213 US App. D.C. 220, 662 F.2d 65, 68-69 (D.C. Cir. 1981). See also, e.g., Hobson v. Wilson, 237 US App. D.C. 219, 737F.2d 1 (D.C. Cir. 1984), cert. denied sub nom Brennan v. Hobson, 470 US 1084, 105 S. Ct. 1843, 85 L. Ed. 2d 142(1985).* With respect to the matter of burden of proof and due diligence, our Circuit Court stated in *Richards*:

When tolling is proper because [**44] the defendants have concealed the very cause of action, or their involvement in a cause of action about which the plaintiff might otherwise be aware, they have the burden of coming forward with any facts showing that the plaintiff could have discovered their involvement or the cause of action if he had exercised due diligence.

662 F.2d at 71.See also Smith v. Nixon, 196 US App.D.C. 276, 606 F.2d 1183, 1191 (D.C. Cir. 1979), cert. denied, 453 US 912, 69 L. Ed. 2d 997, 101 S. Ct. 3147,and cert. denied, 453 US 928, 69 L. Ed. 2d 1024, 101 S. Ct. 892 (1981). The defendant cannot meet this burden. Since 1945, it has concealed the truth concerning the condition and whereabouts of Raoul Wallenberg.

THE MERITS

A

There are few principles of international law, if any, that are as universally [*261] recognized as the principle of diplomatic immunity. The seizure and detention of Raoul Wallenberg presents a clear violation of the law of nations as well as a clear violation of the laws and treaties of the United States and the Soviet Union. Moreover, the record in this action is clear, in that it does not show that the Soviet Union has sought, in [**45] any manner, to justify its conduct toward Wallenberg. Indeed, the 1957 Gromyko Note, *supra* pp. 5-6, characterizes his detention and the concealment of his whereabouts as criminal activity.

The history of the diplomatic immunity doctrine is traced from many recognized sources. *See* D. Michaels, *International Privileges and Immunities*, 7, 1971; 1 L. Oppenheim, International Law § 386 (1905); Restatement of Foreign Relations Law of the United States (Revised)§ 461 (Tent. Draft no. 4, 1983). The concept was a part of the ancient civilizations of China, India and Egypt, *United States v. Enger, 472 F. Supp. 490, 504 (D. N.J.1978).*

The present day consensus of the international community on the protection afforded diplomats has been codified in a number of international agreements, primarily the Vienna Convention on Diplomatic Relations, April 18, 1961, 23 UST. 3227, T.I.A.S. No.7502. Article 29 of the Convention states that the person of a diplomatic agent shall be inviolable. He shall not be liable to any form of arrest or detention. The receiving State shall treat him with due respect and shall take all appropriate steps to prevent any attack on his person, [**46] freedom or dignity.

23 UST. at 3240, T.I.A.S. No. 7502 at 14.Corresponding obligations are imposed upon states other than the receiving state under Article 40 of the Convention. 23 UST. at 3246, T.I.A.S. No. 7502 at20-21.

In the 1970s, the community of nations reaffirmed its commitment to the safety of diplomats by entering into the Convention on the Prevention and Punishment of Crimes Against Internationally Protected Persons, Including Diplomatic Agents,

Whatever Happened to Raoul Wallenberg?

December 14, 1973, 28UST. 1975, T.I.A.S. No. 8532. The Convention requires signatory nations to take steps to punish the" murder, kidnapping or other attack upon the person or liberty of an internationally protected person," 28 UST at 1978, T.I.A.S. No. 8532 at 4, as well as other crimes or threats against them. The Soviet Union is a party to both the Vienna Convention and the 1973 Convention.

Wallenberg's treatment at the hands of the Soviet Union also violates a number of international treaties and conventions relating to human rights, all of which have been signed by the Soviet Union. Under Articles 55 and 56 of the United Nations Charter, each member state pledges to take action to promote "universal respect[**47] for, and observance of, human rights and fundamental freedoms." 59 Stat.1033, 1045-46 (1945). These obligations are given further substance in subsequent documents. Article 3 of the Universal Declaration of Human Rights, G.A. Res. 217A (III), U.N.Doc. A/1810 (1948) mandates the protection of "life, liberty and security of person." Article 9 protects the right not to "be subjected to arbitrary arrest, detention or exile." Article 10 protects each person's right to a fair and public hearing of criminal charges against him. Article 12 protects the right not to "be subjected to arbitrary interference with . . . privacy, family, home or correspondence." The international community—including the Soviet Union—reaffirmed its commitment to these rights in the International Covenant on Civil and Political Rights, G.A. Res. 2200 (XXI), 21 U.N. GAOR Supp. (No. 16) at 52, U.N. Doc. A/6316 (1967), 18andagain in the Final Act of the Conference on Security and Cooperation in Europe (Helsinki 1975), Department of State Bulletin Reprint, Sept. 1, 1975.

18 The United States has signed but not yet ratified this Convention.[**48]

B

United States law has long accepted international standards of diplomatic immunity as part of its common law and has [*262] recognized a private civil cause of action for a violation of diplomatic immunity. *See Tel-Oren v. Libyan Arab Republic, 233 US App. D.C.384, 726 F.2d 774, 814 n.22 (D.C. Cir. 1984).* In *Respublica v. De Longchamps, 1 US (1 Dall.) 111, 1 L. Ed. 59 (Pa. Ct. Oyer & Term. 1784),* the Supreme Court held that the De Longchamps committed "an atrocious violation of the law of nations," when, having first insulted the Consul General of France to the United States, he struck the cane of the diplomat. The Court described De Longchamps' actions as gross insults, and diplomats as "the peculiar objects" of the law of nations.1 US (1 Dall.) at 111, 117.

In 1976, the United States Congress enacted the Act for the Prevention and Punishment of Crimes Against Internationally Protected Persons, *18 USC. §§*

1116,1201, 112, 970, 878 and *11*. That criminal statute proscribes the murder or attempted murder of an internationally protected person, and permits the exercise by the United States of jurisdiction over such an offense "if the alleged offender [**49] is present within the United States, irrespective of the place where the offense was committed or the nationality of the victim or the alleged offender." *18 USC. § 1116(c)*. An "internationally protected person" is defined as including, *inter alia*, any . . . representative, officer, employee, or agent of the United States Government, a foreign government, or international organization who at the time and place concerned is entitled pursuant to international law to special protection against attack upon his person, freedom, or dignity.

18 USC. § 1116((b)(4)(B). Similar prohibitory and jurisdictional language governs the kidnapping of such a person under *18 USC. § 1201(a)(4)* and *(e)*.

At the time of his kidnapping, Raoul Wallenberg was an accredited Swedish diplomat. He was thus an "internationally protected person" within the meaning of *§§ 1116* and *1201(a)(4)* and *(e)*. His kidnapping was therefore a violation of *§ 1201(a)(4)*; if he is no longer alive, *§ 1116* has also been violated. In enacting these statutes, Congress expressly declared its intent to prohibit such acts wherever and by whomever committed, and whatever the nationality of the victim.

Moreover, [**50] this Court has recognized a civil cause of action under federal law on behalf of private plaintiffs pursuant to *18 USC. § 1116*. In *Letelier, 502F. Supp. at 266*, jurisdiction was upheld in a suit brought by the surviving spouses of an exiled Chilean diplomat and his co-worker against those responsible for their murder. The same rationale should apply to *§ 1201(a)(4)* and *(e)*. Under both, plaintiffs are entitled to immediate declaratory relief.

C

The Soviet Union's treatment of Raoul Wallenberg is unlawful even under its own statutes. [19] The Statute on Diplomatic and Consular Representations of Foreign States on the Territory of the USSR, confirmed by edict of the Presidium of the USSR Supreme Soviet on May 23, 1966, set forth in *Collected Legislation of the Union of Soviet Socialist Republics and the Constituent Union Republics* (Butler ed. 1983), affirms the privileges and immunities due to diplomats, Article 1, as well as the primacy of "international treaty rules" on the subject, Article 3. By its terms, the statute applies to diplomatic or consular representations "on the territory of the USSR. "Article 1. The "inviolability" while traveling in the "territory [**51] of the USSR" of diplomats representing a "foreign state in a third country" is specifically assured in Article 18. The detention of Wallenberg plainly violates the diplomatic immunity guaranteed by the statute.

19 In addition to the laws cited in this section, the Soviet Union is party to treaties the terms of which have been violated by the acts against Wallenberg. *See* discussion at slip op. pp. 36-38, *supra.*

Wallenberg's detention is also violative of the Criminal Code of the Russian Soviet Federated Socialist Republic, and corresponding provisions of the Criminal Codes of other Republics of the USSR. Article [*263] 126 of the Federated Socialistic Republic Criminal Code outlaws any deprivation of freedom that was illegal as of the time committed. Article 178 proscribes an arrest or detention which is known to be illegal and which is illegal in fact. Wallenberg's arrest and detention were and continue to be illegal under principles of international law and international agreements, which were in [**52] force in 1945 and to which the USSR was a party. Moreover, the 1957 Gromyko Note acknowledged the illegality of Wallenberg's detention and of the misinformation that made it possible.

The Soviet Union's treatment of Raoul Wallenberg is unlawful under any standard of applicable law. It has never argued otherwise; it has denied and disclaimed its actions, but it has never defended them.

CONCLUSION

In many ways, this action is without precedent in the history of actions against foreign sovereigns. It involves actions, which the Soviet Union has already admitted were unlawful. It involves a gross violation of the personal immunity of a diplomat, one of the oldest and most universally recognized principles of international law. Furthermore, this action involves a deliberate default by a defendant, which has repeatedly demonstrated its familiarity with the proper means for raising a defense of sovereign immunity under the Foreign Sovereign Immunities Act.

There can be little, if any, doubt that both subject matter and personal jurisdiction are conferred through that Act. Whatever sovereign immunity the defendant might have had, is, by the terms of the Act, subject to international [**53] agreements to which the United States was a party when the FSIA was enacted in 1976 which prohibit defendant's actions regarding Mr. Wallenberg.

Additionally, this Court determines that no applicable statute of limitations has begun to run against plaintiff's claims. Because Mr. Wallenberg is still being unlawfully held by the defendants, or alternatively, he is dead, the statute is tolled by the "discovery rule" and/or the law on tolling applicable when one party has fraudulently concealed facts.

For all of these reasons, default judgment is here by entered against the defendant.

Seeking Raoul
Philadelphia lawyer pursues justice in Soviet-era Jailing of Wallenberg.

May 08, 2011|By Carolyn Davis, Inquirer Staff Writer
Source: Philadelphia Inquirer, The (PA);

Lawyer Morris H. Wolff says he believes the long-missing Swedish diplomat Raoul Wallenberg is...

Morris H. Wolff was back at his alma mater, Germantown Friends School, Friday to teach anyone who would listen about a Swedish diplomat and humanitarian hero named Raoul Wallenberg.

Wolff, 74, gave two lessons at once. The overt one was about Wallenberg, a Christian who helped save as many as 100,000 Hungarian Jews from Nazi execution during World War II. The other was about Wolff himself and how passion can fuel a life.

Wolff has spent much of the last 28 years, since Wallenberg's brother phoned to ask for his help, trying to hold the Soviet Union and the current Russian government accountable for Wallenberg—and seeking the truth about what happened to him.

"I think he's still alive," Wolff says.

In 1944, the U.S. War Refugee Board asked Sweden, officially neutral in World War II, to dispatch an envoy who would try to save Hungary's remaining Jews. German forces had just occupied the country and deported about 440,000 Jews to their deaths. Nearly 200,000 remained in Budapest when Wallenberg, a successful

316

businessman with a degree from the University of Michigan, arrived to be chief rescuer.

Wallenberg established social services and safe houses for Jews who held documents from neutral countries. He went beyond his orders by distributing more Swedish protective passports than he was authorized to—and then personally pulled Jews with those documents off trains or out of columns headed for extermination camps.

When the Soviet Union liberated Budapest in 1945, 100,000 Jews were still alive, thanks in large part to Wallenberg and others who worked with him.

It also was in 1945 that Wallenberg disappeared. Years later, Soviet officials admitted they had put him in prison. They claimed he died of natural causes in custody in 1947, when he would have been 35.

Wolff offered possible motives for the Soviets' actions, including suspicion that Wallenberg was a spy for the United States.

Wallenberg's half-brother, Guy Von Dardel, didn't believe Raoul was dead, especially after a freed Russian prisoner said in the 1980s that Wallenberg was still imprisoned. Von Dardel had heard of Wolff, then a Chestnut Hill lawyer and professor of international law at Delaware's Widener University law school, and in 1983, he called him early one day to ask for help.

"If I had any idea what I was taking on, I would have gone back to bed," Wolff said. "I thought I was taking on a mild inquiry."

Wolff found an old legal provision on which to hang a lawsuit in U.S. District Court. In 1984, three years after Congress and President Ronald Reagan made Wallenberg an honorary American citizen, Wolff sued the Soviet Union on behalf of Wallenberg's family and asked for $39 million in damages for illegally imprisoning the diplomat.

He won, but the judgment was reversed in legal manoeuvring that Wolff says was driven by Soviet-U.S. foreign relations.

Wolff loved telling his stories to the Germantown students, in a visit that took place during the National Days of Remembrance. When Harri Plotnick, 18, said she wrote a report on Wallenberg in fourth grade, Wolff beamed and opened his book, *Whatever Happened to Raoul Wallenberg?* When a history teacher greeted

Whatever Happened to Raoul Wallenberg?

him, Wolff asked whether he could speak to the teacher's class; a pop quiz made that impossible.

In September, Wolff plans to file a petition with the U.S. Supreme Court to reinstate the original judgment.

Why does he persevere? Wallenberg's brother has died. The odds seem low that the hero is still alive; he would be 98. Wolff keeps on partly for himself. He has met interesting people and the work has kept his mind and body healthy.

"I know God wants me to do this, and if I do good things, God will keep me healthy," he said.

There's one more reason: "I was overwhelmed by the idea that he was held in custody for 39 years for doing nothing. It was a terrible injustice."

Wolff, who lives in Daytona Beach, Fla., described himself as a "fortunate Jewish man who grew up in Elkins Park" and is grateful that Wallenberg did so much to help Jews.

The copy of his book that Wolff showed the students is thick with handwritten notes. It's printed on-demand, so he constantly revises it as information emerges from Soviet archives and other sources.

So, when does Wolff think the last revision will come?

He is not sure. Whenever it is, Wolff said, he wants to make sure it's done with the same dignity that distinguished Wallenberg's work.

Sabotaged by U.S. Supreme Court Chief...
Attorney Still Fighting for Holocaust Hero
by Sabina Clarke, Chestnut Hill Local 6/23/11

Former Philadelphian and international human rights attorney Morris Wolff, 74, a '54 graduate of Germantown Friends School and an alumnus of Amherst College and Yale University Law School, has been on a 28 year quest to  rescue Holocaust hero Raoul Wallenberg who has been credited with saving at least 100,000 Jews headed for the gas chambers at Auschwitz. Recruited by our government in 1944 to save the remaining Hungarian Jews in Budapest, Wallenberg was later abandoned and left to languish in Soviet prisons ever since his capture by the Russians in 1945. (On August 5, 1981 in a Rose Garden ceremony at the White House, President Ronald Reagan made Wallenberg an American citizen.)

Morris Wolff's fearless journey to free Wallenberg began in 1983 with a 4 AM phone call from Guy Von Dardel, the brother of Raoul Wallenberg. Von Dardel, who had been referred to Wolff by a law professor associate from Chicago, pleaded with Wolff to rescue his brother Raoul and to sue the Russians for his kidnapping and illegal detention. The moment he agreed to take the case, Wolff became the de facto voice of Wallenberg.

Based on Wallenberg's status as an American Citizen, Wolff sent a hand-delivered letter to President Reagan urging him to demand Wallenberg's release by the Soviets. It was not until years later that he learned that Reagan's initial directive to act was sabotaged by the White House and the U.S. State Department and specifically by Reagan's Counsel, Fred Fielding, and his Assistant Counsel John Roberts-- now Chief Justice of the Supreme Court.

Wolff recalls, "It was not until 2005 when I was contacted by E.J. Kessler, investigative reporter for *The Jewish Forward* during the confirmation hearings for Chief Justice Roberts, that I saw a memo from Roberts to President Reagan urging Reagan to 'dodge the Wallenberg issue.' The memo had been buried in the Reagan Library. So with this new information, I asked to be included on the panel for Robert's confirmation hearings and question him on issues of integrity and character. I wanted him to tell the public what he knew about the Wallenberg matter and why he did not encourage President Reagan to use the law I placed in front of him, citing the U.S. Hostages Act, to rescue Wallenberg but I was prevented from doing so because the Chairman of the Senate Judiciary Committee, Arlen Specter, a close friend and a Robert's supporter, knew I would be a hostile witness."

When he received no support from the Reagan administration, Wolff filed his historic lawsuit *Wallenberg versus the U.S.S.R.* in Federal District Court in Washington, D.C. on February 3rd, 1984. He remembers his relief when the judge assigned to his case was Judge Barrington Parker Jr., "He was the grandson of a slave and one of the first African-Americans to enter Yale Law School. He was also a strong supporter of human rights who, despite severe pressure from the White House and the State Department--including a highly improper visit to his judicial chambers by the men in pin striped suits from State-- ordered the Soviets to release Wallenberg and pay damages of $39 million--one million for each year of captivity." Parker, he recalls, called the case 'unique and without precedent in the history of actions against foreign sovereigns.'"

The Wallenberg verdict, handed down on October 15th, 1985, was front-page news in *The New York Times*, *The Washington Post* and *The Philadelphia Inquirer*--and went national. This historic lawsuit that no one thought he could possibly win, paved the way for a new generation of human rights cases.

Then after a series of postponements filed in secret by an insubordinate attorney who infiltrated Wolff's team of lawyers and worked to sabotage the verdict on behalf of his firm's main client, Chase Manhattan Bank, there was a four year delay in implementing Parker's decision. Then, something that has never before occurred in the history of the courts was about to happen. The courts ignored Parker's decision and quietly moved the closed case on Judge Parker's docket to the docket of another judge of equal jurisdiction. "This, according to an associate of mine, the Honorable Arlin M. Adams, a dear friend and retired federal appellate judge on the Third Circuit Court of Appeals, was 'an extreme example of judicial misbehavior.'" Simply put, the Executive Branch of our government interfered with the Judicial Branch of our government violating the separation of powers clause in the U.S. Constitution.

I read with fascination Morris Wolff's spellbinding book *Whatever Happened to Raoul Wallenberg?* chronicling his 28 year quest representing his client Raoul Wallenberg. This true story about his ongoing struggle to free Wallenberg is packed with intrigue, suspense and high drama and trumps a James Bond thriller. It involves encrypted cables between Wallenberg and the U.S. State Department; hidden KGB files, White House memos, secret documents, cloak and dagger meetings, daring rescue attempts, bold disguises, cryptic messages, anonymous phone calls and mysterious deaths under suspect circumstances. It involves former Russian Premier Leonid Brezhnev, who in 1945 was the Red Army's arresting officer and who after arresting Wallenberg, stole the 'Wallenberg Diamonds' from the safe in Wallenberg's office. The jewels had been entrusted to Wallenberg by the Jews on their way to the death camps. This fact was later confirmed to Wolff by several reliable sources including John Erlichman, former President Nixon's Chief Counsel.

Through it all, pointed warnings were given to Morris Wolff from powerful people in high places suggesting that he abandon his lawsuit on behalf of Wallenberg. Yet, Wolff pushed on--ignoring all warnings while taking on the U.S. State Department, the White House, the U.S.S.R. and prestigious law firms who all tried to squash his efforts to secure Wallenberg's release.

Aided, at times, by a few brave individuals who also took considerable personal risks, Wolff uncovered concrete information revealing behind the scenes machinations aimed at stopping his investigation into the disappearance and whereabouts of Raoul Wallenberg. He recalls his friend Earl Silbert, the former Watergate prosecutor saying to him, "I think you may want to back off this case. This is not a game of tennis. There are some pretty strong forces working against you-including the FBI, the CIA and other forces at high levels of government."

When warned by President Reagan's former Assistant Secretary of State Richard Fairbanks that the Russians may try to kill him and that he was "interfering with the conduct of foreign affairs" Wolff replied, "Only a bullet will stop me-and you are not about to order that, are you?"

This is a tale of heroes and villains and a fascinating glimpse into our legal system and its shameful derailment precipitated by the interference of the State Department and the White House and Russia and Sweden and their Wall Street and Washington, D.C. law firms acting as hired guns for the Chase Manhattan Bank in New York and the *Enskilda Bank* of Sweden. All were in bed together. All conspired to squash Wolff's case; and in the end, they almost did.

Wolff's quest for justice for Wallenberg has taken him all over the world collecting first-person recollections from Wallenberg's friends and associates and those who were rescued by Wallenberg. With some, Wolff has forged close and lasting friendships.

Now, 28 years later Wolff plans to go back to court. Encouraged by his friend and associate retired Judge Arlin M. Adams who has reviewed the procedural facts of the case, Wolff is seeking a reversal of Judge Aubrey Robinson's 1989 decision which threw the initial verdict out.

He plans to file a petition with the United States Supreme Court seeking a reinstatement of the Parker decision, the collection of the $39 million with compounded interest and the immediate release of Wallenberg—realizing that the possibility that Wallenberg is still alive is slim. He estimates the current value of the case at $142 million. But, for Wolff, who has worked pro bono all these years, the case has never been about money; it is about getting justice for Raoul Wallenberg.

If he succeeds in getting the Wallenberg case heard before the Supreme Court, any monetary award will   go towards the creation of the Raoul Wallenberg Center for Altruistic Studies, which was agreed upon, by both Wolff and Wallenberg's family from the outset.

He hopes to have the case heard before the Supreme Court citing Article III, Section 2 of the U.S. Constitution that states, *"Cases involving ambassadors, public ministers and consuls can be brought directly to the United States Supreme Court which shall have original jurisdiction over such matters."*

Since Wallenberg qualifies as an ambassador or public minister, his case can be heard directly by the Supreme Court, via petition, with Chief Justice John C. Roberts presiding. "This", says Wolff, "will provide Chief Justice Roberts with an opportunity to correct his earlier error."

Index

Made in the USA
Lexington, KY
14 May 2014